The
Gallup
Poll

Public Opinion 1983

GEORGE H. GALLUP, founder and chairman of
The Gallup Poll, received a Ph.D. in psychology from
the University of Iowa in 1928. From his undergraduate
days he has had three prime interests: survey research,
public opinion, and politics.
Dr. Gallup is the author of many articles on public
opinion and advertising research, and he has published
the following books: *The Pulse of Democracy* (1940);
A Guide Book to Public Opinion Polls (1944); *The Gallup
Political Almanac* (1952); *Secrets of Long Life* (1960);
The Miracle Ahead (1964); *The Sophisticated Poll
Watcher's Guide* (Rev. 1976); *The Gallup Poll,
1935–1971* (1972); *The Gallup Poll: Public Opinion, 1972–1977* (1978);
1978 (1979); *1979* (1980); *1980* (1981); *1981* (1982); *1982* (1983); *1983* (1984).

Other Gallup Poll Publications Available from Scholarly Resources

The Gallup Poll: Public Opinion, 1982
ISBN 0-8420-2214-7 (1983)

The Gallup Poll: Public Opinion, 1981
ISBN 0-8420-2200-7 (1982)

The Gallup Poll: Public Opinion, 1980
ISBN 0-8420-2181-7 (1981)

The Gallup Poll: Public Opinion, 1979
ISBN 0-8420-2170-1 (1980)

The Gallup Poll: Public Opinion, 1978
ISBN 0-8420-2159-0 (1979)

The Gallup Poll: Public Opinion, 1972–1977
2 volumes ISBN 0-8420-2129-9 (1978)

The International Gallup Polls: Public Opinion, 1979
ISBN 0-8420-2180-9 (1981)

The International Gallup Polls: Public Opinion, 1978
ISBN 0-8420-2162-0 (1980)

The
Gallup
Poll

Public Opinion 1983

Dr. George H. Gallup
Founder and Chairman

SR *Scholarly Resources Inc.*
Wilmington, Delaware

ACKNOWLEDGMENTS

The preparation of this volume has involved the entire staff of The Gallup Poll and their contributions are gratefully acknowledged. I particularly wish to thank James Shriver, III, managing editor of The Gallup Poll; and Professor Fred L. Israel of the City College of New York, who has been the principal coordinator of this volume and of the ten volumes that preceded it.

G.H.G.

Scholarly Resources Inc.
104 Greenhill Avenue
Wilmington, DE 19805

Library of Congress Catalog Card Number: 79-56557
International Standard Serial Number: 0195-962X
International Standard Book Number: 0-8420-2220-1

CONTENTS

PREFACE

[This introductory essay by Dr. George Gallup is excerpted from a section entitled "How Polls Operate" from his book *The Sophisticated Poll Watcher's Guide*.]

THE CROSS-SECTION

The most puzzling aspect of modern polls to the layman is the cross-section or sample. How, for example, is it possible to interview 1,000 or 2,000 persons out of a present electorate of about 150 million and be sure that the relatively few selected will reflect accurately the attitudes, interests, and behavior of the entire population of voting age?

Unless the poll watcher understands the nature of sampling and the steps that must be taken to assure its representativeness, the whole operation of scientific polling is likely to have little meaning, and even less significance, to him.

With the goal in mind of making the process understandable, and at the risk of being too elementary, I have decided to start with some simple facts about the nature of sampling—a procedure, I might add, that is as old as man himself.

When a housewife wants to test the quality of the soup she is making, she tastes only a teaspoonful or two. She knows that if the soup is thoroughly stirred, one teaspoonful is enough to tell her whether she has the right mixture of ingredients.

In somewhat the same manner, a bacteriologist tests the quality of water in a reservoir by taking a few samples, maybe not more than a few drops from a half-dozen different points. He knows that pollutants of a chemical or bacteriological nature will disperse widely and evenly throughout a body of water. He can be certain that his tiny sample will accurately reflect the presence of harmful bacteria or other pollutants in the whole body of water.

Perhaps a more dramatic example is to be found in the blood tests given routinely in clinics and hospitals. The medical technician requires only a few drops of blood to discover abnormal conditions. He does not have to draw a quart of blood to be sure that his sample is representative.

These examples, of course, deal with the physical world. People are not as much alike as drops of water, or of blood. If they were, then the world of individuals could be sampled by selecting only a half-dozen persons anywhere. People are widely different because their experiences are widely different.

Interestingly, this in itself comes about largely through a sampling process. Every human being gathers his views about people and about life by his own sampling. And, it should be added, he almost invariably ends with a distorted picture because his experience is unique. For example, he draws conclusions about "California" by looking out of his car or airplane window, by observing the people he meets at the airport or on the streets, and by his treatment in restaurants, hotels, and other places. This individual has no hesitancy in telling his friends back home what California is really like—although his views, obviously, are based upon very limited sampling.

The Black man, living his life in the ghetto, working under conditions that are often unpleasant and for wages that are likely to be less than those of the white man who lives in the suburban community, arrives at his own views about racial equality. His sample, likewise, is unrepresentative even though it may be typical of fellow Blacks living under the same conditions. By the same token, well-to-do whites living in the suburbs with the advantages of a college education and travel have equally distorted views of equality. These distortions come about because their sampling, likewise, is based upon atypical experiences.

Although every individual on the face of the earth is completely unique, in the mass he does conform to certain patterns of behavior. No one has expressed this better than A. Conan Doyle, author of the Sherlock Holmes series. He has one of his characters make this observation:

> While the individual man is an insoluble puzzle, in the aggregate he becomes a mathematical certainty. You can never foretell what any one man will do, but you can say with precision what an average number will be up to. Individuals vary, but averages remain constant.

Whenever the range of differences is great—either in nature or man—the sampling process must be conducted with great care to make certain that all major variations or departures from the norm are embraced.

Since some differences that exist may be unknown to the researcher, his best procedure to be sure of representativeness is to select samples from the population by a chance or random process. Only if he follows this procedure can he be reasonably certain that he has covered all major variations that exist.

This principle can be illustrated in the following manner. Suppose that a government agency, such as the Bureau of the Census, maintained an up-to-date alphabetical list of the names of all persons living in the United States eighteen years of age and older. Such a file, at the present time, would include approximately 148 million names.

Now suppose that a survey organization wished to draw a representative sample of this entire group, a sample, say of 10,000 persons. Such a representative sample could be selected by dividing 150,000,000 by 10,000—which produces a figure of 15,000. If the researcher goes systematically through the entire file and records the name of every 15,000th listed, he can be sure that his sample is representative.

The researcher will find that this chance selection, in the manner described, has produced almost the right percentage of Catholics and Protestants, the proper proportion of persons in each age and educational level. The distribution of persons by occupation, sex, race, and income should be broadly representative and consistent with the best available census data. It is important, however, to emphasize the words "broadly representative." The sample—even of 10,000— most likely would not include a single person belonging to the Fox Indian tribe or a single resident of Magnolia, Arkansas. It might not include a single citizen of Afghanistan heritage or a single Zoroastrian.

For the purposes served by polls, a sample normally needs to be only broadly representative. A study could be designed to discover the attitudes of American Indians, in which case the Fox Indians should be properly represented. And a specially designed study of Arkansas would likely embrace interviews with residents of Magnolia.

But for all practical purposes, individuals making up these groups constitute such a small part of the whole population of the United States that their inclusion, or exclusion, makes virtually no difference in reaching conclusions about the total population or even of important segments of the population.

Unfortunately, there is no master file in the United States of persons over the age of eighteen that is available to the researcher. Moreover, even a few weeks after the decennial census such a file would be out of date. Some citizens would have died, some would have moved, and still others would have reached the age of eighteen.

Unlike some European countries, no attempt is made in the United States to keep voter registration lists complete and up to date. Because of this failure to maintain accurate lists of citizens and of registered voters, survey organizations are forced to devise their own systems to select samples that are representative of the population to be surveyed.

Any number of sampling systems can be invented so long as one all-important goal is kept in mind. Whatever the system, the end result of its use must be to give every individual an equal opportunity of being selected. Actually, not every individual will have an equal chance, since some persons will be hospitalized, some in mental or penal institutions, and some in the armed forces in foreign lands. But while these individuals help make up the total United States citizenry, most are disenfranchised by the voting laws of the various states or find difficulty in implementing their opinions at election time. Typically, therefore, they are not included in survey cross-sections.

The Gallup Poll has designed its sample by choosing at random not individuals as described previously, but small districts such as census tracts, census enumeration districts, and townships. A random selection of these small geographical areas provides a good starting point for building a national sample.

The United States population is first arranged by states in geographical order and then within the individual states by districts, also in geographical order. A sampling interval number is determined by dividing the total population of the nation by the number of interviewing locations deemed adequate for a general purpose sample of the population eighteen years of age and older. In the case of the Gallup Poll sample, the number of locations, so selected, is approximately 300.

At the time of this writing, the population of the United States eighteen years and older is approximately 150,000,000. Dividing 150,000,000 by 300 yields a sampling interval of 500,000. A random starting number is then chosen between 1 and 500,000 in order to select the first location. The remaining 299 locations are determined by the simple process of adding 500,000 successively until all 300 locations are chosen throughout the nation.

A geographical sampling unit having been designated, the process of selection is continued by choosing at random a given number of individuals within each unit. Suppose that the sampling unit is a census tract in Scranton, Pennsylvania. Using block statistics, published by the Census Bureau for cities of this size, a block, or a group of blocks, within the tract is chosen by a random method analogous to the procedure used to select the location.

Within a block or groups of blocks so selected, the interviewer is given a random starting point. Proceeding from this point, the interviewer meets his assignment by taking every successive occupied dwelling. Or, as an alternative procedure, he can be instructed to take every third or every fifth or every tenth dwelling unit and to conduct interviews in these designated homes.

In this systematic selection plan, the choice of the dwelling is taken out of the hands of the interviewer. As a reminder to the reader, it should be pointed out that the area or district has been selected by a random procedure; next, the dwelling within the district has been chosen at random. All that now remains is to select, at random, the individual to be interviewed within the household.

This can be done in several ways. A list can be compiled by the interviewer of all persons of voting age residing within each home. From such a household list, he can then select individuals to be interviewed by a random method. Ingenious methods are employed to accomplish this end. One survey organization in Europe, for example, instructs the interviewer to talk to the person in the household whose birthday falls on the nearest date.

Now the process is complete. The district has been selected at random; the dwelling unit within the district has been selected at random; and the individual within the dwelling unit has been selected at random. The end result is that every individual in the nation of voting age has had an equal chance of being selected.

This is the theory. In actual practice, problems arise, particularly in respect to the last stage of the process. The dwelling unit chosen may be vacant, the individual selected within a household may not be at home when the interviewer calls. Of course, the interviewer can return the next day; in fact, he or she can make a half-dozen call backs without finding the person. Each call back adds that much to the cost of the survey and adds, likewise, to the time required to complete the study.

Even with a dozen call backs, some individuals are never found and are never interviewed. They may be in the hospital, visiting relatives, on vacation, on a business trip, not at home except at very late hours, too old or too ill to be interviewed—and a few may even refuse to be interviewed.

Since no nationwide survey has ever reached every person designated by any random selection procedure, special measures must be employed to deal with this situation. In the early 1950s, the Gallup Poll introduced a system called Time-Place interviewing. After an intensive study of the time of day when different members of a household are at home, an interviewing plan was devised that enabled interviewers to reach the highest proportion of persons at the time of their first call.

Since most persons are employed outside the home, interviewing normally must be done in the late afternoon and evening hours, and on weekends. These are the times when men, and especially younger men, are likely to be at home and therefore available to be interviewed.

In various nations, survey organizations are working out new ways to meet this problem of the individual selected for the sample who is not at home. These new procedures may meet more perfectly the ideal requirements of random sampling.

Many ardent advocates of the procedure described as "quota sampling" are still to be found. This, it should be pointed out, was the system generally employed by the leading survey organizations in the pre-1948 era.

The quota system is simplicity itself. If the state of New York has 10% of the total population of the United States, then 10% of all interviews must come from this state. In the case of a national sample of 10,000, this would mean 1,000 interviews.

Going one step further, since New York City contains roughly 40% of the population of the state, then 40% of the 1,000 interviews must be allocated to New York City, or 400. And since Brooklyn has roughly a third of the total population of New York City, a third of the 400 interviews, or 133, must be made in this borough. In similar fashion, all of the 1,000 interviews made in the state of New York can be distributed among the various cities, towns, and rural areas. Other states are dealt with in similar fashion.

Making still further use of census data, the interviews to be made in each city, town, or rural areas can be assigned on an occupational basis: so many white-collar workers, so many blue-collar workers, so many farmers, so many business and professional people, so many retired persons, and so many on the welfare rolls. The allocation can also be made on the basis of rents paid. The interviewer, for example, may be given a "quota" of calls to be made in residential areas with the highest rental values, in areas with medium priced rentals, and in low rental areas.

Typically, in the quota sampling system, the survey organization predetermines the number of men and women and the age, the income, the occupation, and the race of the individuals assigned to each interviewer.

In setting such quotas, however, important factors may be overlooked. In 1960, for example, a quota sample that failed to assign the right proportion of Catholic voters would have miscalculated John Kennedy's political strength. An individual's religious beliefs, obviously, cannot be ascertained by his appearance or by the place where he dwells; this applies to other factors as well.

Not only do theoretical considerations fault the quota system but so do the problems that face the interviewer. When the selection of individuals is left to him, he tends to seek out the easiest-to-interview respondents. He is prone to avoid the worst slum areas, and consequently he turns up with interviews that are likely to be skewed on the high income and educational side. Typically, a quick look at the results of quota sampling will reveal too many persons with a college education, too many persons with average and above average incomes, and in political polls, too many Republicans. Therefore, one of the many advantages of the random procedure is that the selection of respondents is taken out of the hands of the interviewer. In the random method, the interviewer is told exactly where to go and when to go.

Another consideration with cross-sections is keeping them up to date. Although America's population is highly mobile, fortunately for polltakers the basic structure of society changes little. Perhaps the greatest change in America in recent years has been the rising level of education. In 1935, when the Gallup Poll first published poll results, only 7.2% of the adult population had attended college for one year or more. Today that figure is 27%.

How does a research organization know that the sample it has designed meets proper standards? Normally, examination of the socioeconomic data gathered by the interviewer at the end of each interview provides the answer. As the completed interview forms are returned from the field to the Princeton office of the Gallup Poll, the facts from each are punched into IBM cards. In addition to the questions that have dealt with issues and other matters of interest, the interviewer has asked each person to state his occupation, age, how far he went in school, his religious preference, whether he owns or rents his dwelling, and many other questions of a factual nature.

Since the Census Bureau Current Population Surveys provide data on each one of these factors, even a hasty examination will tell whether the cross-section is fairly accurate—that is, whether the important factors line up properly with the known facts, specifically:
—the educational level of those interviewed
—the age level
—the income level
—the proportion of males to females
—the distribution by occupations

—the proportion of whites to nonwhites
—the geographical distribution of cases
—the city-size distribution.

Typically, when the educational level is correct (that is, when the sample has included the right proportion of those who have attended college, high school, grade school, or no school), when the geographical distribution is right and all areas of the nation have been covered in the correct proportion, when the right proportion of those in each income level has been reached, and the right percentages of whites and nonwhites and of men and women are included—then usually other factors tend to fall in line. These include such factors as religious preference, political party preference, and most other factors that bear upon voting behavior, buying behavior, tastes, interests, and the like.

After checking all of the above "controls," it would be unusual to find that every group making up the total population is represented in the sample in the exact percentage that it should be. Some groups may be slightly larger or smaller than they should be. The nonwhite population eighteen years and older, which makes up 11% of the total population, may be found to be less, or more, than this percentage of the returned interviews. Those who have attended high school in the obtained interviews may number 58%, when actually the true figure should be 54%.

Ways have been developed to correct situations such as these that arise out of the over-representation or under-representation of given groups. The sample can be balanced, that is, corrected so that each group is included in the proportion it represents in the total population. When this procedure is followed, the assumption is made that persons within each group who are interviewed are representative of the group in question. But there are obvious limitations to this. If only a few persons are found in a given category, then the danger is always present that they may not be typical or representative of the people who make up this particular group or cell.

On the whole, experience has shown that this process of weighting by the computer actually does produce more accurate samples. Normally, results are changed by only negligible amounts—seldom by more than 1 or 2 percentage points.

A persistent misconception about polling procedures is that a new sample must be designed for measuring each major issue. Actually, Gallup Poll cross-sections are always based upon samples of the entire voting age population. Every citizen has a right to voice his opinion on every issue and to have it recorded. For this reason, all surveys of public opinion seek to reach a representative cross-section of the entire population of voting age.

Some people ask if we go back to the same persons with different polls. The answer, in the case of the Gallup Poll, is "no"; the same person is not interviewed again. Some survey research is based upon fixed cross-sections or "panels." The same persons are reinterviewed from time to time to measure shifts in opinion.

There are certain advantages to this system—it is possible to determine to what extent overall changes cloak individual changes. But a practical disadvantage is that the size of the sample remains fixed. Unless the panel is very large, reliable information cannot be produced for smaller subgroups. In the case of the Gallup Poll, the same question can be placed on any number of surveys and the total sample expanded accordingly, since the same persons are not reinterviewed.

Panels have other limitations. One has to do with determining the level of knowledge. Having asked a citizen what he knows about a certain issue in the first interview, he may very well take the trouble to read about it when he sees an article later in his newspaper or magazine. There is, moreover, a widespread feeling among researchers that the repeated interviewing of the same person tends to make him a "pro" and to render him atypical for this reason. But the evidence is not clear-cut on this point. The greatest weakness, perhaps, is that panels tend to fall apart; persons change their place of residence and cannot be found for a second or subsequent measurement; some refuse to participate more than once and must be replaced by substitutes.

THE SIZE OF SAMPLES

When the subject of public-opinion polls comes up, many people are quick to say that they do not know of anyone who has ever been polled.

The likelihood of any single individual, eighteen years of age or older, being polled in a sample of 1,500 persons is about one chance in 90,000. With samples of this size, and with the frequency that surveys are scheduled by the Gallup Poll, the chance that any single individual will be interviewed—even during a period of two decades—is less than one in 200.

An early experience of mine illustrates dramatically the relative unimportance of numbers in achieving accuracy in polls and the vital importance of reaching a true cross-section of the population sampled.

In the decade preceding the 1936 presidential election, the *Literary Digest* conducted straw polls during elections, with a fair measure of success. The *Literary Digest*'s polling procedure consisted of mailing out millions of postcard ballots to persons whose names were found in telephone directories or on lists of automobile owners.

The system worked so long as voters in average and above-average income groups were as likely to vote Democratic as Republican; and conversely, those in the lower income brackets—the have-nots—were as likely to vote for either party's candidate for the presidency.

With the advent of the New Deal, however, the American electorate became sharply stratified, with many persons in the above average income groups who had been Democrats shifting to the Republican banner, and those below average to the Democratic.

Obviously, a polling system that reached telephone subscribers and automobile owners—the perquisites of the better-off in this era—was certain to overestimate Republican strength in the 1936 election. And that is precisely what did happen. The *Literary Digest*'s final preelection poll showed Landon winning by 57% and Franklin D. Roosevelt losing with 43% of the two-party popular vote.

Landon did not win, as everyone knows. In fact, Roosevelt won by a whopping majority—62.5% to Landon's 37.5%. The error, more than 19 percentage points, was one of the greatest in polling history.

The outcome of the election spelled disaster for the *Literary Digest*'s method of polling, and was a boon to the new type of scientific sampling that was introduced for the first time in that presidential election by my organization, Elmo Roper's, and Archibald Crossley's.

The *Literary Digest* had mailed out 10,000,000 postcard ballots—enough to reach approximately one family in every three at that point in history. A total of 2,376,523 persons took the trouble to mark their postcard ballots and return them.

Experiments with new sampling techniques had been undertaken by my organization as early as 1933. By 1935 the evidence was clear-cut that an important change had come about in the party orientation of voters—that the process of polarization had shifted higher income voters to the right, lower income voters to the left.

When the presidential campaign opened in 1936, it was apparent that the *Literary Digest*'s polling method would produce an inaccurate figure. Tests indicated that a large majority of individuals who were telephone subscribers preferred Landon to FDR, while only 18% of those persons on relief rolls favored Landon.

To warn the public of the likely failure of the *Literary Digest*, I prepared a special newspaper article that was widely printed on July 12, 1936—at the beginning of the campaign. The article stated that the *Literary Digest* would be wrong in its predictions and that it would probably show Landon winning with 56% of the popular vote to 44% for Roosevelt. The reasons why the poll would go wrong were spelled out in detail.

Outraged, the *Literary Digest* editor wrote: "Never before has anyone foretold what our poll was going to show even before it started . . . Our fine statistical friend (George Gallup) should be advised that the Digest would carry on with those old fashioned methods that have produced correct forecasts exactly one hundred percent of the time."

When the election had taken place, our early assessment of what the *Literary Digest* poll would find proved to be almost a perfect prediction of the *Digest*'s final results—actually within 1 percentage point. While this may seem to have been a foolhardy stunt, actually there was little risk. A sample of only 3,000 postcard ballots had been mailed by my office to the same lists of persons who received the

Literary Digest ballot. Because of the workings of the laws of probability, that 3,000 sample should have provided virtually the same result as the *Literary Digest*'s 2,376,523 which, in fact, it did.

Through its own polling, based upon modern sampling procedures, the Gallup Poll, in the 1936 election, reported that the only sure states for Landon were Maine, Vermont, and New Hampshire. The final results showed Roosevelt with 56% of the popular vote to 44% for Landon. The error was 6.8 percentage points, the largest ever made by the Gallup Poll. But because it was on the "right" side, the public gave us full credit, actually more than we deserved.

The *Literary Digest* is not the only poll that has found itself to be on the "wrong" side. All polls, at one time or another, find themselves in this awkward position, including the Gallup Poll in the election of 1948. Ironically, the error in 1936—a deviation of 6.8 percentage points from the true figure—was greater than the error in 1948—5.4 percentage points. But the public's reaction was vastly different.

The failure of polls to have the winning candidate ahead in final results is seldom due to the failure of the poll to include enough persons in its sample. Other factors are likely to prove to be far more important, as will be pointed out later.

Examination of probability tables quickly reveals why polling organizations can use relatively small samples. But first the reader should be reminded that sampling human beings can never produce findings that are *absolutely* accurate except by mere chance, or luck. The aim of the researcher is to come as close as possible to absolute accuracy.

Since money and time are always important considerations in survey operations, the goal is to arrive at sample sizes that will produce results within acceptable margins of error. Fortunately, reasonably accurate findings can be obtained with surprisingly small samples.

Again, it is essential to distinguish between theory and practice. Probability tables are based upon mathematical theory. In actual survey work, these tables provide an important guide, but they can't be applied too literally.

With this qualification in mind, the size of samples to be used in national surveys can now be described. Suppose, for example, that a sample comprises only 600 individuals. What is the theoretical margin of error? If the sample is a perfectly drawn random sample, then the chances are 95 in 100 that the results of a poll of 600 in which those interviewed divide 60% in favor, 40% opposed (or the reverse) will be within 4 percentage points of the true figure; that is, the division in the population is somewhere between 56% and 64% in favor. The odds are even that the error will be less than 2 percentage points—between 58% and 62% in favor, 42% to 38% opposed.

What this means, in the example cited above, is that the odds are 19 to 1 that in repeated samplings the figure for the issue would vary in the case of those favoring the issue from 56% to 64%; the percentage of those opposed would vary between 44% and 36% in repeated samples. So, on the basis of a national sample of only 600 cases, one could say that the odds are great that the addition of many cases—

even millions of cases—would not likely change the majority side to the minority side.

Now, if this sample is doubled in size—from 600 to 1,200—the error factor using the 95 in 100 criterion or confidence level is decreased from 4 percentage points to 2.8 percentage points; if it is doubled again—from 1,200 to 2,400—there is a further decrease—from 2.8 to 2.0, always assuming a mathematically random sample.

Even if a poll were to embrace a total of 2,000,000 individuals, there would still be a chance of error, although tiny. Most survey organizations try to operate within an error range of 4 percentage points at the 95 in 100 confidence level. Accuracy greater than this is not demanded on most issues, nor in most elections, except, of course, those that are extremely close.

Obviously, in many fields an error factor as large as 4 percentage points would be completely unacceptable. In fact, in measuring the rate of unemployment, the government and the press place significance on a change as small as 0.1%. At present, unemployment figures are based upon nationwide samples carried out by the U.S. Bureau of Labor Statistics in the same general manner as polls are conducted. The government bases its findings on samples of some 50,000 persons. But samples even of this size are not sufficient to warrant placing confidence in a change as small as 0.1%. And yet such a change is often headlined on the front pages as indicating a real and significant change in the employment status of the nation.

Even if one were totally unfamiliar with the laws of probability, empirical evidence would suffice to demonstrate that the amassing of thousands of cases does not change results except to a minor extent.

An experiment conducted early in the Gallup Poll's history will illustrate this point. At the time—in the middle 1930s—the National Recovery Act (N.R.A.) was a hotly debated issue. Survey results were tabulated as the ballots from all areas of the United States were returned. The figures below are those actually obtained as each lot of new ballots was tabulated.

NUMBER OF RETURNED BALLOTS	PERCENT VOTING IN FAVOR OF THE N.R.A.
First 500	54.9%
First 1,000	53.9
First 5,000	55.4
First 10,000	55.4
First 30,000	55.5

From these results it can be seen that if only 500 ballots had been received, the figure would have differed little from the final result. In fact the greatest difference found in the whole series is only 1.6 percentage points from the final result.

This example represents a typical experience of researchers in this field. But one precaution needs to be observed. The returns must come from a representative sample of the population being surveyed; otherwise they could be as misleading as trying to project the results of a national election from the vote registered late in the afternoon of election day in a New Hampshire village.

The theoretical error, as noted earlier, can be used only as a guide. The expected errors in most surveys are usually somewhat larger. In actual survey practice, some sample design elements tend to reduce the range of error, as stratification does; some tend to increase the range of error as, for example, clustering. But these are technical matters to be dealt with in textbooks on statistics.

Survey organizations should, on the basis of their intimate knowledge of their sampling procedures and the analysis of their data, draw up their own tables of suggested tolerances to enable laymen to interpret their survey findings intelligently.

The normal sampling unit of the Gallup Poll consists of 1,500 individuals of voting age, that is, eighteen years and over. A sample of this size gives reasonable assurance that the margin of error for results representing the entire country will be less than 3 percentage points based on the factor of size alone.

The margin for sampling error is obviously greater for subgroups. For example, the views of individuals who have attended college are frequently reported. Since about one-fourth of all persons over eighteen years have attended college, the margin of error must be computed on the basis of one-fourth the total sample of 1,500, or 375. Instead of a margin of error of 3 percentage points, the error factor increases to 6 or 7 percentage points in the typical cluster sample.

In dealing with some issues, interest focuses on the views of subgroups such as Blacks, labor union members, Catholics, or young voters—all representing rather small segments of the total population. Significant findings for these subgroups are possible only by building up the size of the total sample.

This can be done in the case of the Gallup Poll by including the same question or questions in successive surveys. Since different, but comparable, persons are interviewed in each study, subgroup samples can be enlarged accordingly. Thus, in a single survey approximately 165 Blacks and other nonwhites would be interviewed in a sample of 1,500, since they constitute 11% of the total voting-age population. On three successive surveys a total of 495 would be reached—enough to provide a reasonably stable base to indicate their views on important political and social issues.

Since much interest before and after elections is directed toward the way different groups in the population vote, it has been the practice of the Gallup Poll to increase the size of its samples during the final month before election day to be in a position to report the political preferences of the many groups that make up the total population—information that cannot be obtained by analyzing the actual election returns. Election results, for example, do not reveal how women voted as opposed to men, how the different age groups voted, how different religious groups voted, how different income levels voted. Many other facts about the public's voting habits can be obtained only through the survey method.

During the heat of election campaigns, critics have asserted on occasion that the Gallup Poll increases its sample size solely to make more certain of being "right." Examination of trend figures effectively answers this criticism. The results reported on the basis of the standard sampling unit have not varied, on the average, more than 1 or 2 percentage points from the first enlarged sample in all of the national elections of the last two decades, and this, of course, is within the margin of error expected.

Persons unfamiliar with the laws of probability invariably assume that the size of the sample must bear a fixed relationship to the size of the "universe" sampled. For example, such individuals are likely to assume that if a polling organization is sampling opinions of the whole United States, a far larger sample is necessary than if the same kind of survey is to be conducted in a single state, or in a single city. Or, to put this in another way, the assumption is that since the population of the United States is roughly ten times that of New York State, then the sample of the United States should be ten times as large.

The laws of probability, however, do not work in this fashion. Whenever the population to be surveyed is many times the size of the sample (which it typically is), the size of samples must be almost the same. If one were conducting a poll in Baton Rouge, Louisiana, on a mayoralty race, the size of the sample should be virtually the same as for the whole United States. The same principle applies to a state.

Two examples, drawn from everyday life, may help to explain this rather mystifying fact. Suppose that a hotel cook has two kinds of soup on the stove—one in a very large pot, another in a small pot. After thoroughly stirring the soup in both pots, the cook need not take a greater number of spoonsful from the large pot or fewer spoonsful from the small pot to taste the quality of the soup, since the quality should be the same.

The second example, taken from the statistician's world, may shed further light on this phenomenon. Assume that 100,000 black and white balls are placed in a large cask. The white balls number 70,000; the black balls, 30,000. Into another cask, a much smaller one, are placed 1,000 balls, divided in exactly the same proportion: 700 white balls, 300 black balls.

Now the balls in each cask are thoroughly mixed and a person, blindfolded, is asked to draw out of each cask exactly 100 balls. The likelihood of drawing 70 white balls and 30 black balls is virtually the same, despite the fact that one cask contains 100 times as many balls as the other.

If this principle were understood then hours of Senate floor time could have been saved in recent years. Senator Albert Gore, of Tennessee, a few years ago, had this to say about the Gallup Poll's sampling unit of 1,500—as reported in the *Congressional Record*:

As a layman I would question that a straw poll of less than 1 per cent of the people could under any reasonable circumstance be regarded as a fair and meaningful cross-section. This would be something more than 500 times as large a sample as Dr. Gallup takes.

In the same discussion on the Senate floor, Senator Russell Long of Lousiana added these remarks:

I believe one reason why the poll information could not be an accurate reflection of what the people are thinking is depicted in this example. Suppose we should try to find how many persons should be polled in a city the size of New Orleans in order to determine how an election should go. In a city that size, about 600,000 people, a number of 1,000 would be an appropriate number to sample to see how the election was likely to go. . . . In my home town of Baton Rouge, Lousiana, I might very well sample perhaps 300 or 400 people and come up with a fairly accurate guess as to how the city or the parish would go, especially if a scientific principle were used. But if I were to sample only a single person or two or three in that entire city, the chances are slim that I would come up with an accurate guess.

If the reader has followed the explanation of the workings of the laws of probability, and of earlier statements about the size of samples, he will be aware of two errors in the senator's reasoning. Since both cities, New Orleans and Baton Rouge, have populations many times the size of the sample he suggested, both require samples of the same size. The second is his assumption that any good researcher would possibly attempt to draw conclusions about either city on the basis of "a single person or two."

The size of the "universe" to be sampled is typically very great in the case of most surveys; in fact, it is usually many times the size of the samples to be obtained. A different principle applies when the "universe" is small. The size of a sample needed to assess opinions of the residents of a community of 1,000 voters is obviously different from that required for a city that is much larger. A sample of 1,000 in such a town would not be a sample; it would be a complete canvass.

DEVELOPING POLL QUESTIONS

Nothing is so difficult, nor so important, as the selection and wording of poll questions. In fact, most of my time and effort in the field of polling has been devoted to this problem.

The questions included in a national survey of public opinion should meet many tests: they must deal with the vital issues of the day, they must be worded in a way to get at the heart of these issues, they must be stated in language understandable to the least well educated, and finally, they must be strictly impartial in presenting the issue.

If any reader thinks this is easy, let him try to word questions on any present-day issue. It is a tough and trying mental task. And even years of experience do not make the problem less onerous.

One rule must always be followed. No question, no matter how simple, must reach the interviewing stage without first having gone through a thorough pretesting procedure. Many tests must be applied to see that each question meets required standards.

Every survey organization has its own methods of testing the wording of questions. Here it will suffice to describe in some detail how the Gallup Poll goes about this task.

Pretesting of questions dealing with complicated issues is carried on in the Interviewing Center maintained in Hopewell, New Jersey, by the Gallup organizations. Formerly, this center was a motion-picture theater. In the early 1950s it was converted into an interviewing center. The town of Hopewell is located in the middle of an area with a total population of 500,000—an area that includes the cities of Trenton and Princeton, suburban communities, small towns, and rural districts. Consequently, people from many walks of life are available for interviewing.

Pretesting procedures normally start with "in-depth" interviews with a dozen or more individuals invited to come to the center. The purpose of these interviews is to find out how much thought each participant has given to the issue under consideration, the level of his or her knowledge about the issue, and the important facets that must be probed. Most of the questions asked in these sessions are "open" questions—that is, questions which ask: "What do you know about the XX problem? What do you think about it? What should the government do about it?" and so forth.

In conversations evoked by questions of this type, it is possible, in an unhurried manner, to discover how much knowledge average persons have of a given issue, the range of views regarding it, and the special aspects of the issue that need to be probed if a series of questions is to be developed.

The next step is to try out the questions, devised at this first stage, on a new group of respondents, to see if the questions are understandable and convey the meaning intended. A simple test for this can be employed. After reading the question, the respondent is asked to "play back" what it says to him. The answer quickly reveals whether the person being interviewed understands the language used and whether he grasps the main point of the question. This approach can also reveal, to the trained interviewer, any unsuspected biases in the wording of the question. When the language in which a question is stated is not clear to the interviewee, his typical reaction is: "Will you read that question again?" If questions have to be repeated, this is unmistakable evidence that they should be worded in a simpler and more understandable manner.

Another procedure that has proved valuable in testing questions is the self-administered interview. The respondent, without the benefit of an interviewer, writes out the answers to the questions. The advantages of this procedure are many. Answers show whether the individual has given real thought to the issue and reveal, also, the degree of his interest. If he has no opinion, he will typically leave the question blank. If he has a keen interest in the issue, he will spell out his views in some detail. And if he is misinformed, this becomes apparent in what he writes.

Self-administered questionnaires can be filled out in one's own home, or privately in an interviewing center. Since the interviewer is not at hand, many issues, such as those dealing with sex, drug addiction, alcoholism, and other personal matters, can be covered in this manner. The interviewer's function is merely to drop off the questionnaire, and pick it up in a sealed envelope the next day—or the respondent can mail it directly to the Princeton office.

Even with all of these precautions, faulty question wordings do sometimes find their way onto the survey interviewing form. Checks for internal consistency, made when the ballots are returned and are tabulated, usually bring to light these shortcomings.

Most important, the reader himself must be the final judge. The Gallup Poll, from its establishment in 1935, has followed the practice of including the exact wording of questions, when this is important, in the report of the poll findings. The reader is thus in a position to decide whether the question is worded impartially and whether the interpretation of the results, based upon the question asked, is fair and objective.

A United States senator has brought up another point about questions:

> How do pollsters like yourself determine what questions to ask from time to time? It seems to me that pollsters can affect public opinion simply by asking the question. The results could be pro or anti the president depending upon the questions asked and the president's relation to it.

To be sure, a series of questions could be asked that would prove awkward to the administration, even though worded impartially, and interpreted objectively. But this would be self-defeating because it would soon become apparent to readers and commentators that the survey organization was not engaged solely in fact-finding but was trying to promote a cause.

One way to prevent unintentional biases from creeping into survey operations is to have a staff that is composed of persons representing the different shades of political belief—from right to left. If not only the questions but also the written reports dealing with the results have to run this gamut—as is the practice in the Gallup office—the dangers of unintentional bias are decreased accordingly.

Still one more safeguard in dealing with biases of any type comes about through the financial support of a poll. If sponsors represent all shades of political belief, then economic pressures alone help to keep a poll on the straight and narrow path.

So much for bias in the wording and selection of questions. This still does not answer the question posed by some who wish to know what standards or practices are followed in deciding what issues to present to the public.

Since the chief aim of a modern public opinion poll is to assess public opinion on the important issues of the day and to chart the trend of sentiment, it follows that most subjects chosen for investigation must deal with current national and international issues, and particularly those that have an immediate concern for the typical citizen. Newspapers, magazine, and the broadcast media are all useful sources of ideas for polls. Suggestions for poll subjects come from individuals and institutions—from members of Congress, editors, public officials, and foundations. Every few weeks the public itself is questioned about the most important problems facing the nation, as they see them. Their answers to this question establish priorities, and provide an up-to-date list of areas to explore through polling.

A widely held assumption is that questions can be twisted to get any answer you want. In the words of one publisher: "If you word a question one way you get a result which may differ substantially from the result you get if you word the question in a different way."

It's not that easy. Questions can be worded in a manner to bring confusing and misleading results. But the loaded question is usually self-defeating because it is obvious that it is biased.

Hundreds of experiments with a research procedure known as the split-ballot technique (one-half the cross-section gets Question A, the other half Question B) have proved that even a wide variation in question wordings did not bring substantially different results if the basic meaning or substance of the question remained the same.

Change the basic meaning of the question, add or leave out an essential part, and the results will change accordingly, as they should. Were people insensitive to words—if they were unable to distinguish between one concept and another—then the whole *raison d'être* of polling would vanish.

Often the interpreters of poll findings draw inferences that are not warranted or make assumptions that a close reading of the question does not support. Consider, for example, these two questions:

"Do you feel the United States should have gotten involved in Vietnam in the first place?"

"Do you feel the United States should have helped South Vietnam to defend itself?"

While at first glance these questions seem to deal with the same point—America's involvement—actually they are probing widely different aspects of involvement. In the first case, the respondent can read in that we helped Vietnam "with our own troops"; in the second question, that our help would have been limited to materials. Many polls have shown that the American people are willing to give military supplies to almost any nation in the world that is endangered by the communists, but they are unwilling to send troops.

If the two questions cited above did not bring substantially different results, then all the other poll results dealing with this issue would be misleading.

Questions must be stated in words that everyone understands, and results are likely to be misleading to the extent that the words are not fully understood. Ask people whether they are disturbed about the amount of pornography in their magazines and newspapers and you will get one answer; if you talk about the amount of smut you will get another.

Word specialists may insist that every word in the language conveys a slightly different connotation to every individual. While this may be true, the world (and polls) must operate on the principle that commonly used words convey approximately the same meaning to the vast majority. And this fact can easily be established in the pretesting of questions. When a question is read to a respondent and he is then asked to "play it back" in his own words, it becomes quickly evident whether he has understood the words, and in fact, what they mean to him.

Some questions that pass this test can still be faulty. The sophisticated poll watcher should be on the alert for the "desirable goal" question. This type of question ties together a desirable goal with a proposal for reaching this end. The respondent typically reacts to the goal as well as to the means. Here are some examples of desirable goal questions:

"To win the war quickly in Vietnam, would you favor all-out bombing of North Vietnam?"

"To reduce crime in the cities, would you favor increasing jail and prison sentences?"

"In order to improve the quality of education in the United States, should teachers be paid higher salaries?"

These questions, which present widely accepted goals accompanied by the tacit assumption that the means suggested will bring about the desired end, produce results biased on the favorable side.

The more specific questions are, the better. One of the classic arguments between newspapers and television has centered around a question that asks the public: "Where do you get most of your news about what's going on in the world today—from the newspaper, or radio, or television, or magazines, or talking to people, or where?" The answers show TV ahead of daily newspapers. But when this question is asked in a way to differentiate between international news, and local and state news, TV wins on international news, but the daily newspaper has a big lead on local news. A simple explanation is that the phrase, "What is going on in the *world?*" is interpreted by the average citizen to mean in the faraway places—not his home city.

People are extremely literal minded. A farmer in Ontario, interviewed by the Canadian Gallup Poll, was asked at the close of the interview how long he had lived in the same house; specifically, the length of his residence there. The answer that came back was "Twenty-six feet and six inches."

Whenever it is possible, the questions asked should state both sides of the issue. Realistic alternatives should be offered, or implied.

Looking back through more than four decades of polling, this aspect of question wording warrants the greatest criticism. There is probably little need to state the other side, or offer an alternative, in a question such as this: "Should the voting age be lowered to include those eighteen years of age?" The alternative implied is to leave the situation as it is.

An excellent observation has been made by a political scientist on the faculty of a New England college:

> Somehow more realism must be introduced into polls. . . . People often affirm abstract principles but will not be willing to pay the price of their concrete application. For example, would you be willing to pay more for each box of soap you buy in order to reduce ground pollution—or $200 more for your next car in order to reduce air pollution, etc.?

This type of question is similar to the desirable goal question. The public wants to clear the slums, wants better medical care, improved racial relations, better schools, better housing. The real issue is one of priorities and costs. The role of the public opinion poll in this situation is to shed light on the public's concern about each major problem, establish priorities, and then discover whether the people are willing to foot the bill.

The well-informed person is likely to think of the costs involved by legislation that proposes to deal with these social problems. But to the typical citizen there is no immediate or direct relationship between legislation and the amount he has to pay in taxes. Congress usually tries to disguise costs by failing to tie taxes or costs to large appropriations, leaving John Doe with the impression that someone else will pay the bill.

Still another type of question that is suspect has to do with good intentions. Questions of this type have meaning only when controls are used and when the results are interpreted with a full understanding of their shortcomings.

Examples of questions that fall into this category are those asking people if they "plan to go to church," "read a book," "listen to good music," "vote in the coming election," and so forth.

To the typical American the word "intend" or "plan" connotes many things, such as "Do I think this is a good idea?" "Would I like to do it?" "Would it be good for me?" "Would it be good for other people?" These and similar questions of a prestige nature reveal attitudes, but they are a poor guide to action.

Behavior is always the best guide. The person who attended church last Sunday is likely to go next Sunday, if he says he plans to. The citizen who voted in the last election and whose name is now on the registration books is far more likely to vote than the person who hasn't bothered to vote or to register, even though he insists that he "plans" to do both.

Probably the most difficult of all questions to word is the type that offers the respondent several alternatives. Not only is it hard to find alternatives that are mutually exclusive; it is equally difficult to find a series that covers the entire range of opinions. Added to this is the problem of wording each alternative in a way that doesn't give it a special advantage. And finally, in any series of alternatives that ranges from one extreme of opinion to the other, the typical citizen has a strong inclination to choose one in the middle.

As a working principle it can be stated that the more words included in a question, either by way of explanation or in stating alternatives, the greater the possibilities that the question wording itself will influence answers.

A member of the editorial staff of a newsmagazine voiced a common reaction when he observed:

> On more than a few occasions I have found that I could not, were I asked, answer a poll with a "yes" or "no." More likely my answer would be "yes, but" or "yes, if." I wonder whether pollsters can't or just don't want to measure nuances of feeling.

Obviously it is the desire of a polling organization to produce a full and accurate account of the public's views on any given issue, nuances and all.

First, however, it should be pointed out that there are two main categories of questions serving two different purposes—one to *measure* public opinion, the other to *describe* public opinion. The first category has to do with the "referendum" type of question. Since the early years of polling, heavy emphasis has been placed upon this type of question, which serves in effect as an unofficial national referendum on a given issue, actually providing the same results, within a small margin of error, that an official nationwide referendum would if it were held at the same time and on the same issue.

At some point in the decision process, whether it be concerned with an important issue before Congress, a new law before the state legislature, or a school bond issue in Central City, the time comes for a simple "yes" or "no" vote. Fortunately, or unfortunately, there is no lever on a voting machine that permits the voter to register a "yes, if" or a "yes, but" vote. While discussion can and should proceed at length, the only way to determine majority opinion is by a simple count of noses.

If polling organizations limited themselves to the referendum type of question they would severely restrict their usefulness. They can and should use their machinery to reveal the many facets of public opinion of any issue, and to shed light on the reasons why the people hold the views they do; in short, to explore the "why" behind public opinion.

More and more attention is being paid to this diagnostic approach and the greatest improvements in the field of public opinion research in the future are likely to deal with this aspect of polling.

One of the important developments in question technique was the development in the late 1940s of a new kind of question design that permits the investigation of views on any issue of a complex nature.

This design, developed by the Gallup Poll, has been described as the "quintamensional approach" since it probes five aspects of opinion:

1. the respondent's awareness and general knowledge about it,
2. his overall opinions,
3. the reasons why he holds his views,
4. his specific views on specific aspects of the problem,
5. the intensity with which he hold his opinions.

This question design quickly sorts out those who have no knowledge of a given issue—an important function in successful public opinion polling. And it can even reveal the extent or level of knowledge of the interviewee about the issue.

This is how the system works. The first question put to the person being interviewed (on any problem or issue no matter how complex) is this: "Have you heard or read about the XXX problem (proposal or issue)?"

The person being interviewed can answer either "yes" or "no" to this question, or he can add, "I'm not sure." If he answers in the negative, experience covering many years indicates that he is being entirely truthful. If he answers "yes" or "I'm not sure" he is then asked: "Please tell me in your own words what the debate (or the proposal or issue) is about." At this point the person interviewed must produce evidence that reveals whether he has some knowledge of the problem or issue.

The reader might imagine himself in this interviewing situation. You are called upon by an interviewer and in the course of the interview are asked if you have "heard or read about the Bronson proposal to reorganize the Security Council of the United Nations." The answer is likely to be "no." Possibly you might say: "I seem to have heard about it somewhere." Or suppose that, just to impress the interviewer (something that rarely happens) you fall into the trap of saying "yes."

The next question puts you neatly and delicately on the spot. It asks you to describe in your own words what the Bronson proposal is. You have to admit at this point that you do not know, or come up with an answer that immediately indicates you do not know what it is.

At this stage the questioning can be expanded to discover just how well informed you are. If it is an issue or proposal, then you can be asked to give the main arguments for and the main arguments against the plan or issue. In short, by adding questions at this stage, the *level* of knowledge of the respondent can be determined.

The next question in the design is an "open" question that asks simply: "What do you think should be done about this proposal?" or "How do you think this issue should be resolved?" This type of question permits the person being interviewed to give his views without any specifics being mentioned. Answers, of course, are recorded by the interviewer as nearly as possible in the exact words of the respondent.

The third category of questions seeks to find out the "why" behind the respondent's views. This can be done with a simple question asking: "Why do you feel that way?" or variations of this, along with "nondirective" probes such as "What else?" or "Can you explain that in greater detail?"

The fourth category in the design poses specific issues that can be answered in "yes" or "no" fashion. At this fourth stage it is possible to go back to those who were excluded by the first two questions: those who said they had not heard or read about the issue in question or proved, after the second question, that they were uninformed.

By explaining in neutral language to this group what the problem or issue is and the specific proposals that have been made for dealing with it, the uninformed can voice their opinions, which later can be compared with those of the already informed group.

The fifth category attempts to get at the intensity with which opinions are held. How strongly does each side hold to its views? What action is each individual willing to take to see that his opinion prevails? What chance is there that he may change his mind?

This, then, is the quintamensional approach. And its special merit is that it can quickly sort out the informed from the uninformed. The views of the well informed can be compared not only with the less well informed but with those who are learning about the issue for the first time. Moreover, through cross-tabulations, it is possible to show how special kinds of knowledge are related to certain opinions.

The filtering process may screen out nearly all individuals in the sample because they are uninformed, but it is often of interest and importance to know how the few informed individuals divide on a complex issue. When the best informed individuals favor a proposal or issue, experience indicates that their view tends to be accepted by lower echelons as information and knowledge become more widespread.

But this is not the invariable pattern. In the case of Vietnam, it was the best educated and the best informed who reversed their views as the war went on. The least well educated were always more against the war in Vietnam.

It is now proper to ask why, with all of its obvious merits, this question design is not used more often. The answer is that polling organizations generally avoid technical and complex issues, preferring to deal with those on which the vast majority of Americans have knowledge and opinions. Often the design is shortened to embrace only the filter question that seeks to find out if the individual has read or heard about a given issue, and omits the other questions.

In the field of public opinion research, one finds two schools of thought: one is made up largely of those in academic circles who believe that research on public attitudes should be almost entirely descriptive or diagnostic; the other, made up largely of persons in political life or in journalism or allied fields, who want to know the "score." It is the task of the polling organization to satisfy both groups. And to do this, both categories of questions must be included in the surveys conducted at regular intervals.

The long experience of the Gallup Poll points to the importance of reporting trends of opinion on all the continuing problems, the beliefs, the wishes of the people.

In fact, about four out of every ten questions included in a typical survey are for the purpose of measuring trends. Simple "yes" and "no" questions are far better suited to this purpose than "open-ended" questions, and this accounts chiefly for the high percentage of this type of question in the field of polling.

INTERVIEWERS AND INTERVIEWING PROBLEMS

Since the reliability of poll results depends so much on the integrity of interviewers, polling organizations must go to great lengths to see that interviewers follow instructions conscientiously.

A professor at an Ivy League college sums up the problems that have to do with interviewers in this question: "How do you insure quality control over your interviewers, preventing them from either influencing the answers, mis-recording them, or filling in the forms themselves?"

Before these specific points are dealt with, the reader may wish to know who the interviewers are and how they are selected and trained.

Women make the best interviewers, not only in the United States but in virtually every nation where public opinion survey organizations are established. Generally, they are more conscientious and more likely to follow instructions than men. Perhaps the nature of the work makes interviewing more appealing to them. The fact that the work is part-time is another reason why women prefer it.

Most interviewers are women of middle age, with high-school or college education. Most are married and have children.

Very few interviewers devote full time to this work. In fact, this is not recommended. Interviewing is mentally exhausting and the interviewer who works day after day at this task is likely to lose her zeal, with a consequent drop in the quality of her work.

When an area is drawn for the national cross-section, the interviewing department of the polling organization finds a suitable person to serve as the interviewer in this particular district. All the usual methods of seeking individuals who can meet the requirements are utilized, including such sources as school superintendents, newspaper editors, members of the clergy, and the classified columns of the local press.

Training for this kind of work can be accomplished by means of an instruction manual, by a supervisor, or by training sessions. The best training consists of a kind of trial-by-fire process. The interviewer is given test interviews to do after she has completed her study of the instruction manual. The trial interviews prove whether she can do the work in a satisfactory manner; more important, making these interviews enables the interviewer to discover if she really likes this kind of work. Her interviews are carefully inspected and investigated. Telephone conversations often straighten out procedures and clear up any misunderstandings about them.

Special questions added to the interviewing form and internal checks on consistency can be used to detect dishonesty. Also, a regular program of contacting persons who have been interviewed—to see if they in fact have been interviewed—is commonly employed by the best survey organizations.

It would be foolhardy to insist that every case of dishonesty can be detected in this manner, but awareness of the existence of these many ways of checking honesty removes most if not all of the temptation for the interviewers to fill in the answers themselves.

Experience of many years indicates that the temptation to "fudge" answers is related to the size of the work load given to the interviewer. If too many interviews are required in too short a time, the interviewer may hurry through the assignment, being less careful than she otherwise would be and, on occasion, not above the temptation to fill in a last few details.

To lessen this pressure, the assignment of interviews given to Gallup Poll interviewers has been constantly reduced through the years. At the present time, an assignment consists of only five or six interviews, and assignments come at least a week apart. This policy increases the cost per interview but it also keeps the interviewer from being subjected to too great pressure.

In the case of open questions that require the interviewer to record the exact words of the respondent, the difficulties mount. The interviewer must attempt to record the main thought of the respondent as the respondent is talking, and usually without benefit of shorthand. The addition of "probe" questions to the original open-end questions helps to organize the response in a more meaningful way. In certain circumstances, the use of small tape recorders, carried by the interviewer, is highly recommended.

So much for the interviewer's side of this situation. What about the person being interviewed? How honest is he?

While there is no certain way of telling whether a given individual is answering truthfully, the evidence from thousands of surveys is that people are remarkably honest and frank when asked their views in a situation that is properly structured— that is, when the respondent knows the purpose of the interview and is told that his name will not be attached to any of the things he says, and when the questions are properly worded.

It is important to point out that persons reached in a public opinion survey normally do not know the interviewer personally. For this reason, there is little or no reason to try to impress her. And, contrary to a widely held view, people are not inclined to "sound off" on subjects they know little about. In fact, many persons entitled, on the basis of their knowledge, to hold an opinion about a given problem or issue often hesitate to do so. In the development of the quintamensional procedure, described earlier, it was discovered that the opening question could not be stated: "Have you *followed* the discussion about the XX issue?" Far too many said they hadn't. And for this reason the approach had to be changed to ask: "Have you *heard or read* about the XX issue?"

The interviewer is instructed to read the question exactly as it is worded, and not try to explain it or amplify it. If the interviewee says, "Would you repeat that?" (incidentally, this is always the mark of a bad question), the interviewer repeats the question, and if on the second reading the person does not understand or get the point of the question, the interviewer checks the "no opinion" box and goes on to the next question.

But don't people often change their minds? This is a question often asked of poll-takers. The answer is, "Of course." Interviewed on Saturday, some persons may have a different opinion on Sunday. But this is another instance when the law of averages comes to the rescue. Those who shift their views in one direction will almost certainly be counterbalanced by those who change in the opposite direction. The net result is to show no change in the overall results.

Polls can only reflect people as they are—sometimes inconsistent, often uninformed. Democracy, however, does not require that every individual, every voter, be a philosopher. Democracy requires only that the sum total of individual views—the collective judgment—add up to something that makes sense. Fortunately, there now exists some forty years of polling evidence to prove the soundness of the collective judgment of the people.

How many persons refuse to be interviewed? The percentage is very small, seldom more than 10% of all those contacted. Interestingly, this same figure is found in all the nations where public opinion polls are conducted. Refusals are chiefly a function of lack of interviewing skill. Top interviewers are rarely turned down. This does not mean that a man who must get back to work immediately or a woman who has a cake in the oven will take thirty to forty-five minutes to discuss issues of the day. These situations are to be avoided. And that is why the Time-Place interviewing plan was developed by the Gallup Poll.

Readers may wonder how polls allow for the possible embarrassment or guilty conscience factor that might figure in an interviewee's answers to some questions. For example, while a voter might be prepared to vote for a third-party candidate like George Wallace, he might be uneasy about saying so to a stranger sitting in his living room.

When interviews and the interviewing situation are properly structured, however, this does not happen. In the 1968 election campaign, to follow the same example, the Gallup Poll found Wallace receiving at one point as much as 19% of the total vote. Later his popularity declined. The final poll result showed him with 15% of the vote; he actually received 14%. If there had been any embarrassment about admitting being for Wallace, his vote would obviously have been under-estimated by a sizable amount.

Properly approached, people are not reluctant to discuss even personal matters—their private problems, their religion, sex. By using an interesting technique developed in Sweden, even the most revealing facts about the sex life of an individual can be obtained. And the same type of approach is found to be highly successful in finding out the extent of drug use by college students. Many studies about the religious beliefs of individuals have been conducted by the Gallup Poll without meeting interviewing difficulties.

The desire to have one's voice heard on issues of the day is almost universal. An interviewer called upon an elderly man and found him working in his garden. After he had offered his views on many subjects included in the poll, he called to the interviewer who had started for her car, and said: "You know, two of the most important things in my life have happened this week. First, I was asked to serve on a jury, and now I have been asked to give my views in a public opinion poll."

MEASURING INTENSITY

To the legislator or administrator the intensity with which certain voters or groups of voters hold their opinions has special significance. If people feel strongly enough about a given issue they will likely do something about it—write letters, work for a candidate who holds a contrary view, contribute money to a campaign, try to win other voters to their candidate. To cite an example: Citizens who oppose any kind of gun control laws, though constituting a minority of the public, feel so strongly about this issue that they will do anything they can to defeat such legislation. As a result, they have succeeded in keeping strict gun laws from being adopted in most states and by the federal government.

Since most legislation calls for more money, a practical measure of the intensity of feeling about a given piece of legislation is the willingness to have taxes increased to meet the costs.

One politician made this criticism of polling efforts: "Issue polling often fails to differentiate between hard and soft opinion. If the issue is national health insurance, then the real test is not whether the individual favors it but how much more per year he is willing to pay in taxes for such a program."

This is a merited criticism of polls and, as stated earlier, one that points to the need for greater attention on the part of polling organizations. The action that an individual is willing to take—the sacrifice he is willing to undergo—to see that his side of an issue prevails is one of the best ways of sorting out hard from soft opinion.

Questions put to respondents about "how strongly" they feel, "how important it is to them," and "how much they care" all yield added insights into the intensity of opinions held by the public. The fact, however, that they are used as seldom as they are in the regular polls, here and abroad, indicates that the added information gained does not compensate for the time and the difficulties encountered by the survey interviewer. Most attitude scales are, in fact, better suited to the classroom with students as captive subjects than to the face-to-face interviews undertaken by most survey organizations.

The best hope, in my opinion, lies in the development of new questions that are behavior- or action-oriented. Here, then, is an important area where both academicians and practitioners can work together in the improvement of present research procedures.

The specific complaint mentioned above—that of providing a more realistic presentation of an issue—can probably be dealt with best in the question wording, as noted earlier.

While verbal scales to measure intensity can be usefully employed in many situations, two nonverbal scales have gained wide acceptance and use throughout the world. Since they do not depend upon words, language is no barrier to their use in any nation. Moreover, they can be employed in normal interviewing situations, and on a host of problems.

The scales were devised by Jan Stapel of the Netherlands Institute of Public Opinion and by Hadley Cantril and a colleague, F. P. Kilpatrick. While the scales seem to be similar, each has its own special merits.

The Stapel scale consists of a column of ten boxes. The five at the top are white, the five at the bottom black.

The boxes are numbered from +5 to −5. The interviewer carries a reproduction of this scale and at the appropriate time in the interview hands it to the respondent. The interviewer explains the scale in these or similar words: "You will notice that the boxes on this card go from the highest position of plus 5—something you like very much—all the way down to the lowest position of minus 5—or something you dislike very much. Now, how far up the scale, or how far down the scale, would you rate the following?"

After this explanation, the interviewer asks the respondent how far up or down the scale he would rate an individual, political party, product, company, proposal, or almost anything at issue. The person is told "put your finger on the box" that best represents his point of view; or, in other situations, to call off the number opposite the box. The interviewer duly records this number on his interviewing form.

One of the merits of the Stapel Scalometer is that it permits the person being interviewed to answer two questions with one response: whether he has a positive or a negative feeling toward the person or party or institution being rated, and at the same time the degree of his liking or disliking. By simply calling off a number he indicates that he has a favorable or unfavorable opinion of the F.B.I., of Jimmy Carter, or of the Equal Rights Amendment, and how much he likes or dislikes each. In actual use, researchers have found the extreme positions on the scale are most indicative and most sensitive to change. These are the $+4$ and $+5$ positions on the favorable side and the -4 and -5 positions on the negative side. Normally these two positions are combined to provide a "highly favorable" or a "highly unfavorable" rating.

Scale ratings thus obtained are remarkably consistent and remarkably reliable in ranking candidates and parties. In fact, the ratings given to the two major-party candidates have paralleled the relative standings of the candidates in elections, especially when the party ratings are averaged with the candidate ratings.

Cantril and Kilpatrick devised the "Self-Anchoring Scale."* Cantril and his associate, Lloyd Free, used this scale to measure the aspirations and fears of people in different nations of the world—both those living in highly developed countries and those in the least developed. They sought "to get an overall picture of the reality worlds in which people lived, a picture expressed by individuals in their own terms and to do this in such a way . . . as to enable meaningful comparisons to be made between different individuals, groups of individuals, and societies."

The Self-Anchoring scale is so simple that it can be used with illiterates and with people without any kind of formal education. A multination survey in which this measuring instrument was employed included nations as diverse in their educational and living standards as Nigeria, India, the United States, West Germany, Cuba, Israel, Japan, Poland, Panama, Yugoslavia, Philippines, Brazil, and the Dominican Republic.

---

*F. P. Kilpatrick and Hadley Cantril, "Self-Anchoring Scale." *Journal of Individual Psychology,* November 1960.

The scale makes use of a ladder device.

```
———— 10 ————
———— 9 ————
———— 8 ————
———— 7 ————
———— 6 ————
———— 5 ————
———— 4 ————
———— 3 ————
———— 2 ————
———— 1 ————
———— 0 ————
```

The person being interviewed describes his own wishes and hopes, the realization of which would constitute the best possible life. This is the top anchoring point of the scale. At the other extreme, the same individual describes his worries and fears embodied in the worst possible life he can imagine. With the use of this device, he is asked where he thinks he stands on the ladder today. Then he is asked where he thinks he stood in the past, and where he thinks he will stand in the future.

This same procedure was used by Albert Cantril and Charles Roll in a survey called *Hopes and Fears of the American People*—a revealing study of the mood of the American people in the spring of 1971.

Use of this scale would be extremely helpful in pursuing the goal set forth by Alvin Toffler in his book *Future Shock*. He writes:

The time has come for a dramatic reassessment of the directions of change, a reassessment made not by the politicians or the sociologists or the clergy or the elitist revolutionaries, not by technicians or college presidents, but by the people themselves. We need, quite literally, to "go to the people" with a question that is almost never asked of them: *"What kind of a world do you want 10, 20, or 30 years from now?"* We need to initiate, in short, a continuing plebiscite on the future. Toffler points out that "the voter may be polled about specific issues, but not about the general shape of the preferable future."

This is true to a great extent. With the exception of the Cantril-Free studies, this area has been largely overlooked by polling organizations. Toffler advocates a continuing plebiscite in which millions of persons would participate. From a practical point of view, however, sampling offers the best opportunity to discover just what the public's ideas of the future are—and more particularly, the kind of world they want ten years, twenty years, or thirty years from now.

REPORTING AND INTERPRETING POLL FINDINGS

Public opinion polls throughout the world have been sponsored by the media of communication—newspapers, magazines, television, and radio. It is quite proper, therefore, to answer this question: "How well do the various media report and evaluate the results of a given poll?"

Since October 1935, Gallup Poll reports have appeared weekly in American newspapers in virtually all of the major cities. During this period, I am happy to report, no newspaper has changed the wording of poll releases sent to them to make the findings fit the newspaper's editorial or political views. Editors, however, are permitted to write their own headlines because of their own special type and format policies; they can shorten articles or, in fact, omit them if news columns are filled by other and more pressing material.

Since the funds for the Gallup Poll come from this source and since the sponsoring newspapers represent all shades of political belief, the need for strict objectivity in the writing and interpretation of poll results becomes an economic as well as a scientific necessity.

At various stages in the history of the Gallup Poll, charges have been made that the poll has a Republican bias, and at other times, a Democratic bias, largely dependent upon whether the political tide is swinging toward one side or the other. Even a cursory examination of the findings dealing with issues of the day, and of election survey results, will disprove this.

The Gallup Poll is a fact-finding organization, or looked at in another way, a kind of scorekeeper in the political world.

When poll findings are not to the liking of critics there is always a great temptation to try to discredit the poll by claiming that it is "biased," that it makes "secret adjustments" and that it manipulates the figures to suit its fancy, and that it is interfering with "democratic dialogue." Such charges were heard often in earlier years, but time has largely stilled this kind of attack on the poll's integrity.

Limitations of space, in the case of newspapers, and of time in the case of television and radio, impose restrictions on the amount of detail and analysis that can be included in any one report. The news media have a strong preference for "hard" news, the kind that reports the most recent score on candidate or party strength, or the division of opinion on highly controversial subjects. This type of news, it should be added, makes up the bulk of their news budgets.

These space and time requirements do require a different kind of poll report form from one that would be written to satisfy those who prefer a full and detailed description of public opinion.

A political writer for a large metropolitan newspaper has raised this point: "Is it not more accurate to report a point spread instead of a simple single figure? . . . If so, would it not be more responsible to state it that way, even though it would take away some of the sharpness in published reports?"

A degree of error is inherent in all sampling and it is important that this fact be understood by those who follow poll findings. The question is how best to achieve this end. One way, of course, is to educate the public to look at all survey results not as fixed realities or absolutes but as reliable estimates only.

The best examples, as noted earlier, are the monthly figures on unemployment and the cost of living. Should these be published showing a point spread or the margin of error? If they were, then the monthly index of unemployment, based as it is on a sample of 50,000, would read, at a given point in time, not 8.8%, but 8.5% to 9.1%. Reporting the cost of living index in such fashion would almost certainly cause trouble, since many labor contracts are based upon changes as small as 0.1%.

In reporting the trend of opinion, especially on issues, the inclusion of a point spread would make poll reports rather meaningless, particularly if the trend were not a sharp one. The character of the trend curve itself normally offers evidence of the variations due to sample size.

In the case of elections, the reporting of the margin of error can, on occasion, be misleading to the reader. The reason is that polling errors come from many sources, and often the least of these in importance is the size of the sample. Yet, the statistical margin of error relates solely to this one factor.

An example may help to shed light on this point. A telephone poll taken in a mayoralty race in a large eastern city, reported the standings of the candidates and added that they were accurate within "a possible error margin of 3.8%." In short, the newspaper in which the results were published and the polling organization assured readers that the results perforce had to be right within this margin, based upon the laws or probability. Actually, the poll figure was 14 percentage points short on the winning candidate. Factors other than the size of the sample were responsible for this wide deviation.

The best guide to a poll's accuracy is its record. If allowance is to be made for variation in the poll's reported figures, then perhaps the best suggestion, to be reasonably certain that the error will not exceed a stated amount in a national election, is to multiply by 2.5 the average deviation of the poll in its last three or four elections.

Still another way to remind readers and viewers of the presence of some degree of error in all survey findings is to find a word or words that convey this fact. A growing practice among statisticians in dealing with sampling data is to refer to results as "estimates." Unfortunately, this word conveys to some the impression that subjective judgments have entered into the process. A better word needs to be found that removes some of the certainty that is too often attached to poll percentages without, at the same time, erring in the opposite direction. The word "assessment" has been adopted by some survey researchers and it is hoped that it will come into general use in the future.

DESIGN OF THE SAMPLE

The design of the sample used in the Gallup Poll is that of a replicated probability sample down to the block level in the case of urban areas and to segments of townships in the case of rural areas.

After stratifying the nation geographically and by size of community in order to insure conformity of the sample with the latest available estimates by the Census Bureau of the distribution of the adult population, about 350 different sampling locations or areas are selected on a strictly random basis. The interviewers have no choice whatsoever concerning the part of the city or county in which they conduct their interviews.

Interviewers are given maps of the area to which they are assigned, with a starting point indicated, and are required to follow a specified direction. At each occupied dwelling unit, interviewers are instructed to select respondents by following a prescribed systematic method. This procedure is followed until the assigned number of interviews is completed. The standard sample size for most Gallup Polls is 1500 interviews. This is augmented in specific instances where greater survey accuracy is considered desirable.

Since this sampling procedure is designed to produce a sample that approximates the adult civilian population (18 and older) living in private households in the United States (that is, excluding those in prisons and hospitals, hotels, religious institutions, and on military reservations), the survey results can be applied to this population for the purpose of projecting percentages into numbers of people. The manner in which the sample is drawn also produces a sample that approximates the population of private households in the United States. Therefore, survey results also can be projected in terms of numbers of households when appropriate.

SAMPLING TOLERANCES

It should be remembered that all sample surveys are subject to sampling error; that is, the extent to which the results may differ from what would be obtained if the whole population surveyed had been interviewed. The size of such a sampling error depends largely on the number of interviews. Increasing the sample size lessens the magnitude of possible error and vice versa.

The following tables may be used in estimating sampling error. The computed allowances (the standard deviation) have taken into account the effect of the sample design upon sampling error. They may be interpreted as indicating the range (plus or minus the figure shown) within which the results of repeated samplings in the same time period could be expected to vary, 95 percent of the time (or at a confidence level of .5), assuming the same sampling procedure, the same interviewers, and the same questionnaire.

Table A shows how much allowance should be made for the sampling error of a percentage. The table would be used in the following manner: Say a reported percentage is 33 for a group that includes 1500 respondents. Go to the row "percentage near 30" in the table and then to the column headed "1500." The number at this point is three, which means that the 33 percent obtained in the sample is subject to a sampling error of plus or minus 3 points. Another way of saying it is that very probably (95 chances out of 100) the average of repeated samplings would be somewhere between 30 and 36, with the most likely figure being the 33 obtained.

In comparing survey results in two subsamples, such as men and woman, the question arises as to how large must a difference between them be before one can be reasonably sure that it reflects a statistically significant difference. In Table B and C, the number of points that must be allowed for, in such comparisons, is indicated.

For percentages near 20 or 80, use Table B; for those near 50, Table C. For percentages in between, the error to be allowed for is between that shown in the two tables.

Here is an example of how the tables should be used: Say 50 percent of men and 40 percent of women respond the same way to a question—a difference of 10 percentage points. Can it be said with any assurance that the ten-point difference reflects a significant difference between men and women on the question? (Samples, unless otherwise noted, contain approximately 750 men and 750 women.)

Because the percentages are near 50, consult Table C. Since the two samples are about 750 persons each, look for the place in the table where the column and row labeled "750" converge. The number six appears there. This means the allowance for error should be 6 points, and the conclusion that the percentage among men is somewhere between 4 and 16 points higher than the percentage among women would be wrong only about 5 percent of the time. In other words, there is a considerable likelihood that a difference exists in the direction observed and that it amounts to at least 4 percentage points.

If, in another case, male responses amount to 22 percent, and female to 24 percent, consult Table B because these percentages are near 20. The column and row labeled "750" converge on the number five. Obviously, then, the two-point difference is inconclusive.

TABLE A

Recommended Allowance for Sampling Error of a Percentage

In Percentage Points
(at 95 in 100 confidence level)*
Size of the Sample

	3000	1500	1000	750	600	400	200	100
Percentages near 10	2	2	2	3	4	4	5	7
Percentages near 20	2	3	3	4	4	5	7	9
Percentages near 30	2	3	4	4	4	6	8	10
Percentages near 40	3	3	4	4	5	6	9	11
Percentages near 50	3	3	4	4	5	6	9	11
Percentages near 60	3	3	4	4	5	6	9	11
Percentages near 70	2	3	4	4	4	6	8	10
Percentages near 80	2	3	3	4	4	5	7	9
Percentages near 90	2	2	2	3	4	4	5	7

*The chances are 95 in 100 that the sampling error is not larger than the figures shown.

TABLE B

Recommended Allowance for Sampling Error of the Difference Between Two Subsamples

In Percentage Points
(at 95 in 100 confidence level)*

Percentages near 20 or percentages near 80

Size of the Sample	1500	750	600	400	200
1500	3				
750	4	5			
600	5	6	6		
400	6	7	7	7	
200	8	8	8	9	10

TABLE C

Percentages near 50

Size of the Sample	1500	750	600	400	200
1500	4				
750	5	6			
600	6	8	8		
400	7	8	8	9	
200	10	10	11	11	13

*The chances are 95 in 100 that the sampling error is not larger than the figures shown.

RECORD OF
GALLUP POLL ACCURACY

Year	Gallup Final Survey*		Election Result*	
1982	55.0%	Democratic	55.8%	Democratic
1980	47.0	Reagan	50.8	Reagan
1978	55.0	Democratic	54.0	Democratic
1976	48.0	Carter	50.0	Carter
1974	60.0	Democratic	58.9	Democratic
1972	62.0	Nixon	61.8	Nixon
1970	53.0	Democratic	54.3	Democratic
1968	43.0	Nixon	43.5	Nixon
1966	52.5	Democratic	51.9	Democratic
1964	64.0	Johnson	61.3	Johnson
1962	55.5	Democratic	52.7	Democratic
1960	51.0	Kennedy	50.1	Kennedy
1958	57.0	Democratic	56.5	Democratic
1956	59.5	Eisenhower	57.8	Eisenhower
1954	51.5	Democratic	52.7	Democratic
1952	51.0	Eisenhower	55.4	Eisenhower
1950	51.0	Democratic	50.3	Democratic
1948	44.5	Truman	49.9	Truman
1946	58.0	Republican	54.3	Republican
1944	51.5	Roosevelt	53.3**	Roosevelt
1942	52.0	Democratic	48.0	Democratic
1940	52.0	Roosevelt	55.0	Roosevelt
1938	54.0	Democratic	50.8	Democratic
1936	55.7	Roosevelt	62.5	Roosevelt

*The figure shown is the winner's percentage of the Democratic-Republican vote except in the elections of 1948, 1968, and 1976. Because the Thurmond and Wallace voters in 1948 were largely split-offs from the normally Democratic vote, they were made a part of the final Gallup Poll preelection.

**Civilian vote 53.3, Roosevelt soldier vote 0.5 = 53.8% Roosevelt. Gallup final survey based on civilian vote.

estimate of the division of the vote. In 1968 Wallace's candidacy was supported by such a large minority that he was clearly a major candidate, and the 1968 percents are based on the total Nixon-Humphrey-Wallace vote. In 1976, because of interest in McCarthy's candidacy and its potential effect on the Carter vote, the final Gallup Poll estimate included Carter, Ford, McCarthy, and all other candidates as a group.

Average Deviation for 24
    National Elections . . . . 2.3 percentage points

Average Deviation for 17
    National Elections
    Since 1950, inclusive . . . . 1.5 percentage points

Trend in Deviation Reduction

Elections	Average Error
1936–48	4.0
1950–58	1.7
1960–68	1.5
1970–82	1.4
1966–82	1.2

CHRONOLOGY

The chronology is provided to enable the reader to relate poll results to specific events or series of events that may have influenced public opinion.

1982

December 1   Senator Edward M. Kennedy announces that he will not seek the Democratic presidential nomination in 1984.

December 3   The jobless rate climbs to 10.8%; in a labor force of 111 million, about 12 million are unemployed. Congressional leaders of both parties agree that creating jobs is the most important issue before Congress. House Speaker Thomas P. O'Neill and Senate Majority Leader Howard Baker both support a bill allocating $5.5 billion to repair the nation's roads, bridges, and urban transit systems. This program, to be funded by a 5¢ per gallon increase in the federal gasoline tax, is endorsed by President Ronald Reagan. After almost a month of Senate debate, the bill is passed by both congressional houses on December 23 and sent to the president for his signature.

December 21   Yuri Andropov, general secretary of the Soviet Communist party, proposes to reduce the number of Soviet intermediate-range missiles deployed in Europe. The United States rejects his proposal.

1983

January 3   President Reagan appoints a bipartisan panel to find new ways of basing the MX missile.

January 7   The Labor Department announces that unemployment averaged 9.7% for 1982.

January 11	The Defense Department reports a reduction of $8 billion, or 3%, in the defense budget for the 1984 fiscal year, which nevertheless shows a 14.2% increase over fiscal 1983. Most of the increase is planned for weapons production and research.
January 15	The National Commission on Social Security announces a program for saving the system from bankruptcy.
January 18	The Commerce Department discloses that housing starts declined 2.2% in 1982, to the lowest annual total since 1946. The department also reveals that personal income rose 6.4% in 1982, the smallest gain since 1963. The Gross National Product (GNP), adjusted for inflation, fell 1.8% in 1982, the greatest decline since 1946.
January 21	President Reagan certifies to Congress that El Salvador's government has shown progress in reducing human rights abuses and thus is eligible for additional U.S. military aid.
	Dun & Bradstreet figures showed that in the past year about 25,000 businesses had failed, an increase of approximately 50% from 1981.
January 23	Howard Baker announces that he will not run for the Senate in 1984.
January 24	Price agreements within the Organization of Petroleum Exporting Countries (OPEC) begin to unravel. The prospect that oil prices will fall causes the Dow Jones average to drop 22 points.
January 25	President Reagan delivers his State of the Union message.
January 26	The president proposes the abolishment of corporate income taxes.
	The Equal Rights Amendment (ERA) is reintroduced in the Senate.
February 1–6	More than 1,600 U.S. military personnel and 4,000 Honduran soldiers participate with Nicaragua in war games near the Honduran border. Nicaragua claims the exercise is in preparation for an invasion.
February 2	Senator Alan Cranston becomes the first Democrat formally to

announce his candidacy for the 1984 Democratic presidential nomination.

February 4   Unemployment in January fell .4% to 10.4%, the first decline in eighteen months.

February 7   Iran launches a major invasion of Iraq.

February 10   Vice-president George Bush returns to Washington after a twelve-day European trip. His goal was to obtain support for the projected deployment of U.S. intermediate-range missiles in Europe.

February 16   The Commerce Department reports that housing starts in January jumped about 36%, the sharpest increase since records first were kept in 1959.

February 17   Senator Gary Hart announces his candidacy for the Democratic presidential nomination.

February 21   Former Vice-president Walter Mondale announces his candidacy for the Democratic presidential nomination.

              Harold Washington wins the Democratic primary for mayor of Chicago.

February 22   President Reagan pledges border protection to Israel if its troops leave Lebanon.

February 23   Reubin Askew, former governor of Florida, announces his candidacy for the Democratic presidential nomination.

February 26   The president proposes to decontrol natural gas by 1986.

March 1   Pope John Paul II begins a week-long trip to Central America.

March 2   The Commerce Department reports that sales of single-family homes rose 9.9% in January, the largest increase in twenty-eight months.

March 3   A $4.9-billion jobs bill is voted on by the House of Representatives.

              The inflation rate for February remained at 10.4%.

March 6	Chancellor Helmut Kohl's party wins in West Germany. The chancellor strongly supports President Reagan's European missile deployment plan.
March 9	Anne Burford resigns as administrator of the Environmental Protection Agency, while criticism of the agency continues.
March 11	The February unemployment rate remained at 10.2%.
March 14	For the first time in its twenty-three-year history, OPEC agrees to cut oil prices.
March 17	The Senate approves the jobs bill which is expected to create 400,000 jobs in the construction industry and in public service organizations and to provide day-care and home health-related services.
March 24	The House of Representatives passes the compromise bipartisan bill to rescue the Social Security system from bankruptcy, with the hope that the system now will remain solvent for at least seventy-five years.
April 4	The U.S. space shuttle *Challenger* is launched for the first time and will return on April 9. The crew consists of four astronauts, two of whom take the first U.S. space walk in nine years, spending almost four hours outside the vehicle.
April 11	A commission appointed by President Reagan announces its proposals for the production and basing of the MX missile. The president endorses the commission's proposals, stating that the Soviet Union would have no motivation to negotiate arms reduction agreements unless the United States modernizes its land-based missile systems.
April 18	A massive explosion destroys the U.S. embassy in Beirut, killing forty-seven persons and injuring more than one hundred; sixteen Americans are among the dead. A radical Iranian group claims responsibility.
	Senator Ernest Hollings announces his candidacy for the Democratic presidential nomination.
April 20	The Commerce Department reports a 3.1% rise in the GNP for the first quarter of 1983.

President Reagan signs the Social Security rescue bill into law.

April 21   Senator John Glenn announces his candidacy for the Democratic presidential nomination.

April 26   The Dow Jones average closes above 1200 for the first time.

April 27   President Reagan takes an unusual step and addresses a joint session of Congress on a foreign policy issue. He appeals for approval of his requests for economic and military aid to Central America. The president draws heavy applause when he states that he has no intention of sending U.S. combat troops to the area.

May 6   Israel and Lebanon reach an agreement for the withdrawal of Israeli troops from Lebanon, but Israeli acceptance of the U.S.-mediated plan is conditioned on agreement by Syria.

                The Dow Jones average reaches another all-time high of 1232. Economic data released shows that economic recovery continues at a steady pace.

May 13   Syrian President Hafez Assad rejects the U.S. plan and refuses to remove his troops from Lebanon.

June 2   Meeting in Brussels, NATO defense ministers reaffirm their commitment to the deployment of U.S. intermediate-range nuclear missiles in Europe, unless the United States and the Soviet Union reach an agreement in the arms reduction talks by December.

June 3   The Labor Department reports that unemployment fell to 10% in May.

June 9   The British Conservative party, led by Prime Minister Margaret Thatcher, wins a second term in parliamentary elections.

June 10   The Commerce Department reports that retail sales increased a sharp 2.1% in May.

June 15   The U.S. Supreme Court reaffirms its 1973 ruling in *Roe* v. *Wade*, which gave women unrestricted rights to abortions in the first trimester of pregnancy. The next day President Reagan criticizes this decision and calls for legislation to "restore legal protections for the unborn."

June 16	The Commerce Department announces that housing starts climbed 19.1% in May.
	General Secretary Andropov is elected president of the Soviet Union, the third position to which he has been named since the death of Leonid Brezhnev in November 1982. Andropov previously had been chosen as head of the Communist party, and he also had assumed the country's top defense post.
June 16–23	Pope John Paul II returns to Poland for the second time since his elevation to the papacy. His appeal for the restoration of human rights in Poland and his emphasis on Polish nationalism provided tense moments for the Communist government.
June 18	President Reagan announces the reappointment of Paul Volcker as chairman of the Federal Reserve Board.
	Sally Ride becomes the first American woman to travel in space when the space shuttle *Challenger* is launched on its second flight.
June 20	The Commerce Department reports that personal income for all Americans rose 1.2% in May and that consumer spending jumped 1.4%.
June 23	The Supreme Court rules that the "legislative veto" is unconstitutional.
June 24–July 7	Vice-president Bush travels to Europe to firm up allied support for U.S. positions on arms talks. His motorcade is pelted with rocks thrown by persons opposing the deployment of U.S. missiles in Europe, and more than 20,000 demonstrate peacefully near his hotel.
June 28	President Reagan announces that his administration is raising its forecast of economic growth from 4.7% to 5.5% for the fourth quarter of 1983.
	The Senate defeats a proposed constitutional amendment that would permit states and Congress to restrict access to all abortions.
July 5	In a visit to the Soviet Union, Chancellor Kohl of West Germany is warned by Soviet leaders not to permit the planned deployment in his country of U.S. medium-range nuclear missiles.

1

July 6	The Supreme Court rules that an employer-sponsored retirement plan cannot pay women lower monthly pension benefits than it pays men.
July 8	Unemployment fell to 9.8% in June; however, the black unemployment rate remained at a near record high of 20.6%.
	Mehmet Ali Agca, the would-be assassin of Pope John Paul II, tells reporters directly for the first time that the Soviet and Bulgarian secret police were involved in the plot to kill the pontiff.
July 12	President Reagan proposes a constitutional amendment to permit prayer in public schools.
July 13	The Senate votes 50 to 49 to authorize the production of nerve gas weapons.
July 18	The president announces that he will create a commission, headed by former Secretary of State Henry Kissinger, to recommend long-term U.S. policies in Central America.
July 20	The House of Representatives approves funds for the development of the MX missile, followed by the Senate's approval on July 26.
July 21	The GNP rose at an annual rate of 8.7% during the second quarter of 1983.
	Reagan seeks to give assurances that the military activities in Nicaragua are routine, although they surpass in scale any previous training exercises in the area. Panama and Venezuela criticize the planned maneuvers as counterproductive and ill timed.
July 28	Congress votes to repeal legislation passed in 1982 that authorized withholding for taxes of 10% of interest and dividend income.
	The United States and the Soviet Union agree on terms for a new five-year grain purchase deal.
July 29	The Commerce Department announces that the index of leading economic indicators rose 1% in June, the tenth straight monthly advance. In addition, the U.S. trade deficit fell in June after reaching a record high in May.

August 1	The White House cancels a tour by delegates to the convention of the International Federation of Business and Professional Women. On the following day, the president personally apologizes to the delegates, but some find his remarks to be degrading and inappropriate.
	President Reagan creates a study group to investigate the situation of 34.4 million Americans (about 15% of the total population) living in poverty, according to data released by the U.S. Census Bureau. A family of four with an income of less than $9,862 is defined as below the poverty line; the median income for a family in 1982 was $23,430.
August 8	A military coup in Guatemala ousts President Efrain Rios Montt after seventeen months in office. Rios Montt, a born-again Christian, had irritated many in this predominantly Catholic country.
August 18	Soviet President Andropov announces a unilateral moratorium on the deployment of antisatellite weapons.
August 19	The Commerce Department reports that corporate profits jumped 14.7% in the second quarter of 1983.
August 21	Benigno Aquino, Jr., leader of the political opposition to President Ferdinand Marcos, is shot to death on his arrival in the Philippines from exile in the United States.
	Barbara Honegger, a special assistant in the Department of Justice, severely criticizes the Reagan administration's record on women's rights.
August 23	Maureen Reagan, the president's daughter, is hired by the Republican National Committee to help improve the president's image among women.
August 27	The twentieth anniversary of the 1963 March on Washington, led by the Reverend Martin Luther King, Jr., is commemorated by another march in the capital city. More than 250,000 walk for "jobs, peace, and freedom."
August 28	Prime Minister Menachem Begin of Israel announces that he plans to retire for personal reasons.

August 29	President Andropov says that the Soviet Union is prepared to dismantle all missiles it removed from Europe if the Geneva talks on reducing the number of intermediate-range missiles in Europe end successfully.
August 30	The space shuttle *Challenger* is launched on its third mission and carries aloft the first American black astronaut, Air Force Lieutenant Colonel Guion Bluford. The crew also includes the oldest U.S. astronaut to date—Dr. William Thornton, age fifty-four.
September 1	Senator Henry Jackson, a member of Congress for almost forty-three years, dies at age seventy-one.

The Soviet Union shoots down a South Korean airliner. Worldwide indignation, revulsion, and condemnation of the USSR follow news of the deaths of all 269 persons aboard. President Reagan calls the incident a massacre and announces several minor punitive measures against the Soviet Union. |
September 8	The Soviet Union finally admits to shooting down the South Korean KAL jetliner, with the excuse that they did not know it was a civilian aircraft, although they had tracked the plane for more than two hours. This incident brought U.S.-Soviet relations to a new low as each nation hurled charges against the other.
September 13	George McGovern announces his candidacy for the Democratic presidential nomination.
September 19	For the first time, two U.S. Navy ships shell Moslem positions in the hills above Beirut.
September 20	Congressional leaders and the Reagan administration agree to a compromise based on the War Powers Resolution that would allow the administration to keep U.S. troops in Lebanon for eighteen months.
September 30	The National Education Association endorses Walter Mondale for president. On the following day, he is also endorsed by the AFL-CIO.
October 3	As unrest in the Philippines continues, President Reagan postpones his scheduled November trip to that nation.

October 4	The three major automobile companies announce that sales increased almost 17% during the 1983 model year.
October 5	Lech Walesa, founder of the Solidarity union movement in Poland, wins the 1983 Nobel Peace Prize.
October 6	An unidentified American official says that the Soviet Union is preparing to deploy a mobile missile in Syria which would be capable of reaching targets in Lebanon, Israel, and the Mediterranean Sea.
October 7	Syrian-backed Palestinian rebels gain the upper hand over Palestine Liberation Organization (PLO) leader Yasir Arafat. The rebels are preparing to drive Arafat from his remaining stronghold near Tripoli.
	The unemployment rate declined to 9.3% in September.
October 10	The Dow Jones average reaches another all-time high of 1284.
October 13	President Reagan gives his approval for the formation of a committee to work on behalf of his reelection.
	The Commerce Department announces that retail sales increased 1.6% in September.
October 14	William Clark, President Reagan's national security adviser, is named to replace James Watt as secretary of the interior.
October 21	Huge antimissile protests take place throughout Europe.
October 23	A bomb blast in Beirut kills 241 Marines. This is the second worst disaster in Marine Corps history, second only to losses at Iwo Jima in World War II. Radical Iranian terrorists are believed to be responsible.
October 25	The United States invades Grenada.
November 2	President Reagan signs a bill declaring the birthday of Martin Luther King, Jr., a federal holiday.
November 3	Jesse Jackson announces his candidacy for the Democratic presidential nomination.

November 4	The unemployment rate dropped to 8.8% for October.
November 7	A bomb explodes in the Capitol building in Washington, DC.
November 8	President Reagan leaves for a six-day visit to Japan and South Korea.
November 14	American cruise missiles, the first in Europe, arrive at a U.S. air base west of London and provoke outcries from antinuclear protestors.
November 15	The ERA amendment fails to pass the House of Representatives.
November 20	More than 100 million adults watch the ABC television movie "The Day After," which depicts the nuclear annihilation of Kansas City and the nightmarish aftermath. The movie was preceded by weeks of heavy publicity and public debate.
November 22	The twentieth anniversary of John F. Kennedy's assassination is marked by remembrances throughout the nation.
December 2	The unemployment rate dropped to 8.4% in November, a two-year low.
December 4	Targets in Syria are bombed by U.S. planes. Two aircraft are shot down, and an American naval flier, Robert Goodman, is taken prisoner by the Syrians.
	Eight Marines are killed in Lebanon.
December 12	The U.S. embassy in Kuwait is attacked; seven persons are killed and more than sixty are injured.
December 13	American ships attack Syrian positions near Beirut.
	A presidential commission urges twenty-one as the national drinking age.
December 14	The U.S.S. *New Jersey* shells Syrian antiaircraft positions.
December 15	The Reagan administration agrees to give Israel $1.4 billion in military aid during 1984.
	The last American combat troops leave Grenada.

December 17   Members of the PLO begin evacuation from Tripoli on Italian ships.

December 29   The United States formally announces its intention to withdraw from the United Nations Educational, Scientific and Cultural Organization.

                 Jesse Jackson leaves for Syria to negotiate the release of the captured American flier.

	Better	Worse	Same	No opinion
Japan	20	17	41	22
France	18	42	36	4
Netherlands	16	49	30	5
Denmark	14	47	31	8
West Germany	13	22	53	12
Luxembourg	8	56	33	3
Belgium	7	60	26	7
Austria	6	45	43	6
Average	27	38	28	7
Grand total average	29%	36%	26%	9%

JANUARY 2
THE FUTURE

Interviewing Date: 11/19–28/82 (U.S. Only)
Special Telephone Survey

Asked in a twenty-seven-nation Gallup International Survey: So far as you are concerned, do you think that 1983 will be better or worse than 1982?

Developing Nations

	Better	Worse	Same	No opinion
Colombia	54%	24%	12%	10%
Brazil	45	27	19	9
Uruguay	34	35	20	11
Argentina	34	36	20	10
Philippines	26	23	31	20
Chile	21	15	15	49
Peru	12	67	19	2
Average	32	33	19	16

Industrial Nations

	Better	Worse	Same	No opinion
Greece	59%	18%	10%	13%
Spain	53	13	24	10
United States	50	32	10	8
Norway	44	40	12	4
Great Britain	43	30	22	5
Canada	40	30	25	5
Australia	32	46	16	6
Italy	27	56	15	2
Finland	26	36	37	1
Switzerland	24	29	42	5
Ireland	23	55	18	4
Sweden	22	35	40	3

National Trend
(United States)

Predictions for	Better	Worse	Same	No opinion
1983	50%	32%	10%	8%
1982	41	44	11	4
1981	49	26	19	6
1980	31	56	*	13
1979	33	55	*	12
1978	45	30	18	7
1972	57	22	**	21
1960	56	7	28	9

*No "same" category
**"Same" responses were recorded with "no opinion" responses.

Note: Despite concern over the present high rate of unemployment, Americans are more optimistic in their outlook for the year 1983 than at the outset of any of the last five years. Although current expectations are relative to one's assessment of the year just past, 50% of adults predict that 1983 will be better than 1982 in terms of their own personal lives, while three in ten say it will be worse. Another 10% anticipate little change.

Americans today are more upbeat about the coming twelve months than they have been at comparable points since the start of 1978. They are also more optimistic than all but the people of the industrial countries of Spain and Greece in a recent twenty-seven-nation Gallup International Survey, in which nearly 30,000 representative citizens were interviewed.

The predictions of people around the globe of

what lies ahead is of considerable significance in view of the increasing economic interdependence of nations. The twenty-seven-nation total shows 29% saying 1983 will be better than 1982, and 36% holding the view that it will be worse. The twenty-nation total for the industrial countries shows pessimism outweighing optimism by about a 3-to-2 ratio while the seven-nation total for the developing countries shows optimism matching pessimism.

JANUARY 6
PRESIDENTIAL TRIAL HEATS

Interviewing Date: 12/10–13/82
Survey #206-G

> *Asked of registered voters: Suppose the 1984 presidential elections were being held today. If President Ronald Reagan were the Republican candidate and Senator John Glenn were the Democratic candidate, which would you like to see win? [Those who were undecided were asked: As of today, do you lean more to Reagan, the Republican, or to Glenn, the Democrat?]*

Reagan 39%
Glenn 54
Other; undecided 7

By Sex
Male

Reagan 43%
Glenn 52
Other; undecided 5

Female

Reagan 36%
Glenn 56
Other; undecided 8

By Race
White

Reagan 44%
Glenn 51
Other; undecided 5

Nonwhite

Reagan 7%
Glenn 77
Other; undecided 16

By Education
College

Reagan 48%
Glenn 47
Other; undecided 5

High School

Reagan 37%
Glenn 56
Other; undecided 7

Grade School

Reagan 25%
Glenn 67
Other; undecided 8

By Region
East

Reagan 30%
Glenn 66
Other; undecided 4

Midwest

Reagan 47%
Glenn 48
Other; undecided 5

South

Reagan 35%
Glenn 52
Other; undecided 13

West

Reagan 44%
Glenn 52
Other; undecided 4

By Age

18–29 Years

Reagan 41%
Glenn 52
Other; undecided 7

30–49 Years

Reagan 38%
Glenn 53
Other; undecided 9

50 Years and Over

Reagan 39%
Glenn 56
Other; undecided 5

By Politics

Republicans

Reagan 76%
Glenn 20
Other; undecided 4

Democrats

Reagan 14%
Glenn 79
Other; undecided 7

Independents

Reagan 44%
Glenn 47
Other; undecided 9

Asked of registered voters: Suppose the 1984 presidential elections were being held today. If President Ronald Reagan were the Republican candidate and Walter Mondale were the Democratic candidate, which would you like to see win? [Those who were undecided were then asked: As of today, do you lean more to Reagan, the Republican, or to Mondale, the Democrat?]

Reagan 40%
Mondale 52
Other; undecided 8

By Sex

Male

Reagan 44%
Mondale 52
Other; undecided 4

Female

Reagan 36%
Mondale 53
Other; undecided 11

By Race

White

Reagan 45%
Mondale 48
Other; undecided 7

Nonwhite

Reagan 3%
Mondale 82
Other; undecided 15

By Education

College

Reagan 51%
Mondale 43
Other; undecided 6

High School

Reagan 37%
Mondale 54
Other; undecided 9

Grade School

Reagan 24%
Mondale 69
Other; undecided 7

By Region

East

Reagan 33%
Mondale 61
Other; undecided 6

Midwest

Reagan	47%
Mondale	47
Other; undecided	6

South

Reagan	33%
Mondale	52
Other; undecided	15

West

Reagan	46%
Mondale	50
Other; undecided	4

By Age

18–29 Years

Reagan	45%
Mondale	50
Other; undecided	5

30–49 Years

Reagan	39%
Mondale	50
Other; undecided	11

50 Years and Over

Reagan	38%
Mondale	55
Other; undecided	7

By Politics

Republicans

Reagan	82%
Mondale	14
Other; undecided	4

Democrats

Reagan	12%
Mondale	80
Other; undecided	8

Independents

Reagan	42%
Mondale	47
Other; undecided	11

Note: As the political attention of the nation turns toward the 1984 presidential elections, two possible Democratic contenders, Senator John Glenn of Ohio and former Vice-president Walter Mondale, take early leads over President Ronald Reagan in test races. Glenn currently holds a 54%-to-39% lead over Reagan among a national sample of registered voters, while Mondale outscores the president by a similar margin, 52% to 40%.

JANUARY 9
MOST ADMIRED MAN

Interviewing Date: 12/10–13/82
Survey #206-G

What man that you have heard or read about, living today in any part of the world, do you admire the most? Who is your second choice?

The following are listed in order of frequency of mention with first and second choices combined:

Ronald Reagan
Pope John Paul II
Billy Graham
Jimmy Carter
Edward Kennedy
Lech Walesa
Menachem Begin
Henry Kissinger
Jesse Jackson
Gerald Ford

Note: Receiving mention but not listed in the top ten were Howard Baker, George Bush, Clint Eastwood, Barry Goldwater, Bob Hope, Walter Mondale, Paul Newman, Richard Nixon, Thomas "Tip" O'Neill, Burt Reynolds, and Andrew Young.

By way of comparison, the following are the 1981 and 1980 results:

Most Admired Man, 1981

Ronald Reagan
Pope John Paul II
Jimmy Carter
Billy Graham
Edward Kennedy
Menachem Begin
Bob Hope
Gerald Ford
Henry Kissinger
Jesse Jackson

Most Admired Man, 1980

Pope John Paul II
Jimmy Carter
Anwar Sadat
Billy Graham
Ronald Reagan
Henry Kissinger
Richard Nixon
Gerald Ford
Edward Kennedy
Menachem Begin

Survey respondents in these studies, which have been conducted for more than three decades, are asked to give their choices without a list of names. This procedure, while opening the field to all possible choices, tends to favor those persons who are currently in the news.

JANUARY 10
MOST ADMIRED WOMAN

Interviewing Date: 12/10–13/82
Survey #206-G

What woman that you have heard or read about, living today in any part of the world, do you admire the most? Who is your second choice?

The following are listed in order of frequency of mention with first and second choices combined:

Margaret Thatcher
Mother Teresa of Calcutta
Nancy Reagan

Jane Fonda
Princess Diana
Barbara Walters
Queen Elizabeth II
Betty Ford
Sandra Day O'Connor
Rosalynn Carter

By Sex

Male

Margaret Thatcher
Mother Teresa of Calcutta
Nancy Reagan
Barbara Walters
Jane Fonda
Rosalynn Carter
Sandra Day O'Connor
Indira Gandhi
Queen Elizabeth II
Jane Byrne

Female

Mother Teresa of Calcutta
Margaret Thatcher
Nancy Reagan
Princess Diana
Betty Ford
Jane Fonda
Queen Elizabeth II
Sandra Day O'Connor
Coretta King
Rosalynn Carter

Note: Receiving mention but not listed in the top ten were Jane Byrne, Shirley Chisholm, Indira Gandhi, Coretta King, and Jacqueline Kennedy Onassis. All but one of the ten most admired women appeared in the 1981 list as well. Princess Diana was in fifth place this year, but was not among the top ten in the 1981 survey.

Absent from the current top ten was former First Lady Jacqueline Kennedy Onassis. As the wife of President John Kennedy and subsequently as his widow, Mrs. Onassis appeared in the top ten in every Gallup audit from 1960 to 1981, a total of seventeen times. Another First Lady, Eleanor Roosevelt, dominated the list from the first audit in 1948 until her death in 1962. She was the top vote-getter in thirteen of the fourteen audits conducted during this period, placing second to Sister Kenny in 1951.

Survey respondents in these studies are asked to give their choices without the aid of a prearranged list of names. This procedure, while opening the field to all possible choices, tends to favor those persons who are currently or have recently been in the news.

JANUARY 11
EARLY FRONT-RUNNERS
ARE GENERALLY LOSERS*

When Edward Kennedy withdrew as a contender for the 1984 Democratic presidential nomination, there was good news for Walter Mondale—he clearly became the front-runner in the polls. But he also had bad news; more often than not, Democratic front-runners lose their support and do not get the nomination.

In the last eight presidential elections, there have been ten contests for the Democratic and Republican nominations (excluding cases where the incumbent president was likely to run again). In only half of these contests did the candidate who enjoyed the most popular support among members of his own party maintain that position over an eighteen-month period to the nomination. But the handicap on early front-runners is much greater when only Democratic races are considered. Four times out of five, the Democratic candidate who had the greatest early public support for the nomination lost that support to a rival by convention time.

*This Gallup analysis was written by Andrew Kohut, president of the Gallup Organization Inc.

Democratic Nomination Contests

Election	Front-runner*	Eventual nominee
1976	E. Kennedy	Carter
1972	Muskie	McGovern
1960	Stevenson	J. Kennedy
1956	Stevenson	Stevenson
1952	Eisenhower	Stevenson

Republican Nomination Contests

Election	Front-runner*	Eventual nominee
1980	Reagan	Reagan
1968	Nixon	Nixon
1964	Rockefeller	Goldwater
1960	Nixon	Nixon
1952	Eisenhower	Eisenhower

Candidates who have early leads in the polls lose their support in a variety of ways, but the public generally does not change its allegiances until the primaries actually begin. In fact, a front-runner typically will lose that position as an outcome of the primaries. Such was the case in 1976 when Jimmy Carter rather than Kennedy became the top choice of Democrats nationally, based on his primary victories. As late as January 1976, Carter hardly registered in the national polls; a Gallup Poll at that time found only 4% of Democrats selecting the former Georgia governor as their top choice for the nomination. However, he became the favorite of Democrats nationally in March 1976 after consecutive primary victories.

In other instances, public opinion will react strongly to campaign incidents. George Romney telling the press he was brainwashed by American officials in Vietnam in 1967–68 and Edmund Muskie's tears at a primary press conference both led to significant declines in support.

*The front-runner is the candidate with the largest proportion of his own party members making him their first choice for the nomination in January and December polls, eighteen months before the nominating conventions.

Candidates generally become early front-runners because they are familiar to members of their own party. The challenge they face is from little-known candidates handicapped by the lack of name awareness, but potentially representing fresh faces to the voters. Certainly, familiarity is a two-edged sword for Mondale. As a result of familiarity he is now the front-runner, but he may also suffer from it if he is defined as a legacy of the Carter years. The current polls show little nostalgia for Carter despite dissatisfaction with Ronald Reagan.

Recent political history indicates that fresh faces have more appeal to Democratic voters than to Republicans, who tend to stick with front-runners to a greater degree. This tendency was certainly to the Republicans' advantage in 1951, when the front-runner for both parties' nomination was the same man, Dwight Eisenhower.

JANUARY 13
DEMOCRATIC PRESIDENTIAL CANDIDATES

Interviewing Date: 12/10–13/82
Survey #206-G

Asked of Democrats and independents: Would you please look over this list [respondents were handed a card listing sixteen names] and tell me which of these persons, if any, you have heard something about? Those who replied in the affirmative were asked: Can you tell me something about these persons?

Democrats Only

	Heard something about	Know something about
Walter Mondale	86%	59%
George McGovern	73	41
Edmund (Jerry) Brown, Jr.	70	46
John Glenn	69	50
Jay Rockefeller	49	22
Morris Udall	45	20
Daniel (Pat) Moynihan	39	21
Robert Strauss	33	12
Alan Cranston	30	14
Bill Bradley	29	14
John Y. Brown	26	11
Reubin Askew	23	10
Gary Hart	22	9
Lloyd Bentsen	17	6
Ernest Hollings	15	5
Bruce Babbitt	12	3

Independents Only

	Heard something about	Know something about
Mondale	88%	62%
Brown (Jerry)	81	59
McGovern	79	51
Glenn	77	56
Rockefeller	55	24
Udall	55	25
Moynihan	52	27
Cranston	40	17
Strauss	35	14
Brown (John Y.)	34	18
Bradley	32	18
Hart	26	12
Askew	25	8
Hollings	21	5
Bentsen	19	8
Babbitt	13	4

Asked of Democrats and independents: Which one of these persons [respondents were handed a card listing sixteen names and titles of possible nominees] would you like to see nominated as the Democratic party's candidate for president in 1984?

Choice of Democrats

Mondale	32%
Glenn	14
McGovern	6
Brown (Jerry)	5
Others*	17
None; don't know	26

Choice of Independents

Glenn	22%
Mondale	15
Brown (Jerry)	6

McGovern 6
Others* 18
None; don't know 33

*All others on the list each received 3% or less of the vote of survey respondents.

Asked of Democrats and independents: Suppose the choice for president in the Democratic convention in 1984 narrows down to Walter Mondale and John Glenn. Which one would you prefer to have the Democratic convention select?

Choice of Democrats

Mondale 59%
Glenn 28
Undecided 13

Choice of Independents

Mondale 41%
Glenn 40
Undecided 19

Note: Former Vice-president Walter Mondale currently enjoys a 2-to-1 advantage over Senator John Glenn among Democratic voters to be their party's nominee in the 1984 presidential elections. In the first Gallup test for the nomination since Senator Edward Kennedy withdrew from the race in early December, Mondale receives the first-place votes of 32% of Democrats to 14% for Glenn, 6% for 1972 nominee George McGovern, and 5% for former California governor Jerry Brown. None of the others on a list of sixteen gets more than 3% of Democrats' votes.

When the race is narrowed to the two front-runners, Mondale is the choice of 59% of Democrats to be their party's 1984 standard-bearer, while 28% pick Glenn and 13% are undecided.

In earlier Gallup contests, Kennedy was a strong favorite for the Democratic nomination. In a survey conducted last summer, for example, he won 43% of Democrats' first-place votes from a list of fifteen possible candidates, to 13% for Mondale and 7% for Glenn.

The two-way nomination contest is a toss-up,

however, among political independents, with 41% expressing a preference for Mondale and 40% for Glenn. Independent voters, who may participate in primary elections in some states, constitute about one-fourth of the electorate. Also, Glenn leads Mondale among independents when tested against the full line-up of Democratic candidates. The Ohio senator beats Mondale, 22% to 15%, with McGovern and Brown each getting 6% of votes for the Democratic nomination from voters espousing neither of the two major parties.

To a considerable extent, the current choices for the Democratic nomination are a result of name awareness. A majority of Democrats in the survey has heard of only four of the sixteen persons tested and claims to know something about only one of the sixteen.

Although the current figures show that many Democratic hopefuls have a long way to go before they are known to a majority of the electorate, they can take encouragement from the dramatic example of Jimmy Carter, who two years before the 1976 primaries was known to few people outside his native Georgia. In fact, it was not until mid-1975 that as many as one Democrat in four had heard of Carter. At that point he was the choice of merely 1% of Democrats to be their party's nominee in the 1976 presidential race.

JANUARY 16
PRESIDENT REAGAN

Interviewing Date: 12/10–13/82
Survey #206-G

Do you approve or disapprove of the way Ronald Reagan is handling his job as president?

Approve 41%
Disapprove 50
No opinion 9

By Sex
Male

Approve 47%
Disapprove 46
No opinion 7

Female

Approve 36%
Disapprove 54
No opinion 10

By Race
White

Approve 46%
Disapprove 45
No opinion 9

Nonwhite

Approve 9%
Disapprove 85
No opinion 6

By Education
College

Approve 51%
Disapprove 44
No opinion 5

High School

Approve 40%
Disapprove 51
No opinion 9

Grade School

Approve 25%
Disapprove 61
No opinion 14

By Region
East

Approve 36%
Disapprove 57
No opinion 7

Midwest

Approve 46%
Disapprove 44
No opinion 10

South

Approve 38%
Disapprove 52
No opinion 10

West

Approve 46%
Disapprove 48
No opinion 6

By Age
18–24 Years

Approve 42%
Disapprove 50
No opinion 8

25–29 Years

Approve 47%
Disapprove 46
No opinion 7

30–49 Years

Approve 39%
Disapprove 52
No opinion 9

50–64 Years

Approve 39%
Disapprove 52
No opinion 9

65 Years and Over

Approve 41%
Disapprove 50
No opinion 9

By Income
$25,000 and Over

Approve 56%
Disapprove 41
No opinion 3

$15,000 and Over

Approve 50%
Disapprove 44
No opinion 6

Under $15,000

Approve 30%
Disapprove 59
No opinion 11

By Politics
Republicans

Approve 76%
Disapprove 17
No opinion 7

Democrats

Approve 21%
Disapprove 71
No opinion 8

Independents

Approve 42%
Disapprove 49
No opinion 9

By Religion
Protestants

Approve 42%
Disapprove 49
No opinion 9

Catholics

Approve 41%
Disapprove 50
No opinion 9

National Trend
(Over Last Six Months of 1982)

	Approve	Dis-approve	No opinion
November 19–22	43%	47%	10%
November 5–8	43	47	10
October 15–18	42	48	10
September 17–20	42	48	10
August 27–30	42	46	12
August 13–16	41	49	10
July 30–August 2	41	47	12
July 23–26	42	46	12

Note: After two years in office, President Ronald Reagan's job performance rating is not only his lowest to date, but is substantially lower than the ratings given his four elected predecessors—Presidents Jimmy Carter, Richard Nixon, John Kennedy, and Dwight Eisenhower—at mid-point of their first terms in office. In the latest survey, 41% of Americans say they approve of the way Reagan is handling his job as chief executive while 50% disapprove, the least favorable set of findings since he took office nearly two years ago.

After two years in office, Carter had a rating of 51% approval; Nixon, 52%; Kennedy, 76%; and Eisenhower, 69%. Presidents Gerald Ford and Lyndon Johnson were not elected to their first periods in office.

Not only is Reagan's national approval rating lower than those of his predecessors' at this point in time, but it is also lower among most key groups in the population as well. The most dramatic differences are found in terms of racial background, with only 9% of nonwhites currently expressing approval of the president's performance. By way of comparison, Carter's rating among nonwhites was 64%; Nixon's, 33%; Kennedy's, 93%; and Eisenhower's, 57%.

Reagan's current rating is lower than his predecessors' among both men and women, particularly the latter. At present, 47% of men and 36% of women express approval of the way the president is discharging his duties.

A relatively bright spot for Reagan in these comparative ratings is his showing among members of his own party. He wins approval of 76% of Republicans, nearly matching the figure recorded for another Republican, Nixon, and a better showing than Carter's, who had the approval of only 62% of Democrats at this point in his tenure.

President Reagan's job performance rating is closely tied to public concern over the economy. Because of this, his ratings will likely register gains if the economy shows signs of improvement in the months ahead.

The following tables compare Reagan's approval ratings after two years in office with those of his four elected predecessors:

Presidential Popularity

(Percent Approving at End of Second Year)

Reagan (1982) 41%
Carter (1978) 51
Nixon (1970) 52
Kennedy (1962) 76
Eisenhower (1954) 69

By Sex

Male

Reagan 47%
Carter 49
Nixon 56
Kennedy 74
Eisenhower 70

Female

Reagan 36%
Carter 54
Nixon 47
Kennedy 77
Eisenhower 68

By Race

White

Reagan 46%
Carter 49
Nixon 53
Kennedy 74
Eisenhower 70

Nonwhite

Reagan 9%
Carter 64
Nixon 33
Kennedy 93
Eisenhower 57

By Education

College

Reagan 51%
Carter 48
Nixon 54
Kennedy 75
Eisenhower 71

High School

Reagan 40%
Carter 50
Nixon 53
Kennedy 79
Eisenhower 71

Grade School

Reagan 25%
Carter 61
Nixon 56
Kennedy 72
Eisenhower 63

By Region

East

Reagan 36%
Carter 49
Nixon 52
Kennedy 79
Eisenhower 78

Midwest

Reagan 46%
Carter 54
Nixon 45
Kennedy 80
Eisenhower 69

South

Reagan 38%
Carter 52
Nixon 59
Kennedy 69
Eisenhower 65

West

Reagan	46%
Carter	49
Nixon	50
Kennedy	73
Eisenhower	78

By Age
18–29 Years

Reagan	44%
Carter	53
Nixon	50
Kennedy	85
Eisenhower	65

30–49 Years

Reagan	39%
Carter	49
Nixon	52
Kennedy	75
Eisenhower	70

50 Years and Over

Reagan	40%
Carter	51
Nixon	53
Kennedy	72
Eisenhower	71

By Politics
Republicans

Reagan	76%
Carter	32
Nixon	79
Kennedy	55
Eisenhower	89

Democrats

Reagan	21%
Carter	62
Nixon	34
Kennedy	92
Eisenhower	54

Independents

Reagan	42%
Carter	50
Nixon	51
Kennedy	71
Eisenhower	67

By Religion
Protestants

Reagan	42%
Carter	53
Nixon	55
Kennedy	71
Eisenhower	73

Catholics

Reagan	41%
Carter	51
Nixon	50
Kennedy	88
Eisenhower	63

JANUARY 20
PRESIDENT REAGAN

Interviewing Date: 12/10–13/82
Survey #206-G

Would you like to see Ronald Reagan run for president in 1984, or not?

Would	37%
Would not	56
No opinion	7

By Politics
Republicans

Would	69%
Would not	28
No opinion	3

Democrats

Would	18%
Would not	75
No opinion	7

Independents

Would 40%
Would not 51
No opinion 9

National Trend

	Would	Would not	No opinion
August 13–16, 1982	36%	51%	13%
March 12–15, 1982	35	52	13

Regardless of whether or not you would like to see him run, do you think Reagan will run for president in 1984, or not?

Will 74%
Will not 16
No opinion 10

By Politics

Republicans

Will 78%
Will not 15
No opinion 7

Democrats

Will 73%
Will not 16
No opinion 11

Independents

Will 74%
Will not 18
No opinion 8

National Trend

	Will	Will not	No opinion
August 13–16, 1982	67%	21%	12%
March 12–15, 1982	59	30	11

Note: President Ronald Reagan begins his third year in office amid broad public speculation that he will seek reelection in 1984. Although no more voters than a year ago indicate they would welcome such a move, three in four (74%) now say they expect Reagan will try for a second term, up sharply from the 59% who expressed this view last March.

In the latest Gallup survey, only about one-third of all voters (37%) say they would like to see Reagan seek a second term, virtually unchanged from the 35% recorded last March. Conversely, 56% of the public now say they would not support a reelection bid by the president, a marginal increase from 52% in the earlier survey.

Predictably, the public's expressed desire to see Reagan run next year follows party lines, with far more Republicans (69%) than Democrats (18%) or independents (40%) thinking this way. These figures represent little change from those recorded in the March 1982 survey, with Republicans backing a Reagan reelection bid as strongly as ever.

Aside from Republicans, greater opposition than support is found in almost all major population groups, including those with a Republican bias. College-educated respondents, for instance, oppose a Reagan bid for reelection by 50% to 44%. Even persons whose family income is $25,000 a year or more are narrowly divided, with 49% saying they would like to see the president run again, compared to 46% who would not.

While public opinion on wanting Reagan to run for a second term is sharply divided along political lines, no such division is found on whether or not he will run. In the latest survey, 78% of Republicans, 73% of Democrats, and 74% of independents say they think Reagan will try for another four years in the White House.

JANUARY 23
RELIGION

Interviewing Date: Seven selected weeks during 1982
Various Surveys

Do you happen to be a member of a church or synagogue?

	Yes
National	67%

National Trend

	Yes
1981	68%
1980	69
1978	68
1976	71
1965	73
1952*	73
1947	76
1942	75
1939	72
1937	73

*Figures prior to 1955 were based on a single annual survey.

Did you, yourself, happen to attend church or synagogue in the last seven days?

	Yes
National	41%

National Trend

	Yes
1981	41%
1980	40
1979	40
1978	41
1977	41
1972	40
1969	42
1967	43
1962	46
1958	49
1957	47
1955	49
1954	46
1950	39
1940	37
1939	41

National Trend

	Protestants	Catholics
1981	40%	53%
1980	39	53
1979	40	52
1978	40	52
1968	38	65
1958	44	74

Note: Four adults in every ten (41%) attended church or synagogue in a typical week in 1982, matching the figure recorded for 1981. Church-going has remained remarkably constant since 1969, after having declined from the high points of 49% recorded in 1955 and 1958. Attendance has not varied by more than 2 percentage points since 1969.

The rate of churchgoing is higher among women than men, and among older persons than younger. Attendance is highest in the East, where the greatest proportion of Catholics is found, and is lowest in the West. In 1982, 51% of Catholics nationwide attended Mass in a typical week, compared to 41% of Protestants, figures that closely approximate those from the 1981 audit.

Since 1958, a peak year for church attendance, the decline in churchgoing has been sharpest among Catholics. Attendance at Mass has fallen 23 points since 1958, while Protestant churchgoing has remained remarkably stable during the same time period.

The proportion of adults who say they are church members also has changed little in recent years, with two-thirds of Americans (67%) now claiming membership in a church or synagogue. The 1981 figure was 68%, statistically the same as the latest percentage. The highest level of church membership (76%) was found in 1947, close to the 73% recorded in the first Gallup audit in 1937.

It is important to bear in mind that the membership figures reported here are self-classifications, representing the proportions of people who say they are members of a church or synagogue, and may include some who are not actually on the rolls of local churches. It should also be stressed that adherents of certain faiths—for example, the Roman Catholic and Eastern Orthodox churches—are considered members at birth.

JANUARY 27
LEGAL DRINKING AGE

Interviewing Date: 12/10–13/82
Survey #206-G

Do you favor or oppose a national law that would raise the legal drinking age in all states to 21?

Favor 77%
Oppose 20
No opinion 3

By Sex
Male

Favor 74%
Oppose 23
No opinion 3

Female

Favor 79%
Oppose 17
No opinion 4

By Education
College

Favor 70%
Oppose 28
No opinion 2

High School

Favor 80%
Oppose 17
No opinion 3

Grade School

Favor 78%
Oppose 14
No opinion 8

By Region
East

Favor 81%
Oppose 16
No opinion 2

Midwest

Favor 78%
Oppose 18
No opinion 4

South

Favor 70%
Oppose 24
No opinion 6

West

Favor 76%
Oppose 21
No opinion 3

By Age
18–20 Years

Favor 58%
Oppose 38
No opinion 4

21–29 Years

Favor 72%
Oppose 24
No opinion 4

30–49 Years

Favor 77%
Oppose 20
No opinion 3

50 Years and Over

Favor 83%
Oppose 14
No opinion 3

Note: If the American people were voting today in a referendum making 21 the national minimum drinking age, the large majority, including young people, would vote "yes." Adults of all ages express support for a uniform national drinking age. Even 18, 19, and 20 year olds vote for the proposed legislation, by a 3-to-2 ratio. These young men and women would not be able legally to buy or drink alcoholic beverages if such a law were enacted. At present, thirty-four states and the District of Columbia permit adults under 21 to drink.

The strongest backing (6-to-1) for the proposal comes from persons 50 and older, with proportionately less support as age decreases. Thus, 83% of those 50 and older favor a national minimum-age law, compared to 77% of 30 to 49 year olds, 72% of 21 to 29 year olds, and 58% of 18 to 20 year olds. Also, men and persons who attended college—population groups in which there is a high incidence of drinking—express somewhat greater opposition to the proposed law.

When the 26th Amendment to the U.S. Constitution was ratified in 1971, giving 18, 19, and 20 year olds the right to vote in national elections, many states lowered their minimum legal drinking age. This reflected the belief that, if young people were old enough to vote, marry, and serve in the armed forces, they were mature enough to drink responsibly. However, with teen-agers disproportionately involved in alcohol-related auto accidents, state legislators have been reassessing their drinking-age laws. As recently as 1979, twelve states permitted 18 year olds to drink; today only five do.

Spurred by parents of children killed in accidents involving drunk drivers, President Ronald Reagan last year named a thirty-two-member commission to study the drunk-driving problem, which reportedly causes 25,000 auto fatalities and costs the nation some $24 billion each year. Some states which have taken tough measures to deal with drunk driving, including raising the legal drinking age, report sharp reductions in alcohol-related accidents. One of the commission's key recommendations urged states to raise the legal age for buying or consuming alcoholic beverages to 21.

Another principal argument for raising the legal age is that it would help prevent high-school seniors, many of whom are now of legal age, from buying alcoholic beverages for their younger schoolmates.

Gallup surveys have shown strong public support for raising the minimum drinking age in states where it is legal to drink at ages 18 or 19. However, a 1981 Gallup Youth Survey of 13 to 18 year olds found that far fewer teen-agers living in states with lower drinking ages favored raising the legal age, while in states with higher limits, many more teen-agers expressed a preference for lowering the drinking age.

JANUARY 30
JOGGING/EXERCISE

Interviewing Date: 11/5–8/82*
Survey #204-G

Do you happen to jog, or not?

	Yes
National	19%

By Age

13–15 years	53%
16–18 years	50
Teen-agers (total)	52
18–24 years	30
25–29 years	24
30–49 years	12
50–64 years	6
65 years and over	2
Adults (total)	14

*Teen-age results are based on telephone interviews with a representative national cross-section of boys and girls, 13 to 18 years old, conducted during July 1982.

Asked of joggers: On the average, how far do you usually jog, in terms of miles or fractions of miles?

	Adults	Teens
Less than one mile	20%	19%
One mile and fractions	28	30
Two miles and fractions	25	22
Three miles or more	24	28
Not sure	3	1

Aside from any work you do, here at home or at a job, do you do anything regularly—that is, on a daily basis—that helps you keep physically fit?

	Yes
National	47%

By Age

18–24 years	59%
25–29 years	50
30–49 years	44
50–64 years	39
65 years and over	48

Note: Jogging's rapid growth appears to have leveled off, with about one adult in seven (14%) currently jogging regularly. This represents no significant change from the 12% participation recorded in 1980 and 11% in 1977. In the first Gallup audit, in 1961, only 6% of adults were joggers. In addition to adult participation, as many as half the teen-age population (52%) are joggers. And although its forward momentum may have slowed, jogging remains one of the nation's most popular recreational activities.

In the latest Gallup survey, the average distance covered by adult joggers in their typical run was 2.3 miles; in the 1977 survey the figure was 1.6 miles. Teen-age joggers, too, appear to have lengthened the distances they cover in their typical outings, from an average of 2.2 miles in 1980 to 2.6 in 1982, an 18% increase. All told, adult and teen-age joggers cover an estimated 28 million miles each day, or the equivalent of sixty round trips to the moon. This suggests that jogging is maturing as a sport and fitness regimen from the fad status it held during its formative years.

Sex and education play important roles in the popularity of jogging. Substantially more men (18%) than women (11%) are joggers, and persons who attended college (21%) are more apt to be joggers than are those with less formal education (11%). But the most important dimension to jogging is age. As shown in the current survey, almost as many older teen-agers (16 to 18 years old) as younger (13 to 15) are joggers, but jogging rapidly loses popularity as adults grow older. From a peak of 30% among 18 to 24 year olds, participation falls off to merely 2% among those 65 and older.

The demographic pattern of involvement in a fitness regimen is quite different from the jogging profile. Where jogging was found to drop sharply as age increased, exercising is almost as prevalent among older as younger survey participants.

FEBRUARY 3
PRESIDENT REAGAN

Interviewing Date: 1/14–17/83
Survey #207-G

Do you approve or disapprove of the way Ronald Reagan is handling his job as president?

Approve	37%
Disapprove	54
No opinion	9

By Politics
Republicans

Approve	68%
Disapprove	22
No opinion	10

Democrats

Approve	18%
Disapprove	76
No opinion	6

Independents

Approve	42%
Disapprove	49
No opinion	9

Note: President Ronald Reagan begins his third year in office at a time when only 37% of voters approve of his job performance, the lowest rating recorded during his tenure. In the same survey, 54% disapprove and 9% are uncommitted.

In the Gallup Poll's last audit (mid-December), the president's popularity stood at 41% approval, with 50% disapproving. During 1982, Reagan's performance rating averaged 44% approval. Only 8 percentage points separate his high for the year

(49%, in early January) and his low of 41% in December.

Comparison with other recent elected presidents after their second year in office shows Reagan's 44% average approval to be only marginally below the 47% average approval score accorded Jimmy Carter in 1978, but far lower than Richard Nixon's 57% in 1970, John Kennedy's 72% in 1962, and Dwight Eisenhower's 65% in 1954. Equally interesting is that three of the four— Carter, Nixon, and Kennedy—declined in popularity during their third year in office.

The table below compares Reagan's average popularity during his first two years with that of his elected predecessors during their first three years:

Presidential Performance Ratings

(Average Approval for Year in Office)

	First year	Second year	Third year
Ronald Reagan	58%	44%	?%
Jimmy Carter	62	47	38
Richard Nixon	61	57	50
John Kennedy	75	72	64
Dwight Eisenhower	69	65	71

Comparison of the findings of the last two surveys shows decreases in Reagan's popularity in almost all major population groups. With the exception of Republicans, 68% of whom give the president a favorable job rating, Reagan's current approval score does not top 50% in any group, including persons from households in which the chief wage earner is employed in business or the professions and persons from families with $25,000 or more yearly income.

Reagan's present 68% approval among Republicans is slightly better than the 59% positive rating Democrats accorded Carter at a similar point in his tenure. However, Nixon, Kennedy, and Eisenhower each had the approval of over 80% of their own party members at comparable periods.

The polarization of President Reagan's political support is illustrated by the fact that only 18% of Democrats and 42% of independents now approve of his job performance. These figures are well below the approval ratings of nonparty members recorded for any of Reagan's four elected predecessors at this time in their tenure, as shown in the table below:

National Trend of Presidential Performance Ratings

(By Percent Approving)

Reagan (January 1983) 37%
Carter (January 1979) 50
Nixon (January 1971) 56
Kennedy (February 1963) 70
Eisenhower (February 1955) 72

Republicans

Reagan (January 1983) 68%
Carter (January 1979) 33
Nixon (January 1971) 83
Kennedy (February 1963) 47
Eisenhower (February 1955) 90

Democrats

Reagan (January 1983) 18%
Carter (January 1979) 59
Nixon (January 1971) 38
Kennedy (February 1963) 85
Eisenhower (February 1955) 61

Independents

Reagan (January 1983) 42%
Carter (January 1979) 50
Nixon (January 1971) 57
Kennedy (February 1963) 66
Eisenhower (February 1955) 79

FEBRUARY 6
PRESIDENT REAGAN

Interviewing Date: 1/14–17/83
Survey #207-G

Now let me ask you about specific foreign and domestic problems. As I read off each problem, one at a time, would you tell me whether you approve or disapprove of the way President Reagan is handling that problem:

Economic conditions in this country?

Approve 29%
Disapprove 64
No opinion 7

By Politics
Republicans

Approve 57%
Disapprove 36
No opinion 7

Democrats

Approve 12%
Disapprove 82
No opinion 6

Independents

Approve 33%
Disapprove 60
No opinion 7

National Trend

	Approve	Dis-approve	No opinion
July–August 1982	31%	59%	10%
June 1982	35	58	7
April–May 1982	37	55	8
March 1982	38	54	8
February 1982	38	53	9
January 1982	41	51	8
November 1981	43	48	9
October 1981	44	47	9

Inflation?

Approve 36%
Disapprove 56
No opinion 8

By Politics
Republicans

Approve 62%
Disapprove 29
No opinion 9

Democrats

Approve 20%
Disapprove 73
No opinion 7

Independents

Approve 40%
Disapprove 53
No opinion 7

National Trend

	Approve	Dis-approve	No opinion
July–August 1982	33%	58%	9%
June 1982	37	58	5
April–May 1982	36	57	7
March 1982	37	54	9
February 1982	37	53	10
January 1982	37	53	10
October 1981	42	48	10
August 1981	53	35	12

Unemployment?

Approve 19%
Disapprove 73
No opinion 8

By Politics
Republicans

Approve 37%
Disapprove 50
No opinion 13

Democrats

Approve 9%
Disapprove 86
No opinion 5

Independents

Approve 21%
Disapprove 72
No opinion 7

National Trend

	Approve	Dis-approve	No opinion
July–August 1982	22%	66%	12%
June 1982	22	70	8
April–May 1982	23	67	10
March 1982	25	64	11
February 1982	27	63	10
January 1982	26	63	11
October 1981	33	53	14
August 1981	39	38	23

National defense?

Approve 44%
Disapprove 43
No opinion 13

By Politics
Republicans

Approve 64%
Disapprove 26
No opinion 10

Democrats

Approve 33%
Disapprove 53
No opinion 14

Independents

Approve 45%
Disapprove 41
No opinion 14

National Trend

	Approve	Dis-approve	No opinion
July–August 1982	47%	38%	15%
April–May 1982	49	38	13
March 1982	51	36	13
February 1982	55	34	11
October 1981	61	28	11
June 1981	57	26	17

Foreign policy?

Approve 36%
Disapprove 41
No opinion 23

By Politics
Republicans

Approve 57%
Disapprove 22
No opinion 21

Democrats

Approve 25%
Disapprove 50
No opinion 25

Independents

Approve 37%
Disapprove 43
No opinion 20

National Trend

	Approve	Dis-approve	No opinion
July–August 1982	36%	41%	23%
April–May 1982	42	38	20
March 1982	36	44	20
February 1982	44	38	18
October 1981	56	29	15
August 1981	52	26	22

Relations with the Soviet Union?

Approve 41%
Disapprove 37
No opinion 22

By Politics
Republicans

Approve 62%
Disapprove 22
No opinion 16

Democrats

Approve 31%
Disapprove 45
No opinion 24

Independents

Approve 40%
Disapprove 40
No opinion 20

National Trend

	Approve	Dis-approve	No opinion
July–August 1982	44%	34%	22%
April–May 1982	45	32	23
March 1982	41	36	23
February 1982	49	33	18
October 1981	53	25	22
June 1981	48	25	27

The Middle East situation?

Approve 35%
Disapprove 38
No opinion 27

By Politics
Republicans

Approve 53%
Disapprove 21
No opinion 26

Democrats

Approve 25%
Disapprove 47
No opinion 28

Independents

Approve 36%
Disapprove 39
No opinion 25

Note: Although President Ronald Reagan's overall job performance rating has declined to its lowest point since he took office, approval of his handling of foreign policy issues has shown relatively little slippage since the previous survey in October.

The president's overall rating is currently 37% approval. However, on handling relations with the Soviet Union, Reagan receives a 41% approval rating, nearly matching the 40% reported in October. On foreign policy, 36% approve of the president's performance, close to the 38% recorded earlier. On handling national defense, 44% express approval, only moderately less positive than the 47% recorded in the earlier survey.

Offsetting the public support given the president on foreign policy issues has been growing public disapproval of his handling of domestic economic issues. Last fall, 36% approved of Reagan's handling of economic conditions; today 29% do so. Public perceptions of the state of the economy are clearly taking a serious toll on the president's current job performance rating, yet if, as many economists predict, the economy takes an upturn, such a trend is likely to be reflected in the president's overall approval rating.

On the issue of unemployment, the public's assessment of the president's performance is least favorable (19% approval), although virtually no change has occurred in this figure since the earlier survey. Even on an issue for which the Reagan administration can claim considerable credit—reducing inflation—public opinion remains more negative than positive. Today, 36% approve of Reagan's handling of inflation, compared to 41% in the October survey. This drop in approval came despite the fact that the Consumer Price Index shows the rate of inflation in 1982 to have increased only 3.9%, compared to 8.9% in 1981 and 12.4% in 1980.

While the decline in approval during Reagan's term has been greater on his handling of economic issues than on international affairs, the fall-off has been across the board. In the early months of his presidency, solid majorities expressed approval of Reagan's handling of the specific areas covered in the current survey, with one exception: at no point did the president enjoy majority approval for his handling of unemployment.

On each of the seven issues covered in the current survey, nonwhites are far more likely than whites to express disapproval of the president's performance, particularly on domestic economic issues. Women, too, are far more negative than men on six of the seven issues, especially those relating to foreign policy. On the issue of inflation, women and men give Reagan similar ratings.

FEBRUARY 10
REAGANOMICS

Interviewing Date: 1/14–17/83
Survey #207-G

What effect do you think the Reagan admin-istration's economic policies will have on your own and your family's financial situation? Do you feel your financial situation will be much better, somewhat better, somewhat worse, or much worse as a result of the Reagan economic policies?

Better 25%
Worse 52
Same (volunteered) 18
No opinion 5

By Sex
Male

Better 30%
Worse 47
Same (volunteered) 17
No opinion 6

Female

Better 19%
Worse 57
Same (volunteered) 19
No opinion 5

By Race
White

Better 26%
Worse 50
Same (volunteered) 19
No opinion 5

Nonwhite

Better 18%
Worse 63
Same (volunteered) 12
No opinion 7

By Education
College

Better 32%
Worse 44
Same (volunteered) 21
No opinion 3

High School

Better 24%
Worse 55
Same (volunteered) 17
No opinion 4

Grade School

Better 13%
Worse 57
Same (volunteered) 16
No opinion 14

By Region
East

Better 26%
Worse 56
Same (volunteered) 13
No opinion 5

Midwest

Better 25%
Worse 50
Same (volunteered) 19
No opinion 6

South

Better 25%
Worse 48
Same (volunteered) 20
No opinion 7

West

Better 22%
Worse 55
Same (volunteered) 21
No opinion 2

By Age

18–24 Years

Better 31%
Worse 50
Same (volunteered) 13
No opinion 6

25–29 Years

Better 29%
Worse 49
Same (volunteered) 18
No opinion 4

30–49 Years

Better 29%
Worse 55
Same (volunteered) 14
No opinion 2

50 Years and Over

Better 17%
Worse 51
Same (volunteered) 24
No opinion 8

By Income

$25,000 and Over

Better 34%
Worse 45
Same (volunteered) 19
No opinion 2

$15,000 and Over

Better 29%
Worse 49
Same (volunteered) 19
No opinion 3

Under $15,000

Better 18%
Worse 57
Same (volunteered) 17
No opinion 8

By Politics

Republicans

Better 43%
Worse 31
Same (volunteered) 20
No opinion 6

Democrats

Better 15%
Worse 65
Same (volunteered) 15
No opinion 5

Independents

Better 25%
Worse 51
Same (volunteered) 19
No opinion 5

National Trend

	Better	Worse	Same	No opinion
August 1982	23%	56%	15%	6%
June 1982	29	51	15	5
March 1982	28	51	15	6
February 1982 ...	31	44	25*	
Oct.–Nov. 1981 ..	34	45	15	6
August 1981	48	36	16*	

*Volunteered "same" response recorded with "no opinion."

How about the nation? What effect do you think the Reagan administration's economic policies will have on the nation's economic situation? Do you feel the nation's economic situation will be much better, somewhat better, somewhat worse, or much worse as a result of the Reagan economic policies?

Better 32%
Worse 54
Same (volunteered) 7
No opinion 7

By Politics

Republicans

Better 59%
Worse 28
Same (volunteered) 7
No opinion 6

Democrats

Better 17%
Worse 68
Same (volunteered) 8
No opinion 7

Independents

Better 35%
Worse 53
Same (volunteered) 6
No opinion 6

National Trend

	Better	Worse	Same	No opinion
August 1982	32%	54%	7%	7%
March 1982	40	48	5	7
February 1982 ...	40	44	16*	
Oct.–Nov. 1981 ..	44	42	7	7

*Volunteered "same" response recorded with "no opinion."

Note: Despite mounting evidence that the economy is starting to emerge from recession, the heavy weight of public opinion continues to be that one's own finances and the nation's economic health will worsen rather than improve as a result of the Reagan administration's economic policies.

In the latest Gallup survey, 25% of respondents say their financial situation will improve, while twice that number (52%) say their finances will become worse because of the Reagan policies. The public's confidence in the administration's economic program has gradually eroded since the first Gallup assessment in May 1981, when almost half, 48%, were optimistic while 37% were pessimistic.

Growing pessimism also is recorded on the impact of Reaganomics on the nation as a whole, with 32% at present maintaining that the nation's economy will improve as a result of these policies and 54% saying it will be worse. In October 1981, when this question was first asked, 53% thought the economy would improve and 37% thought it would not.

Respondents consistently have been less sanguine about Reaganomics' effect on their own economic health than on the nation's, suggesting a willingness to undergo personal sacrifice if it meant the United States as a whole would benefit. There also has been a tendency in past surveys for the public to express greater optimism about personal finances and the national economy as the time reference is projected into the future, "one year from now," for example, or "in the long run."

Major differences of opinion are found among various population groups. Far more whites (26%) than blacks (18%) think Reaganomics will improve their financial situation. Other groups with a more positive outlook include men, persons who attended college, those with family incomes of $15,000 or more per year, and Republicans. On the other hand, those with a more negative outlook toward the success of Reaganomics include women, those with no college training, persons with family incomes under $15,000, Democrats, and, as mentioned, blacks.

There is a strong correlation between approval of President Reagan's job performance and assessments of the economic consequences of Reaganomics. Fully 48% of those who approve of the way Reagan is handling his presidential duties are bullish about Reaganomics' effect on their family finances, compared to only 8% of those whose overall evaluation of Reagan is negative.

FEBRUARY 13
FEDERAL DEFICIT

Interviewing Date: 11/19–22/82
Survey #205-G

Do you happen to know whether the federal government is or is not operating at a loss?

Is (correct) 63%
Is not 8
Don't know 29

By Education
College

Is (correct) 81%
Is not 4
Don't know 15

High School

Is (correct) 58%
Is not 9
Don't know 33

Grade School

Is (correct) 45%
Is not 13
Don't know 42

Asked of those who replied that the federal government is operating at a loss: Just your best guess, what is the estimated size of the federal deficit for fiscal 1983?

$200 billion or more 16%
$150–$199 billion 9
$100–$149 billion 9
$50–$99 billion 3
Less than $50 billion 10
"Billions" 9
"Millions" 1
"High" 4
Don't know 39

By Education
College

$200 billion or more 20%
$150–$199 billion 13
$100–$149 billion 10
$50–$99 billion 3
Less than $50 billion 13
"Billions" 8
"Millions" .... *
"High" 5
Don't know 28

High School and Grade School

$200 billion or more 14%
$150–$199 billion 6
$100–$149 billion 8
$50–$99 billion 2
Less than $50 billion 9
"Billions" 9
"Millions" 2
"High" 4
Don't know 46

*Less than 1%

Interviewing Date: 1/14–17/83
Survey #207-G

It is estimated that the federal government will have a deficit of as much as $200 billion for fiscal 1984—that is, it will spend more than it takes in—unless some steps are taken to reduce the deficit. Basically, there are only a few ways this deficit can be reduced. Please tell me whether you approve or disapprove of each of the following:

Raise income taxes?

Approve 18%
Disapprove 77
No opinion 5

By Sex
Male

Approve 21%
Disapprove 76
No opinion 3

Female

Approve 16%
Disapprove 78
No opinion 6

By Race
White

Approve 19%
Disapprove 76
No opinion 5

Nonwhite

Approve 15%
Disapprove 79
No opinion 6

By Education
College

Approve 26%
Disapprove 70
No opinion 4

High School

Approve 15%
Disapprove 81
No opinion 4

Grade School

Approve 15%
Disapprove 74
No opinion 11

By Region
East

Approve 21%
Disapprove 75
No opinion 4

Midwest

Approve 18%
Disapprove 78
No opinion 4

South

Approve 16%
Disapprove 78
No opinion 6

West

Approve 19%
Disapprove 76
No opinion 5

By Income
$25,000 and Over

Approve 22%
Disapprove 76
No opinion 2

$15,000 and Over

Approve 18%
Disapprove 79
No opinion 3

Under $15,000

Approve 19%
Disapprove 73
No opinion 8

By Politics
Republicans

Approve 19%
Disapprove 76
No opinion 5

Democrats

Approve 20%
Disapprove 75
No opinion 5

Independents

Approve 16%
Disapprove 80
No opinion 4

Make further cuts in government spending for social programs?

Approve 41%
Disapprove 52
No opinion 7

By Sex
Male

Approve 41%
Disapprove 51
No opinion 8

Female

Approve 40%
Disapprove 52
No opinion 8

By Race
White

Approve 45%
Disapprove 48
No opinion 7

Nonwhite

Approve 22%
Disapprove 70
No opinion 8

By Education
College

Approve 44%
Disapprove 53
No opinion 3

High School

Approve 41%
Disapprove 51
No opinion 8

Grade School

Approve 31%
Disapprove 53
No opinion 16

By Region
East

Approve 36%
Disapprove 58
No opinion 6

Midwest

Approve 44%
Disapprove 49
No opinion 7

South

Approve 43%
Disapprove 48
No opinion 9

West

Approve 40%
Disapprove 53
No opinion 7

By Income
$25,000 and Over

Approve 50%
Disapprove 46
No opinion 4

$15,000 and Over

Approve 47%
Disapprove 47
No opinion 6

Under $15,000

Approve 32%
Disapprove 58
No opinion 10

By Politics
Republicans

Approve 56%
Disapprove 35
No opinion 9

Democrats

Approve 30%
Disapprove 63
No opinion 7

Independents

Approve 47%
Disapprove 47
No opinion 6

Make cuts in defense spending?

Approve 57%
Disapprove 35
No opinion 8

By Sex
Male

Approve 55%
Disapprove 40
No opinion 5

Female

Approve 58%
Disapprove 32
No opinion 10

By Race
White

Approve 57%
Disapprove 36
No opinion 7

Nonwhite

Approve 58%
Disapprove 32
No opinion 10

By Education
College

Approve 66%
Disapprove 29
No opinion 5

High School

Approve 53%
Disapprove 39
No opinion 8

Grade School

Approve 51%
Disapprove 35
No opinion 14

By Region
East

Approve 65%
Disapprove 30
No opinion 5

Midwest

Approve 59%
Disapprove 35
No opinion 6

South

Approve 48%
Disapprove 42
No opinion 10

West

Approve 55%
Disapprove 36
No opinion 9

By Income
$25,000 and Over

Approve 58%
Disapprove 39
No opinion 3

$15,000 and Over

Approve 58%
Disapprove 36
No opinion 6

Under $15,000

Approve 55%
Disapprove 35
No opinion 10

By Politics
Republicans

Approve 47%
Disapprove 47
No opinion 6

Democrats

Approve 51%
Disapprove 31
No opinion 8

Independents

Approve 61%
Disapprove 33
No opinion 6

Make cuts in "entitlement" programs such as Social Security, Medicaid, and the like?

Approve 12%
Disapprove 83
No opinion 5

By Sex

Male

Approve 14%
Disapprove 81
No opinion 5

Female

Approve 11%
Disapprove 85
No opinion 4

By Race

White

Approve 13%
Disapprove 82
No opinion 5

Nonwhite

Approve 7%
Disapprove 87
No opinion 6

By Education

College

Approve 17%
Disapprove 79
No opinion 4

High School

Approve 10%
Disapprove 86
No opinion 4

Grade School

Approve 8%
Disapprove 83
No opinion 9

By Region
East

Approve 12%
Disapprove 85
No opinion 3

Midwest

Approve 12%
Disapprove 84
No opinion 4

South

Approve 13%
Disapprove 80
No opinion 7

West

Approve 11%
Disapprove 84
No opinion 5

By Income
$25,000 and Over

Approve 16%
Disapprove 80
No opinion 4

$15,000 and Over

Approve 15%
Disapprove 82
No opinion 3

Under $15,000

Approve 9%
Disapprove 84
No opinion 7

By Politics

Republicans

Approve 20%
Disapprove 75
No opinion 5

Democrats

Approve 7%
Disapprove 88
No opinion 5

Independents

Approve 13%
Disapprove 82
No opinion 5

Note: If the American people had the task of reducing the federal government's budget deficit, projected to be as much as $200 billion for fiscal 1984, they would favor cuts in defense spending as the best way to accomplish this.

Six in ten Americans (57%) would approve of cuts in defense spending, while 41% choose further cuts in government spending for social programs to reduce the deficit. These two approaches are far more popular than the other two tested in a recent Gallup survey—raising income taxes and making cuts in "entitlement" programs such as Social Security, Medicaid, and the like. A total of 18% and 12%, respectively, favors these courses of action.

Sharp divisions are found along political party lines, with Republicans leaning in favor of further cuts in social programs and Democrats (joined by independent voters) choosing reductions in military spending. Neither Republicans, Democrats, nor independents are enthusiastic about raising taxes as a way to reduce the expected flow of red ink.

President Ronald Reagan's proposed budget of $848 billion for fiscal 1984, which begins this October 1, projects a deficit of $189 billion. The budget for next year calls for $239 billion in military spending, up 14% from the $209 budgeted for this purpose in 1983. Because nondefense spending would rise only 2% in the proposed 1984 budget, the military's share of the total budget would increase to 28% from 25.9% this fiscal year.

While Americans strongly endorse a balanced budget, many are unaware that the nation is operating in the red or have an inaccurate idea of the size of the projected deficit. Specifically, a recent Gallup survey shows that more than one-third of the public as a whole—and as many as one-fifth of persons with a college background—are not aware that the federal government is operating at a loss. Of those who are aware that the government is operating in the red, only one-fourth—and one-third of the college group—have an accurate idea of the size of the deficit; that is, they give responses in the $150- to $200-billion or over range.

FEBRUARY 17
REPUBLICAN PRESIDENTIAL CANDIDATES

Interviewing Date: 1/21–24/83
Survey #208-G

Asked of Republicans and independents: Would you please look over this list [respondents were handed a card listing seventeen names] and tell me which of these persons, if any, you have heard something about? Those who replied in the affirmative were asked: Now will you please tell me which of these persons you know something about?

Republicans Only

	Heard something about	Know something about
George Bush	96%	71%
Howard Baker	80	49
John Connally	78	48
Robert Dole	77	49
John Anderson	76	41
Charles Percy	62	35
Jesse Helms	57	28

Jack Kemp	43	20
Orrin Hatch	34	13
Philip Crane	33	15
Lowell Weicker	32	15
Paul Laxalt	30	13
William Armstrong	27	8
John Danforth	21	4
Richard Lugar	20	8
Robert Packwood	19	7
David Durenberger	11	5

Independents Only

	Heard something about	Know something about
Bush	92%	64%
Connally	73	43
Anderson	73	41
Baker	72	45
Dole	65	38
Percy	56	29
Helms	48	25
Kemp	39	20
Armstrong	30	10
Hatch	29	11
Weicker	28	14
Crane	25	11
Laxalt	21	10
Danforth	21	6
Lugar	17	7
Packwood	17	7
Durenberger	9	3

Asked of Republicans and independents: If Ronald Reagan decides not to stand for re-election, which one would you like to see nominated as the Republican party's candidate for president in 1984? And who would be your second choice?

First Choice of Republicans

Bush	23%
Baker	20
Dole	6
Kemp	4
Percy	4
Anderson	3

Connally	3
Others*	7
Don't know	30

First Choice of Independents

Bush	16%
Baker	15
Anderson	14
Connally	4
Dole	3
Helms	3
Kemp	3
Others**	10
Don't know	32

First and Second Choices of Republicans

Bush	40%
Baker	29
Dole	14
Connally	8
Percy	8
Anderson	7
Kemp	6
Helms	5
Laxalt	3
Others	**

First and Second Choices of Independents

Bush	28%
Baker	25
Anderson	20
Dole	8
Connally	8
Percy	7
Kemp	5
Helms	4
Others	**

*All others on the list each received 1% or less of the vote of survey respondents.
**All others on the list each received 2% or less of the vote of survey respondents.

Note: Vice-president George Bush and Senate Majority Leader Howard Baker are the early top choices of Republicans to be their party's 1984 presidential nominee if President Ronald Reagan chooses not to run. In the latest Gallup survey, Bush receives 23% of Republicans' first-place votes for the GOP nomination to 20% for Baker, a stand-off considering the margin of error for survey samples of this size.

Baker announced last month that he would not seek reelection to the Senate seat he has held since 1967, and that he would be a candidate for the 1984 GOP presidential nomination if Reagan decides not to run. Baker's announcement seems to have given a boost to his candidacy; in a Gallup survey last August, he received only half as many Republican first-place votes as Bush, 15% to 32%.

Next most often mentioned by Republicans in the current survey are Senator Robert Dole (6%), Representative Jack Kemp (4%), Senator Charles Percy (4%), 1982 independent presidential candidate John Anderson (3%), and former Texas governor John Connally (3%). None of the others on the list of seventeen possible contenders receives more than 1% of Republicans' votes.

The choices of political independents, who may participate in the party primaries in some states, generally parallel the selections of Republican voters, with one important exception: John Anderson, whose name was not included in the early survey, is in a virtual three-way tie for the GOP nomination, based on the choices of independent voters.

When the list is expanded by adding first and second choices, Bush becomes the clear choice of Republicans, followed by Baker. However, the selections of independents are narrowly divided among Bush, Baker, and Anderson.

Republican strategists are pressing the president for an early decision on whether he plans to seek reelection. Aspirants for the nomination would need an early start to put together their organizations and begin their campaigns. Some political observers believe there is no obvious GOP successor to Reagan if he chooses not to run, and GOP strategists fear that a power struggle within the party might develop if Reagan puts off his decision too long.

Among the public the belief has grown steadily that Reagan will run again in 1984. In a December survey, 74% of voters said they thought Reagan would try for another four years in the White House, up from 67% who expressed that view in an August survey and 59% last March. However, only 37% in the December survey said they would like to see Reagan run again.

To a considerable extent, the current choices for the Republican nomination are a result of name awareness. A majority of Republicans has heard of only seven of the seventeen persons tested, and Vice-president Bush is the only person of the seventeen about whom a majority of Republicans claims to know something. The nomination choices closely parallel awareness levels at this early stage and clearly show the importance of candidates becoming known to the public.

FEBRUARY 20
CRIME

Interviewing Date: 1/28–31/83
Survey #209-G

Is there any area right around here—that is, within a mile—where you would be afraid to walk alone at night?

	Yes
National	45%

By Sex

Male	26%
Female	62

By Race

White	43%
Nonwhite	57

By Region

East	47%
Midwest	38
South	44
West	53

By Age

18–29 years	.45%
30–49 years	.39
50–64 years	.47
65 years and over	.54

By Income

$25,000 and over	.37%
$15,000 and over	.41
Under $15,000	.50

By Community Size

One million and over	.56%
500,000–999,999	.49
50,000–499,999	.54
2,500–49,999	.40
Under 2,500; rural	.29
Center cities	.61%
Suburbs	.45
Rural areas	.33

National Trend

1982	.48%
1981	.45
1979	.42
1977	.45
1972	.42
1965	.34

How about at home at night—do you feel safe and secure, or not?

	Unsafe and unsecure
National	16%

By Sex

Male	11%
Female	.20

By Race

White	.14%
Nonwhite	.21

By Region

East	.17%
Midwest	.10
South	.19
West	.15

By Age

18–29 years	.16%
30–49 years	.16
50–64 years	.12
65 years and over	.16

By Income

$25,000 and over	.12%
$15,000 and over	.14
Under $15,000	.18

By Community Size

One million and over	.21%
500,000–999,999	.14
50,000–499,999	.16
2,500–49,999	.16
Under 2,500; rural	.12
Center cities	.10%
Suburbs	.14
Rural areas	.13

National Trend

1981	.16%
1977	.15
1975	.20
1972	.17

How about during the daytime? Is there any area within a mile of here where you would be afraid to walk alone during the daytime?

	Yes
National	13%

By Sex

Male	7%
Female	.19

By Race

White 11%
Nonwhite 22

By Region

East 13%
Midwest 10
South 12
West 18

By Age

18–29 years 12%
30–49 years 12
50–64 years 15
65 years and over 14

By Income

$25,000 and over 10%
$15,000 and over 10
Under $15,000 17

By Community Size

One million and over 20%
500,000–999,999 14
50,000–499,999 16
2,500–49,999 7
Under 2,500; rural 8

Center cities 22%
Suburbs 12
Rural areas 8

Is there more crime in this area than there was a year ago, or less?

More 37%
Less 17
Same 36
Don't know 10

National Trend

	More	Less	Same	Don't know
1982	47%	17%	28%	8%
1981	54	8	29	9
1977	43	17	32	8
1975	50	12	29	9
December 1972	51	10	27	12
March 1972	35	11	42	12

Note: Fear of crime is pervasive in American society, with nearly 45% of its citizens fearful of walking alone at night in their neighborhoods. The proportion rises to 76% among women living in heavily urbanized areas of the nation. Not only are half of U.S. citizens afraid to walk alone in their neighborhoods at night, but 13% fear doing so even in broad daylight, with the figure rising to 31% in the case of urban women.

The current level of fear, as determined by the 1983 annual Gallup survey of crime, is up sharply from the 1960s (for example, 31% were afraid of venturing out at night in 1967) but is no higher than the level recorded during the last decade.

Furthermore, 16% of the populace admits to being fearful at night in their homes. Most fearful are women, older persons, those who live in the larger cities, and blacks, who customarily have been the chief victims of crime.

Although the fear of crime has shown little sign of abatement, fewer today than in 1982 or 1981 perceive an increase in crime in their communities or neighborhoods, which suggests that the crime wave of recent years may be starting to level off. In the current survey, 37% say there is more crime in their area than a year ago, compared to 47% who held this view in 1982.

FEBRUARY 21
CRIME

Interviewing Date: 1/28–31/83
Survey #209-G

During the last twelve months, have any of these happened to you? [Respondents were handed a card listing crimes.]

                                              Yes
Money or property stolen 12%
Property vandalized 11

Home broken into or attempt made 8
Assaulted or mugged; money or
   property taken by force or
   threat of force 5
Car stolen 2

By Sex
Male

Money or property stolen 12%
Property vandalized 11
Home broken into or attempt made 5
Assaulted or mugged; money or
   property taken by force or
   threat of force 3
Car stolen 2

Female

Money or property stolen 12%
Property vandalized 11
Home broken into or attempt made 10
Assaulted or mugged; money or
   property taken by force or
   threat of force 6
Car stolen 3

By Race
White

Money or property stolen 12%
Property vandalized 12
Home broken into or attempt made 8
Assaulted or mugged; money or
   property taken by force or
   threat of force 5
Car stolen 3

Nonwhite

Money or property stolen 11%
Property vandalized 9
Home broken into or attempt made 7
Assaulted or mugged; money or
   property taken by force or
   threat of force 5
Car stolen 2

By Age
18–29 Years

Money or property stolen 16%
Property vandalized 16
Home broken into or attempt made 9
Assaulted or mugged; money or
   property taken by force or
   threat of force 7
Car stolen 3

30–49 Years

Money or property stolen 14%
Property vandalized 11
Home broken into or attempt made 10
Assaulted or mugged; money or
   property taken by force or
   threat of force 4
Car stolen 4

50 Years and Over

Money or property stolen 8%
Property vandalized 8
Home broken into or attempt made 5
Assaulted or mugged; money or
   property taken by force or
   threat of force 2
Car stolen 1

By Community Size
One Million and Over

Money or property stolen 13%
Property vandalized 11
Home broken into or attempt made 9
Assaulted or mugged; money or
   property taken by force or
   threat of force 8
Car stolen 2

500,000–999,999

Money or property stolen 17%
Property vandalized 18
Home broken into or attempt made 9
Assaulted or mugged; money or
   property taken by force or
   threat of force 4
Car stolen 5

50,000–499,999

Money or property stolen 13%
Property vandalized 10
Home broken into or attempt made 13
Assaulted or mugged; money or
  property taken by force or
    threat of force 5
Car stolen 4

2,500–49,999

Money or property stolen 7%
Property vandalized 12
Home broken into or attempt made 4
Assaulted or mugged; money or
  property taken by force or
    threat of force 3
Car stolen .... *

Under 2,500; Rural

Money or property stolen 12%
Property vandalized 9
Home broken into or attempt made 4
Assaulted or mugged; money or
  property taken by force or
    threat of force 3
Car stolen 1

*Less than 1%

Total of Sample Victimized at Least Once

National............................25%

By Sex

Male 25%
Female 25

By Race

White 25%
Nonwhite 24

By Age

18–29 years 31%
30–49 years 29
50 years and over 17

By Income

$25,000 and over 27%
$15,000 and over 26
Under $15,000 23

By Community Size

One million and over 28%
500,000–999,999 32
50,000–499,999 27
2,500–49,999 21
Under 2,500; rural 20

Center cities 30%
Suburbs 26
Rural areas 21

Asked of those who have been victimized during the last twelve months: Did you report this to the police, or not?

	Crime incidence	Reported to police
Money or property stolen................	12%	7%
Property vandalized	11	
Home broken into or attempt made	8	6
Assaulted or mugged; money or property taken by force or threat of force	5	3
Car stolen	2	2

Note: The latest Gallup crime victimization audit shows that as many as one-fourth (25%) of U.S. households were victimized by crime during the twelve months preceding the survey. These were crimes either against property (money or property stolen or vandalized) or against persons (robberies or assaults).

The level of victimization has changed little over the last five years. In the 1982 audit, 25% also reported they had been victimized.

FEBRUARY 27
DEFENSE SPENDING

Interviewing Date: 1/14–17/83
Survey #207-G

There is much discussion as to the amount of money the government in Washington should spend for national defense and military purposes. How do you feel about this? Do you think we are spending too much, too little, or about the right amount?

Too much 45%
Too little 14
About right 33
No opinion 8

By Sex
Male

Too much 43%
Too little 16
About right 35
No opinion 6

Female

Too much 46%
Too little 12
About right 32
No opinion 10

By Race
White

Too much 43%
Too little 15
About right 35
No opinion 7

Nonwhite

Too much 56%
Too little 9
About right 24
No opinion 11

By Education
College

Too much 52%
Too little 12
About right 33
No opinion 3

High School

Too much 43%
Too little 14
About right 36
No opinion 7

Grade School

Too much 36%
Too little 16
About right 29
No opinion 19

By Region
East

Too much 54%
Too little 10
About right 32
No opinion 4

Midwest

Too much 45%
Too little 12
About right 34
No opinion 9

South

Too much 36%
Too little 16
About right 37
No opinion 11

West

Too much 43%
Too little 19
About right 31
No opinion 7

By Politics

Republicans

Too much	32%
Too little	17
About right	47
No opinion	4

Democrats

Too much	51%
Too little	12
About right	28
No opinion	9

Independents

Too much	47%
Too little	14
About right	31
No opinion	8

National Trend

	Too much	Too little	About right	No opinion
November 1982	41%	16%	31%	12%
March 1982	36	19	36	9
1981	15	51	22	12
1976	36	22	32	10
1973	46	13	30	11
1971	50	11	31	8
1969	52	8	31	9
1960	18	21	45	16

Note: With the stage in Washington now set for a showdown between the Reagan administration and Congress over the size of the defense budget for fiscal 1984, there is stronger public support today than in a decade for a reduction in military spending. In the latest Gallup survey, a 45% plurality says the government is spending too much for defense compared to 14% who say too little. A continuation of the present level of military spending is favored by 33% of Americans. Not since 1973 has public opinion been as supportive of a reduction in defense spending as it is today.

Only two years ago, the situation was the reverse. In an early 1981 survey, 51% of Americans said they believed too little was being spent on defense, while 22% thought the budget was adequate and only 15% believed that too much was budgeted for military purposes.

As might be expected, there are strong political overtones to public opinion on defense spending. Far more Democrats (51%) than Republicans (32%) believe the government has budgeted too much for military purposes. Nevertheless, the weight of Republican opinion is also that too much is spent for defense (32%) rather than that too little is budgeted for this purpose (17%).

MARCH 3
IDEAL FAMILY SIZE

Interviewing Date: 1/14–17/83
Survey #207-G

What do you think is the ideal number of children for a family to have?

One	3%
Two	54
Three	21
Four	11
Five	1
Six or more	2
None	3
Don't know	5

Those Saying Four or More Children

By Sex

Male	14%
Female	16

By Race

White	13%
Nonwhite	22

By Education

College	10%
High school	14
Grade school	28

By Age

18–29 years	13%
30–49 years	12
50 years and over	19

By Religion

Protestants	13%
Catholics	19

By Marital Status

Single	13%
Married	13

National Trend

(Those Saying
Four or More Children)

1980	14%
1978	17
1974	19
1971	23
1968	41
1963	42
1960	45
1957	38
1953	41
1947	47
1945	49
1941	41
1936	34

Note: The long downtrend in the appeal of large families appears to have leveled out, with 14% in the latest Gallup survey saying the ideal number of children is four or more. In 1980, 14% also cited this family size. As recently as 1968, 41% thought the model family would include four or more children, three times the proportion who now favor families of this size.

In the current survey, approximately half of the respondents (54%) say the ideal number of children is two. Only 3% favor single-child families.

In the Gallup Poll's first measurement on ideal family size in 1936, 34% said that four or more children represented this ideal. By 1945, 49% chose four or more children as the best number, presaging the postwar "baby boom." The percentage trended slowly downward between 1947 and 1968, but subsequently dropped sharply.

Significant differences now are found by major population groups. Persons who have had only a grade-school education are far more likely to prefer large families than are those with more formal education. Similarly, persons 50 years of age and older are somewhat more inclined to favor larger families. Catholics are more apt to prefer large families than are Protestants. Men and women hold similar views, as do both married and single persons. And nonwhites are considerably more inclined than whites to say the ideal number of children is four or more.

The views of Americans regarding the ideal number of children have consistently reflected actual population trends. The high cost of rearing children and uncertainty about the world situation are undoubtedly factors in the long-term trend away from large families.

MARCH 6
PRESIDENT REAGAN

Interviewing Date: 1/14–17; 21–24; 28–31/83
Survey #207-G; 208-G; 209-G

Do you approve or disapprove of the way Ronald Reagan is handling his job as president?

Performance Ratings

(Three-Survey Average Approval)

	Both sexes	Men	Women
National	37%	40%	33%

By Race

White	40%	44%	37%
Black	10	16	6

By Education

College	46%	49%	42%
High school	36	39	33
Grade school	20	23	16

By Region

East	34%	36%	32%
Midwest	38	41	36
South	36	40	32
West	38	44	32

By Age

18–29 years	41%	46%	36%
30–49 years	36	40	31
50 years and over	34	35	33

By Family Income

$20,000 and over	44%	45%	43%
Under $20,000	31	35	27

By Politics

Republicans	68%	74%	62%
Democrats	19	19	18
Independents	39	43	34

By Religion

Protestants	38%	43%	35%
Catholics	37	41	33
Jews	21	23	20

By Occupation

Professional and business	48%	52%	45%
Clerical and sales	34	37	32
Manual workers	33	35	30
Skilled	38	41	34
Unskilled	27	28	26
Nonlabor force	31	35	28
Labor union households	30	30	29
Nonunion households	38	43	34

Note: Since he took office, President Ronald Reagan has been plagued by a gender gap; he receives markedly lower assessments of his policies and performance in office from women voters than from men. This sex differential cuts across all social and economic boundaries and is found in every region of the nation.

A special Gallup analysis of more than 4,500 interviews conducted in January permits a detailed examination of this gender gap for the first time. In these surveys, 37% of adult Americans say they approve of the way Reagan is handling the duties of his office, while 54% disapprove and 9% are uncommitted. During this period 40% of men but only 33% of women had a favorable opinion of Reagan's job performance, a significant 7-percentage point difference.

This discrepancy by sex is found to a greater or lesser degree in each of the forty-one national surveys Gallup has conducted since Reagan took office. A summary is shown below:

National Trend of
Reagan Performance Ratings

(Average Percent Approving)

	Both sexes	Men	Women
1983 (3 surveys)	37%	40%	33%
1982 (19 surveys)	44	48	40
1981 (19 surveys)	58	62	53
Average to date	50	54	45

These differences by sex are not found in the public's assessments of Reagan's predecessors. As shown in the following table, the greatest previous disparity was during Richard Nixon's presidency, when 50% of men and 47% of women approved of his job performance:

National Trend of
Presidential Performance Ratings

(Average Percent Approving)

	Both sexes	Men	Women
Reagan	50%	54%	45%
Carter	47	46	47
Ford	46	45	46
Nixon	49	50	47
Johnson	55	56	54
Kennedy	70	70	70
Eisenhower	64	63	65

In a single January survey, the gender gap extended to men's and women's assessment of Reagan's handling of the economy (33% of men approved, but only 25% of women did), inflation (43% and 30%), unemployment (21% and 18%), and, especially, to his defense program (53% and 36%).

The president's gender gap actually began before the 1982 presidential election, in which men voted for Reagan to a greater extent than did women. The reasons underlying this discrepancy generally are considered to center on the peace issue—with women more likely than men to believe Reagan might get the United States into war—

and on women's consistently more liberal stance on many social issues.

The political differences between the two sexes take on special significance because of changes in the composition of the voting public. According to the U.S. Census, in each election a progressively larger percentage of the electorate is female. Census studies show that for the first time in history equal proportions of men and women reported voting in the 1980 election. As a consequence, women now represent a majority of the voting public. If the trend persists, this will constitute an even larger majority.

Not only are women less supportive than men of the Reagan administration on the national level, but also the gender gap is found in every major population subgroup, as well. Among groups which have included the administration's staunchest supporters, 42% of college-educated women compared to 49% of college-educated men approve of Reagan's conduct in office. Among Republicans, a 12-percentage point gap between the sexes exists, with 74% of men but only 62% of women approving of the president. In households in which the chief wage earner is employed in business or the professions, 52% of men and 45% of women approve.

The principle also embraces population groups which have been least supportive of Reagan. Among blue-collar groups, for example, 35% of men and 30% of women give the president a favorable rating. Also, 16% of black men but only 6% of black women approve of Reagan's job performance. The gender gap is found in each of the four major geographic regions, with the greatest disparity in the far western states.

National Trend of Reagan Performance Ratings

(Average Percent Approving)

	Both sexes	Men	Women
January 28–31, 1983	35%	39%	32%
January 21–24, 1983	37	39	35
January 14–17, 1983	37	42	32
December 1982	41	47	36
November 1982	43	48	39
October 1982	42	46	38
September 1982	42	47	37
August 1982	41	44	38
July 1982	42	48	38
June 1982	45	51	39
May 1982	45	47	43
April 1982	43	49	38
March 1982	46	52	41
February 1982	47	51	42
January 1982	49	53	45

MARCH 8
SOCIAL SECURITY—A CREDIBLE CRISIS*

As national crises go, the one facing the Social Security system is very credible to the American public. Consequently, it is willing to consider changes in the system, if necessary, to stave off its collapse. By contrast, for nearly a decade the polls showed that Americans simply did not believe in the energy crisis and, as such, they rejected most proposals to deal with it. Recent polling finds that Americans have no such doubts about the possibility of an insolvent Social Security system.

A 1982 Gallup survey for the U.S. Chamber of Commerce indicated that 63% of employed Americans were afraid they might not receive benefits at all when they reached retirement age, while another 16% believed benefits might not be as good as they are now. Other polls have shown as much, if not more, public doubt about the viability of the Social Security system. A January 1983 CBS/*New York Times* Poll found only 27% of the public believing that the Social Security system will have the money available for the benefits they expect upon retirement.

The polls have been less clear on what changes the public is willing to accept to save the system, but they seem to indicate public willingness to accept some change. Here is what recent surveys have shown:

1) Delays in retirement age. When the Gallup

*This Gallup analysis was written by Andrew Kohut, president of the Gallup Organization Inc.

Poll and the NBC/Associated Press Poll asked their respondents if moving back the age for retirement was acceptable, large majorities said no. However, when the proposition was to increase benefits for those who delay their retirement (ABC/ *Washington Post*) or reduce benefits for those who retire early (NBC/Associated Press), solid majorities responded positively. In effect, the public favors both negative and positive incentives for later retirement, but resists any proposals for doing away with retirement at age 65 for those who want it.

2) The inclusion of federal employees. All the polls have shown large majorities in favor of bringing federal employees into the Social Security system.

3) Delays in cost-of-living increases. The public tends to be more or less evenly divided on delays in cost-of-living increases, but slight majorities favored this principle in the CBS/*New York Times* and ABC/*Washington Post* polls. Similarly, the Gallup Poll found a slight plurality favoring tying future Social Security benefit increases to wages rather than prices.

4) Tax increases. The greatest difference between the polls has been on the public's willingness to accept further increases in Social Security premiums. As a general rule, polls showed acceptance of higher Social Security taxes to the extent that the wording of the question pitted acceptance of higher taxes against the alternative of cutting benefits or allowing the system to collapse. Gallup found only 34% approved when increased employee or employer payments were proposed as a means of "making the system pay for itself," but the Harris Poll found 55% approving and 42% disapproving of a rise in Social Security taxes "to keep benefits as they are now." NBC/ Associated Press found the largest margin favoring taxes when it asked respondents simply to choose between increasing taxes (51%) or reducing benefits (34%).

The driving force in public opinion about Social Security is preservation of the system as it exists now with regard to age of eligibility and level of benefits. There appears to be some give on the part of the public when it comes to cost-of-living increases, and there is acceptance of the concept of monetary incentives to delayed retirement. The sacred cow is the level of benefits. For now, at least, the public is willing to accept changes in the system and increased taxes to preserve the existing level of benefits for current and future retirees.

The political consequence of a public focus on preserving benefits is advantageous to the Democratic party and dangerous for the Republican party. The *Los Angeles Times* Poll showed that while both parties are judged about equally capable of putting the system back on its feet, the Republican party is seen as more likely to slash benefits and to reduce the number of workers who are eligible. However, the bipartisan plan to save the system, which comes up for a vote this month, may have taken some of the political sting out of the Social Security issue.

A *Newsweek* Poll found a majority (53%) of respondents reacting favorably to a description of the compromise worked out between the administration and the Democratic leadership, but as many as 38% were opposed. The most controversial element in the plan is the taxing of Social Security benefits for upper-income retirees. The public is about evenly divided on the acceptability of such taxation.

Nonetheless, the compromise achieved in Washington is in keeping with the mood of the public as measured by the polls: a deep concern that the Social Security payout might not be there in years to come, overriding specific objections to changes that will preserve the system.

MARCH 10
POLITICAL AFFILIATION

Interviewing Date: November 1982–January 1983
Six National Surveys

In politics, as of today, do you consider your-self a Republican, a Democrat, or an independent?

Republican 25%
Democrat 45
Independent 30

The following table shows the political affiliation of major population groups from November 1982 through January 1983. The groups are ranked in order of Republican strength. (Persons who said they belong to other parties or have no party allegiance have been excluded.)

Political Affiliation

(November 1982–January 1983)

	Republicans	Democrats	Independents
Farmers	39%	31%	30%
Professional and business $25,000 and over	33	35	32
income	30	37	33
Protestants	30	43	27
2,500–49,999 population	30	37	33
College educated	29	38	33
Under 2,500 population	28	42	30
50 years and older	28	51	21
Whites	28	40	32
West	27	44	29
Midwest	27	38	35
Clerical and sales	27	45	28
Nonunion households	26	43	31
$20,000–$24,999 income	25	43	32
National	25	45	30
Women	25	47	28
Men	25	42	33
$15,000–$19,999 income	25	45	30
East	24	46	30
Nonlabor force	24	52	24
High-school educated	24	45	31
18–24 years	24	39	37
$10,000–$14,999 income	24	48	28
50,000–499,999 population	23	46	31
25–29 years	23	41	36
South	22	52	26
Skilled workers	22	43	35
One million and over population	21	54	25
500,000–999,999 population	21	46	33
$5,000–$9,999 income	20	53	27
Catholics	19	50	31
Labor union households	19	52	29
Grade-school educated	19	60	21
Jews	15	65	20
Under $5,000 income	14	60	26
Blacks	6	77	17

The following percentages represent the trend in political affiliation since 1946:

National Trend

	Republicans	Democrats	Independents
1983 (January)	24%	45%	31%
1982 (4th quarter)	26	45	29
1982 (3d quarter)	27	45	28
1982 (2d quarter)	26	46	28
1982 (1st quarter)	26	44	30
1981	28	42	30
1980	24	46	30
1979	22	45	33
1975	22	45	33
1972	38	43	29
1968	27	46	27
1964	25	53	22
1960	30	47	23
1954	34	46	20
1950	33	45	22
1946	40	39	21

Note: The proportion of adults who regard themselves as Republicans has declined since the early months of the Reagan presidency in 1981, with only one person in four currently claiming affiliation with the GOP. In three January surveys, 25% classify themselves as Republicans, 45% as Democrats, and 30% as independents. In 1981, the percentages were Republicans 28%, Democrats 42%, and independents 30%, representing the highest level of GOP affiliation in a decade.

The current findings, which show Democrats outnumbering Republicans by nearly a 2-to-1 margin, clearly point up the challenge facing Republican presidential hopefuls. To win, GOP candidates in the past have had not only to win a very high percentage of the votes of their own party members but also the support of a majority of independents and some Democratic votes as well.

MARCH 13
COST OF LIVING

Interviewing Date: 1/14-17; 21-24/83
Survey #207-G; 208-G

On the average, about how much does your family spend on food, including milk, each week?

	Median average
National	$69*

By Region

East	$74
Midwest	$63
South	$65
West	$71

By Income

$15,000 and over	$76
Under $15,000	$53

By Size of Household

Single person	$40
Two-person family	$53
Three-person family	$69
Four-person family	$78
Five-person family	$99

*Farm families were excluded from the survey because many farmers raise their own food.

National Trend

	Median average
1983	$69
1982	$70
1981	$62
1980	$59
1979	$53
1977	$48
1976	$48
1975	$47
1974	$42
1973	$37
1971	$35
1970	$34
1969	$33
1959	$29
1949	$25
1937	$11

Note: Thanks to a mild winter, increased productivity, and lower farm prices, Americans currently are spending about the same amount to feed their families as they did at this time last year. The 1983 Gallup audit of food expenditures shows the median amount spent by a representative, nonfarm U.S. household now is about $69 per week, statistically unchanged from the $70 recorded in 1982.

Since the Gallup Poll began charting food expenditures in 1937, the weekly amount has increased six-fold, from $11 in the first audit to the current $69. During the twenty-year period between 1949 and 1969, the figure grew from $25 per week to $33 per week, an increase of only 32%. However, from 1970 to the present—a span of only fourteen years—food costs have doubled, from $34 per week to $69 this year.

As in the past, food costs take a smaller bite out of the family budget of midwesterners and southerners than those living elsewhere in the nation. Persons in the survey whose annual family income is over $15,000 report spending almost half again as much on food as do those with lower incomes. However, food costs represent a larger portion of total expenditures of families in the lower-income category than is true of upper-income households.

MARCH 17
PRESIDENT REAGAN

Interviewing Date: 1/28–31; 2/25–28/83
Survey #209-G; 210-G

Do you approve or disapprove of the way Ronald Reagan is handling his job as president?

Reagan Performance Ratings

(Percent Approving)

	February	January	Difference
National	40%	35%	+ 5

By Sex

Male	43%	39%	+ 4
Female	37	32	+ 5

By Race

White	45%	39%	+ 6
Black	10	10	0

By Education

College	51%	43%	+ 8
High school	38	36	+ 2
Grade school	25	16	+ 9

By Age

18–29 years	40%	40%	0
30–49 years	44	34	+ 10
50 years and over	37	33	+ 4

By Income

$20,000 and over	49%	39%	+ 10
Under $20,000	33	31	+ 2

By Politics

Republicans	79%	69%	+ 10
Democrats	17	19	− 2
Independents	46	34	+ 12

Interviewing Date: 2/25–28/83
Survey #210-G

President Reagan has said that the recession is ending and recovery has begun. Do you tend to agree or disagree with him on this?

Agree	39%
Disagree	53
No opinion	8

By Politics

Republicans

Agree	66%
Disagree	26
No opinion	8

Democrats

Agree	22%
Disagree	71
No opinion	7

Independents

Agree	46%
Disagree	48
No opinion	6

Those Who Approve of Reagan

Agree	68%
Disagree	24
No opinion	8

Those Who Disapprove of Reagan

Agree	17%
Disagree	78
No opinion	5

Note: President Ronald Reagan's approval rating with the American people has shot up 5 percentage points amid signs that the economy may be starting to improve. In a late-February Gallup survey, 40% of the public approved of the way Reagan is handling his presidential duties, while 50% disapproved. A month earlier the president had the approval of only 35% of Americans, while 56% disapproved.

Another survey question showed 39% of the public agreeing with Reagan that the recession is ending and that recovery has begun. About half (53%) disagreed with the president's contention. Two thirds (68%) of those in the survey who approve of Reagan's overall job performance agree with him that economic recovery is at hand; only 17% of persons who have an unfavorable opinion of the president's handling of his job are optimistic about the recession's end.

Not unexpectedly, the public's perception has a strong political cast, with 66% of Republicans but only 22% of Democrats agreeing with Reagan's claim that recovery has begun. Independents are evenly divided on the issue, with 46% in agreement and 48% in disagreement.

The improvement in Reagan's overall popularity rating stems mostly from renewed confidence on the part of Republicans, as well as in population groups with a tradition of GOP loyalty. During the one-month period between the late January and late February surveys, Reagan's approval rating climbed 10 percentage points—from 69%

to 79% positive—among Republicans. Among Democrats, on the other hand, he registered a 2-point decline, from 19% to 17% approval.

Similarly, his popularity rose 8 points among people with at least some exposure to college but only 2 points among those with less formal education. Among members of families with incomes of $20,000 or more per year his current 49% approval rating is 10 points higher than the 39% recorded in the January survey.

Reagan's improved standing traces mainly to whites (up 6 points). Among blacks there was no discernible change, with 10% in both the January and February surveys approving of his handling of his presidential duties. Men and women participated about equally in bolstering Reagan's overall approval rating. Nevertheless, significantly fewer women (37%) than men (43%) continue to approve.

MARCH 20
PRESIDENTIAL TRIAL HEATS

Interviewing Date: 2/25–28/83
Survey #210-G

Asked of registered voters: Suppose the 1984 presidential elections were being held today. If President Ronald Reagan were the Republican candidate and Senator John Glenn were the Democratic candidate, which would you like to see win? [Those who named another candidate or who were undecided were asked: As of today, do you lean more to Reagan, the Republican, or to Glenn, the Democrat?]

Reagan 40%
Glenn 45
Other 3
Undecided 12

By Politics
Republicans

Reagan 76%
Glenn 15
Other 1
Undecided 8

Democrats

Reagan 19%
Glenn 66
Other 4
Undecided 11

Independents

Reagan 44%
Glenn 35
Other 3
Undecided 18

Asked of registered voters: Suppose the 1984 presidential elections were being held today. If President Ronald Reagan were the Republican candidate and Walter Mondale were the Democratic candidate, which would you like to see win? [Those who named another candidate or who were undecided were asked: As of today, do you lean more to Reagan, the Republican, or to Mondale, the Democrat?]

Reagan 41%
Mondale 47
Other 3
Undecided 9

By Politics
Republicans

Reagan 83%
Mondale 11
Other 2
Undecided 4

Democrats

Reagan 15%
Mondale 73
Other 4
Undecided 8

Independents

Reagan 46%
Mondale 34
Other 3
Undecided 17

Note: Former Vice-president Walter Mondale and Senator John Glenn, the current top choices of Democratic voters for the 1984 nomination, continue to lead President Ronald Reagan in the latest test elections, but by smaller margins than in December.

Mondale leads Reagan 47% to 41% among registered voters, while Glenn holds a similar 45%-to-40% margin. In the previous (December) trial heats, Mondale led the president 52% to 40%, and Glenn outscored Reagan by a 54%-to-39% margin.

Reagan's improved showing undoubtedly reflects public reaction to signs that the economy may be starting to improve: the latest Gallup survey shows approval of the president's performance in office up 5 points from a January measurement, from 35% to 40% approval.

In the first Reagan-Mondale trial heat (October 1981), the president held a comfortable 54%-to-37% lead. However, Reagan's support ebbed in subsequent measurements and reached its lowest point last December.

Reagan vs. Mondale

(Based on Registered Voters)

	Reagan	Mondale	Other	Unde-cided
February 1983	41%	47%	3%	9%
December 1982	40	52	2	6
October 1982	47	44	3	6
June 1982	43	49	1	7
April 1982	46	46	1	7
October 1981	54	37	1	8

President Reagan was matched against Glenn for the first time in December:

Reagan vs. Glenn

(Based on Registered Voters)

	Reagan	Glenn	Other	Unde-cided
February 1983	40%	45%	3%	12%
December 1982	39	54	1	5

Mondale and Glenn are the top choices of Democrats nationwide for their party's nominee

in 1984. In a recent Gallup Poll in which respondents were asked to choose from a list of sixteen possible nominees, Mondale and Glenn outstripped the rest of the field. However, in a nomination test between just the two men, Mondale leads Glenn 52% and 30% among Democrats. The fact that Glenn makes nearly as good a showing as Mondale in test races against Reagan is due to the fact that he is currently as popular as Mondale among independents in the latest trial heats, and even slightly stronger than the former vice-president among voters who classify themselves as Republicans.

MARCH 24
PRESIDENTIAL TRIAL HEATS

Interviewing Date: 2/25–28/83
Survey #210-G

Asked of registered voters: Suppose the 1984 presidential elections were being held today. If Vice-president George Bush were the Republican candidate and Walter Mondale were the Democratic candidate, which would you like to see win? [Those who named another candidate or who were undecided were asked: As of today, do you lean more to Bush, the Republican, or to Mondale, the Democrat?]

Bush	37%
Mondale	48
Other	2
Undecided	13

By Politics
Republicans

Bush	74%
Mondale	12
Other	1
Undecided	13

Democrats

Bush	15%
Mondale	74
Other	3
Undecided	8

Independents

Bush 43%
Mondale 33
Other 2
Undecided 22

Asked of registered voters: Suppose the 1984 presidential elections were being held today. If Vice-president George Bush were the Republican candidate and Senator John Glenn were the Democratic candidate, which would you like to see win? [Those who named another candidate or who were undecided were asked: As of today, do you lean more to Bush, the Republican, or to Glenn, the Democrat?]

Bush 36%
Glenn 47
Other 2
Undecided 15

By Politics
Republicans

Bush 70%
Glenn 16
Other 1
Undecided 13

Democrats

Bush 15%
Glenn 70
Other 2
Undecided 13

Independents

Bush 40%
Glenn 36
Other 1
Undecided 23

Asked of registered voters: Suppose the 1984 presidential elections were being held today. If Senator Howard Baker were the Republican candidate and Walter Mondale were the Democratic candidate, which would you like to see win? [Those who named another candidate or who were undecided were asked: As of today, do you lean more to Baker, the Republican, or to Mondale, the Democrat?]

Baker 34%
Mondale 48
Other 2
Undecided 16

By Politics
Republicans

Baker 67%
Mondale 18
Other 1
Undecided 14

Democrats

Baker 13%
Mondale 72
Other 2
Undecided 13

Independents

Baker 40%
Mondale 33
Other 3
Undecided 24

Asked of registered voters: Suppose the 1984 presidential elections were being held today. If Senator Howard Baker were the Republican candidate and Senator John Glenn were the Democratic candidate, which would you like to see win? [Those who named another candidate or who were undecided were asked: As of today, do you lean more to Baker, the Republican, or to Glenn, the Democrat?]

Baker 34%
Glenn 45
Other 2
Undecided 19

By Politics

Republicans

Baker	63%
Glenn	20
Other	1
Undecided	17

Democrats

Baker	17%
Glenn	64
Other	2
Undecided	17

Independents

Baker	38%
Glenn	34
Other	3
Undecided	25

Asked of Republicans: Suppose President Reagan decides not to run for reelection and the choice for president in the Republican convention in 1984 narrows down to George Bush and Howard Baker. Which one would you prefer to have the Republican convention select?

Bush	55%
Baker	27
Undecided	18

Note: Vice-president George Bush and Senate Majority Leader Howard Baker—likely contenders for the 1984 Republican presidential nomination if President Ronald Reagan chooses not to seek reelection—both lose in test elections to the Democratic front-runners, former Vice-president Walter Mondale and Senator John Glenn.

If the election were being held today, the latest Gallup survey found, Mondale would be a 48%-to-37% victor over Bush among registered voters. Mondale would also beat Senator Baker, 48% to 34%. The 3-point difference in the votes for the two GOP candidates is statistically meaningless.

Almost identical results are found in test races pitting Glenn against each possible Republican nominee. Bush loses 36% to 47% in a contest

against Glenn. And Glenn beats Baker by a similar 45%-to-34% margin. In each case, registered voters who name other candidates or who are undecided make up the balance of the vote.

Though neither Republican fares much better against Mondale or Glenn in test elections for the presidency, Vice-president Bush is the clear GOP winner in a head-to-head nomination contest, with 55% of Republicans choosing Bush and 27% Baker for the GOP nomination, if Reagan does not run.

Mondale and Glenn are the clear leaders for their party's nomination, outstripping fourteen other possible Democratic candidates in a recent Gallup survey. Thus, in the present political climate—even one which produced a 5-percentage-point improvement in Reagan's overall standing with the public—none of the three most plausible GOP nominees would defeat either Democratic front-runners Mondale or Glenn.

MARCH 27
COST OF LIVING

Interviewing Date: 1/14–17; 21–24/83
Survey #207-G; 208-G

What is the smallest amount of money a family of four (husband, wife, and two children) needs each week to get along in this community?

	Median average
National	$296*

By Region

East	$304
Midwest	$288
South	$289
West	$309

By Type of Community

Center cities	$301
Suburban areas	$307
Rural areas	$260

What is the smallest amount of money your family needs each week to get along in this community?

	Median average
National	$249*

By Size of Household

Single person	$180
Two-person family	$208
Three-person family	$258
Four-person family	$297
Five-person family	$306

*Farm families were excluded from the survey because many farmers raise their own food.

Note: Americans believe it takes a minimum of $296 weekly for a husband, wife, and two children to make ends meet. This median amount is identical to last year's, marking the first time in five years that a significant year-to-year increase has not occurred. By comparison, last year's $296 median represented a $19 increase over the $277 median amount for 1981. This, in turn, was $27 higher than the $250 figure recorded in 1980.

These annual audits of the public's perception of living costs have tended to closely conform to the Consumer Price Index (CPI) compiled by the U.S. Bureau of Labor Statistics. According to the CPI, living costs during 1982 rose only 3.9% over the comparable 1981 period.

The last time there was no significant year-to-year increase in the Gallup audit was in 1978, when the public's consensus that it took $201 per week for a four-person family to get by was statistically the same as the figure of $199 recorded the year before. For three consecutive years, 1952–1954, the median estimate stood at $60 per week. And for the four-year period ending in 1951 it remained at $50 per week.

In 1937, when the Gallup Poll first surveyed Americans' perception of weekly living costs for a family of four, the median response was $30, or one-tenth the current amount. By 1947, the figure had climbed to $43. It did not hit three-digit proportions until 1967, when the median estimate was $101. It took only twelve years, until 1978, for living costs to pass the $200 mark.

The trend of the minimum amount needed for a family of four since the inception of the cost-of-living survey in 1937 is presented below:

National Trend

	Median average
1983	$296
1982	$296
1981	$277
1980	$250
1979	$223
1978	$201
1977	$199
1976	$177
1975	$161
1974	$152
1973	$149
1971	$127
1970	$126
1969	$120
1967	$101
1966	$ 99
1964	$ 81
1961	$ 84
1959	$ 79
1957	$ 72
1954	$ 60
1953	$ 60
1952	$ 60
1951	$ 50
1950	$ 50
1949	$ 50
1948	$ 50
1947	$ 43
1937	$ 30

Americans' own life-styles tend to be reflected in their estimates of the minimum cost of living in their neighborhoods. The median amount cited by college-educated respondents, for instance, is $307 per week, while the comparable figures for persons with a high-school education and for those with even less formal education are $293 and $245, respectively. Similarly, $303 per week is the median estimate of persons whose family income is $15,000 per year or more; those in the survey with less than $15,000 annual income estimate it takes $260 per week for a four-person family to get by.

As in past surveys, living costs are perceived to be slightly higher by easterners ($304) and westerners ($309) than by residents of the Midwest ($288) and South ($289).

The type of communities in which Americans live also contributes to their perception of living costs. Residents of the nation's center cities say it takes $301 per week to keep a family of four going. People living in the generally wealthier suburban areas report that a family requires $307 weekly. And for those who live in nonmetropolitan or rural areas, the median estimate is $260.

MARCH 31
EL SALVADOR

Interviewing Date: 3/11–14/83
Survey #211-G

Have you heard or read about the situation in El Salvador?

	Yes
National	87%

Asked of those who replied in the affirmative: President Reagan has asked Congress to approve an additional $60 million in military aid for El Salvador. Do you think Congress should or should not approve this request?

Should	22%
Should not	68
No opinion	10

By Sex
Male

Should	25%
Should not	62
No opinion	13

Female

Should	18%
Should not	74
No opinion	8

By Race
White

Should	23%
Should not	66
No opinion	11

Nonwhite

Should	13%
Should not	78
No opinion	9

By Education
College

Should	26%
Should not	62
No opinion	12

High School

Should	19%
Should not	72
No opinion	9

Grade School

Should	22%
Should not	67
No opinion	11

By Region
East

Should	24%
Should not	68
No opinion	8

Midwest

Should	23%
Should not	67
No opinion	10

South

Should	19%
Should not	70
No opinion	11

West

Should	19%
Should not	66
No opinion	15

By Age
18–24 Years

Should	17%
Should not	74
No opinion	9

25–29 Years

Should	14%
Should not	81
No opinion	5

30–49 Years

Should	23%
Should not	68
No opinion	9

50–64 Years

Should	27%
Should not	59
No opinion	14

65 Years and Over

Should	23%
Should not	64
No opinion	13

By Income
$25,000 and Over

Should	26%
Should not	64
No opinion	10

$15,000 and Over

Should	25%
Should not	65
No opinion	10

Under $15,000

Should	16%
Should not	72
No opinion	12

By Politics
Republicans

Should	36%
Should not	48
No opinion	16

Democrats

Should	16%
Should not	77
No opinion	7

Independents

Should	20%
Should not	69
No opinion	11

Also asked of those who replied in the affirmative: The Reagan administration plans to increase the number of U.S. advisers in El Salvador to about fifty-five. Do you approve or disapprove of this?

Approve	32%
Disapprove	59
No opinion	9

By Sex
Male

Approve	38%
Disapprove	55
No opinion	7

Female

Approve	26%
Disapprove	63
No opinion	11

By Race
White
Approve 34%
Disapprove 57
No opinion 9

Nonwhite
Approve 19%
Disapprove 68
No opinion 13

By Education
College
Approve 38%
Disapprove 55
No opinion 7

High School
Approve 30%
Disapprove 60
No opinion 10

Grade School
Approve 24%
Disapprove 64
No opinion 12

By Region
East
Approve 33%
Disapprove 60
No opinion 7

Midwest
Approve 32%
Disapprove 61
No opinion 7

South
Approve 35%
Disapprove 53
No opinion 12

West
Approve 27%
Disapprove 62
No opinion 11

By Age
18–24 Years
Approve 28%
Disapprove 62
No opinion 10

25–29 Years
Approve 36%
Disapprove 58
No opinion 6

30–49 Years
Approve 31%
Disapprove 61
No opinion 8

50–64 Years
Approve 35%
Disapprove 53
No opinion 12

65 Years and Over
Approve 33%
Disapprove 57
No opinion 10

By Income
$25,000 and Over
Approve 39%
Disapprove 56
No opinion 5

$15,000 and Over
Approve 37%
Disapprove 56
No opinion 7

Under $15,000

Approve 25%
Disapprove 63
No opinion 12

By Politics
Republicans

Approve 48%
Disapprove 41
No opinion 11

Democrats

Approve 28%
Disapprove 64
No opinion 8

Independents

Approve 29%
Disapprove 64
No opinion 7

*Also asked of those who replied in the affir-
mative: How likely do you think it is that the
U.S. involvement in El Salvador could turn
into a situation like Vietnam—that is, that
the United States would become more and
more deeply involved as time goes on? Would
you say this is very likely, fairly likely, not
very likely, or not at all likely?*

Very likely 37%
Fairly likely 31
Not very likely 20
Not at all likely 6
No opinion 6

By Sex
Male

Very likely 35%
Fairly likely 28
Not very likely 25
Not at all likely 7
No opinion 5

Female

Very likely 39%
Fairly likely 32
Not very likely 16
Not at all likely 5
No opinion 8

By Race
White

Very likely 35%
Fairly likely 31
Not very likely 22
Not at all likely 6
No opinion 6

Nonwhite

Very likely 54%
Fairly likely 24
Not very likely 10
Not at all likely 6
No opinion 6

By Education
College

Very likely 27%
Fairly likely 34
Not very likely 26
Not at all likely 9
No opinion 4

High School

Very likely 42%
Fairly likely 29
Not very likely 18
Not at all likely 5
No opinion 6

Grade School

Very likely 44%
Fairly likely 26
Not very likely 16
Not at all likely 3
No opinion 11

By Region

East

Very likely	33%
Fairly likely	30
Not very likely	25
Not at all likely	7
No opinion	5

Midwest

Very likely	39%
Fairly likely	32
Not very likely	20
Not at all likely	4
No opinion	5

South

Very likely	35%
Fairly likely	32
Not very likely	19
Not at all likely	7
No opinion	7

West

Very likely	43%
Fairly likely	27
Not very likely	17
Not at all likely	6
No opinion	7

By Age

18–24 Years

Very likely	41%
Fairly likely	32
Not very likely	16
Not at all likely	7
No opinion	4

25–29 Years

Very likely	36%
Fairly likely	32
Not very likely	22
Not at all likely	3
No opinion	7

30–49 Years

Very likely	33%
Fairly likely	33
Not very likely	23
Not at all likely	6
No opinion	5

50–64 Years

Very likely	36%
Fairly likely	28
Not very likely	20
Not at all likely	10
No opinion	6

65 Years and Over

Very likely	42%
Fairly likely	26
Not very likely	19
Not at all likely	4
No opinion	9

By Income

$25,000 and Over

Very likely	28%
Fairly likely	35
Not very likely	26
Not at all likely	8
No opinion	3

$15,000 and Over

Very likely	32%
Fairly likely	32
Not very likely	25
Not at all likely	7
No opinion	4

Under $15,000

Very likely	44%
Fairly likely	29
Not very likely	14
Not at all likely	5
No opinion	8

By Politics

Republicans

Very likely	26%
Fairly likely	27
Not very likely	35
Not at all likely	8
No opinion	4

Democrats

Very likely	43%
Fairly likely	30
Not very likely	16
Not at all likely	5
No opinion	6

Independents

Very likely	36%
Fairly likely	33
Not very likely	17
Not at all likely	7
No opinion	7

Also asked of those who replied in the affirmative: If the rebel forces succeed in taking over the government in El Salvador, how likely do you think it is that the same kind of thing will happen in other Latin American countries—very likely, fairly likely, not very likely, or not at all likely?

Very likely	39%
Fairly likely	36
Not very likely	12
Not at all likely	3
Don't know	10

By Sex

Male

Very likely	39%
Fairly likely	34
Not very likely	18
Not at all likely	3
Don't know	6

Female

Very likely	40%
Fairly likely	38
Not very likely	7
Not at all likely	2
Don't know	13

By Race

White

Very likely	38%
Fairly likely	38
Not very likely	12
Not at all likely	2
Don't know	10

Nonwhite

Very likely	46%
Fairly likely	22
Not very likely	13
Not at all likely	8
Don't know	11

By Education

College

Very likely	36%
Fairly likely	37
Not very likely	18
Not at all likely	2
Don't know	7

High School

Very likely	40%
Fairly likely	36
Not very likely	10
Not at all likely	3
Don't know	11

Grade School

Very likely	45%
Fairly likely	32
Not very likely	10
Not at all likely	2
Don't know	11

By Region

East

Very likely 35%
Fairly likely 43
Not very likely 11
Not at all likely 2
Don't know 9

Midwest

Very likely 40%
Fairly likely 37
Not very likely 14
Not at all likely 2
Don't know 7

South

Very likely 41%
Fairly likely 33
Not very likely 12
Not at all likely 4
Don't know 10

West

Very likely 42%
Fairly likely 29
Not very likely 14
Not at all likely 1
Don't know 14

By Age

18–24 Years

Very likely 27%
Fairly likely 43
Not very likely 15
Not at all likely 6
Don't know 9

25–29 Years

Very likely 29%
Fairly likely 46
Not very likely 18
Not at all likely 2
Don't know 5

30–49 Years

Very likely 39%
Fairly likely 36
Not very likely 14
Not at all likely 2
Don't know 9

50–64 Years

Very likely 50%
Fairly likely 27
Not very likely 9
Not at all likely 3
Don't know 11

65 Years and Over

Very likely 45%
Fairly likely 34
Not very likely 9
Not at all likely 2
Don't know 10

By Income

$25,000 and Over

Very likely 38%
Fairly likely 39
Not very likely 16
Not at all likely 2
Don't know 5

$15,000 and Over

Very likely 39%
Fairly likely 37
Not very likely 14
Not at all likely 2
Don't know 8

Under $15,000

Very likely 39%
Fairly likely 34
Not very likely 10
Not at all likely 3
Don't know 14

By Politics

Republicans

Very likely	42%
Fairly likely	33
Not very likely	18
Not at all likely	1
Don't know	6

Democrats

Very likely	41%
Fairly likely	35
Not very likely	10
Not at all likely	4
Don't know	10

Independents

Very likely	34%
Fairly likely	40
Not very likely	12
Not at all likely	2
Don't know	12

Note: Fearing another Vietnam, the public overwhelmingly votes against President Ronald Reagan's proposal to spend an additional $60 million in military aid for El Salvador. It also rejects the president's plan to increase the number of U.S. military advisers there. The public takes this stand despite its widespread concern that other Latin American governments will fall if the rebel forces succeed in taking over the government in El Salvador.

Of the nine in ten in the latest Gallup survey who are aware of the El Salvador situation, 68% oppose sending $60 million in additional military aid and 59% disapprove of increasing the number of U.S. advisers. A total of 68% believe it is either very or fairly likely that the U.S. involvement in El Salvador could turn into a situation like Vietnam. Also, three in four (75%) think it is either very or fairly likely that, if the rebel forces succeed in taking over the government in El Salvador, the same kind of thing will happen in other Latin American countries.

Republicans and Democrats have similar views on the likelihood of other Latin American governments falling if the rebels in El Salvador succeed, but major differences are found between members of the two parties on the likelihood of a Vietnam-like involvement and on the desirability of sending military aid and additional advisers. Democrats vote 77% to 16% against sending a greater amount of military aid, while far fewer Republicans do so, 48% to 36%. On the issue of sending additional advisers, Democrats are 64% to 28% opposed, but Republicans lean in favor, 48% to 41%. Finally, Democrats are far more convinced than are Republicans that U.S. involvement in El Salvador could turn into another Vietnam, with 73% of Democrats saying this is very or fairly likely, compared to 53% of Republicans.

President Reagan recently declared the three-year-old civil war in El Salvador to be a direct threat to U.S. interests. To allay fears that a rerun of Vietnam was in the making, the president pledged to keep the U.S. role strictly limited. "We will not Americanize this conflict," he said. "American combat troops are not going to El Salvador." Critics of the president's proposals, however, worry about a protracted U.S. involvement and maintain that a resolution of the conflict should be sought through negotiations rather than on the battlefield.

APRIL 3
"FAIRNESS" ISSUE

Interviewing Date: 2/25–28/83
Survey #210-G

As I read off some groups, one at a time, would you tell me whether you feel that that group is being treated fairly or unfairly by the Reagan administration:

Let's start with poor people. Do you feel the poor are being treated fairly or unfairly by the Reagan administration?

Fairly	30%
Unfairly	62
No opinion	8

By Politics

Republicans

Fairly 53%
Unfairly 37
No opinion 10

Democrats

Fairly 16%
Unfairly 60
No opinion 24

Independents

Fairly 34%
Unfairly 57
No opinion 9

The average citizen?

Fairly 40%
Unfairly 50
No opinion 10

By Politics

Republicans

Fairly 73%
Unfairly 22
No opinion 5

Democrats

Fairly 25%
Unfairly 65
No opinion 10

Independents

Fairly 43%
Unfairly 49
No opinion 8

Blacks?

Fairly 50%
Unfairly 36
No opinion 14

By Politics

Republicans

Fairly 77%
Unfairly 12
No opinion 11

Democrats

Fairly 35%
Unfairly 51
No opinion 14

Independents

Fairly 55%
Unfairly 31
No opinion 14

Women?

Fairly 55%
Unfairly 31
No opinion 14

By Politics

Republicans

Fairly 75%
Unfairly 14
No opinion 11

Democrats

Fairly 42%
Unfairly 44
No opinion 14

Independents

Fairly 62%
Unfairly 26
No opinion 12

Wealthy people?

Fairly 90%
Unfairly 3
No opinion 7

By Politics
Republicans
Fairly 97%
Unfairly 1
No opinion 2

Democrats
Fairly 89%
Unfairly 4
No opinion 7

Independents
Fairly 91%
Unfairly 4
No opinion 5

Middle-income people?
Fairly 41%
Unfairly 49
No opinion 10

By Politics
Republicans
Fairly 63%
Unfairly 31
No opinion 6

Democrats
Fairly 32%
Unfairly 58
No opinion 10

Independents
Fairly 41%
Unfairly 49
No opinion 10

Elderly people?
Fairly 27%
Unfairly 66
No opinion 7

By Politics
Republicans
Fairly 52%
Unfairly 45
No opinion 3

Democrats
Fairly 14%
Unfairly 81
No opinion 5

Independents
Fairly 32%
Unfairly 61
No opinion 7

People like yourself?
Fairly 42%
Unfairly 51
No opinion 7

By Politics
Republicans
Fairly 70%
Unfairly 28
No opinion 2

Democrats
Fairly 27%
Unfairly 66
No opinion 7

Independents
Fairly 46%
Unfairly 48
No opinion 6

Business executives?
Fairly 78%
Unfairly 5
No opinion 17

By Politics

Republicans

Fairly	83%
Unfairly	5
No opinion	12

Democrats

Fairly	78%
Unfairly	5
No opinion	17

Independents

Fairly	78%
Unfairly	5
No opinion	17

Small-business people?

Fairly	29%
Unfairly	54
No opinion	17

By Politics

Republicans

Fairly	48%
Unfairly	42
No opinion	10

Democrats

Fairly	19%
Unfairly	62
No opinion	19

Independents

Fairly	32%
Unfairly	53
No opinion	15

Farmers?

Fairly	26%
Unfairly	58
No opinion	16

By Politics

Republicans

Fairly	45%
Unfairly	45
No opinion	10

Democrats

Fairly	15%
Unfairly	67
No opinion	18

Independents

Fairly	29%
Unfairly	57
No opinion	14

Interviewing Date: 3/11–14/83
Survey #211-G

Do you approve or disapprove of the way Ronald Reagan is handling his job as president?

Approve	41%
Disapprove	49
No opinion	10

By Politics

Republicans

Approve	78%
Disapprove	17
No opinion	5

Democrats

Approve	23%
Disapprove	66
No opinion	11

Independents

Approve	41%
Disapprove	48
No opinion	11

Note: Although the Reagan administration is generally seen by the public as not treating all groups in the population equitably, women and blacks, who have been among the administration's harshest critics, are perceived as having received relatively fairer treatment than others. In fact, of the groups included in a recent Gallup study, only wealthy people and business executives are thought by the public to have received better treatment than women and blacks. Faring far less well, in the public's eyes, have been farmers, the elderly, small-business people, and the poor.

In the light of their markedly lower assessment of the way President Ronald Reagan is handling his job, women and men almost exactly agree, perhaps surprisingly, about whether women are treated fairly or unfairly by the administration. Blacks and whites, on the other hand, are in sharp disagreement about the administration's treatment of blacks. Three in four blacks in the survey (73%) compared to three in ten whites (30%) say they believe blacks are unfairly treated.

Asked to judge each of eleven population groups on the basis of their treatment by the administration, the public most widely thinks the affluent and business executives have received a fair deal. Specifically, 90% of the public believes wealthy Americans are fairly treated and 78% think the same about business executives. In sharp contrast, poor people and the owners of small businesses are widely considered to have been dealt with unfairly.

Next highest on the list, ranked in order of their treatment by the administration, are women and blacks. Women are thought to be fairly treated by 55% of the public compared to 31% who disagree. One-half of the public believes blacks are receiving fair treatment from the administration, while 36% think they are not.

In the mid-range of the positive to negative ranking are three centrist or middle-of-the road population groups: "middle-income people," "people like you," and "the average citizen." In the case of each of these categories, about half of the public thinks their treatment has been unfair, while four in ten believe they have been dealt with fairly by the Reagan administration. Interestingly, these perceptions almost exactly coincide with the public's assessment of Reagan's job performance. In the latest survey, 41% approve of the way the

president is handling the duties of his office, while 49% disapprove and 10% are uncommitted.

At the bottom of the list, with roughly two negative votes for each positive one in terms of the perceived equity of their treatment, are poor people, small-business people, the elderly, and farmers.

Not unexpectedly, Republicans are much more likely than Democrats to characterize as fair the administration's treatment of all groups included in the study. But more than one Republican in three brands as unfair the administration's dealings with the elderly (45% negative), farmers (45%), small-business people (42%), and the poor (37%). Majorities of Democrats express the opinion that all but three of the groups—women, business executives, and the wealthy—are receiving unfair treatment.

APRIL 7
REAGANOMICS

Interviewing Date: 3/11–14/83
Survey #211-G

What effect do you think the Reagan administration's economic policies will have on your own and your family's financial situation? Do you feel your financial situation will be much better, somewhat better, somewhat worse, or much worse as a result of the Reagan economic policies?

Better 34%
Worse 44
Same (volunteered) 15
No opinion 7

By Sex
Male

Better 37%
Worse 18
Same (volunteered) 39
No opinion 6

Female

Better	30%
Worse	12
Same (volunteered)	50
No opinion	8

By Race

White

Better	36%
Worse	16
Same (volunteered)	41
No opinion	7

Nonwhite

Better	18%
Worse	66
Same (volunteered)	8
No opinion	8

By Education

College

Better	47%
Worse	36
Same (volunteered)	13
No opinion	4

High School

Better	28%
Worse	48
Same (volunteered)	17
No opinion	7

Grade School

Better	26%
Worse	43
Same (volunteered)	14
No opinion	17

By Region

East

Better	30%
Worse	47
Same (volunteered)	16
No opinion	7

Midwest

Better	31%
Worse	45
Same (volunteered)	14
No opinion	10

South

Better	36%
Worse	44
Same (volunteered)	14
No opinion	6

West

Better	38%
Worse	39
Same (volunteered)	17
No opinion	6

By Age

18–24 Years

Better	29%
Worse	47
Same (volunteered)	18
No opinion	6

25–29 Years

Better	37%
Worse	49
Same (volunteered)	9
No opinion	5

30–49 Years

Better	40%
Worse	41
Same (volunteered)	13
No opinion	6

50 Years and Over

Better	28%
Worse	45
Same (volunteered)	17
No opinion	10

By Income

$25,000 and Over

Better 45%
Worse 37
Same (volunteered) 14
No opinion 4

$15,000 and Over

Better 41%
Worse 37
Same (volunteered) 17
No opinion 5

Under $15,000

Better 24%
Worse 53
Same (volunteered) 13
No opinion 10

By Politics

Republicans

Better 56%
Worse 18
Same (volunteered) 17
No opinion 9

Democrats

Better 23%
Worse 57
Same (volunteered) 14
No opinion 6

Independents

Better 35%
Worse 44
Same (volunteered) 15
No opinion 6

National Trend

	Better	Worse	Same	No opinion
January 1983	25%	52%	18%	5%
August 1982	23	56	15	6
February 1982	31	44	17	8
May 1981	48	37	—	15*

*Volunteered "same" response recorded with "no opinion."

How about the nation? What effect do you think the Reagan administration's economic policies will have on the nation's economic situation? Do you feel the nation's economic situation will be much better, somewhat better, somewhat worse, or much worse as a result of the Reagan economic policies?

Better 42%
Worse 44
Same (volunteered) 8
No opinion 6

By Politics

Republicans

Better 73%
Worse 18
Same (volunteered) 5
No opinion 4

Democrats

Better 29%
Worse 57
Same (volunteered) 8
No opinion 6

Independents

Better 41%
Worse 41
Same (volunteered) 10
No opinion 8

Edmund (Jerry) Brown, Jr. 4
Alan Cranston 3
All others* 15
None; don't know 27

First Choice of Independents

Walter Mondale 21%
John Glenn 18
George McGovern 6
Edmund (Jerry) Brown, Jr. 5
All others* 16
None; don't know 34

*All others on the list each received 2% or less of the votes: Reubin Askew, Bruce Babbitt, Lloyd Bentsen, Bill Bradley, John Y. Brown, Dale Bumpers, Gary Hart, Ernest Hollings, Daniel (Pat) Moynihan, Jay Rockefeller, and Robert Strauss.

Interviewing Date: 2/25–28/83
Survey #210-G

> Asked of Democrats and independents: Suppose in 1984 the choice for president in the Democratic convention narrows down to Walter Mondale and John Glenn. Which one would you prefer to have the Democratic convention select?

Choice of Democrats

Mondale 52%
Glenn 30
Undecided 18

Choice of Independents

Mondale 42%
Glenn 35
Undecided 23

The following table is based on a combination of two surveys* to provide a larger sample base of Democrats, which showed the choices of Democrats from the full list of sixteen candidates:

*Surveys #206-G and #211-G dated 12/10–13/82 and 3/11–14/83

Mondale vs. Glenn

Mondale 32%
Glenn 14
All others 28
None; no opinion 26

By Sex
Male

Mondale 31%
Glenn 15
All others 29
None; no opinion 25

Female

Mondale 33%
Glenn 13
All others 25
None; no opinion 29

By Race
White

Mondale 31%
Glenn 16
All others 38
None; no opinion 15

Nonwhite

Mondale 36%
Glenn 6
All others 26
None; no opinion 32

By Education
College

Mondale 28%
Glenn 15
All others 43
None; no opinion 14

High School

Mondale 34%
Glenn 14
All others 26
None; no opinion 26

Grade School

Mondale 31%
Glenn 12
All others 18
None; no opinion 39

By Region
East

Mondale 32%
Glenn 14
All others 26
None; no opinion 28

Midwest

Mondale 40%
Glenn 21
All others 20
None; no opinion 19

South

Mondale 31%
Glenn 10
All others 39
None; no opinion 20

West

Mondale 25%
Glenn 11
All others 41
None; no opinion 23

By Age
18–29 Years

Mondale 25%
Glenn 14
All others 36
None; no opinion 25

30–49 Years

Mondale 28%
Glenn 16
All others 31
None; no opinion 25

50 Years and Over

Mondale 39%
Glenn 12
All others 19
None; no opinion 30

By Religion
Protestants

Mondale 31%
Glenn 10
All others 30
None; no opinion 29

Catholics

Mondale 33%
Glenn 15
All others 28
None; no opinion 24

Labor Union Members

Mondale 32%
Glenn 18
All others 30
None; no opinion 20

Nonlabor Union Members

Mondale 21%
Glenn 12
All others 38
None; no opinion 29

Note: Former Vice-president Walter Mondale and Senator John Glenn of Ohio continue to lead the field of Democratic hopefuls in the race for the 1984 nomination. In a just-completed national survey, 32% of Democratic voters, asked to choose from a list of sixteen possible Democratic presidential candidates, select Mondale. Glenn is number two in the current rankings, but with only 13% of the vote he trails front-runner Mondale by a wide margin.

While the current standings of the two front-runners are a virtual carbon copy of the findings from the December survey,* Glenn has made some

*December 10–13, 1982

headway in a two-way head-to-head match with Mondale, when all Democrats surveyed are asked to choose only between these two men. Mondale has a 52%-to-30% lead over Glenn in this test, but in December the margin was wider, 59% to 28%.

Next in the current choices are former California governor Jerry Brown, with 6% of the support of his fellow Democrats; former senator George McGovern, with 4%; and California senator Alan Cranston with 3% of the vote.

It should be noted that the current rankings are in some measure a reflection of name recognition; as the lesser known candidates gain in recognition, they will move up in the rankings.

APRIL 14
DEMOCRATIC PRESIDENTIAL CANDIDATES

Interviewing Date: 3/11–14/83
Survey #211-G

Asked of Democrats: Would you please look over this list [respondents were handed a card listing sixteen names] and tell me which of these persons, if any, you have heard something about? Those who replied in the affirmative were asked: Can you tell me something about these persons?

Democrats Only

	Heard something about	Know something about
Walter Mondale	91%	68%
George McGovern	79	48
Edmund (Jerry) Brown, Jr.	78	55
John Glenn	76	56
Jay Rockefeller	59	23
Daniel (Pat) Moynihan	44	23
Alan Cranston	42	21
Robert Strauss	38	15
Bill Bradley	33	17
John Y. Brown	32	14

Reubin Askew	32	11
Gary Hart	27	12
Lloyd Bentsen	23	9
Ernest Hollings	17	6
Dale Bumpers	17	5
Bruce Babbitt	12	3

*Asked of Democrats: Now, would you tell me which of the other persons on the list you would consider as the Democratic candidate for president in 1984?**

Possible Democratic Nominees

(First and Second Choices, Plus "Would Consider")

	Based on all Democrats	Based on Democrats aware of each man
Mondale	52%	59%
Glenn	37	51
McGovern	21	24
Brown (Jerry)	19	28
Cranston	10	24
Moynihan	9	20
Rockefeller	9	15
Hart	8	30
Askew	6	20
Bradley	6	20
Bentsen	5	23
Brown (John Y.)	4	13
Strauss	3	9
Hollings	2	14
Bumpers	2	10
Babbitt	1	11

*Respondents previously had been asked their preference for the 1984 Democratic presidential nomination. See April 10 release.

Note: At this early stage in the electoral process the names of only five persons mentioned as possible Democratic presidential nominees in 1984 are known to at least half of Democratic voters. Two of the five— Edmund "Jerry" Brown, Jr., and George McGovern—generally are not considered active candidates.

Democrats who have announced their availability for their party's nomination and the percentage of rank-and-file Democrats who have heard of each are as follows: Walter Mondale, 91%; Alan Cranston, 42%; Reuben Askew, 32%; Gary Hart, 27%. John Glenn, who has not yet formally declared his candidacy, is known to 76% of Democrats.

As reported on April 10, Mondale is the 32% front-runner among Democrats asked to choose from a list of sixteen possible nominees. Glenn is in second place with 13% of the votes. Glenn, however, fares much better in a head-to-head contest with Mondale. None of the others on the list receives more than 6% of Democrats' votes for the nomination.

Presidential aspirants with low recognition scores may be heartened by the classic example of Jimmy Carter, who in January 1976 won the votes of only 4% of Democrats for the nomination, but went on to win the nomination and the presidency. Another dimension of familiarity is the extent to which voters say they know something about each of the possible nominees. Only three men—Mondale, Brown, and Glenn—are this familiar to one-half or more of Democrats.

In addition to asking Democrats for their first and second choices, the latest survey asked which other persons on the list they would consider for the nomination. The aggregated positive responses to these three questions provide a measure of net positive votes for each potential nominee.

APRIL 17
BLACK PRESIDENTIAL
CANDIDATE

Interviewing Date: 3/11–14/83
Survey #211-G

If your party nominated a generally well-qualified man for president and he happened to be a black, would you vote for him?

Yes 77%
No 16
No opinion 7

By Sex
Male

Yes 77%
No 16
No opinion 7

Female

Yes 78%
No 15
No opinion 7

By Race
White

Yes 76%
No 18
No opinion 6

Black

Yes 85%
No 4
No opinion 11

By Education
College

Yes 85%
No 10
No opinion 5

High School

Yes 78%
No 15
No opinion 7

Grade School

Yes 59%
No 29
No opinion 12

By Region
East

Yes 82%
No 12
No opinion 6

Midwest

Yes 77%
No 19
No opinion 4

South

Yes 68%
No 22
No opinion 10

West

Yes 86%
No 6
No opinion 8

By Age
18–24 Years

Yes 86%
No 10
No opinion 4

25–29 Years

Yes 87%
No 10
No opinion 3

30–49 Years

Yes 80%
No 15
No opinion 5

50–64 Years

Yes 74%
No 15
No opinion 11

65 Years and Over

Yes 64%
No 26
No opinion 10

By Politics
Republicans

Yes 75%
No 19
No opinion 6

Democrats

Yes 77%
No 16
No opinion 7

Northern Democrats

Yes 81%
No 14
No opinion 5

Southern Democrats

Yes 68%
No 20
No opinion 12

Independents

Yes 80%
No 14
No opinion 6

By Occupation
Professional and Business

Yes 83%
No 13
No opinion 4

Clerical and Sales

Yes 83%
No 15
No opinion 2

Manual Workers

Yes 81%
No 14
No opinion 5

Nonlabor Force

Yes 72%
No 18
No opinion 10

National Trend

	Yes	No	No opinion
1978	77%	18%	5%
1971	70	23	7
1969	67	23	10
1967	54	40	6
1965	59	34	7
1963	47	45	8
1958	38	53	9

Note: The election of Harold Washington as Chicago's first black mayor focuses attention on the broader subject of blacks in high national political office. As black leaders debate whether or not to mount a campaign for a black for president, the latest Gallup Poll finds the mood of the electorate to be far more inclined toward such a candidacy than a quarter century ago, although views have changed little over the last five years.

In the latest survey, 77% say they would vote for a black president, compared to half this proportion (38%) in 1958. While the electorate is currently far more receptive to a black presidential candidate than in earlier years, such a candidate continues to have a major liability: one fourth of voters today either say they would not vote for a black man (16%) or express uncertainty (7%).

Analysis of the current findings shows that young adults (18 to 29 years old) are more willing to vote for a black than are older persons—86% compared to 64% for those 65 and older. Northern whites (81%) are more receptive to a black candidacy than are southern whites (64%), and northern Democrats (81%) also are more open to the idea than are southern Democrats (68%).

A marked difference is found on the basis of level of education, with 85% of persons with a college background saying they would be willing to vote for a black compared to 59% among persons with only a grade-school background.

APRIL 21
NUCLEAR ARMS FREEZE

Interviewing Date: 3/11–14/83
Survey #211-G

Would you favor or oppose an agreement between the United States and the Soviet Union for an immediate verifiable freeze on the testing, production, and deployment of nuclear weapons?

Favor 70%
Oppose 21
No opinion 9

By Sex
Male

Favor 71%
Oppose 23
No opinion 6

Female

Favor 69%
Oppose 20
No opinion 11

By Race
White

Favor 71%
Oppose 21
No opinion 8

Nonwhite

Favor 65%
Oppose 17
No opinion 18

By Education
College

Favor 75%
Oppose 22
No opinion 3

High School

Favor 71%
Oppose 21
No opinion 8

Grade School

Favor 56%
Oppose 18
No opinion 26

By Region
East

Favor 74%
Oppose 19
No opinion 7

Midwest

Favor 68%
Oppose 23
No opinion 9

South

Favor 65%
Oppose 23
No opinion 12

West

Favor 74%
Oppose 18
No opinion 8

By Age
18–24 Years

Favor 73%
Oppose 21
No opinion 6

25–29 Years

Favor 81%
Oppose 15
No opinion 4

30–49 Years

Favor 73%
Oppose 23
No opinion 4

50–64 Years

Favor 64%
Oppose 23
No opinion 13

65 Years and Over

Favor 63%
Oppose 18
No opinion 19

By Income
$25,000 and Over

Favor 76%
Oppose 21
No opinion 3

$15,000 and Over

Favor 73%
Oppose 22
No opinion 5

Under $15,000

Favor 67%
Oppose 19
No opinion 4

By Politics
Republicans

Favor 69%
Oppose 25
No opinion 6

Democrats

Favor 70%
Oppose 20
No opinion 10

Independents

Favor 72%
Oppose 19
No opinion 9

By Religion

Protestants

Favor 67%
Oppose 22
No opinion 11

Catholics

Favor 70%
Oppose 23
No opinion 7

National Trend

November 1982

Favor 71%
Oppose 20
No opinion 9

At the present time, which nation do you feel is stronger in terms of nuclear weapons, the United States or the Soviet Union—or do you think they are about equal in nuclear strength?

United States 15%
Soviet Union 42
About equal 35
No opinion 8

By Education

College

United States 13%
Soviet Union 41
About equal 41
No opinion 5

High School

United States 15%
Soviet Union 43
About equal 34
No opinion 8

Grade School

United States 18%
Soviet Union 42
About equal 25
No opinion 15

By Politics

Republicans

United States 14%
Soviet Union 48
About equal 33
No opinion 5

Democrats

United States 16%
Soviet Union 40
About equal 35
No opinion 9

Independents

United States 12%
Soviet Union 42
About equal 38
No opinion 8

National Trend

April–May 1982

United States 40%
Soviet Union 17
About equal 32
No opinion 11

In your opinion, which of the following increases the chances of nuclear war more— a continuation of the nuclear arms buildup here and in the Soviet Union, or the United States falling behind the Soviet Union in nuclear weaponry?

Continuation of arms buildup 38%
U.S. falling behind 47
No opinion 15

By Sex

Male

Continuation of arms buildup 37%
U.S. falling behind 52
No opinion 11

Female

Continuation of arms buildup 39%
U.S. falling behind 42
No opinion 19

By Race

White

Continuation of arms buildup 37%
U.S. falling behind 49
No opinion 14

Nonwhite

Continuation of arms buildup 44%
U.S. falling behind 31
No opinion 25

By Education

College

Continuation of arms buildup 45%
U.S. falling behind 47
No opinion 8

High School

Continuation of arms buildup 36%
U.S. falling behind 47
No opinion 17

Grade School

Continuation of arms buildup 28%
U.S. falling behind 43
No opinion 29

By Region

East

Continuation of arms buildup 41%
U.S. falling behind 46
No opinion 13

Midwest

Continuation of arms buildup 35%
U.S. falling behind 53
No opinion 12

South

Continuation of arms buildup 36%
U.S. falling behind 43
No opinion 21

West

Continuation of arms buildup 41%
U.S. falling behind 44
No opinion 15

By Age

18–24 Years

Continuation of arms buildup 43%
U.S. falling behind 43
No opinion 14

25–29 Years

Continuation of arms buildup 57%
U.S. falling behind 31
No opinion 12

30–49 Years

Continuation of arms buildup 36%
U.S. falling behind 54
No opinion 10

50–64 Years

Continuation of arms buildup 34%
U.S. falling behind 47
No opinion 19

65 Years and Over

Continuation of arms buildup 31%
U.S. falling behind 45
No opinion 24

By Income

$25,000 and Over

Continuation of arms buildup 42%
U.S. falling behind 49
No opinion 9

$15,000 and Over

Continuation of arms buildup 41%
U.S. falling behind 48
No opinion 11

Under $15,000

Continuation of arms buildup 34%
U.S. falling behind 44
No opinion 22

By Politics

Republicans

Continuation of arms buildup 33%
U.S. falling behind 56
No opinion 11

Democrats

Continuation of arms buildup 42%
U.S. falling behind 41
No opinion 17

Independents

Continuation of arms buildup 37%
U.S. falling behind 49
No opinion 14

By Religion

Protestants

Continuation of arms buildup 34%
U.S. falling behind 50
No opinion 16

Catholics

Continuation of arms buildup 42%
U.S. falling behind 44
No opinion 14

National Trend

August 1982*

Continuation of arms buildup 43%
U.S. falling behind 46
No opinion 11

*Survey conducted by the Gallup Organization for the *Wall Street Journal*

Do you think the United States is or is not doing all it can to keep peace in the world?

Yes, is 58%
No, is not 34
No opinion 8

By Sex

Male

Yes, is 61%
No, is not 33
No opinion 6

Female

Yes, is 55%
No, is not 35
No opinion 10

By Race

White

Yes, is 59%
No, is not 34
No opinion 7

Nonwhite

Yes, is 50%
No, is not 35
No opinion 15

By Education

College

Yes, is 52%
No, is not 44
No opinion 4

High School

Yes, is 58%
No, is not 32
No opinion 10

Grade School

Yes, is 68%
No, is not 21
No opinion 11

By Region
East

Yes, is 56%
No, is not 38
No opinion 6

Midwest

Yes, is 59%
No, is not 31
No opinion 10

South

Yes, is 59%
No, is not 32
No opinion 9

West

Yes, is 57%
No, is not 36
No opinion 7

By Age
18–24 Years

Yes, is 49%
No, is not 41
No opinion 10

25–29 Years

Yes, is 53%
No, is not 42
No opinion 5

30–49 Years

Yes, is 54%
No, is not 37
No opinion 9

50–64 Years

Yes, is 64%
No, is not 28
No opinion 8

65 Years and Over

Yes, is 69%
No, is not 23
No opinion 8

By Income
$25,000 and Over

Yes, is 53%
No, is not 40
No opinion 7

$15,000 and Over

Yes, is 57%
No, is not 37
No opinion 6

Under $15,000

Yes, is 58%
No, is not 31
No opinion 11

By Politics
Republicans

Yes, is 71%
No, is not 25
No opinion 4

Democrats

Yes, is 52%
No, is not 37
No opinion 11

Independents

Yes, is 55%
No, is not 38
No opinion 7

By Religion
Protestants

Yes, is 59%
No, is not 32
No opinion 9

Catholics

Yes, is 59%
No, is not 36
No opinion 5

National Trend
November 1981

Yes, is 54%
No, is not 39
No opinion 7

Do you think the USSR is or is not doing all it can to keep peace in the world?

Yes, is 8%
No, is not 81
No opinion 11

By Sex
Male

Yes, is 8%
No, is not 83
No opinion 9

Female

Yes, is 8%
No, is not 78
No opinion 14

By Race
White

Yes, is 8%
No, is not 82
No opinion 10

Nonwhite

Yes, is 11%
No, is not 69
No opinion 20

By Education
College

Yes, is 5%
No, is not 88
No opinion 7

High School

Yes, is 9%
No, is not 80
No opinion 11

Grade School

Yes, is 12%
No, is not 65
No opinion 23

By Region
East

Yes, is 8%
No, is not 84
No opinion 8

Midwest

Yes, is 8%
No, is not 79
No opinion 13

South

Yes, is 8%
No, is not 79
No opinion 13

West

Yes, is 8%
No, is not 82
No opinion 10

By Age

18–24 Years

Yes, is 10%
No, is not 76
No opinion 14

25–29 Years

Yes, is 8%
No, is not 84
No opinion 8

30–49 Years

Yes, is 5%
No, is not 87
No opinion 8

50–64 Years

Yes, is 8%
No, is not 78
No opinion 14

65 Years and Over

Yes, is 11%
No, is not 74
No opinion 15

By Income

$25,000 and Over

Yes, is 6%
No, is not 88
No opinion 6

$15,000 and Over

Yes, is 6%
No, is not 86
No opinion 8

Under $15,000

Yes, is 10%
No, is not 74
No opinion 16

By Politics

Republicans

Yes, is 5%
No, is not 86
No opinion 9

Democrats

Yes, is 10%
No, is not 78
No opinion 12

Independents

Yes, is 8%
No, is not 80
No opinion 12

By Religion

Protestants

Yes, is 8%
No, is not 79
No opinion 13

Catholics

Yes, is 7%
No, is not 86
No opinion 7

National Trend

November 1981

Yes, is 7%
No, is not 84
No opinion 9

Note: A total of 70% of Americans votes in favor of an agreement between the United States and the Soviet Union for an immediate verifiable freeze on the testing, production, and deployment of nuclear weapons.

The latest survey also shows that about a third of Americans (35%) say the Soviet Union and the United States are equal in nuclear strength, while 42% believe the Soviet Union is stronger and 15% believe the United States has the advantage in nuclear weapons. By the margin of 47% to 38%, the public holds the view that the United States falling behind in nuclear weaponry increases the chances of nuclear war to a greater extent than does a continuation of the nuclear arms buildup in the two nations.

Finally, a majority of 58% of Americans believes the United States is doing all it can to keep peace in the world, but one-third (34%) hold the opposite view. Far fewer believe the Soviet Union is dong all it can to keep peace, with only 8% holding this view.

By Age

18–24 years	67%
25–29 years	82
30–49 years	73
50–64 years	58
65 years and over	42

By Religion

Protestants	58%
Catholics	76

APRIL 24
ALCOHOLIC BEVERAGES

Interviewing Date: 3/11–14/83
Survey #211-G

Do you have occasion to use alcoholic beverages such as liquor, wine, or beer, or are you a total abstainer?

	Those who drink
National	65%

By Sex

Male	71%
Female	58

By Race

White	66%
Nonwhite	52

By Education

College	78%
High school	65
Grade school	35

By Region

East	71%
Midwest	68
South	53
West	67

National Trend

	Those who drink
1981	70%
1976	71
1974	68
1966	65
1960	62
1958	55
1952	60
1947	63
1946	67
1939	58

Asked of those who replied in the affirmative (65% of the sample): About how often would you say you drink alcoholic beverages?

Every day	9%
Almost every day	8
About 2 or 3 times per week	20
Once per week	20
About 2 or 3 times per month	13
Once per month	11
About once every 2 or 3 months	7
Every 6 months or so	5
Almost never	5
Don't know	2

Various Interviewing Dates
Special Survey*

Asked in thirteen nations: In your country today, how serious a problem do you think alcoholism is?

	Very serious
France	74%
Italy	74
United States	71
Ireland, Republic of	71
Spain	66
Ireland, Northern	61
Denmark	61
West Germany	56
Holland	54
Canada	52
Belgium	45
Great Britain	44
Japan	17

Note: The percentage of Americans who drink alcoholic beverages, 65% in the latest survey, remains at the same relatively low level found in an August survey, lower than recorded at any time after 1969. Examination of the trend in alcohol use since 1939 offers evidence that periods of economic hardship, such as the recent recession, are often accompanied by a decrease in the use of alcoholic beverages. About six adult drinkers in ten (57%) drink once a week or more often, while one in six (17%) drinks every day or almost every day.

*This survey was conducted by Gallup-affiliated organizations for the Amsterdam-based European Value Systems study group. Surveys in the United States and Canada were conducted by Gallup organizations for the Washington-based Center for Applied Research in the Apostolate (CARA).

APRIL 28
THE 65-AND-OLDER GROUP—
A REVIEW

Various Surveys

Recent Gallup survey results dispel the notion sometimes held that the 65-and-older group in the population is an inactive and disinterested segment of society. For example, 36% of this group, comprising about one fifth of the adult population, are involved in charitable activities compared to 31% of younger (under 65) adults. In addition, the proportion of the older group who belong to voluntary organizations (33%) is statistically as high as the proportion among the younger group (34%). The over-65 group also is more likely to have given money to charity (71%) during the twelve-month period tested than persons under this age (66%).

Other interesting comparisons in the attitude and behavior of older and younger adults are:

1) Older persons are as likely as younger to exercise regularly, with 48% of the 65-and-older group saying they perform some kind of daily exercise, compared to 47% among the under-65 group.

2) Older persons (79%) are far more likely than younger people (66%) to be members of a church or synagogue, to attend church in a typical week (50% against 38%), and to say religion is "very important" in their lives (50% compared to 38% among those younger than 65).

3) Senior citizens are more fearful of walking in their neighborhoods at night (54% compared to 43% of their younger counterparts), but they are no more likely to be fearful of walking in their communities during the daylight hours. And they are as likely as persons under 65 to feel secure in their homes. In addition, persons over 65 are only about half as likely as younger adults to have been victims of assault or a housebreaking during a twelve-month period; the figures are 15% and 27%, respectively.

4) Older persons have a better record in terms of being currently registered to vote (83% compared to 69%) and are more likely to say they "always" vote in national elections—57% compared to 37%.

The GOP can claim a greater proportion of the

over-65 group than the younger segment, as seen in the table below:

Political Affiliation

65 Years and Older

Republicans 30%
Democrats 52
Independents 18

Under 65 Years

Republicans 23%
Democrats 45
Independents 32

Similarly, the older group tends more to a conservative political philosophy than do persons under 65, as seen below:

Political Philosophy

65 Years and Older

Right 35%
Center 41
Left 12
No opinion 12

Under 65 Years

Right 32%
Center 37
Left . . . . , ...21
No opinion 10

The older group is more likely than its younger counterparts to espouse traditional values, although the differences are not great in the case of certain values tested. Not surprisingly, they are less likely to favor more acceptance of sexual freedom and marijuana use, as seen below:

Religious Beliefs Playing a Greater Role in People's Lives

65 years and older .88%
Under 65 years 74

More Respect for Authority

65 years and over .94%
Under 65 years 88

Less Emphasis on Working Hard

65 years and over .23%
Under 65 years 29

Less Emphasis on Money

65 years and over .66%
Under 65 years 72

More Emphasis on Traditional Family Ties

65 years and over .95%
Under 65 years 92

More Acceptance of Sexual Freedom

65 years and over 7%
Under 65 years 28

More Acceptance of Marijuana Use

65 years and over 1%
Under 65 years 16

Any notion that older persons, because of age-related health and other problems, are less content than the rest of the adult population is dispelled by results showing that 55% of the 65-and-older group say they are "very happy" compared to 49% among the under-65 group. And finally, the 65-and-older group is even slightly more satisfied than the younger group with the way things are going in their personal lives and hold views which are closely comparable about the way things are going in the nation, as seen below:

Satisfied/Dissatisfied With Way Things Are Going in Personal Lives

65 Years and Over

Satisfied 78%
Dissatisfied 20
No opinion 2

Under 65 Years

Satisfied 74%
Dissatisfied 24
No opinion 2

Satisfied/Dissatisfied With Way Things Are Going in Nation

65 Years and Over

Satisfied 24%
Dissatisfied 73
No opinion 3

Under 65 Years

Satisfied 23%
Dissatisfied 72
No opinion 5

MAY 1
PRESIDENT REAGAN AND BLACK AMERICANS

Interviewing Date: 1/14–17; 21–24; 28–31; 2/25–28; 3/11–14/83
Survey #207-G; 208-G; 209-G; 210-G; 211-G

Do you approve or disapprove of the way Ronald Reagan is handling his job as president?

	Yes White	Yes Black
National	42%	10%

By Sex

Male	46%	13%
Female	39	7

By Education

College	50%	16%
High school or less	38	9

By Region

South	44%	13%
Nonsouth	42	8

By Age

18–29 years	46%	12%
30–49 years	43	9
50 years and over	38	9

By Income

$15,000 and over	47%	11%
Under $15,000	34	10

By Occupation

White collar	49%	13%
Blue collar	39	9
Labor union households	36%	8%
Nonlabor union households ...	44	11

Note: Despite signs of economic recovery, only one black American in ten approves of President Ronald Reagan's performance in office, according to recent Gallup surveys. This is far lower than the positive ratings blacks accorded other Republican presidents at the same point in their tenure.

Approval is slightly higher among younger blacks, men, those who attended college, and blacks living in the South. But in every black subgroup, disapproval of the president outweighs approval by a wide margin. It should be emphasized, however, that in no major black subgroup does approval of Reagan exceed 20%, and in no major white group does it fall below this proportion.

Reagan's current approval rating among blacks is far lower than that of his elected predecessors at the same point in their presidencies. As shown in the table below, in the first quarter of 1971 President Richard Nixon had the confidence of 30% of blacks. And President Dwight Eisenhower's rating among blacks at this time in 1955 was 63% approval:

Presidential Performance Ratings
(Percent Approving in First Quarter of Third Year in Office)

	National	Black	White
1983 Reagan	38%	10%	42%
1979 Carter	43	51	42
1971 Nixon	52	30	55
1963 Kennedy	70	92	68
1955 Eisenhower	70	63	74

One factor in the poor rating Reagan receives from blacks is that comparatively few are now optimistic about their personal finances. While 47% of whites in the latest survey expect their financial situation will be better a year from now than it currently is, only 28% of blacks share this outlook. In fact, comparison of the latest findings with the results of a November survey shows a 6-percentage-point increase in the proportion of whites who expect to be better off in a year's time, but a 6-point decrease among blacks.

Here is the question asked and the comparative findings:

Looking ahead, do you expect that at this time next year you will be financially better off than now, or worse off than now?

Blacks—March 1983

Better	28%
Same	21
Worse	37
No opinion	14

Whites—March 1983

Better	47%
Same	24
Worse	20
No opinion	9

National Trend

Blacks—November 1982

Better	34%
Same	21
Worse	30
No opinion	15

Whites—November 1982

Better	41%
Same	29
Worse	21
No opinion	9

In assessing the views of blacks toward Reagan's job performance, it is important to bear in mind that only 5% of blacks consider themselves Republicans, while 78% say they are Democrats and 17% independents:

Political Party Affiliation

(First Quarter, 1983)

	National	Black	White
Republicans	24%	5%	27%
Democrats	46	78	41
Independents	30	17	32

MAY 5
EDUCATION REFORMS

Special Survey*

The American people have long endorsed many of the reforms recently cited by a federal commission as necessary to prevent further deterioration of public education in the United States. The bipartisan National Commission on Excellence in Education, in a highly critical report on the public schools, said: "The educational foundations of our society are presently being eroded by a rising tide of mediocrity that threatens our very future as a nation and as a people." Some of the specific changes recommended by the commission and the findings of recent Gallup surveys that bear on these points are described below.

The commission urged the schools to strengthen their requirements in the "new basics" of mathematics, English, science, social studies, and computer science and, for students planning to attend college, foreign languages. A 1981 Gallup survey showed the public narrowly favoring concentration on "fewer basic courses" over "a wide variety of courses." Here is the question and the national trend:

*The adult questions were asked in surveys conducted by the Gallup Organization for the National Association of Secondary School Principals, the National Association of Elementary School Principals, the Institute for the Development of Educational Activities (IDEA), and Phi Delta Kappa, a professional education fraternity.

Public high schools can offer students a wide variety of courses, or they can concentrate on fewer basic courses such as English, mathematics, history, and science. Which of these two policies do you think the local high schools should follow in planning their curriculum—a wide variety or fewer but more basic courses?

	1981	1979
Favor wide variety	43%	44%
Favor fewer, more basic	52	49
No opinion	5	7

In the same 1981 survey, respondents were asked what subjects they would require high-school students who were planning to go to college to take, if they were the ones to decide. Here are the leading responses:

	Would require subject	Number of years
Mathematics	94%	4
English	91	4
History/U.S. government	83	4
Science	76	4
Business	60	2
Foreign language	54	2

The survey also found 43% of the public would require computer instruction for all high-school students.

Students, according to the commission, should be given far more homework. The Gallup Youth Survey of teen-agers (13 through 18 years) consistently has found that students themselves think their school work and homework are too easy. Here are the questions asked in a 1979 survey, and the results:

In general, do you think elementary-school children in the public schools here are made to work too hard in school and on homework, or not hard enough?

Teen-agers Only*

Too hard	10%
About right	29
Not hard enough	58
No opinion	3

What about students in the public high schools here—in general, are they required to work too hard or not hard enough?

·*The Gallup Youth Survey findings are based on a representative cross-section of telephone interviews with teen-agers, ages 13 to 18.

Teen-agers Only

Too hard	22%
About right	30
Not hard enough	45
No opinion	3

Gallup surveys have found increasing support for requiring students to demonstrate competence before graduation. Here is the question and the trend:

Should all high-school students in the United States be required to pass a standard nationwide examination in order to get a high-school diploma?

	1981	1976	1958
Yes	69%	65%	50%
No	26	31	39
No opinion	5	4	11

Teen-agers interviewed by the Gallup Youth Survey also back the nationwide exam, 63% in favor to 34% opposed.

One of the commission's more sweeping conclusions was that America is in great danger of losing its primacy in world affairs if it continues to neglect its educational system. In the latest Gallup survey on the subject this question was asked:

Some observers say the United States is losing its lead in science and technology to Japan and Germany. Do you think this is true or not true?

True 48%
Not true 38
No opinion 14

Other commission recommendations were that the school day should be lengthened from the present six hours to seven hours, and that the school year should be increased from 180 to as many as 220 days. A 1982 Gallup survey found the public opposing both these proposals by almost identical margins. Here are the questions and the results:

In some nations, students attend school as many as 240 days a year as compared to 180 in the United States. How do you feel about extending the public school year in this community by 30 days, making the school year about 210 days or 10 months long? Do you favor or oppose this idea?

Favor 37%
Oppose 53
No opinion 10

How do you feel about extending the school day in the public schools in this community by one hour? Do you favor or oppose this idea?

Favor 37%
Oppose 55
No opinion 8

Finally, there is little doubt that the public believes that America's future rests more on developing the best educational system in the world than on developing the most efficient industrial production system or the strongest military force, as seen in responses to this question:

In determining America's strength in the future—say, twenty-five years from now—how important do you feel each of the following

factors will be: very important, fairly important, not too important, or not at all important:

Developing the best educational system in the world?

Very important 84%
Fairly important 13
Not too important 1
Not at all important .... *
Don't know 2

*Less than 1%

Developing the most efficient industrial production system in the world?

Very important 66%
Fairly important 26
Not too important 3
Not at all important 1
Don't know 4

Building the strongest military force in the world?

Very important 47%
Fairly important 37
Not too important 11
Not at all important 2
Don't know 3

MAY 8
MOST IMPORTANT PROBLEM

Interviewing Date: 4/15–18/83
Survey #212-G

What do you think is the most important problem facing this country today?

Unemployment; recession 54%
Inflation; high cost of living 18
Fear of war 11
Economy (general)...................... 8
Excessive government spending.......... 5
Moral decline in society................. 4
Reagan budget cuts 3
High interest rates 2

International problems	2
Crime	2
All others	9
Don't know	2
	110%*

National Trend

October 1982

Unemployment; recession	62%
Inflation; high cost of living	18
Fear of war	3
Economy (general)	11
Excessive government spending	4
Moral decline in society	3
Reagan budget cuts	3
High interest rates	4
International problems	2
Crime	3
All others	9
Don't know	2
	114%*

August 1982

Unemployment; recession	48%
Inflation; high cost of living	23
Fear of war	6
Economy (general)	16
Excessive government spending	5
Moral decline in society	4
Reagan budget cuts	5
High interest rates	8
International problems	3
Crime	3
All others	6
Don't know	3
	130%*

*Total adds to more than 100% due to multiple responses.

All persons who named a problem were then asked: Which political party do you think can do a better job of handling the problem you have just mentioned—the Republican party or the Democratic party?

Republican	20%
Democratic	41
No difference (volunteered)	26
No opinion	13

By Sex

Male

Republican	22%
Democratic	41
No difference (volunteered)	27
No opinion	10

Female

Republican	19%
Democratic	41
No difference (volunteered)	25
No opinion	15

By Race

White

Republican	23%
Democratic	36
No difference (volunteered)	28
No opinion	13

Nonwhite

Republican	4%
Democratic	67
No difference (volunteered)	17
No opinion	12

By Education

College

Republican	31%
Democratic	33
No difference (volunteered)	26
No opinion	10

High School

Republican	17%
Democratic	44
No difference (volunteered)	27
No opinion	12

Grade School

Republican 14%
Democratic 40
No difference (volunteered) 27
No opinion 19

By Region
East

Republican 16%
Democratic 42
No difference (volunteered) 29
No opinion 13

Midwest

Republican 21%
Democratic 39
No difference (volunteered) 29
No opinion 11

South

Republican 22%
Democratic 43
No difference (volunteered) 21
No opinion 14

West

Republican 23%
Democratic 37
No difference (volunteered) 27
No opinion 13

By Income
$25,000 and Over

Republican 32%
Democratic 34
No difference (volunteered) 23
No opinion 11

$15,000 and Over

Republican 26%
Democratic 35
No difference (volunteered) 28
No opinion 11

Under $15,000

Republican 14%
Democratic 48
No difference (volunteered) 24
No opinion 14

By Politics
Republicans

Republican 62%
Democratic 9
No difference (volunteered) 21
No opinion 8

Democrats

Republican 4%
Democratic 69
No difference (volunteered) 16
No opinion 11

Independents

Republican 18%
Democratic 23
No difference (volunteered) 42
No opinion 17

National Trend

	October 1982	August 1982
Republican	29%	26%
Democratic	41	35
No difference (volunteered)	21	27
No opinion	9	12

Note: Although evidence of recovery from the recession dominates the economic headlines, unemployment continues to be perceived by Americans as the most urgent problem facing the nation. In the latest (mid-April) Gallup survey, 54% cite unemployment as the nation's top problem, three times greater than the 18% who name inflation or the high cost of living as most urgent. Other concerns in the forefront of voters' minds are fear of war, mentioned by 11%; the poor shape of the economy in general (8%); and excessive government spending (5%).

The proportion of the public who now think

unemployment is the greatest cause for national concern has slipped by 8 percentage points since October, when 62% said joblessness was the most pressing problem. As in past surveys, unemployment is cited more often by easterners and midwesterners than by persons living elsewhere in the nation. However, the percentages are lower now than in October in all geographic regions, as shown below:

Most Important Problem

(Percent Naming Unemployment)

	April 1983	October 1982
National	54%	62%

By Region

East	56%	62%
Midwest	62	71
South	47	58
West	49	58

Blacks, unskilled workers, persons whose formal education ended at the high-school level, and Democrats continue to regard unemployment as a more serious national problem than do persons from different backgrounds.

The proportion of voters citing the possibility of war as the greatest national problem, though still at a relatively low level, has grown significantly from 3% in October to 11% in the current survey. Fear of war is more acute among 18 to 24 year olds, mentioned by 19%, making it second only to unemployment (58%) as the most pressing national problem. Fear of war is not restricted to young men, many of whom would be eligible for a possible military draft; in fact, 21% of women 18 to 24, compared to 17% of men in this bracket, name the chance of war as the most important problem facing the United States.

In the latest survey, 41% of all voters say they believe the Democratic party is better able to deal with the problems they consider uppermost, while 20% name the Republican party. Another 39% perceive no difference between the parties or do not express an opinion. The 21-percentage-point advantage now held by the Democrats over the Republicans is the greatest difference between the

parties recorded since October 1977. At that time, the Democratic party enjoyed a 38%-to-14% lead over the Republican party, a 24-point advantage. As recently as October 1981, the Republicans held a small but significant 32%-to-29% edge over the Democrats on this issue.

MAY 12
PRESIDENT REAGAN

Interviewing Date: 4/15–18/83
Survey #212-G

> Now, let me ask you about specific foreign and domestic problems. As I read off each problem, one at a time, would you tell me whether you approve or disapprove of the way President Ronald Reagan is handling that problem:

National defense?

Approve	43%
Disapprove	42
No opinion	15

By Politics
Republicans

Approve	64%
Disapprove	23
No opinion	13

Democrats

Approve	33%
Disapprove	52
No opinion	15

Independents

Approve	45%
Disapprove	41
No opinion	14

Inflation?

Approve	39%
Disapprove	52
No opinion	9

By Politics

Republicans

Approve	69%
Disapprove	24
No opinion	7

Democrats

Approve	23%
Disapprove	62
No opinion	15

Independents

Approve	45%
Disapprove	47
No opinion	8

Relations with the Soviet Union?

Approve	37%
Disapprove	41
No opinion	22

By Politics

Republicans

Approve	56%
Disapprove	24
No opinion	20

Democrats

Approve	28%
Disapprove	50
No opinion	22

Independents

Approve	38%
Disapprove	39
No opinion	23

Economic conditions?

Approve	34%
Disapprove	58
No opinion	8

By Politics

Republicans

Approve	67%
Disapprove	28
No opinion	5

Democrats

Approve	17%
Disapprove	77
No opinion	6

Independents

Approve	38%
Disapprove	51
No opinion	11

The energy situation?

Approve	34%
Disapprove	48
No opinion	18

By Politics

Republicans

Approve	54%
Disapprove	28
No opinion	18

Democrats

Approve	24%
Disapprove	60
No opinion	16

Independents

Approve	38%
Disapprove	43
No opinion	19

The environment?

Approve	33%
Disapprove	50
No opinion	17

By Politics

Republicans

Approve 55%
Disapprove 31
No opinion 14

Democrats

Approve 23%
Disapprove 62
No opinion 15

Independents

Approve 36%
Disapprove 44
No opinion 20

Foreign policy?

Approve 32%
Disapprove 44
No opinion 24

By Politics

Republicans

Approve 51%
Disapprove 26
No opinion 23

Democrats

Approve 23%
Disapprove 55
No opinion 22

Independents

Approve 35%
Disapprove 41
No opinion 24

The Middle East situation?

Approve 32%
Disapprove 42
No opinion 26

By Politics

Republicans

Approve 48%
Disapprove 24
No opinion 28

Democrats

Approve 26%
Disapprove 50
No opinion 24

Independents

Approve 34%
Disapprove 42
No opinion 24

Unemployment?

Approve 20%
Disapprove 71
No opinion 9

By Politics

Republicans

Approve 44%
Disapprove 44
No opinion 12

Democrats

Approve 9%
Disapprove 85
No opinion 6

Independents

Approve 22%
Disapprove 67
No opinion 11

Note: If the 1984 presidential election is close, as many political observers expect it will be, the views of the large group of independent voters on Ronald Reagan's handling of key issues could be crucial. In general, the political views of independents, who represent more than one-fourth of all registered voters in the United States, fall mid-way between those of Democrats and Republicans and closely reflect the views of the nation as a whole.

Survey respondents were asked whether they approve or disapprove of the president's handling of nine specific domestic and international problems. Independent voters give highest approval to his handling of national defense and inflation, with 45% approving in each case. Their lowest approval (22%) goes to Reagan's dealing with unemployment.

MAY 15
EL SALVADOR

Interviewing Date: 4/29–5/8/83*
Special Telephone Survey

Have you heard or read about the situation in El Salvador?

	April 29– May 8, 1983 Yes	March 11–14, 1983** Yes
National	79%	87%

Asked of those who replied in the affirmative: How likely do you think it is that the U.S. involvement in El Salvador could turn into a situation like Vietnam—that is, that the United States would become more and more deeply involved as time goes on? Would you say this is very likely, fairly likely, not very likely, or not at all likely?

	April 29– May 8, 1983 Very likely; fairly likely	March 11–14, 1983** Very likely; fairly likely
National	67%	68%

Also asked of the aware group: If the rebel forces succeed in taking over the government in El Salvador, how likely do you think it is that the same kind of thing will happen in other Latin American countries—very likely, fairly likely, not very likely, or not at all likely?

	April 29– May 8, 1983 Very likely; fairly likely	March 11–14, 1983** Very likely; fairly likely
National	72%	75%

*On April 27, President Ronald Reagan delivered a televised speech on Central America before both houses of Congress.
**Included for comparison purposes. See March 31 release for breakdown of these survey results.

MAY 19
PRESIDENTIAL TRIAL HEATS

Interviewing Date: 4/29–5/2/83
Survey #213-G

Asked of registered voters: Suppose the 1984 presidential election were being held today. If President Ronald Reagan were the Republican candidate and Senator John Glenn were the Democratic candidate, which would you like to see win? [Those who named another candidate or who were undecided were asked: As of today, do you lean more to Reagan, the Republican, or to Glenn, the Democrat?]

Reagan 37%
Glenn 54
Other; undecided 9

By Politics
Republicans

Reagan 75%
Glenn 18
Other; undecided 7

Democrats

Reagan 15%
Glenn 74
Other; undecided 11

Independents

Reagan 42%
Glenn 49
Other; undecided 9

National Trend

	Reagan	Glenn	Other; undecided
February 25–28, 1983	40%	45%	15%
December 1982	39	54	7

Asked of registered voters: Suppose the 1984 presidential election were being held today. If President Ronald Reagan were the Republican candidate and Walter Mondale were the Democratic candidate, which would you like to see win? [Those who named another candidate or who were undecided were asked: As of today, do you lean more to Reagan, the Republican, or to Mondale, the Democrat?]

Reagan 42%
Mondale 49
Other; undecided 9

By Politics

Republicans

Reagan 82%
Mondale 13
Other; undecided 5

Democrats

Reagan 19%
Mondale 72
Other; undecided 9

Independents

Reagan 52%
Mondale 38
Other; undecided 10

National Trend

	Reagan	Mondale	Other; undecided
February 25–28, 1983	41%	47%	12%
December 1982	40	52	8
June 1982	43	49	8
October 1981	54	37	9

Note: Senator John Glenn is now seen as a stronger vote-getter than former Vice-president Walter Mondale, as determined by the latest nationwide Gallup test elections. Glenn now leads President Ronald Reagan 54% to 37% among registered voters, having widened his margin since February, when he led by 45% to 40%. Mondale's current edge over Reagan is 49% to 42%; this figure contrasts with February, when Mondale had a similar lead, 47% to 41%.

In the first Mondale-Reagan trial heat in October 1981, the president held a comfortable 54%-to-37% lead. However, Reagan's support ebbed in subsequent measurements, reaching its lowest point last December, when he trailed Mondale 40% to 52%. Reagan was matched against Glenn for the first time in December and lost to the Ohio senator, 39% to 54%.

Glenn's stronger showing against Reagan now than in February can be traced, at least in part, to his improved standing with independents. In February, both Mondale and Glenn beat the president among all registered voters, but lost to Reagan by similar margins among independents.

MAY 22
DEMOCRATIC PRESIDENTIAL CANDIDATES

Interviewing Date: 4/29–5/2/83
Survey #213-G

Asked of Democrats and independents: Which one of these persons [respondents were handed a card listing eleven names and titles of possible nominees] would you like to see nominated as the Democratic party's candidate for president in 1984?

First Choices of Democrats

Walter Mondale 29%
John Glenn 23
Gary Hart 4
Alan Cranston 3
Others* 10
None; don't know 31

*All others on the list each received 2% or less of the vote of survey respondents: Reubin Askew, Lloyd Bentsen, Bill Bradley, John Y. Brown, Ernest Hollings, Daniel (Pat) Moynihan, and Jay Rockefeller.

National Trend

	March 11–14, 1983	December 1982
Mondale	32%	32%
Glenn	13	14
Cranston	3	2
Hart	2	2
Others	23	24
None; don't know	27	26

First Choices of Independents

Glenn	22%
Mondale	17
Cranston	3
Hart	3
Moynihan	3
Rockefeller	3
Others	7
None; don't know	42

National Trend

	March 11–14, 1983	December 1982
Mondale	21%	15%
Glenn	18	22
Cranston	3	1
Hart	2	2
Moynihan	2	3
Rockefeller	2	2
Others	17	22
None; don't know	35	33

Note: Former Vice-president Walter Mondale continues to be the favorite of Democrats for the 1984 presidential nomination. But Senator John Glenn, an underdog as recently as March, now trails Mondale by only 6 percentage points. In the latest Gallup survey, Mondale is the choice of 29% of Democrats for the nomination to 23% for Glenn. In March, 19 percentage points separated the two front-runners, with Mondale receiving 32% of Democrats' first-place votes to 13% for Glenn.

Next in the current choices are Colorado Senator Gary Hart, with 4% of the support of Democrats, and California Senator Alan Cranston, with 3%. The two other announced candidates for the

nomination, former Florida Governor Reubin Askew and Senator Ernest Hollings of South Carolina, are each selected by 1% of Democrats.

As reported recently, Glenn is now a stronger Democratic challenger to President Ronald Reagan than Mondale. Glenn currently leads Reagan 54% to 37% in a test election among registered voters, while Mondale's edge over the president is a narrower 49% to 42%. In February, Reagan trailed both Democrats by similar margins.

Glenn's improved showing against Reagan traces largely to his present popularity with political independents. The president defeated both Glenn and Mondale in test elections in February among independents. In the current survey, however, Mondale loses to Reagan 38% to 52% among registered independents, but Glenn beats the president 49% to 42%.

It should be noted that the current rankings are in some measure a reflection of name recognition; it can be expected that as the lesser-known candidates gain in recognition, they will move up in the rankings. In January of the 1976 presidential year, for example, then little-known Jimmy Carter received the support of only 4% of Democrats in a Gallup survey.

In the current survey, only three men, Mondale (91%), Glenn (77%), and West Virginia Governor Jay Rockefeller (53%), are known to a majority of Democrats. Also, only the two leaders are sufficiently familiar to Democratic voters for a majority to say they know enough about them to have an opinion of them—65% in the case of Mondale and 54% in Glenn's case. None of the others on the list is known to this extent by as many as 20% of Democrats.

MAY 26
TANDEM-TRUCK RIGS

Interviewing Date: 4/29–5/2/83
Survey #213-G

Would you favor or oppose a law in this state that would prohibit tandem-truck rigs—that is, large trucks with two trailers attached— on major interstate highways?

Favor 45%
Oppose 43
No opinion 12

By Sex
Male

Favor 42%
Oppose 49
No opinion 9

Female

Favor 47%
Oppose 37
No opinion 16

By Region
East

Favor 49%
Oppose 37
No opinion 14

Midwest

Favor 42%
Oppose 45
No opinion 13

South

Favor 47%
Oppose 40
No opinion 13

West

Favor 38%
Oppose 53
No opinion 9

Would you favor or oppose a law in this state that would prohibit such vehicles on other roads?

Favor 57%
Oppose 32
No opinion 11

By Sex
Male

Favor 59%
Oppose 33
No opinion 8

Female

Favor 55%
Oppose 32
No opinion 13

By Region
East

Favor 57%
Oppose 31
No opinion 12

Midwest

Favor 57%
Oppose 33
No opinion 10

South

Favor 57%
Oppose 32
No opinion 11

West

Favor 56%
Oppose 35
No opinion 9

Those Who Favor a Ban on Interstate Highways

Favor 84%
Oppose 14
No opinion 2

Those Who Oppose a Ban on Interstate Highways

Favor 39%
Oppose 59
No opinion 2

Note: The Federal Highway Administration's controversial plan to permit tandem trailer trucks to use interstate highways has about equal numbers of supporters and detractors in the general population. However, the public, by almost a 2-to-1 ratio, opposes allowing these big trucks to use other federal highways.

In the latest Gallup survey, 45% of adult Americans favor laws prohibiting the big rigs from operating on their major state highways while 43% oppose such laws. For samples of the size used in this survey, the 2 percentage-point difference is considered insignificant.

Almost twice the proportion of respondents favor (57%) as oppose (32%) banning the vehicles from other noninterstate roads. In all, almost four respondents in ten (38%) favor legislation that would make all roads in their states, whether interstates or noninterstates, off limits to tandem-truck rigs.

The U.S. Department of Transportation recently announced a plan that would permit wider use of federal highways by the big trucks. This move, it is maintained, would greatly increase the efficiency and productivity of the trucking industry and would help to offset the April tax increase of 5 cents per gallon on gasoline and diesel fuels. Some state authorities, particularly those in the densely populated northeast region of the nation, have opposed the plan on the ground that permitting the big trucks to use their roads would create a major safety hazard. Transportation Secretary Elizabeth Dole has said that the Highway Administration would try to reconcile its views on the safety issue with those of state officials.

Men and women differ slightly in their views on the issue, with men narrowly opposed to state laws prohibiting big trucks from the interstates, while women favor these laws by a 47% to 37% vote. The greatest regional difference is found between the views of westerners, in whose states the double-trailer rigs have long been permitted, and those living in other sections of the country. Westerners themselves oppose restrictive laws 53% to 38%. Finally, state laws banning tandem-trailer trucks on roads other than interstates are heavily favored in all major population groups, with no significant regional differences found.

MAY 29
INTERRACIAL AND INTERFAITH MARRIAGES

Interviewing Date: 4/29–5/2/83
Survey #213-G

Do you approve or disapprove of marriage between blacks and whites?

Approve 43%
Disapprove 50
No opinion 7

By Sex
Male

Approve 45%
Disapprove 47
No opinion 8

Female

Approve 41%
Disapprove 53
No opinion 6

By Race
White

Approve 38%
Disapprove 56
No opinion 6

Nonwhite

Approve 71%
Disapprove 20
No opinion 9

By Education
College

Approve 61%
Disapprove 32
No opinion 7

High School

Approve 39%
Disapprove 55
No opinion 6

Grade School

Approve 23%
Disapprove 68
No opinion 9

By Region
East

Approve 46%
Disapprove 46
No opinion 8

Midwest

Approve 40%
Disapprove 52
No opinion 8

South

Approve 34%
Disapprove 60
No opinion 6

West

Approve 58%
Disapprove 37
No opinion 5

By Age
18–24 Years

Approve 61%
Disapprove 32
No opinion 7

25–29 Years

Approve 66%
Disapprove 26
No opinion 8

30–49 Years

Approve 45%
Disapprove 48
No opinion 7

50–64 Years

Approve 32%
Disapprove 62
No opinion 6

65 Years and Over

Approve 18%
Disapprove 76
No opinion 6

By Income
$25,000 and Over

Approve 51%
Disapprove 44
No opinion 5

$15,000 and Over

Approve 46%
Disapprove 48
No opinion 6

Under $15,000

Approve 40%
Disapprove 53
No opinion 7

By Religion
Protestants

Approve 38%
Disapprove 57
No opinion 5

Catholics

Approve 47%
Disapprove 46
No opinion 7

By Occupation
Professional and Business

Approve 56%
Disapprove 35
No opinion 9

Clerical and Sales

Approve 47%
Disapprove 44
No opinion 9

Manual Workers

Approve 48%
Disapprove 46
No opinion 6

Nonlabor Force

Approve 33%
Disapprove 62
No opinion 5

National Trend

	Approve	Dis-approve	No opinion
1983	43%	50%	7%
1978	36	54	10
1972	29	60	11
1968	20	72	8

Do you approve or disapprove of marriage between Catholics and Protestants?

Approve 79%
Disapprove 10
No opinion 11

By Sex
Male

Approve 80%
Disapprove 9
No opinion 11

Female

Approve 79%
Disapprove 11
No opinion 10

By Race
White

Approve 80%
Disapprove 10
No opinion 10

Nonwhite

Approve 77%
Disapprove 8
No opinion 15

By Education
College

Approve 87%
Disapprove 6
No opinion 7

High School

Approve 82%
Disapprove 8
No opinion 10

Grade School

Approve 55%
Disapprove 25
No opinion 20

By Region
East

Approve 85%
Disapprove 8
No opinion 7

Midwest

Approve 82%
Disapprove 9
No opinion 9

South

Approve 70%
Disapprove 13
No opinion 17

West

Approve 83%
Disapprove 10
No opinion 7

By Age

18–24 Years

Approve 89%
Disapprove 6
No opinion 5

25–29 Years

Approve 87%
Disapprove 5
No opinion 8

30–49 Years

Approve 79%
Disapprove 9
No opinion 12

50–64 Years

Approve 78%
Disapprove 10
No opinion 12

65 Years and Over

Approve 66%
Disapprove 20
No opinion 14

By Income

$25,000 and Over

Approve 87%
Disapprove 5
No opinion 8

$15,000 and Over

Approve 85%
Disapprove 7
No opinion 8

Under $15,000

Approve 73%
Disapprove 14
No opinion 13

By Religion

Protestants

Approve 74%
Disapprove 13
No opinion 13

Catholics

Approve 89%
Disapprove 6
No opinion 5

By Occupation

Professional and Business

Approve 86%
Disapprove 6
No opinion 8

Clerical and Sales

Approve 86%
Disapprove 7
No opinion 7

Manual Workers

Approve 82%
Disapprove 8
No opinion 10

Nonlabor Force

Approve 74%
Disapprove 14
No opinion 12

National Trend

	Approve	Dis-approve	No opinion
1983	79%	10%	11%
1978	73	13	14
1972	72	13	15
1968	63	22	15

Do you approve or disapprove of marriage between Jews and non-Jews?

Approve 77%
Disapprove 10
No opinion 13

By Sex
Male
Approve 78%
Disapprove 8
No opinion 14

Female
Approve 77%
Disapprove 10
No opinion 13

By Race
White
Approve 77%
Disapprove 10
No opinion 13

Nonwhite
Approve 77%
Disapprove 8
No opinion 15

By Education
College
Approve 86%
Disapprove 5
No opinion 9

High School
Approve 79%
Disapprove 8
No opinion 13

Grade School
Approve 55%
Disapprove 23
No opinion 22

By Region
East
Approve 82%
Disapprove 9
No opinion 9

Midwest
Approve 78%
Disapprove 9
No opinion 13

South
Approve 69%
Disapprove 12
No opinion 19

West
Approve 82%
Disapprove 7
No opinion 11

By Age
18–24 Years
Approve 86%
Disapprove 5
No opinion 9

25–29 Years
Approve 87%
Disapprove 3
No opinion 10

30–49 Years
Approve 77%
Disapprove 9
No opinion 14

50–64 Years
Approve 78%
Disapprove 10
No opinion 12

65 Years and Over

Approve	60%
Disapprove	21
No opinion	19

By Income
$25,000 and Over

Approve	85%
Disapprove	6
No opinion	9

$15,000 and Over

Approve	83%
Disapprove	7
No opinion	10

Under $15,000

Approve	71%
Disapprove	13
No opinion	16

By Religion*
Protestants

Approve	73%
Disapprove	12
No opinion	15

Catholics

Approve	86%
Disapprove	6
No opinion	8

By Occupation
Professional and Business

Approve	86%
Disapprove	5
No opinion	9

*Among the small number in the sample, Jewish opinion closely matches that of non-Jews.

Clerical and Sales

Approve	82%
Disapprove	7
No opinion	11

Manual Workers

Approve	80%
Disapprove	7
No opinion	13

Nonlabor Force

Approve	71%
Disapprove	14
No opinion	15

National Trend

	Approve	Dis-approve	No opinion
1983	77%	10%	13%
1978	69	14	17
1972	67	14	19
1968	59	21	20

Note: One of the most interesting chapters in U.S. social history has been a decline in racial and religious prejudice. Compelling evidence that Americans are becoming more tolerant is found in the public's attitude toward interracial and inter-faith marriages during the last decade and a half.

Since 1968 the proportion of Americans who say they approve of marriage between whites and blacks has grown from 20% to 43%, while those approving of marriage between Catholics and Protestants has increased from 63% to 79%. In the case of marriage between Jews and non-Jews, the percentage has risen from 59% in 1968 to 77% today.

The sharpest change in tolerance is recorded in public attitudes toward marriage between whites and blacks. In the current survey, as in 1972, nonwhites are found to be about twice as likely as whites to express approval of interracial marriages.

One of the key factors in the growth of racial and religious tolerance has been the increase in college training. The proportion of the population with at least some college education has more than tripled since the Gallup Poll was founded in 1935. College-educated persons in every survey have been more tolerant than those without a college background.

JUNE 2
DEFORMED INFANTS

Interviewing Date: 5/13–16/83
Survey #214-G

When a badly deformed baby who could live only a few years was born in a Midwest city, the parents asked the doctors not to keep the baby alive. Would you take the same position as the parents did, or not?

Yes, would 43%
No, would not 40
No opinion 17

By Sex
Male

Yes, would 45%
No, would not 37
No opinion 18

Female

Yes, would 41%
No, would not 43
No opinion 16

By Race
White

Yes, would 45%
No, would not 38
No opinion 17

Black

Yes, would 28%
No, would not 59
No opinion 13

By Education
College

Yes, would 54%
No, would not 33
No opinion 13

High School

Yes, would 38%
No, would not 43
No opinion 19

Grade School

Yes, would 42%
No, would not 42
No opinion 16

By Age
18–24 Years

Yes, would 46%
No, would not 44
No opinion 10

25–29 Years

Yes, would 42%
No, would not 42
No opinion 16

30–49 Years

Yes, would 42%
No, would not 42
No opinion 16

50 Years and Over

Yes, would 44%
No, would not 35
No opinion 21

By Religion
Protestants

Yes, would 43%
No, would not 38
No opinion 19

Catholics

Yes, would 40%
No, would not 47
No opinion 13

By Marital Status

Married

Yes, would 43%
No, would not 41
No opinion 16

Single

Yes, would 52%
No, would not 34
No opinion 14

Note: The U.S. public is evenly divided on the controversial issue of whether severely handicapped or deformed infants should be kept alive or allowed to die. In the latest Gallup survey, 43% of respondents say that if they had to make the decision, they would ask the doctors not to keep a badly deformed baby alive, while 40% take the opposite position.

While the nation as a whole is divided on this issue, sharp differences are found on the basis of race, religion, education, and marital status. Blacks are 2 to 1 of the opinion the baby should be kept alive; Catholics are somewhat more likely to favor keeping the baby alive than are Protestants; persons with a college background lean heavily, 54% to 33%, toward letting a newborn child die if born with a serious deformity; and married persons and women are more in favor of keeping the baby alive than single persons and men.

The issue is now in federal court. On one side, federal law prohibits withholding medical treatment and requires hospitals to post notices warning employees that such a practice is illegal. On the other side, many in the medical profession contend that the new government rules could lead to overtreatment of handicapped infants and merely prolong the process of dying.

The rules, which took effect March 22, resulted from the death last year of a Bloomington, Indiana, infant afflicted with Down's Syndrome and other medical complications requiring surgery. The infant died when the parents, doctors, and a state court permitted food and treatment to be withheld.

JUNE 5
PRESIDENTIAL TRIAL HEATS

Interviewing Date: 5/13–16/83
Survey #214-G

Asked of registered voters: Suppose the 1984 presidential election were being held today. If President Ronald Reagan were the Republican candidate and Walter Mondale were the Democratic candidate, which would you like to see win? [Those who named another person or who were undecided were asked: As of today, do you lean more to Reagan, the Republican, or to Mondale, the Democrat?]

Reagan 42%
Mondale 47
Other; undecided 11

By Sex

Male

Reagan 47%
Mondale 42
Other; undecided 11

Female

Reagan 38%
Mondale 51
Other; undecided 11

By Race

White

Reagan 46%
Mondale 43
Other; undecided 11

Black

Reagan 10%
Mondale 80
Other; undecided 10

By Education
College
Reagan 52%
Mondale 38
Other; undecided 10

High School
Reagan 38%
Mondale 50
Other; undecided 12

Grade School
Reagan 36%
Mondale 55
Other; undecided 9

By Region
East
Reagan 39%
Mondale 51
Other; undecided 10

Midwest
Reagan 42%
Mondale 45
Other; undecided 13

South
Reagan 43%
Mondale 47
Other; undecided 10

West
Reagan 47%
Mondale 45
Other; undecided 8

By Age
18–29 Years
Reagan 40%
Mondale 47
Other; undecided 13

30–49 Years
Reagan 42%
Mondale 47
Other; undecided 11

50 Years and Over
Reagan 44%
Mondale 47
Other; undecided 9

By Politics
Republicans
Reagan 84%
Mondale 12
Other; undecided 4

Democrats
Reagan 16%
Mondale 73
Other; undecided 11

Independents
Reagan 46%
Mondale 37
Other; undecided 17

Asked of registered voters: If the 1984 presidential election were being held today and President Ronald Reagan were the Republican candidate, running against Walter Mondale, the Democratic candidate, and Rev. Jesse Jackson, an independent candidate, which would you like to see win? [Those who named another person or who were undecided were asked: As of today, do you lean more to Reagan, the Republican; Mondale, the Democrat; or to Jackson, the independent?]

Reagan 41%
Mondale 40
Jackson 9
Other; undecided 10

By Sex

Male

Reagan	45%
Mondale	35
Jackson	11
Other; undecided	9

Female

Reagan	37%
Mondale	45
Jackson	8
Other; undecided	10

By Race

White

Reagan	46%
Mondale	41
Jackson	4
Other; undecided	9

Black

Reagan	7%
Mondale	29
Jackson	48
Other; undecided	16

By Education

College

Reagan	51%
Mondale	32
Jackson	8
Other; undecided	9

High School

Reagan	37%
Mondale	43
Jackson	10
Other; undecided	10

Grade School

Reagan	34%
Mondale	49
Jackson	8
Other; undecided	9

By Region

East

Reagan	39%
Mondale	43
Jackson	6
Other; undecided	12

Midwest

Reagan	42%
Mondale	40
Jackson	9
Other; undecided	9

South

Reagan	42%
Mondale	39
Jackson	12
Other; undecided	7

West

Reagan	44%
Mondale	37
Jackson	14
Other; undecided	5

By Age

18–29 Years

Reagan	37%
Mondale	35
Jackson	16
Other; undecided	12

30–49 Years

Reagan	41%
Mondale	40
Jackson	9
Other; undecided	10

50 Years and Over

Reagan	44%
Mondale	43
Jackson	6
Other; undecided	7

By Politics

Republicans

Reagan 84%
Mondale 12
Jackson 2
Other; undecided 2

Democrats

Reagan 15%
Mondale 60
Jackson 13
Other; undecided 12

Independents

Reagan 46%
Mondale 34
Jackson 8
Other; undecided 12

Note: If President Ronald Reagan runs again in 1984, his chances for reelection would be enhanced if black leader Rev. Jesse Jackson were to enter the race as an independent. In the first of two just-completed test elections, Democratic challenger Walter Mondale beats Reagan 47% to 42%, not significantly different from the 49%-to-42% vote recorded in a survey conducted two weeks earlier. However, in a second test election, also pitting Reagan against Mondale but adding Jackson as an independent, Reagan is the choice of 41% of registered voters to 40% for Mondale and 9% for Jackson. Virtually all of Jackson's support would come at the expense of Mondale, as shown below:

Presidential Trial Heats

(Choice of Registered Voters)

	Two-way race	Three-way race	Differ-ence
Reagan	42%	41%	−1
Mondale	47	40	−7
Jackson	—	9	+9
Other; undecided	11	10	−1

The recent mayoral election victory of Harold Washington in Chicago and primary victory of Wilson Goode in Philadelphia have focused public attention on the subject of blacks in high national political office. Civil-rights activist Jackson has said he is considering running as an independent candidate for president in 1984, causing immediate speculation about the impact such a move would have on the two major party candidates.

Jackson also said recently that a black presidential candidate in 1984 could win, but added that it was too early for a black to announce. The latest survey evidence suggests that he would hurt the Democratic candidate far more than the Republican. In the event of a close presidential contest, his entry into the race could tip the balance toward the GOP.

In the three-way contest, Jackson wins about half (48% of registered blacks' votes and 4% of whites'). However, Jackson's entry would likely have an impact transcending race alone. A black presidential candidate, many observers believe, would sharply increase black voter registration and focus national attention on issues of paramount importance to blacks, such as chronic high unemployment among minority groups. Critics, however, think that no black candidate has a chance of winning and the splinter effect might hurt rather than help blacks' concerns.

Efforts among black leaders to register members of their race have paid substantial dividends in recent years, with nearly as high a proportion of blacks (68%) as whites (72%) saying they are registered to vote. At the same time, however, fewer blacks than whites usually get to the polls on election day. In the 1980 presidential election, for example, 61% of eligible whites reported having voted, compared to 50.5% of blacks.

JUNE 9
PRESIDENT REAGAN/CONGRESS

Interviewing Date: 5/20–23/83
Survey #215-G

Do you approve or disapprove of the way Ronald Reagan is handling his job as president?

	May 20–23, 1983 Approve	January 14–17, 1983 Approve	Difference
National	46%	37%	+ 9
By Sex			
Male	49%	42%	+ 7
Female	43	32	+11
By Race			
White	49%	41%	+ 8
Black	21	14	+ 7
By Education			
College	50%	45%	+ 5
High school	46	37	+ 9
Grade school	34	21	+13
By Region			
East	45%	35%	+10
Midwest	44	41	+ 3
South	45	35	+10
West	50	35	+15
By Age			
18–29 years	44%	40%	+ 4
30–49 years	48	39	+ 9
50 years and over	45	33	+12
By Income			
$15,000 or over	54%	44%	+10
Under $15,000	34	28	+ 6
By Politics			
Republicans	78%	68%	+10
Democrats	26	18	+ 8
Independents	49	42	+ 7
By Union Membership			
Labor union households	45%	27%	+18
Nonlabor union households	46	39	+ 7

Note: President Ronald Reagan's job performance rating has improved steadily since the beginning

of the year, with 46% in the latest survey compared to 37% in January expressing approval of his handling of his presidential duties. The current findings represent the highest level of approval in over a year and also mark the first time in fifteen months that the president has received significantly higher approval than disapproval ratings. Reagan's popularity gains are recorded among all population groups, including men and women, whites and blacks, and Republicans and Democrats.

The upturn in the president's job performance ratings—which undoubtedly reflects, at least in part, the strengthening of the economy—runs counter to the historical pattern observed for his elected predecessors at a similar point in their tenure. Jimmy Carter, Richard Nixon, and John Kennedy suffered significant declines during this period, while Dwight Eisenhower in May 1955 stood about where he began the year. At the start of 1983, Reagan's approval rating was below that accorded his predecessors; his latest rating tops President Carter's and is only 4 percentage points lower than President Nixon's. Details are shown below:

Presidential Performance Ratings

(Percent Approving)

	May	January	Difference
1983—Reagan	46%	37%	+ 9
1979—Carter	32	43	− 11
1971—Nixon	50	56	− 6
1963—Kennedy	65	74	− 9
1955—Eisenhower	69	70	− 1

Reagan Performance Ratings

	Approve	Disapprove	No opinion
1983			
May 20–23	46%	43%	11%
May 13–16	43	45	12
April 29–May 2	43	46	11
April 15–18	41	49	10
March 11–14	41	49	10
February 25–28	40	50	10
January 28–31	35	56	9

January 21–24	37	53	10
January 14–17	37	54	9

1982

December	41	50	9
November	43	47	10
October	42	48	10
September	42	48	10
August	41	49	10
July	42	46	12
June	45	45	10
May	45	44	11
April	43	47	10
March	46	45	9
February	47	43	10
January	49	40	11

Interviewing Date: 4/29–5/2/83
Survey #213-G

Do you approve or disapprove of the way Congress is handling its job?

Approve 33%
Disapprove 43
No opinion 24

By Sex
Male

Approve 33%
Disapprove 46
No opinion 21

Female

Approve 33%
Disapprove 40
No opinion 27

By Race
White

Approve 33%
Disapprove 44
No opinion 23

Nonwhite

Approve 23%
Disapprove 47
No opinion 30

By Education
College

Approve 39%
Disapprove 47
No opinion 14

High School

Approve 33%
Disapprove 40
No opinion 27

Grade School

Approve 23%
Disapprove 45
No opinion 32

By Region
East

Approve 34%
Disapprove 43
No opinion 23

Midwest

Approve 32%
Disapprove 43
No opinion 25

South

Approve 32%
Disapprove 42
No opinion 26

West

Approve 35%
Disapprove 44
No opinion 21

By Age
18–29 Years

Approve 37%
Disapprove 34
No opinion 29

30–49 Years

Approve 33%
Disapprove 47
No opinion 20

50 Years and Over

Approve 30%
Disapprove 46
No opinion 24

By Politics
Republicans

Approve 28%
Disapprove 52
No opinion 20

Democrats

Approve 36%
Disapprove 39
No opinion 25

Independents

Approve 33%
Disapprove 44
No opinion 23

National Trend

	Approve	Dis-approve	No opinion
April 29–May 2, 1983	33%	43%	24%
June 1981	38	40	22
June 1979	19	61	20
September 1978	29	49	22
June 1977	34	42	24
June 1975	29	54	17
August 1974	48	35	17

Note: President Ronald Reagan's current 46% positive job rating is substantially higher than the 33% rating the public accords Congress for the way it is handling its duties. Analysis of the latest survey findings shows that while Reagan enjoys disproportionately higher ratings among men, whites, the college-educated, and Republicans, the profile of congressional approval is remarkably even. Proportionately as many blacks as whites, for example, give the Congress favorable marks for its performance. Similarly, congressional approval is about the same among Republicans as it is among Democrats.

JUNE 12
LABOR UNION ENDORSEMENT

Interviewing Date: 5/13–16/83
Survey #214-G

Labor unions are going to announce their choice of a presidential candidate before next year's presidential primaries. Would the endorsement by labor unions of a presidential candidate make you more likely or less likely to vote for that candidate?

More likely 18%
Less likely 35
No difference (volunteered) 41
No opinion 6

By Sex
Male

More likely 18%
Less likely 35
No difference (volunteered) 43
No opinion 4

Female

More likely 17%
Less likely 35
No difference (volunteered) 39
No opinion 9

By Race
White

More likely 16%
Less likely 38
No difference (volunteered) 40
No opinion 6

Nonwhite

More likely 26%
Less likely 20
No difference (volunteered) 44
No opinion 10

By Education

College

More likely 15%
Less likely 40
No difference (volunteered) 43
No opinion 2

High School

More likely 19%
Less likely 34
No difference (volunteered) 39
No opinion 8

Grade School

More likely 17%
Less likely 32
No difference (volunteered) 41
No opinion 10

By Region

East

More likely 18%
Less likely 31
No difference (volunteered) 48
No opinion 3

Midwest

More likely 16%
Less likely 35
No difference (volunteered) 42
No opinion 7

South

More likely 19%
Less likely 35
No difference (volunteered) 36
No opinion 10

West

More likely 18%
Less likely 42
No difference (volunteered) 35
No opinion 5

By Politics

Republicans

More likely 10%
Less likely 52
No difference (volunteered) 33
No opinion 5

Democrats

More likely 25%
Less likely 26
No difference (volunteered) 43
No opinion 6

Independents

More likely 14%
Less likely 37
No difference (volunteered) 42
No opinion 7

By Occupation

Professional and Business

More likely 13%
Less likely 42
No difference (volunteered) 42
No opinion 3

Clerical and Sales

More likely 22%
Less likely 35
No difference (volunteered) 38
No opinion 5

Manual Workers

More likely 21%
Less likely 30
No difference (volunteered) 42
No opinion 7

Nonlabor Force

More likely 16%
Less likely 34
No difference (volunteered) 40
No opinion 10

Labor Union Families

More likely 32%
Less likely 18
No difference (volunteered) 47
No opinion 3

Nonlabor Union Families

More likely 14%
Less likely 40
No difference (volunteered) 39
No opinion 7

Note: Although leading Democratic presidential hopefuls are eagerly vying for trade union support, results of a just-completed Gallup Poll reveal that a candidate might be hurt more than helped by organized labor's endorsement. For every voter who said he or she would be more likely to vote for a candidate who receives the endorsement of labor unions, there are two voters who say they would be less likely to do so.

The AFL-CIO has approved a plan to endorse a candidate before the start of the presidential primaries next year. Under the plan, introduced by president Lane Kirkland, all ninety-eight affiliated unions would be bound to support that candidate in the primaries. In the past, the AFL-CIO has not endorsed any candidate until after the nominating process. The new approach is intended to increase its influence by making it a major broker in the Democratic nomination process.

As might be expected, the sharpest divergence of opinion is found between members of labor-union families versus those from nonunion homes. The union group, by a 5-to-3 margin, say they would be more likely to vote for a labor-endorsed candidate; nonunionists, who represent 80% of the sample, say labor's support would make them less likely to back such a candidate, by a 3-to-1 ratio.

Among Republicans and independents, organized labor's endorsement of a candidate would hurt more than help his or her chances. Even among Democrats, with their traditional prolabor stance,

the union endorsement would hurt as much as it would help a candidate.

JUNE 15
SIGNIFICANT PARALLELS IN PUBLIC RESPONSE TO REAGAN AND THATCHER*

As Ronald Reagan's approval ratings improve with each succeeding month into the recovery, the Thatcher victory looms over the American political scene. What happened in England this year has implications for 1984. Three key ingredients in Margaret Thatcher's success may also exist for Reagan next year—political momentum, economic hope, and a third party to splinter the opposition.

Prime Minister Thatcher found political momentum in the Falkland Islands. Prior to the war the Conservative leader had abysmal opinion ratings, far worse than Reagan's were at the depths of the U.S. recession. Britons rallied around her leadership during the South Atlantic war, and for the most part, have not left her since.

Reagan has been gaining political momentum since February. Virtually every poll during the past five months has indicated some increase in public support for the president. How long it will last and how far it will go is hard to calculate. Gallup historical analyses have shown that upticks in presidential popularity associated with dramatic events tend to have a life span of six months. Reagan's current climb is not related to some specific event, but is a political dividend of the recovery.

Unfortunately for Reagan, he cannot call for an election as his British counterpart did. His political momentum has to carry him to November 1984. But Reagan has passed the first hurdle; his approval ratings have responded to the stimulus of an improving economy.

Economic hope was a key ingredient in Great Britain as it is here. Actual conditions in England

*This Gallup analysis was written by Andrew Kohut, president of the Gallup Organization Inc.

remain very poor. While inflation has been tamed, unemployment is a crushing 12%, and in the industrial north it is far higher than that. But there is hope. The British Gallup Poll found the percentage expecting the economy to be better next year has climbed by 10 percentage points in the past five months. Americans are showing a parallel increase in economic hope, even though economic indicators have changed very little and unemployment remains the dominant national concern. From a political point of view, the expectation of better times is as potent as the realization. But on the expectation/reality continuum, timing is crucial.

It would seem that Mrs. Thatcher owes a great deal to the widely heralded Liberal/SD Alliance. This merger of an old, ineffective third party with a new centrist party claimed much attention because of its potential to capture the center of the British electorate. In point of fact its 12% of the vote was an impressive showing. Indeed, the alliance may have captured the center of the British electorate, but the center itself is inadequate; a plurality is what is required, and the Conservatives obtained the plurality in a three-way race.

This is in keeping with the overall track record of third-party races. Republicans generally do better than Democrats in elections in which there is a third-party candidate (witness 1980 and 1968). Compared to the opposition, Republicans or Conservatives are more politically homogeneous and harmonious. Their levels of political commitment are greater, and they are less subject to the appeals of new parties and/or candidates.

In 1984 a principal concern of the Republicans has to be the intensity of Reagan's critics—blacks, women, the unemployed, labor, the freeze groups, and all the others who believe they have been treated unfairly by the Reagan administration. The polls show that the president's critics are deeply committed in their opposition to him, more so than for past presidents at comparable points of time. A third-party or even fourth-party candidate defraying some of that opposition would certainly be an asset to the Republicans. For example, the Gallup Poll found that Jesse Jackson as an independent would make it easier for Reagan in a race

against Mondale, and the same is probably true for a race that included John Anderson.

The alliance made it easier for Mrs. Thatcher. She achieved a landslide without achieving a majority of the vote. Of course, the poor campaign performance of the Labour party was a central factor in her victory. The success of the Democrats in mobilizing significant elements of the anti-Reagan vote in the 1982 congressional election suggests that the president cannot count on a similarly ineffective opposition. But a third-party candidate certainly would be more of an asset to the Republicans than to the Democrats.

Mrs. Thatcher and Reagan have shared many parallels in the course of their political careers, the most obvious being that they are conservative leaders who inherited electorates favorably disposed to more liberal policies than those they espoused. Both came to office with a specific mandate—to improve economic conditions. In a broad overview, the pattern of public response to Mrs. Thatcher and Reagan have been very similar. They have weathered the same economic cycle. Prime Minister Thatcher, with somewhat more control over the situation, timed it very nicely. For President Reagan, the clock is ticking in his favor—at least for now.

JUNE 16
WOMAN FOR PRESIDENT

Interviewing Date: 4/29–5/2/83
Survey #213-G

If your party nominated a woman for president, would you vote for her if she were qualified for the job?

Yes 80%
No 16
Not sure 4

By Sex
Male

Yes 80%
No 16
Not sure 4

Female

Yes 80%
No 16
Not sure 4

By Education
College

Yes 87%
No 10
Not sure 3

High School

Yes 80%
No 17
Not sure 3

Grade School

Yes 69%
No 22
Not sure 9

By Region
East

Yes 85%
No 12
Not sure 3

Midwest

Yes 80%
No 17
Not sure 3

South

Yes 75%
No 18
Not sure 7

West

Yes 82%
No 15
Not sure 3

By Age
18–29 Years

Yes 89%
No 8
Not sure 3

30–49 Years

Yes 83%
No 14
Not sure 3

50–64 Years

Yes 72%
No 22
Not sure 6

65 Years and Over

Yes 68%
No 25
Not sure 7

By Income
$20,000 and Over

Yes 86%
No 12
Not sure 2

Under $20,000

Yes 77%
No 18
Not sure 5

By Politics
Republicans

Yes 74%
No 22
Not sure 4

Democrats

Yes 79%
No 17
Not sure 4

Independents

Yes 88%
No 9
Not sure 3

By Religion

Protestants

Yes 78%
No 18
Not sure 4

Catholics

Yes 84%
No 12
Not sure 4

National Trend

	Yes	No	Not sure
April 29–May 3, 1983	80%	16%	4%
1978	76	19	5
1975	73	23	4
1971	66	29	5
1969	54	39	7
1967	57	39	4
1955	52	44	4
1949	48	48	4
1937	31	65	4

Note: Prime Minister Margaret Thatcher's resounding victory in Great Britain recently could give new impetus to the women-in-politics movement in the United States. A recent Gallup Poll shows the American people to be more receptive to a woman president than ever before.

In the survey, five Americans in six indicate they would have no trouble voting for a qualified female presidential candidate. The trend in the proportion saying they would be willing to vote for a woman is one of the most striking in Gallup annals, having grown from 31% in 1937 to 80% today.

Heavy support for a woman as chief executive is found in all population groups, with men and women backing the concept by identical 80% to 16% votes. Greater support is expressed by younger Americans (18-29 years), the college-educated, persons from upper-income families, Catholics, and independents—groups which customarily share more liberal political views. Conversely, support is somewhat lower among groups of a more conservative stamp—persons 65 and older, those with only a grade-school education, persons from lower-income households, southerners, and Republicans.

JUNE 19
HANDGUN LAWS

Interviewing Date: 5/20–23/83
Survey #215-G

In general, do you feel that the laws covering the sale of handguns should be made more strict, less strict, or kept as they are now?

More strict 59%
Less strict 4
Kept same 31
No opinion 6

By Sex

Male

More strict 51%
Less strict 6
Kept same 39
No opinion 4

Female

More strict 67%
Less strict 3
Kept same 23
No opinion 7

By Race

White

More strict 58%
Less strict 4
Kept same 33
No opinion 5

Nonwhite

More strict 66%
Less strict 6
Kept same 20
No opinion 8

By Education

College

More strict	.67%
Less strict	4
Kept same	25
No opinion	4

High School

More strict	.58%
Less strict	5
Kept same	31
No opinion	6

Grade School

More strict	.51%
Less strict	3
Kept same	38
No opinion	8

By Region

East

More strict	.70%
Less strict	1
Kept same	23
No opinion	6

Midwest

More strict	.58%
Less strict	5
Kept same	33
No opinion	4

South

More strict	.57%
Less strict	5
Kept same	32
No opinion	6

West

More strict	.51%
Less strict	7
Kept same	36
No opinion	6

By Age

18–29 Years

More strict	.66%
Less strict	3
Kept same	27
No opinion	4

30–49 Years

More strict	.59%
Less strict	7
Kept same	29
No opinion	5

50 Years and Over

More strict	.55%
Less strict	3
Kept same	35
No opinion	7

All Gun Owners

More strict	.47%
Less strict	6
Kept same	44
No opinion	3

Handgun Owners Only

More strict	.39%
Less strict	9
Kept same	50
No opinion	2

Nonowners

More strict	.68%
Less strict	3
Kept same	22
No opinion	7

National Trend

	More strict	Less strict	Kept same	No opinion
May 1983	59%	4%	31%	6%
1982	65	3	30	2
1980	59	6	29	6
1975	69	3	24	4

In your opinion, if the laws on handguns were stricter than they are now, would this reduce the number of crimes a great deal, quite a lot, not very much, or not at all?

Great deal	17%
Quite a lot	24
Not very much	31
Not at all	25
No opinion	3

All Gun Owners

Great deal	10%
Quite a lot	19
Not very much	35
Not at all	35
No opinion	1

Handgun Owners Only

Great deal	11%
Quite a lot	15
Not very much	31
Not at all	42
No opinion	1

Nonowners

Great deal	22%
Quite a lot	28
Not very much	28
Not at all	18
No opinion	4

If the laws on handguns were stricter than they are now, would this reduce the number of people killed by guns in family arguments a great deal, quite a lot, not very much, or not at all?

Great deal	26%
Quite a lot	28
Not very much	25
Not at all	18
No opinion	3

All Gun Owners

Great deal	18%
Quite a lot	22
Not very much	31
Not at all	27
No opinion	2

Handgun Owners Only

Great deal	13%
Quite a lot	20
Not very much	30
Not at all	33
No opinion	4

Nonowners

Great deal	32%
Quite a lot	32
Not very much	21
Not at all	12
No opinion	3

If the laws on handguns were stricter than they are now, would this reduce the number of accidental deaths caused by guns a great deal, quite a lot, not very much, or not at all?

Great deal	26%
Quite a lot	27
Not very much	26
Not at all	17
No opinion	4

All Gun Owners

Great deal	18%
Quite a lot	22
Not very much	32
Not at all	25
No opinion	3

Handgun Owners Only

Great deal	16%
Quite a lot	19
Not very much	31
Not at all	31
No opinion	3

Nonowners

Great deal 32%
Quite a lot 30
Not very much 22
Not at all 12
No opinion 4

Note: The American people do not agree with President Ronald Reagan that handgun laws should be less strict and, in fact, believe that tougher laws would reduce the number of gun deaths resulting from family arguments and cut down on the number of accidental deaths caused by guns.

In the latest Gallup survey, 59% of all respondents—including 47% of gun owners—say the laws governing handgun sales should be stricter. Three persons in ten (31%) and 44% of gun owners would like the present laws retained. Merely 4% of respondents—and 6% of gun owners—want the laws relaxed. The latest findings represent a decrease since 1975 and in 1982 in the proportion opting for stricter gun laws but are the same as those recorded in 1980.

As shown, together with the 47% plurality of gun owners who favor stricter handgun laws are four handgun owners in ten (39%). Women are substantially more likely than men to opt for more restrictions on handgun sales. Also, young adults (18–29 years), the college educated, and easterners back tougher laws. The percentage favoring less strict handgun sales does not surpass 10% among any major population group.

JUNE 20
HANDGUN LAWS

Interviewing Date: 5/20–23/83
Survey #215-G

Some communities have passed laws banning the sale and possession of handguns. Would you favor or oppose having such a law in this city/community?

Favor 44%
Oppose 48
No opinion 8

By Sex
Male

Favor 36%
Oppose 59
No opinion 5

Female

Favor 52%
Oppose 37
No opinion 11

By Race
White

Favor 44%
Oppose 48
No opinion 8

Nonwhite

Favor 45%
Oppose 45
No opinion 10

By Education
College

Favor 47%
Oppose 48
No opinion 5

High School

Favor 43%
Oppose 48
No opinion 9

Grade School

Favor 41%
Oppose 47
No opinion 12

By Region
East

Favor 58%
Oppose 34
No opinion 8

Midwest

Favor 41%
Oppose 50
No opinion 9

South

Favor 35%
Oppose 55
No opinion 10

West

Favor 42%
Oppose 52
No opinion 6

By Age
18–29 Years

Favor 51%
Oppose 41
No opinion 8

30–49 Years

Favor 43%
Oppose 51
No opinion 6

50 Years and Over

Favor 40%
Oppose 49
No opinion 11

By Community Size
One Million and Over

Favor 58%
Oppose 31
No opinion 11

500,000–999,999

Favor 52%
Oppose 40
No opinion 8

50,000–499,999

Favor 47%
Oppose 45
No opinion 8

2,500–49,999

Favor 33%
Oppose 60
No opinion 7

Under 2,500; Rural

Favor 31%
Oppose 60
No opinion 9

All Gun Owners

Favor 28%
Oppose 68
No opinion 4

Handgun Owners Only

Favor 19%
Oppose 79
No opinion 2

Nonowners

Favor 55%
Oppose 34
No opinion 11

Those Who Favor Stricter Gun Laws

Favor 65%
Oppose 30
No opinion 5

Those Who Oppose Stricter Gun Laws

Favor 11%
Oppose 81
No opinion 8

Do you have any guns in the house? Is it a pistol, shotgun, or rifle?

Yes 40%
  Handgun 18

```
Rifle  . . . . . . . . . . . . . . . . . . . . . . . . . .25
Shotgun  . . . . . . . . . . . . . . . . . . . . . . .24
No  . . . . . . . . . . . . . . . . . . . . . . . . . . . . .60
```

National Trend

	Yes	Hand-gun	Rifle	Shot-gun	No
1980	44%	*	*	*	56%
1975	44	18	26	26	56
1972	43	16	26	27	57
1968	50	17	34	33	50
1965	48	16	24	33	52
1959	49	16	27	32	51

*Not asked

Asked of gun owners: What is the total number of handguns kept in your house?

```
Own one or more  . . . . . . . . . . . . . . . . . . . .18%
  One  . . . . . . . . . . . . . . . . . . . . . . . . . . . 9
  Two  . . . . . . . . . . . . . . . . . . . . . . . . . . . 4
  Three  . . . . . . . . . . . . . . . . . . . . . . . . . . 2
  Four or more  . . . . . . . . . . . . . . . . . . . . 1
  Don't know; no answer  . . . . . . . . . . . . . 2
```

Note: The Chicago suburb of Morton Grove, Illinois, made national headlines two years ago when it became the first municipality in the United States to enact an ordinance prohibiting both the sale and private possession of handguns. The Morton Grove ordinance has so far survived all legal challenges; the U.S. Supreme Court is expected to decide whether or not to hear the case at its next session.

Last November, Californians defeated a state-wide ballot initiative that would have placed stringent controls on the purchase and possession of handguns. The initiative would have required the registration of handguns, prohibited their sale through the mails, mandated a six-month jail sentence for anyone carrying an unregistered handgun, and restricted the future sale of handguns to law enforcement personnel.

The Gallup Poll has periodically made public opinion soundings on many of these handgun control measures and has consistently found Americans throughout the nation and from all walks of life supportive of stricter handgun laws. However, while the public heavily endorses more stringent controls, it has stopped short of favoring an outright ban on the sale or private possession of handguns.

There are major differences of opinion on this issue, not only on the basis of gun ownership, as would be expected, but also by demographic factors. Women, for example, favor a community ban on handguns by a convincing 15-percentage point edge. On the other hand, men oppose the ban by an even larger 23-point margin. In addition, the community handgun ban is favored by young adults (18–24 years), white-collar workers, and easterners. It is opposed by persons 30 and older, those whose education ended at the high-school level or earlier, blue-collar workers, and those from regions other than the East. It is interesting to note that even among the 59% majority in the survey who favor stricter laws governing the sale of handguns, some 30%—or about 18% of the total sample—nevertheless oppose a community prohibition on their sale and possession.

Residents of the nation's large cities (population of one-half million or over) favor a ban on the sale and possession of handguns, while residents of smaller communities and rural areas say they would vote against such a ban. The vote is nearly 2-to-1 in the largest cities (one million and more), 5-to-4 in favor among the next tier of cities (one-half million to one million), about evenly divided in the 50,000 to half-million group, but decidedly opposed among smaller cities and rural areas. Taking the views of the American public as a whole, opposition slightly outweighs support, 48% to 44%. At the same time, however, a 59% majority of Americans want stiffer handgun laws, as reported in an earlier poll.

If community laws banning handgun possession were enacted, a great many weapons would be involved. In the latest survey, 18% of the respondents say that someone in their household owns a handgun, and about half this proportion owns more than one.

Although reported ownership of any type of gun (40%) is somewhat lower than that recorded in earlier surveys, the handgun figure has not varied by more than 1 or 2 percentage points since these Gallup audits began in 1959.

JUNE 26
PRESIDENT REAGAN

Interviewing Date: 5/20–23/83
Survey #215-G

Do you approve or disapprove of the way Ronald Reagan is handling his job as president?

Approve 45%
Disapprove 43
No opinion 12

Would you like to see Ronald Reagan run for president in 1984, or not?

Would 36%
Would not 54
No opinion 10

By Politics
Republicans

Would 67%
Would not 26
No opinion 7

Democrats

Would 20%
Would not 72
No opinion 8

Independents

Would 38%
Would not 50
No opinion 12

National Trend

	Would	Would not	No opinion
December 1982	37%	56%	7%
August 1982	36	51	13
March 1982	35	52	13

Regardless of whether or not you would like to see him run, do you think Ronald Reagan will run for president in 1984, or not?

Will 79%
Will not 12
No opinion 9

By Politics
Republicans

Will 81%
Will not 10
No opinion 9

Democrats

Will 76%
Will not 16
No opinion 8

Independents

Will 83%
Will not 9
No opinion 8

National Trend

	Will	Will not	No opinion
December 1982	74%	16%	10%
August 1982	67	21	12
March 1982	59	30	11

Note: Speculation continues to mount that President Ronald Reagan will seek reelection in 1984, with four voters in five (79%) now expecting such a move. At about this time last year substantially fewer, 59%, thought Reagan would try for a second term. At the same time, however, two out of three Republicans (67%) in the latest Gallup survey say they would like to see Reagan run again, virtually unchanged from the 68% who expressed this view last year.

Currently, 36% of all voters say they would like to see Reagan stand for reelection, similar to the 35% recorded earlier. In four surveys conducted at regular intervals since March 1982, the proportion of adult Americans reporting they would like the president to run again has varied by no more than 2 percentage points. Although far more Republicans (67%) than independents (38%) or Democrats (20%) would like Reagan to run again, one-third of GOP members either would not like to see this (26%) or are uncommitted (7%). These figures, too, have changed little during the past fourteen months.

Aside from Republicans, greater opposition than support is found in almost all major population groups, including those with a Republican predisposition. College-educated respondents, for instance, oppose a Reagan bid for reelection by 51% to 42%. Even persons whose family income is $25,000 a year or more are narrowly divided, with 47% saying they would like to see the president run again, compared to 43% who would not.

Regardless of party affiliation, the proportion of the public indicating a desire for a Reagan rebid has consistently lagged behind the proportion approving of the way Reagan is handling his presidential duties. In the current survey, for example, Reagan's overall approval rating of 45% is 9 points higher than the 36% who would like to see him try for another term in the White House. In each of the four surveys, one voter in five who approved of his job performance nevertheless indicated he or she would not welcome a Reagan bid for a second term.

JUNE 26
BRITISH ELECTIONS

The British Gallup Poll's estimate of the outcome of their recent election was on the mark. The final preelection estimate showed a deviation of only 1.5 percentage points from the actual popular vote for both the Conservative and Labour parties and no deviation in the case of the Liberal/SD Alliance, as seen in the following table:

	Popular vote	British Gallup estimate	Deviation
Conservative	44%	45.5%	+ 1.5
Labour	28	26.5	− 1.5
Alliance	26	26.0	—
Others	2	2.0	—

JUNE 30
DEMOCRATIC PRESIDENTIAL CANDIDATES

Interviewing Date: 6/10–13/83
Survey #216-G

Asked of Democrats and independents: Which one of these persons would you like to see nominated as the Democratic party's candidate for president in 1984? [Respondents were handed a card listing the six announced candidates.]

Choice of Democrats

	June 10–13, 1983	April 29– May 2, 1983*	Point change
Walter Mondale ...	41%	31%	+ 10
John Glenn	24	25	− 1
Alan Cranston	8	4	+ 4
Gary Hart	3	4	− 1
Reubin Askew	3	1	+ 2
Ernest Hollings	1	2	− 1
None; don't know	20	33	− 13

Choice of Independents

Mondale	25%	25%	—
Glenn	28	19	+ 9
Cranston	7	3	+ 4
Hart	7	3	+ 4
Askew	2	2	—
Hollings	2	1	+ 1
None; don't know	29	47	− 18

With the Rev. Jesse Jackson considering the race for the Democratic nomination, the survey sought to measure his strength among Democratic voters nationwide, as well as his likely impact on the other candidates currently in the race. When Jackson is added to the list of announced candidates, he is found to win 8% of the vote, which puts him into a virtual tie with Cranston in the present rankings. A Jackson candidacy would appear to hurt Mondale to a somewhat greater extent than Glenn.

*This earlier survey included five more names on the list (unannounced candidates but considered possible nominees). To facilitate a comparison with the latest figures, support for these five candidates was reallocated to the six announced candidates on the basis of second choices.

The following table compares the current rankings with and without Jackson:

Choice of Democrats

	Jackson in	Jackson out
Mondale	36%	40%
Glenn	22	24
Jackson	8	—
Cranston	7	8
Askew	4	4
Hart	3	3
Hollings	1	1
None; don't know	19	20

Choice of Independents

Glenn	26%	27%
Mondale	24	25
Jackson	5	—
Cranston	7	8
Hart	5	6
Hollings	2	2
Askew	2	2
None; don't know	29	30

Asked of Democrats: Suppose the choice for president in the Democratic convention in 1984 narrows down to Walter Mondale and John Glenn. Which one would you prefer to have the Democratic convention select?

Mondale	57%
Glenn	31
Undecided	12

Note: Former Vice-president Walter Mondale has stretched his lead over Senator John Glenn of Ohio and the four other presently announced Democratic presidential candidates in the latest test of nomination support. Mondale is currently the choice of 41% of Democratic voters nationwide, up a full 10 points since an early May survey, to 24% for runner-up Glenn whose support has leveled off after a dramatic uptrend between December and early May.

JULY 3
PRESIDENTIAL TRIAL HEATS

Interviewing Date: 6/10–13/83
Survey #216-G

Asked of registered voters: Suppose the 1984 presidential election were being held today. If President Ronald Reagan were the Republican candidate and Walter Mondale were the Democratic candidate, which would you like to see win? [Those who named another candidate or who were undecided were asked: As of today, do you lean more to Reagan, the Republican, or to Mondale, the Democrat?]

Reagan	41%
Mondale	50
Other	3
Undecided	6

By Politics
Republicans

Reagan	81%
Mondale	14
Other	1
Undecided	4

Democrats

Reagan	16%
Mondale	77
Other	3
Undecided	4

Independents

Reagan	54%
Mondale	31
Other	4
Undecided	11

National Trend

	Reagan	Mondale	Other; undecided
June 1983	41%	50%	9%
April–May 1983 . .	43	49	8
February 1983. . . .	41	47	12
December 1982 . . .	40	52	8

Asked of registered voters: Suppose the 1984 presidential elections were being held today. If President Ronald Reagan were the Republican candidate and Senator John Glenn were the Democratic candidate, which would you like to see win? [Those who named another candidate or who were undecided were asked: As of today, do you lean more to Reagan, the Republican, or to Glenn, the Democrat?]

Reagan 38%
Glenn 53
Other 1
Undecided 8

By Politics
Republicans

Reagan 78%
Glenn 17
Other 1
Undecided 4

Democrats

Reagan 17%
Glenn 75
Other 2
Undecided 6

Independents

Reagan 42%
Glenn 43
Other 1
Undecided 14

National Trend

	Reagan	Glenn	Other; undecided
June 1983	38%	53%	9%
April–May 1983 . .	37	54	9
February 1983. . . .	40	45	15
December 1982 . . .	39	54	7

Note: Former Vice-president Walter Mondale and Senator John Glenn continue to lead President Ronald Reagan in the latest nationwide Gallup test elections by about the same margins as recorded in a previous survey. Mondale leads Reagan, 50% to 41%, in the latest matchup; these findings also closely parallel those from the earlier survey, which were 49% to 43%. Glenn runs a stronger race against the president than does Mondale; he currently leads Reagan 53% to 38%, closely paralleling the results of the previous results (54% to 37%) in late April–early May.

JULY 3
PRESIDENT REAGAN

Interviewing Date: 6/10–13/83
Survey #216-G

Do you approve or disapprove of the way Ronald Reagan is handling his job as president?

Approve 43%
Disapprove 45
No opinion 12

National Trend in 1983

	Approve
June 10–13	43%
May 20–23	45
May 13–16	43
April 29–May 2	43
April 15–18	41
March 11–14	41
February 25–28	40
January 28–31	35
January 21–24	37
January 14–17	37

Note: After an increase of nine percentage points since January, President Ronald Reagan's approval rating has leveled off in the latest survey, with 43% expressing approval and 45% disapproval of his performance in office. Statistically, these findings represent virtually no change from the previous (late April–early May) findings when 46% approved.

JULY 7
AIDS—ACQUIRED IMMUNE DEFICIENCY SYNDROME

Interviewing Date: 6/10–13/83
Survey #216-G

> Have you heard or read about a disease called AIDS—Acquired Immune Deficiency Syndrome?

	Yes
National	77%

> Asked of those who replied in the affirmative: Do you think this disease is likely to reach epidemic proportions?

Yes, likely	43%
No, not likely	35
No opinion	22

By Sex
Male

Yes, likely	37%
No, not likely	41
No opinion	22

Female

Yes, likely	48%
No, not likely	29
No opinion	23

By Race
White

Yes, likely	41%
No, not likely	37
No opinion	22

Nonwhite

Yes, likely	55%
No, not likely	16
No opinion	29

By Education
College

Yes, likely	38%
No, not likely	43
No opinion	19

High School

Yes, likely	46%
No, not likely	31
No opinion	23

Grade School

Yes, likely	39%
No, not likely	28
No opinion	33

By Region
East

Yes, likely	43%
No, not likely	38
No opinion	19

Midwest

Yes, likely	36%
No, not likely	38
No opinion	26

South

Yes, likely	45%
No, not likely	31
No opinion	24

West

Yes, likely	47%
No, not likely	31
No opinion	22

By Age
18–29 Years
Yes, likely 52%
No, not likely 30
No opinion 18

30–49 Years
Yes, likely 42%
No, not likely 39
No opinion 19

50 Years and Over
Yes, likely 37%
No, not likely 34
No opinion 29

Also asked of the aware group: Do you think a cure for this disease will or will not be found during the next year or two?

Yes, will be found 33%
No, will not 45
No opinion 22

By Sex
Male
Yes, will be found 36%
No, will not 43
No opinion 21

Female
Yes, will be found 31%
No, will not 46
No opinion 23

By Race
White
Yes, will be found 33%
No, will not 46
No opinion 21

Nonwhite
Yes, will be found 36%
No, will not 39
No opinion 25

By Education
College
Yes, will be found 35%
No, will not 47
No opinion 18

High School
Yes, will be found 34%
No, will not 43
No opinion 23

Grade School
Yes, will be found 24%
No, will not 51
No opinion 25

By Region
East
Yes, will be found 34%
No, will not 47
No opinion 19

Midwest
Yes, will be found 34%
No, will not 41
No opinion 25

South
Yes, will be found 32%
No, will not 44
No opinion 24

West
Yes, will be found 33%
No, will not 47
No opinion 20

By Age
18–29 Years
Yes, will be found 38%
No, will not 44
No opinion 18

30–49 Years

Yes, will be found .31%
No, will not 50
No opinion 19

50 Years and Over

Yes, will be found .32%
No, will not 41
No opinion 27

Note: Despite repeated statements by health authorities that for the vast majority of Americans there is little or no risk of falling victim to AIDS (Acquired Immune Deficiency Syndrome), many U.S. adults fear the disease is likely to reach epidemic proportions and do not believe an immediate cure will be found. Of those in a just-completed Gallup survey who have heard or read about the disease, 43% think AIDS will become an epidemic, and 35% do not believe a cure will be found in the next year or two. And 77% of Americans say they have heard or read about AIDS—a high percentage considering the disease was virtually unknown to the public a few months ago.

Health and Human Services Secretary Margaret Heckler, in a recent address to the 51st annual meeting of the U.S. Conference of Mayors, called AIDS, the cause of which is unknown, her agency's major public health priority. In her address, Heckler asked the mayors' help in stemming a tide of what she called "unnecessary and unjustified" fear about AIDS. "For the overwhelming majority of Americans," she said, "there appears to be little or no risk of falling victim to this disease—in particular through normal daily social contact."

Heckler said AIDS, which destroys a body's ability to fight infection, had killed 595 people in the United States. Of the 1,552 reported cases as of the time of Heckler's speech, 94% had occurred in homosexual or bisexual males with multiple sex partners, intravenous drug abusers, recent immigrants from Haiti, and people with hemophilia.

JULY 10
BALANCED BUDGET AMENDMENT

Interviewing Date: 6/10–13/83
Survey #216-G

Have you heard or read about the proposal for a constitutional amendment which would require the federal government to balance the national budget each year?

                                                              Yes
National 53%

Asked of those who replied in the affirmative: A proposed amendment to the Constitution would require Congress to approve a balanced federal budget each year. Government spending would have to be limited to no more than expected revenues, unless a three-fifths majority of Congress voted to spend more than expected revenues. Would you favor or oppose this amendment to the Constitution?

Favor 71%
Oppose 21
No opinion 8

By Education
College

Favor 70%
Oppose 24
No opinion 6

High School

Favor 75%
Oppose 18
No opinion 7

Grade School

Favor 54%
Oppose 23
No opinion 23

By Region

East

Favor 68%
Oppose 23
No opinion 9

Midwest

Favor 76%
Oppose 20
No opinion 4

South

Favor 69%
Oppose 18
No opinion 13

West

Favor 69%
Oppose 25
No opinion 6

By Politics

Republicans

Favor 77%
Oppose ....:15
No opinion 8

Democrats

Favor 66%
Oppose 26
No opinion 8

National Trend

	Favor	Oppose	No opinion
June 10–13, 1983	71%	21%	8%
May 1982	74	17	9
September 1981	73	19	8
April 1981	70	22	8

Note: Seven out of every ten Americans familiar with the proposal favor a constitutional amendment that would require Congress to balance the federal budget each year. Actually, the wishes of those who favor such an amendment may be coming closer to realization. Missouri recently became the 32nd state to pass a resolution calling for a constitutional convention to consider the balanced budget amendment. If only two more states approve similar resolutions, Congress will have to call such a meeting.

The last constitutional convention was held in 1787, two years before George Washington was elected president. Since 1787 all proposed amendments to the Constitution have been suggested by Congress after being approved by a two-thirds vote of both houses. But there is another legal method according to Article V of the Constitution: "on the application of the legislature of two-thirds of the several states, [Congress] shall call a convention for proposed amendments. . . ."

In the current survey, support among those familiar with the proposal far outweighs opposition in each of the four major regions of the nation. Republicans view the proposed amendment more favorably than do Democrats.

JULY 14
FUTURE THREAT TO COUNTRY

Interviewing Date: 5/13–16/83
Survey #214-G

In your opinion, which of the following will be the biggest threat to the country in the future—big business, big labor, or big government?

Big business 19%
Big labor 18
Big government 51
No opinion 13
                                    ————
                                    101%*

By Education

College

Big business 21%
Big labor 21
Big government 52
No opinion 8
                                    ————
                                    102%*

High School

Big business	19%
Big labor	16
Big government	53
No opinion	12

Grade School

Big business	14%
Big labor	19
Big government	43
No opinion	26
	102%*

By Region

East

Big business	21%
Big labor	20
Big government	47
No opinion	13
	101%*

Midwest

Big business	18%
Big labor	16
Big government	57
No opinion	10
	101%*

South

Big business	19%
Big labor	16
Big government	49
No opinion	17
	101%*

West

Big business	19%
Big labor	19
Big government	53
No opinion	9

By Age

18–29 Years

Big business	20%
Big labor	14
Big government	56
No opinion	11
	101%*

30–49 Years

Big business	18%
Big labor	19
Big government	55
No opinion	8

50 Years and Over

Big business	19%
Big labor	20
Big government	45
No opinion	18
	102%*

By Politics

Republicans

Big business	15%
Big labor	31
Big government	49
No opinion	7
	102%*

Democrats

Big business	21%
Big labor	12
Big government	53
No opinion	14

Independents

Big business	20%
Big labor	16
Big government	53
No opinion	13
	102%*

By Occupation

Professional and Business

Big business 18%
Big labor 24
Big government 53
No opinion 6
                                  ———
                                  101%*

Clerical and Sales

Big business 15%
Big labor 16
Big government 58
No opinion 11

Blue Collar Workers

Big business 21%
Big labor 13
Big government 54
No opinion 12

Labor Union Households

Big business 25%
Big labor 12
Big government 53
No opinion 11
                                  ———
                                  101%*

Nonlabor Union Households

Big business 18%
Big labor 20
Big government 51
No opinion 13
                                  ———
                                  102%*

*Total adds to more than 100% due to multiple responses.

National Trend

	Business	Labor	Government	No opinion
May 13–16,				
1983	19%	18%	51%	13%
1981	22	22	46	10
1979	28	17	43	12
1977	23	26	39	12

1968	12	26	46	16
1967	14	21	49	16
1959	15	41	14	30

Note: Far more Americans think that "big government" poses a threat to the nation than does either "big business" or "big labor," perhaps reflecting the huge federal deficits forecast for fiscal 1984 and beyond. In a recent Gallup survey, 51% name big government, 19% big business, and 18% big labor as cause for concern. The proportion currently citing big government is the highest recorded since these measurements began in 1959. In that first survey, merely 14% considered big government the greatest threat, compared to 41% who named big labor and 15% big business.

Roughly equal proportions of Republicans (49%), Democrats (53%), and independents (53%) currently cite big government as the greatest threat. A sizeable 31% minority of Republicans, however, compared to 16% of independents and 12% of Democrats, singles out big labor.

JULY 17
PRESIDENTIAL TRIAL HEATS

Interviewing Date: 6/10–13/83
Survey #216-G

Asked of registered voters: Suppose the 1984 presidential election were being held today. If President Ronald Reagan were the Republican candidate, running against Walter Mondale, the Democratic candidate, and John Anderson, an independent candidate, which would you like to see win? [Those who were undecided or who named another candidate were asked: As of today, do you lean more to Reagan, the Republican; to Mondale, the Democrat; or to Anderson, the independent?]

Reagan 38%
Mondale 40
Anderson 15
Other; undecided 7

By Sex

Male

Reagan 42%
Mondale 38
Anderson 14
Other; undecided 6

Female

Reagan 34%
Mondale 42
Anderson 17
Other; undecided 7

By Race

White

Reagan 43%
Mondale 36
Anderson 15
Other; undecided 6

Nonwhite

Reagan 7%
Mondale 69
Anderson 14
Other; undecided 10

By Education

College

Reagan 45%
Mondale 32
Anderson 20
Other; undecided 3

High School

Reagan 37%
Mondale 41
Anderson 14
Other; undecided 8

Grade School

Reagan 28%
Mondale 55
Anderson 6
Other; undecided 11

By Region

East

Reagan 30%
Mondale 43
Anderson 18
Other; undecided 9

Midwest

Reagan 43%
Mondale 40
Anderson 14
Other; undecided 3

South

Reagan 42%
Mondale 36
Anderson 13
Other; undecided 9

West

Reagan 39%
Mondale 40
Anderson 17
Other; undecided 4

By Age

18–29 Years

Reagan 35%
Mondale 37
Anderson 24
Other; undecided 4

30–49 Years

Reagan 41%
Mondale 39
Anderson 15
Other; undecided 5

50 Years and Over

Reagan 37%
Mondale 42
Anderson 12
Other; undecided 9

By Politics

Republicans

Reagan 88%
Mondale 11
Anderson 8
Other; undecided 3

Democrats

Reagan . . . . , ... 14%
Mondale 64
Anderson 15
Other; undecided 7

Independents

Reagan 48%
Mondale 19
Anderson 25
Other; undecided 8

Note: John Anderson's recent announcement of his intention to run as a third-party candidate for president in 1984 has renewed speculation about the impact such a move could have on the election. In a three-way test election for 1984, the Gallup Poll has found that Anderson is backed by 15% of registered voters nationwide, compared to 38% for President Ronald Reagan and 40% for Walter Mondale, presently the top choice of Democrats for their party's nomination.

Anderson's present level of support is somewhat lower than it was in the spring of 1980 when he began his campaign as an independent presidential candidate. In nine three-way test elections conducted between March 1980 and the Republican convention in July, Anderson's support from registered voters ranged from a low of 18% in April to a high of 24% in mid-June, averaging 21%. After the Republican and Democratic conventions, this support waned. In Gallup's final preelection survey, Anderson was the choice of 8% of likely voters; he received 6.7% of the popular vote in the election itself.

In the current survey, as in those conducted in 1980, Anderson demonstrates greater appeal for college-educated survey respondents, those under 30 years of age, and political independents. Most of his backing now comes from registered independents (25% of whom say they would vote for Anderson if the 1984 elections were being held now) and Democrats (15%). Only 8% of Republicans indicate a preference for the former GOP congressman from Illinois.

Contrary to the evidence of the 1980 surveys, in which Anderson's support came about equally from major-party opponents Jimmy Carter and Reagan, Anderson now draws much more backing from possible Democratic nominee Mondale than he does from the president. As reported recently, Mondale is now the choice of 50% of registered voters to 41% for Reagan in a two-way test election. Analysis shows that the addition of Anderson, making it a three-way contest, causes the Mondale vote to decline by 10 percentage points while Reagan loses only 3 points:

Test Elections Comparison

(Based on Registered Voters)

	Two-way	Three-way	Com-parison
Reagan	41%	38%	− 3
Mondale	50	40	− 10
Anderson	−	15	+ 15
Other; undecided	9	7	− 2

One probable reason why many voters deserted Anderson toward the end of the 1980 campaign was the fact that fewer voters than earlier in the later stages of the campaign perceived him to be middle-of-the-road, or were uncertain about where to place him on a political spectrum. Historically, presidential candidates who have veered too far to the left or to the right of the political ideology of the electorate have failed to win the election. Two examples are Senator George McGovern in 1972 and Senator Barry Goldwater in 1964.

The attractiveness of the center in American politics is seen in the fact that a proposed new "center party" has wide appeal for American voters. In fact, a political alignment which would include a center party in addition to the Republican and Democratic parties might have the support of

25% of voters. Interestingly, this is exactly the percentage won by the centrist SDP in the recent election in Great Britain.

JULY 21
CENTRAL AMERICA

Interviewing Date: 6/24–27/83
Survey #217-G

Have you heard or read about the situation in El Salvador?

	Yes
National	82%

Asked of those who replied in the affirmative: How likely do you think it is that the U.S. involvement in El Salvador could turn into a situation like Vietnam—that is, that the United States would become more and more deeply involved as time goes on? Would you say this is very likely, fairly likely, not very likely, or not at all likely?

Very likely	37%
Fairly likely	34
Not very likely	19
Not at all likely	5
No opinion	5

By Sex
Male

Very likely	36%
Fairly likely	31
Not very likely	22
Not at all likely	7
No opinion	5

Female

Very likely	39%
Fairly likely	36
Not very likely	16
Not at all likely	3
No opinion	6

By Race
White

Very likely	37%
Fairly likely	35
Not very likely	20
Not at all likely	4
No opinion	4

Nonwhite

Very likely	44%
Fairly likely	28
Not very likely	12
Not at all likely	7
No opinion	9

By Education
College

Very likely	32%
Fairly likely	36
Not very likely	25
Not at all likely	5
No opinion	2

High School

Very likely	41%
Fairly likely	35
Not very likely	15
Not at all likely	3
No opinion	6

Grade School

Very likely	42%
Fairly likely	22
Not very likely	15
Not at all likely	10
No opinion	11

By Region
East

Very likely	35%
Fairly likely	33
Not very likely	22
Not at all likely	5
No opinion	5

Midwest

Very likely	39%
Fairly likely	38
Not very likely	18
Not at all likely	3
No opinion	2

South

Very likely	38%
Fairly likely	29
Not very likely	19
Not at all likely	7
No opinion	7

West

Very likely	40%
Fairly likely	35
Not very likely	14
Not at all likely	5
No opinion	6

By Age
18–24 Years

Very likely	33%
Fairly likely	38
Not very likely	20
Not at all likely	4
No opinion	5

25–29 Years

Very likely	30%
Fairly likely	41
Not very likely	20
Not at all likely	3
No opinion	6

30–49 Years

Very likely	44%
Fairly likely	32
Not very likely	17
Not at all likely	3
No opinion	4

50 Years and Over

Very likely	36%
Fairly likely	31
Not very likely	20
Not at all likely	7
No opinion	6

By Politics
Republicans

Very likely	26%
Fairly likely	34
Not very likely	28
Not at all likely	9
No opinion	3

Democrats

Very likely	47%
Fairly likely	36
Not very likely	10
Not at all likely	3
No opinion	4

Independents

Very likely	34%
Fairly likely	31
Not very likely	23
Not at all likely	4
No opinion	8

Those Who Approve of Reagan's Overall Job Performance

Very, fairly likely	60%
Not very, not at all likely	34
No opinion	6

Those Who Disapprove of Reagan's Overall Job Performance

Very, fairly likely	84%
Not very, not at all likely	13
No opinion	3

Those Who Approve of Reagan's Handling of Central American Situation

Very, fairly likely	53%
Not very, not at all likely	43
No opinion	4

Those Who Disapprove of Reagan's Handling of Central American Situation

Very, fairly likely 85%
Not very, not at all likely 12
No opinion 3

Do you approve or disapprove of the way President Ronald Reagan is handling the situation in Central America?

Approve 25%
Disapprove 46
No opinion 29

By Sex
Male

Approve 30%
Disapprove 49
No opinion 21

Female

Approve 21%
Disapprove 43
No opinion 36

By Race
White

Approve 27%
Disapprove 43
No opinion 30

Nonwhite

Approve 15%
Disapprove 60
No opinion 25

By Education
College

Approve 30%
Disapprove 49
No opinion 21

High School

Approve 24%
Disapprove 44
No opinion 32

Grade School

Approve 21%
Disapprove 45
No opinion 34

By Region
East

Approve 24%
Disapprove 45
No opinion 31

Midwest

Approve 22%
Disapprove 48
No opinion 30

South

Approve 32%
Disapprove 40
No opinion 28

West

Approve 22%
Disapprove 52
No opinion 26

By Age
18–24 Years

Approve 22%
Disapprove 45
No opinion 33

25–29 Years

Approve 19%
Disapprove 51
No opinion 30

30–49 Years

Approve 28%
Disapprove 47
No opinion 25

50 Years and Over

Approve 26%
Disapprove 44
No opinion 30

By Politics
Republicans

Approve 45%
Disapprove 29
No opinion 26

Democrats

Approve 17%
Disapprove 58
No opinion 25

Independents

Approve 24%
Disapprove 41
No opinion 35

Note: A majority of Americans continues to fear that greater U.S. involvement in El Salvador could develop into a situation like Vietnam, despite assurances from Washington to the contrary. In the latest Gallup survey, 71% of persons familiar with the El Salvador situation—82% of the total—believe it is at least fairly likely the United States will become more deeply enmeshed with the passage of time. In contrast, 19% think this is not very likely and merely 5% that it is not at all likely to occur.

In the same survey, one person in four, 25%, expresses approval of President Ronald Reagan's handling of the Central American situation, while 46% disapprove and 29% are uncommitted. This represents a modest improvement since an April survey, when only 21% approved and 49% disapproved of Reagan's efforts.

The public's assessment of the president's actions is closely linked to its fears of a Vietnam-like involvement. As shown in the table below, only 20% of those in the survey who say the United States is very or fairly likely to become more deeply embroiled approve of Reagan's handling of the Central American situation, while 60% disapprove. However, among the minority who are not too concerned about the U.S. involvement, 49% approve of his conduct there.

Reagan's handling of Central American situation	Likelihood of Another Vietnam		
	Total U.S.	Very, fairly likely	Not very, not at all likely
Approve	25%	20%	49%
Disapprove	46	60	26
No opinion	29	20	25

Evidence of the widespread public fear that our El Salvador involvement could turn into another Vietnam is seen in the fact that even among those most supportive of the administration's actions—Republicans, persons approving of Reagan's overall job performance, and those approving of the president's handling of the Central American situation—majorities think it is at least fairly likely El Salvador could become a problem resembling Vietnam.

JULY 24
PRESIDENT REAGAN

Interviewing Date: 6/24–27/83
Survey #217-G

Do you approve or disapprove of the way Ronald Reagan is handling his job as president?

Approve 47%
Disapprove............................44
No opinion............................9

Asked of those who replied that they approve: How strongly would you say you approve/disapprove—very strongly or not so strongly?

Approve
Very strongly 21%
Not so strongly 26
Disapprove
Not so strongly 15
Very strongly 29
                                  91%

By Sex
Male

Approve
Very strongly 26%
Not so strongly 26
Disapprove
Not so strongly 16
Very strongly 26
                                  94%

Female

Approve
Very strongly 17%
Not so strongly 25
Disapprove
Not so strongly 15
Very strongly 31
                                  88%

By Race
White

Approve
Very strongly 24%
Not so strongly 27
Disapprove
Not so strongly 16
Very strongly 25
                                  92%

Nonwhite

Approve
Very strongly 4%
Not so strongly 18
Disapprove
Not so strongly 17
Very strongly 47
                                  86%

By Politics
Republicans

Approve
Very strongly 54%
Not so strongly..................... 28
Disapprove
Not so strongly..................... 6
Very strongly 7
                                      95%

Democrats

Approve
Very strongly 9%
Not so strongly..................... 19
Disapprove
Not so strongly..................... 21
Very strongly 43
                                      92%

Independents

Approve
Very strongly 17%
Not so strongly..................... 33
Disapprove
Not so strongly..................... 15
Very strongly 23
                                      88%

Note: President Ronald Reagan's job performance rating is at its highest level in sixteen months, defying the third-year downturn in approval ratings usually accorded chief executives. In the most recent (late June) survey, 47% approve of the way he is handling his job as president, while 44% disapprove, statistically matching his scores (46% and 43%) in a late May survey. The last time Reagan's rating was as high was in February 1982, when his score was also 47%.

From a high point of 68% in May 1981, the president's approval rating, with only brief periods of stabilization, trended downward, dipping to 35% in late January of this year. Since then his rating has climbed slowly but steadily.

The upturn in Reagan's job performance ratings—which undoubtedly reflects, at least in part, the strengthening of the economy—runs counter to the historical pattern observed for his elected predecessors during the third year of their tenure. Presidents Jimmy Carter, Richard Nixon, and John Kennedy suffered significant declines during this period, while Dwight Eisenhower in May 1955 stood about where he began the year. At the start of 1983, Reagan's approval rating was below those of his predecessors; his latest rating tops Carter's and is only 4 percentage points lower than Nixon's.

JULY 28
CIGARETTE SMOKING

Interviewing Date: 4/15–18/83
Survey #212-G

Have you, yourself, smoked any cigarettes in the past week?

	Yes
National	38%

By Sex

Male	40%
Female	36

By Race

White	38%
Nonwhite	37

By Education

College	30%
High school	43
Grade school	35

By Region

East	41%
Midwest	39
South	39
West	31

By Age

18–29 years	44%
30–49 years	42
50–64 years	36
65 years and over	20

By Income

$20,000 and over	36%
Under $20,000	39

By Occupation

Professional and business	29%
Clerical and sales	46
Blue collar—Total	49
Skilled workers	40
Unskilled workers	54

National Trend

1983	38%
1981	35
1978	36
1977	38
1974	40
1973	40
1972	43
1971	42
1969	40
1958	45
1957	42
1954	45
1949	44
1944	41

Note: Despite strong health warnings on cigarette packages and a stiff new federal cigarette tax, the incidence of cigarette smoking in the United States has not declined during the last two years. In the latest Gallup audit, 38% of survey respondents have smoked cigarettes during the week prior to being interviewed. This is statistically unchanged from the 35% recorded in 1981. However, the proportion of smokers in the adult population has declined since the Surgeon General's historic 1964 report linking smoking to serious health hazards such as cancer and heart disease.

As in past Gallup surveys, more men (40%) than women (36%) are smokers. Another important demographic determinant is education; substantially smaller numbers of persons who attended college are smokers (30%) than are those whose education ended at the high-school (43%) or grade-school (35%) level.

A related factor is occupation. Only 29% of

survey respondents from households in which the chief wage earner is employed in business or the professions are smokers, compared to 46% in homes headed by workers in other white-collar occupations and 48% in blue-collar households. A large difference is found in the percentage of cigarette smokers from homes headed by skilled workers (40%) versus unskilled workers (54%).

In the current survey, the incidence of cigarette smoking drops sharply as age increases, from 44% of persons 18 to 29 years old, to 42% of 30 to 49 year olds, to 36% of those ages 50 to 64, to 20% of persons 65 and older. Cigarette smoking is influenced to only a minor degree by race, family income, or geographic region.

JULY 28
PROTECTIONISM AND CONSUMER OPINION AT ODDS*

At least one likely legacy of the 1981–82 recession is a mild case of American consumer schizophrenia in the matter of imported products. Opinion polls show that, on the one hand, Americans strongly favor greater trade restrictions on imports, but on the other, they have a healthy respect for the quality and value offered by imported goods.

Virtually all opinion polls on the subject show the public favoring greater trade restrictions to protect American industries and jobs, even if it means some consumer sacrifice. A May *Newsweek* Poll by Gallup found 55% favoring increased taxes on imports to protect jobs, while 36% opposed these taxes "which might lead to higher consumer prices." Similarly, a *Los Angeles Times* Poll in May had an even larger majority (68%) believing there should be a policy to restrict foreign imports "in order to protect American industry and jobs." Only 26% were opposed "in order to permit the widest choice and lowest price for consumers." Consistently, Americans say policy

*This Gallup analysis was written by Andrew Kohut, president of the Gallup Organization Inc.

should favor protection of jobs over protection of consumer choice or value.

That is the case at the policy level, but at the consumer level Americans are candid about acting in their own self-interest. Reflecting their current views about trade policy, people now say they are less apt to buy imported products than they were ten years ago. In 1973, a Gallup survey found only 34% were "less inclined to purchase imports." Throughout the 1970s, there was a steady increase in that sentiment; by 1983, the *Newsweek* Poll found 53% expressing this view. But market shares and international trade statistics belie Americans' expressed desire not to buy imports.

The *Newsweek* Poll found close to eight in ten (78%) of its respondents reporting that they buy the best product for them whether it is American-made or not. The same poll showed in an experiment that when all things are equal, 94% will choose an American brand over an imported brand, but when the American brand costs as little as ten percent more, consumer preference divides evenly between it and the import. To a greater extent than in years past, Americans want to buy American, but in tough economic times this is often a desire which cannot be realized.

The *Los Angeles Times* and the *Newsweek/Gallup* polls both show that in many product areas imports, especially Japanese imports, are seen as rivals in quality to American brands. With specific regard to autos, the *Los Angeles Times* found that Japanese automobiles are seen as equal if not better in quality than American automobiles and are even more clearly seen as a better value. Some 40% thought Japanese automobiles are a better value for the money, while only 22% believed they are not.

Despite such consumer views and behavior, public pressure for import restrictions seems resolute. In the January *New York Times*/CBS Poll, competition from foreign products was cited more often than any other factor, except high interest rates, as a cause of unemployment in the United States. Since then Gallup found for *Newsweek* that voters now regard import restrictions as one of the three most important campaign issues for 1984.

Opinion is as intense as it is because Americans see cheap labor as the main reason for the success of imports; over seven in ten see lower labor costs behind the success of imported brands in the United States. Many fewer believe that better engineering and design (39%), better management (36%), or obsolete American manufacturing plants (34%) account for the popularity of imports in the United States. However, the public sees overseas workers as taking more pride in their work (55%) and overseas managers as putting more emphasis on quality.

Although a need for restricting imports and a desire to buy American is evident among respondents of all ages, young people seem the least concerned about the import problem. Consumers under 30 years of age pay less attention to country of origin, are not as inclined to buy American, and have a more favorable opinion of imported brands. For example, only one-third of Gallup/ *Newsweek*'s young respondents are less inclined to buy imports compared to 64% of those age 50 and over. Only 39% of young people think that American cars are superior to imports, while 57% of those age 50 and over hold that opinion.

Although young people are far less nationalistic in their consumer views, they agree with their elders when it comes to the issue of more protection for American jobs from overseas competition. A majority of Americans of all ages embraces that notion, even though as consumers they continue to regard imports favorably and to purchase them eagerly.

	1983	1981*
Favor	50%	45%
Oppose	43	46
No opinion	7	9

*Included for comparative purposes. The 1981 results are based on Survey #173-G; Interviewing Date: May 8–11, 1981.

By Sex
Male

Favor	56%	47%
Oppose	37	44
No opinion	7	9

Female

Favor	46%	43%
Oppose	48	49
No opinion	6	8

By Race
White

Favor	52%	46%
Oppose	42	46
No opinion	6	8

Nonwhite

Favor	44%	38%
Oppose	45	51
No opinion	11	11

By Education
College

Favor	60%	58%
Oppose	35	35
No opinion	5	7

High School

Favor	49%	41%
Oppose	44	49
No opinion	7	10

Grade School

Favor	36%	33%
Oppose	54	59
No opinion	10	8

JULY 31
ABORTION

Interviewing Date: 6/24–27/83
Survey #217-G

The U.S. Supreme Court has ruled that a woman may go to a doctor to end her pregnancy at any time during the first three months of pregnancy. Do you favor or oppose this ruling?

By Region

East

Favor	59%	51%
Oppose	36	38
No opinion	5	11

Midwest

Favor	43%	37%
Oppose	49	54
No opinion	8	9

South

Favor	47%	40%
Oppose	46	52
No opinion	7	8

West

Favor	54%	57%
Oppose	39	37
No opinion	7	6

By Age

18–24 Years

Favor	52%	44%
Oppose	44	46
No opinion	4	10

25–29 Years

Favor	58%	48%
Oppose	38	43
No opinion	4	9

30–49 Years

Favor	51%	50%
Oppose	44	43
No opinion	5	7

50 Years and Over

Favor	47%	40%
Oppose	42	51
No opinion	11	9

By Politics

Republicans

Favor	48%	47%
Oppose	45	45
No opinion	7	8

Democrats

Favor	50%	41%
Oppose	44	50
No opinion	6	9

Independents

Favor	54%	39%
Oppose	39	55
No opinion	7	6

By Religion

Protestants

Favor	50%	45%
Oppose	43	46
No opinion	7	9

Catholics

Favor	47%	37%
Oppose	48	56
No opinion	5	7

National Trend

	Favor	Oppose	No opinion
1983	50%	43%	7%
1981	45	46	9
1974	47	44	9

Do you think abortions should be legal under any circumstances, legal under only certain circumstances, or illegal in all circumstances?

Legal, any circumstances	23%
Legal, certain circumstances	58
Illegal, all circumstances	16
No opinion	3

By Sex

Male

Legal, any circumstances 24%
Legal, certain circumstances 57
Illegal, all circumstances 16
No opinion 3

Female

Legal, any circumstances 22%
Legal, certain circumstances 58
Illegal, all circumstances 17
No opinion 3

By Race

White

Legal, any circumstances 23%
Legal, certain circumstances 60
Illegal, all circumstances 15
No opinion 2

Nonwhite

Legal, any circumstances 23%
Legal, certain circumstances 46
Illegal, all circumstances 26
No opinion 5

By Education

College

Legal, any circumstances 32%
Legal, certain circumstances 56
Illegal, all circumstances 10
No opinion 2

High School

Legal, any circumstances 22%
Legal, certain circumstances 59
Illegal, all circumstances 16
No opinion 3

Grade School

Legal, any circumstances 10%
Legal, certain circumstances 55
Illegal, all circumstances 29
No opinion 6

By Region

East

Legal, any circumstances 29%
Legal, certain circumstances 53
Illegal, all circumstances 16
No opinion 2

Midwest

Legal, any circumstances 21%
Legal, certain circumstances 60
Illegal, all circumstances 17
No opinion 2

South

Legal, any circumstances 17%
Legal, certain circumstances 60
Illegal, all circumstances 19
No opinion 4

West

Legal, any circumstances 27%
Legal, certain circumstances 58
Illegal, all circumstances 12
No opinion 3

By Age

18–24 Years

Legal, any circumstances 20%
Legal, certain circumstances 58
Illegal, all circumstances 21
No opinion 1

25–29 Years

Legal, any circumstances 31%
Legal, certain circumstances 57
Illegal, all circumstances 10
No opinion 2

30–49 Years

Legal, any circumstances 26%
Legal, certain circumstances 58
Illegal, all circumstances 14
No opinion 2

50 Years and Over

Legal, any circumstances 19%
Legal, certain circumstances 58
Illegal, all circumstances 18
No opinion 5

By Politics

Republicans

Legal, any circumstances 21%
Legal, certain circumstances 61
Illegal, all circumstances 15
No opinion 3

Democrats

Legal, any circumstances 23%
Legal, certain circumstances 56
Illegal, all circumstances 17
No opinion 4

Independents

Legal, any circumstances 24%
Legal, certain circumstances 59
Illegal, all circumstances 16
No opinion 1

By Religion

Protestants

Legal, any circumstances 20%
Legal, certain circumstances 62
Illegal, all circumstances 15
No opinion 3

Catholics

Legal, any circumstances 22%
Legal, certain circumstances 57
Illegal, all circumstances 19
No opinion 2

National Trend

	Legal, any	Legal, certain	Illegal, all	No opinion
1983	23%	58%	16%	3%
1981	23	52	21	4
1980	25	53	18	4
1979	22	54	19	5
1977	22	55	19	4
1975	21	54	22	3

Note: In the aftermath of the U.S. Supreme Court's recent reaffirmation of its historic ruling on abortion ten years ago, the public remains closely divided on this vital issue. In the latest survey, 50% agree with the Court's ruling that a woman may go to a doctor to end her pregnancy at any time during the first three months, while 43% are opposed. These findings represent a slight increase in support for the Court's decision since a 1981 survey, when 45% were in favor and 46% opposed. In a 1974 survey, 47% backed the Court's ruling, while 44% were in opposition.

The increase in support since the 1981 survey has been somewhat more pronounced among Catholics (up 10 percentage points) than Protestants (5 points), with the result that the two groups currently hold views on the Court decision that are comparable. Although marginally more women now (46%) than in 1981 (43%) take a liberal stand on abortion, the views of men have grown substantially in this direction, from 47% in favor in 1981 to 56% at present.

The recent 6-to-3 Court decision struck down laws in Ohio and Missouri requiring that abortions after the first trimester of pregnancy be performed in hospitals rather than clinics. The Court said the government cannot interfere with a woman's fundamental right to have an abortion in any place or manner, unless the decision is based on accepted medical practice.

The 1973 decision, reaffirmed in the recent Court review, said that the states cannot place restrictions on a woman's right to an abortion during the first three months of pregnancy. In the second three months the Court said that the state still has no authority to prevent abortion, but that it can regulate certain of the medical aspects involved. Only during the final three months, when medical experts generally agree that the fetus is capable of living outside the womb, can states impose restrictions on a woman's right to an abortion.

Another survey question sought to determine what changes, if any, have come about in the proportions of Americans who believe abortions should be "legal under any circumstances" and those who hold the belief that abortions should be "illegal in all circumstances." Paralleling the small increase in public support for the 1973 ruling, the current survey shows a 5 percentage-point decline since 1981 in the proportion who think that abortions should be outlawed, from 21% to 16%, and a concomitant increase of 6 points in those believing that circumstances should dictate the legality of abortions, from 52% to 58%.

AUGUST 4
HONESTY AND ETHICAL STANDARDS

Interviewing Date: 5/20–23/83
Survey #215-G

How would you rate the honesty and ethical standards of people in these different fields— very high, high, average, low, or very low:

Clergymen?

Very high; high 64%
Average 27
Low; very low 5
No opinion 4

Druggists; pharmacists?

Very high; high 61%
Average 33
Low; very low 4
No opinion 2

Medical doctors?

Very high; high 53%
Average 35
Low; very low 10
No opinion 2

Dentists?

Very high; high 51%
Average 41
Low; very low 5
No opinion 3

College teachers?

Very high; high 47%
Average 38
Low; very low 5
No opinion 10

Engineers?

Very high; high 46%
Average 39
Low; very low 3
No opinion 12

Policemen?

Very high; high 42%
Average 45
Low; very low 11
No opinion 2

Bankers?

Very high; high 38%
Average 49
Low; very low 9
No opinion 4

Television reporters; commentators?

Very high; high 33%
Average 47
Low; very low 15
No opinion 5

Funeral directors?

Very high; high 29%
Average 43
Low; very low 19
No opinion 9

Newspaper reporters?

Very high; high 26%
Average 52
Low; very low 16
No opinion 6

Lawyers?

Very high; high	24%
Average	43
Low; very low	27
No opinion	6

Stockbrokers?

Very high; high	19%
Average	45
Low; very low	11
No opinion	25

Business executives?

Very high; high	18%
Average	55
Low; very low	20
No opinion	7

Senators?

Very high; high	17%
Average	48
Low; very low	29
No opinion	6

Building contractors?

Very high; high	17%
Average	54
Low; very low	23
No opinion	6

Local political officeholders?

Very high; high	16%
Average	49
Low; very low	29
No opinion	6

Congressmen?

Very high; high	14%
Average	43
Low; very low	38
No opinion	5

Realtors?

Very high; high	13%
Average	52
Low; very low	28
No opinion	7

State political officeholders?

Very high; high	13%
Average	49
Low; very low	31
No opinion	7

Insurance salesmen?

Very high; high	13%
Average	49
Low; very low	34
No opinion	4

Labor union leaders?

Very high; high	12%
Average	35
Low; very low	44
No opinion	9

Advertising practitioners?

Very high; high	8%
Average	43
Low; very low	39
No opinion	10

Car salesmen?

Very high; high	6%
Average	34
Low; very low	55
No opinion	5

Note: Of twenty-four occupations studied, the public rates clergymen and pharmacists highest in terms of their perceived honesty and ethical standards. Although some occupations receive low ratings in these studies, it is important to bear in mind that the findings reflect the public's perceptions, and are not necessarily indicative of the true ethical standards of the groups studied. At the same time, however, the results suggest a need for remedial efforts on the part of poorly rated professions and occupations.

Clergymen, as in each of the earlier surveys, come out at the top of the scale, with 64% of respondents giving them a very high or high rating. Next are pharmacists or druggists, with a 61% positive rating. Following closely are medical doctors, dentists, college teachers, engineers, and policemen, with positive scores ranging from 53% to 42%. In the next tier are bankers, television reporters or commentators, funeral directors, newspaper reporters, and lawyers, with ratings from 38% to 24%.

Ten occupational groups are given very high or high ratings by 19% to 12%: stockbrokers, business executives, senators, building contractors, local political officeholders, congressmen, realtors, state political officeholders, insurance salesmen, and labor union leaders. The range of positive ratings for the four political offices tested varies by only four percentage points, from 17% to 13%, and offers evidence of the poor public image of politicians in the United States. Advertising practitioners and car salesmen occupy the lowest two positions, receiving positive ratings from only 8% to 6% of survey respondents, respectively.

Collectively, the occupations that receive the lowest scores for honesty and ethics are those that involve selling. Only about one person in ten rates the ethics of realtors, insurance salesmen, advertising practitioners, and auto salesmen in positive terms. In contrast, about three persons in ten rate each of these occupations as very low or low. These findings suggest that occupations which depend heavily on personal salesmanship to promote their products and services have done a poor job of selling themselves.

AUGUST 7
PRESIDENT REAGAN'S GENDER GAP—A SUMMARY

Despite the administration's efforts to minimize President Ronald Reagan's gender gap—proportionately fewer women than men approve of the president and his programs—recent surveys contain no evidence that this is being accomplished. The president's latest approval rating of 47% is up sharply since January, in tempo with the economy. It now stands at its highest level in almost one and one-half years. Nevertheless, in terms of the gender gap, Reagan ended the first six months of 1983 where he began the year, with a 10-percentage point deficit in the proportion of women (42%) versus men (52%) approving of the way he is handling his presidential duties.

Women have given Reagan lower competency ratings than have men in each of the forty-nine national Gallup surveys conducted since he took office. The discrepancy has ranged from a low of 3 percentage points (April 1983 and January 1982) to a high of 16 (September 1981) and has averaged 9 points during Reagan's tenure.

The following table shows the full trend for 1983 and a summary of the record to date:

Reagan Performance Ratings

(Percent Approving)

1983	Both sexes	Men	Women
June 24–27	47%	52%	42%
June 10-13	43	47	40
May 20–23	46	49	43
May 13–16	43	50	36
April 29–May 2	43	48	38
April 15–18	41	42	39
March 11–14	41	47	35
February 25–28	40	43	37
January 28–31	35	39	32
January 21–24	37	39	35
January 14–17	37	42	32
Averages			
Entire tenure	49%	53%	44%
1983 to date	41	45	37
1982	44	48	40
1981	58	62	53

As shown below, major differences by sex are not found in the public's assessments of Reagan's predecessors. The figures show Reagan's average for his tenure to date and the full tenure of his predecessors:

Presidential Performance Ratings

(Percent Approving)

	Both sexes	Men	Women
Reagan	49%	53%	44%
Carter	47	46	47
Ford	46	45	46
Nixon	49	50	47
Johnson	55	56	54
Kennedy	70	70	70
Eisenhower	64	63	65

The reasons underlying the gender gap generally are considered to center on the peace issue—with women more likely than men to think Reagan might lead the United States into war—and on women's more liberal stance on some social issues. Women, for instance, have been more opposed than men to the death penalty and to relaxing environmental standards. They also have tended more than men to perceive the Reagan administration's economic programs as treating minorities, the elderly, and low-income groups unfairly.

In a speech before the American Bar Association last week, President Reagan strongly defended his record on women. Not only had he appointed the first woman to the U.S. Supreme Court and three women to his cabinet, the president said, but he has named more women to top government positions than did any preceding administration. Reagan also cited as evidence of his concern over women's rights the reduction of the "marriage penalty" tax and the increase in tax credits for child care.

AUGUST 11
PRESIDENT REAGAN

Interviewing Date: 7/22–25/83
Survey #218-G

Do you approve or disapprove of the way Ronald Reagan is handling his job as president?

Approve 42%
Disapprove 47
No opinion 11

Note: President Ronald Reagan's job performance rating declined by 5 percentage points in late July, after having reached a sixteen-month peak one month earlier. In a Gallup survey completed on July 25, 42% of the public expressed approval of the way Reagan was handling his presidential duties, while 47% disapproved. In late June, the figures were almost reversed: 47% approved, 44% disapproved.

Reagan's drop in approval can be attributed almost entirely to a loss of confidence on the part of women, among whom the president suffered an 8-point decline since the earlier survey, from 42% to 34% approval. Among men, Reagan's job performance score was statistically unchanged, with 51% in the latest survey compared to 52% in June approving.

The president's current gender gap of 17 percentage points—the difference in the proportions of men and women approving of his job performance—is the largest recorded in fifty Gallup surveys conducted since Reagan took office. In the June survey his deficit among women was 10 points, about the same as the 9-point average throughout his tenure.

The table below summarizes Reagan's approval ratings from men and women:

Reagan Performance Ratings

(Percent Approving)

1983	Both sexes	Men	Women
July 22–25	42%	51%	34%
June 24–27	47	52	42
Second quarter	44	48	40
First quarter	38	42	34
1982	44	48	40
1981	58	62	53
Tenure to date	48	53	44

There are no measurements in the new survey that would permit examination of a possible link between the president's sudden drop in popularity and the recent developments in Central America. However, it bears noting that in past surveys women have been particularly sensitive to what they perceive as threats to world peace, and, on the day the latest survey began, Reagan unveiled his administration's plan for a substantial increase in U.S. military involvement in the region.

AUGUST 14
DEMOCRATIC PRESIDENTIAL CANDIDATES

Interviewing Date: 7/22–25/83
Survey #218-G

Asked of Democrats and independents: Which one of these persons [respondents were handed a card listing seven names and titles of possible nominees] would you like to see nominated as the Democratic party's candidate for president in 1984? And who would be your second choice?

Choice of Democrats

(Without Edward Kennedy on List)

Walter Mondale	41%
John Glenn	25
Alan Cranston	7
Gary Hart	4
Reubin Askew	2
Ernest Hollings	2
None; don't know	19

Choice of Independents

(Without Edward Kennedy on List)

Mondale	32%
Glenn	31
Cranston	4
Hart	4
Askew	2
Hollings	2
None; don't know	25

Choice of Democrats

(With Edward Kennedy on List)

Kennedy	32%
Mondale	26
Glenn	18
Cranston	5
Askew	2
Hart	2
Hollings	2
None; don't know	13

Choice of Independents

(With Edward Kennedy on List)

Kennedy	23%
Mondale	23
Glenn	23
Cranston	3
Askew	3
Hart	2
Hollings	2
None; don't know	21

Note: With one year remaining until the Democrats convene in San Francisco to choose their 1984 presidential nominee, Walter Mondale holds a wide 8-to-5 lead over Senator John Glenn for the post. A late July Gallup survey found Mondale the choice of 41% of Democrats to 25% for Glenn, virtually unchanged from the findings of a survey conducted six weeks earlier. Next in the latest ranking is Senator Alan Cranston with 7%, followed by Senator Gary Hart with 4%, and former Florida Governor Reubin Askew and Senator Ernest Hollings, each with 2% of Democrats' votes.

Despite his determined noncandidate status, speculation continues over how Senator Edward Kennedy would fare against the announced candidates for the Democratic nomination. When Kennedy's name is entered into these test election contests, as shown below, he wins more of Democrats' votes than either Mondale or Glenn.

Among independents, with Kennedy in the nomination the contest becomes a three-way dead heat between Glenn, Kennedy, and Mondale, with each man receiving 23% of independents' votes.

In the nomination contest among Democrats, Mondale benefits twice as much as Glenn when Kennedy's name is omitted. However among independents, Kennedy's vote splits about evenly between the two front-runners.

AUGUST 18
PRESIDENTIAL TRIAL HEATS

Interviewing Date: 7/29–8/1/83
Survey #219-G

Asked of registered voters: Suppose the 1984 presidential election were being held today. If President Ronald Reagan were the Republican candidate and Walter Mondale were the Democratic candidate, which would you like to see win? [Those who named another candidate or who were undecided were asked: As of today, do you lean more to Reagan, the Republican, or to Mondale, the Democrat?]

Reagan 44%
Mondale 42
Other; undecided 14

By Sex
Male

Reagan 48%
Mondale 38
Other; undecided 14

Female

Reagan 41%
Mondale 46
Other; undecided 13

By Race
White

Reagan 50%
Mondale 37
Other; undecided 13

Nonwhite

Reagan 7%
Mondale 72
Other; undecided 21

By Education
College

Reagan 50%
Mondale 37
Other; undecided 13

High School

Reagan 45%
Mondale 42
Other; undecided 13

Grade School

Reagan 28%
Mondale 55
Other; undecided 17

By Region
East

Reagan 39%
Mondale 44
Other; undecided 17

Midwest

Reagan 51%
Mondale 41
Other; undecided 8

South

Reagan 41%
Mondale 45
Other; undecided 14

West

Reagan 46%
Mondale 38
Other; undecided 16

By Age
18–29 Years

Reagan 49%
Mondale 40
Other; undecided 11

30–49 Years

Reagan	44%
Mondale	42
Other; undecided	14

50 Years and Over

Reagan	42%
Mondale	43
Other; undecided	15

By Politics
Republicans

Reagan	85%
Mondale	11
Other; undecided	4

Democrats

Reagan	18%
Mondale	65
Other; undecided	17

Independents

Reagan	51%
Mondale	34
Other; undecided	15

National Trend

	Reagan	Mondale	Other; undecided
July 29–August 1, 1983	44%	42%	14%
June 10–13, 1983	41	50	9
May 13–16, 1983	42	47	11
April 29–May 2, 1983	43	49	8
February 25–28, 1983	41	47	12
December 1982	40	52	8
October 1982	47	44	9
June 1982	43	49	8
April 1982	46	46	8
October 1981	54	37	9

Asked of registered voters: Suppose the 1984 presidential elections were being held today.

If President Ronald Reagan were the Republican candidate and Senator John Glenn were the Democratic candidate, which would you like to see win? [Those who named another candidate or who were undecided were asked: As of today, do you lean more to Reagan, the Republican, or to Glenn, the Democrat?]

Reagan	41%
Glenn	45
Other; undecided	14

By Sex
Male

Reagan	45%
Glenn	41
Other; undecided	14

Female

Reagan	37%
Glenn	49
Other; undecided	14

By Race
White

Reagan	46%
Glenn	42
Other; undecided	12

Nonwhite

Reagan	11%
Glenn	67
Other; undecided	22

By Education
College

Reagan	45%
Glenn	40
Other; undecided	15

High School

Reagan	41%
Glenn	45
Other; undecided	14

Grade School

Reagan 29%
Glenn 58
Other; undecided 13

By Region

East

Reagan 35%
Glenn 48
Other; undecided 17

Midwest

Reagan 46%
Glenn 44
Other; undecided 10

South

Reagan 38%
Glenn 46
Other; undecided 16

West

Reagan 44%
Glenn 41
Other; undecided 15

By Age

18–29 Years

Reagan 43%
Glenn 43
Other; undecided 14

30–49 Years

Reagan 42%
Glenn 44
Other; undecided 14

50 Years and Over

Reagan 39%
Glenn 47
Other; undecided 14

By Politics

Republicans

Reagan 81%
Glenn 13
Other; undecided 6

Democrats

Reagan 16%
Glenn 68
Other; undecided 16

Independents

Reagan 47%
Glenn 38
Other; undecided 15

National Trend

	Reagan	Glenn	Other; undecided
July 29–August 1, 1983	41%	45%	14%
June 10–13, 1983	38	53	9
April 29–May 2, 1983	37	54	9
February 25–28, 1983	40	45	15
December 1982	39	54	7

Asked of registered voters: Suppose the 1984 presidential election were being held today. If President Ronald Reagan were the Republican candidate and the Reverend Jesse Jackson were the Democratic candidate, which would you like to see win? [Those who named another candidate or who were undecided were asked: As of today, do you lean more to Reagan, the Republican, or to Jackson, the Democrat?]

Reagan 61%
Jackson 22
Other; undecided 17

By Sex

Male

Reagan	64%
Jackson	20
Other; undecided	16

Female

Reagan	58%
Jackson	23
Other; undecided	19

By Race

White

Reagan	69%
Jackson	15
Other; undecided	16

Nonwhite

Reagan	15%
Jackson	66
Other; undecided	19

Black

Reagan	12%
Jackson	71
Other; undecided	17

By Education

College

Reagan	63%
Jackson	21
Other; undecided	16

High School

Reagan	63%
Jackson	21
Other; undecided	16

Grade School

Reagan	48%
Jackson	29
Other; undecided	23

By Region

East

Reagan	60%
Jackson	22
Other; undecided	18

Midwest

Reagan	65%
Jackson	19
Other; undecided	16

South

Reagan	59%
Jackson	27
Other; undecided	14

West

Reagan	61%
Jackson	19
Other; undecided	20

By Age

18–29 Years

Reagan	60%
Jackson	23
Other; undecided	17

30–49 Years

Reagan	62%
Jackson	25
Other; undecided	13

50 Years and Over

Reagan	61%
Jackson	19
Other; undecided	20

By Politics

Republicans

Reagan	89%
Jackson	5
Other; undecided	6

Democrats

Reagan 43%
Jackson 35
Other; undecided 22

Independents

Reagan 68%
Jackson 15
Other; undecided 17

Note: President Ronald Reagan has made considerable headway in recent weeks against his two most likely Democratic challengers. If the 1984 elections were held now, the latest Gallup test elections suggest there would be a standoff between Reagan and either Senator John Glenn or former Vice-president Walter Mondale. As recently as mid-June, the president was the distinct underdog in trial heat contests against each Democrat.

Pitted against Mondale, Reagan currently makes his strongest showing since last fall. In the new survey, Reagan is the choice of 44% of registered voters to 42% for Mondale—a statistical tie. In surveys conducted at regular intervals since last October, Mondale has taken Reagan's measure every time, though in most cases by narrow margins. An October 1982 trial heat in which the president edged Mondale by a slim 47%-to-44% vote was the last time Reagan had prevailed.

The president fares marginally less well against potential challenger Glenn, narrowly losing to the Ohio senator, 41% to 45%. In the mid-June survey, Reagan trailed Glenn by 15 percentage points, 38% to 53%. Reagan's current 4-point deficit is the smallest to separate the two since the Reagan-Glenn test elections were begun last December.

With the Reverend Jesse Jackson reportedly considering an entry into the Democratic nomination contest, the latest survey measured his election strength against Reagan. The president beats Jackson by almost a 3-to-1 ratio, 61% to 22%. Not only does he win by overwhelming margins among both Republicans and independents, but also the president holds a 43% plurality to Jackson's 35% among Democratic voters. Among black voters, Jackson beats Reagan by a lopsided 71%

to 12% vote. But blacks also choose Mondale and Glenn over Reagan by equally impressive margins.

AUGUST 21
CENTRAL AMERICA

Interviewing Date: 7/29–8/1/83
Survey #219-G

Have you heard or read about the situation in El Salvador?

	Yes
National	86%

Asked of those who replied in the affirmative: The U.S. Defense Department has recommended increasing the number of U.S. military advisers in El Salvador from fifty-five to about one hundred twenty-five. Would you favor or oppose this?*

Favor 24%
Oppose 63
No opinion 13

By Sex
Male

Favor 31%
Oppose 60
No opinion 9

Female

Favor 18%
Oppose 64
No opinion 18

By Race
White

Favor 25%
Oppose 62
No opinion 13

Nonwhite

Favor 22%
Oppose 63
No opinion 15

By Education

College

Favor 25%
Oppose 65
No opinion 10

High School

Favor 23%
Oppose 63
No opinion 14

Grade School

Favor 27%
Oppose 54
No opinion 19

By Region

East

Favor 19%
Oppose 67
No opinion 14

Midwest

Favor 25%
Oppose 63
No opinion 12

South

Favor 33%
Oppose 52
No opinion 15

West

Favor 18%
Oppose 69
No opinion 13

By Age

18–24 Years

Favor 23%
Oppose 68
No opinion 9

25–29 Years

Favor 27%
Oppose 63
No opinion 10

30–49 Years

Favor 24%
Oppose 63
No opinion 13

50 Years and Over

Favor 25%
Oppose 59
No opinion 16

By Politics

Republicans

Favor 36%
Oppose 53
No opinion 11

Democrats

Favor 19%
Oppose 68
No opinion 13

Independents

Favor 24%
Oppose 63
No opinion 13

Also asked of those who replied in the affirmative: U.S. advisers in El Salvador have not been permitted to enter combat areas, a policy which the U.S. Defense Department now wants to change. Would you favor or oppose *permitting U.S. military advisers to enter combat areas in El Salvador?**

Favor 21%
Oppose 69
No opinion 10

By Sex
Male

Favor 22%
Oppose 72
No opinion 6

Female

Favor 20%
Oppose 66
No opinion 14

By Race
White

Favor 21%
Oppose 70
No opinion 9

Nonwhite

Favor 18%
Oppose 66
No opinion 16

By Education
College

Favor 20%
Oppose 74
No opinion 6

*Combining the results of these two questions, 12% favor both an increase in the number of U.S. advisers and permitting them to enter combat areas; 53% are opposed to both new options; and the remaining 35% give mixed responses.

High School

Favor 22%
Oppose 66
No opinion 12

Grade School

Favor 20%
Oppose 67
No opinion 13

By Region
East

Favor 21%
Oppose 71
No opinion 8

Midwest

Favor 20%
Oppose 70
No opinion 10

South

Favor 25%
Oppose 62
No opinion 13

West

Favor 17%
Oppose 73
No opinion 10

By Age
18–24 Years

Favor 21%
Oppose 72
No opinion 7

25–29 Years

Favor 23%
Oppose 68
No opinion 9

30–49 Years

Favor 22%
Oppose 68
No opinion 10

50 Years and Over

Favor 19%
Oppose 69
No opinion 12

By Politics
Republicans

Favor 23%
Oppose 68
No opinion 9

Democrats

Favor 15%
Oppose 74
No opinion 11

Independents

Favor 26%
Oppose 65
No opinion 9

Also asked of those who replied in the affirmative: How likely do you think it is that the U.S. involvement in El Salvador could turn into a situation like Vietnam—that is, that the United States would become more and more deeply involved as time goes on? Would you say this is very likely, fairly likely, not very likely, or not at all likely?

Very likely 41%
Fairly likely 31
Not very likely 16
Not at all likely 5
No opinion 7

By Sex
Male

Very likely 40%
Fairly likely 28
Not very likely 21
Not at all likely 7
No opinion 4

Female

Very likely 41%
Fairly likely 34
Not very likely 12
Not at all likely 4
No opinion 9

By Race
White

Very likely 39%
Fairly likely 33
Not very likely 17
Not at all likely 5
No opinion 6

Nonwhite

Very likely 48%
Fairly likely 21
Not very likely 12
Not at all likely 5
No opinion 14

By Education
College

Very likely 37%
Fairly likely 33
Not very likely 22
Not at all likely 5
No opinion 3

High School

Very likely 42%
Fairly likely 33
Not very likely 13
Not at all likely 5
No opinion 7

Grade School

Very likely 43%
Fairly likely 21
Not very likely 15
Not at all likely 7
No opinion 14

By Region
East

Very likely 40%
Fairly likely 33
Not very likely 16
Not at all likely 5
No opinion 6

Midwest

Very likely 42%
Fairly likely 28
Not very likely 19
Not at all likely 5
No opinion 6

South

Very likely 34%
Fairly likely 32
Not very likely 17
Not at all likely 6
No opinion 11

West

Very likely 47%
Fairly likely 30
Not very likely 12
Not at all likely 5
No opinion 6

By Age
18–24 Years

Very likely 33%
Fairly likely 39
Not very likely 16
Not at all likely 6
No opinion 6

25–29 Years

Very likely 37%
Fairly likely 41
Not very likely 15
Not at all likely 4
No opinion 3

30–49 Years

Very likely 43%
Fairly likely 31
Not very likely 14
Not at all likely 4
No opinion 8

50 Years and Over

Very likely 42%
Fairly likely 25
Not very likely 18
Not at all likely 7
No opinion 8

By Politics
Republicans

Very likely 27%
Fairly likely 33
Not very likely 26
Not at all likely 8
No opinion 6

Democrats

Very likely 48%
Fairly likely 30
Not very likely 13
Not at all likely 3
No opinion 6

Independents

Very likely 41%
Fairly likely 32
Not very likely 14
Not at all likely 6
No opinion 7

National Trend

	July–August 1983	June 1983	March 1983
Very likely	41%	37%	37%
Fairly likely	31	34	31
Not very likely	16	19	20
Not at all likely	5	5	6
No opinion	7	5	6

Also asked of those who replied in the affirmative: Some people say the United States should give military assistance to governments in Central America that are friendly to us. Others say we should not get involved in the internal affairs of these nations. Which point of view comes closer to the way you feel—that we should give military assistance to these nations or that we should not get involved?

Military assistance 35%
Not get involved 55
No opinion 10

By Sex

Male

Military assistance 45%
Not get involved 48
No opinion 7

Female

Military assistance 25%
Not get involved 62
No opinion 13

By Race

White

Military assistance 36%
Not get involved 54
No opinion 10

Nonwhite

Military assistance 27%
Not get involved 62
No opinion 11

Black

Military assistance 25%
Not get involved 62
No opinion 13

By Education

College

Military assistance 43%
Not get involved 50
No opinion 7

High School

Military assistance 33%
Not get involved 57
No opinion 10

Grade School

Military assistance 26%
Not get involved 57
No opinion 17

By Region

East

Military assistance 34%
Not get involved 57
No opinion 9

Midwest

Military assistance 33%
Not get involved 55
No opinion 12

South

Military assistance 42%
Not get involved 46
No opinion 12

West

Military assistance 31%
Not get involved 62
No opinion 7

By Age

18–24 Years

Military assistance 36%
Not get involved 57
No opinion 7

25–29 Years

Military assistance 32%
Not get involved 58
No opinion 10

30–49 Years

Military assistance 40%
Not get involved 41
No opinion 9

50 Years and Over

Military assistance 32%
Not get involved 57
No opinion 11

By Politics

Republicans

Military assistance 44%
Not get involved 46
No opinion 10

Democrats

Military assistance 28%
Not get involved 62
No opinion 10

Independents

Military assistance 39%
Not get involved 52
No opinion 9

Hispanic–Americans Only

Military assistance 35%
Not get involved 58
No opinion 7

Note: The American people continue to fear greater
U.S. involvement in Central America, despite
President Ronald Reagan's assurances that the
United States does not seek a larger military presence in the region. In the latest Gallup survey,
conducted soon after the president's July 26 press
conference in which he defended his administration's plans for military exercises in Central
America, the public expressed these views:

1) They currently oppose, by a 5-to-2 ratio,
increasing the number of U.S. military advisers
in El Salvador. (In March the public had voted
heavily against the first proposed increase in the
number of advisers to fifty-five.)

2) By an even larger 69% to 21% majority,
the public now rejects a Defense Department plan
to permit U.S. advisers to enter combat areas in
El Salvador.

3) The proportion of the public fearing that
U.S. intervention in El Salvador could turn into
another Vietnam remains at a very high level, with
72% saying this is at least fairly likely to occur.

4) Americans' desire for a hands-off military
policy in El Salvador extends to other nations in
the region as well. By a 55% to 35% vote, the
weight of public opinion is that the United States
should not get involved in the internal affairs of
friendly Central American nations, rather than
provide them with military assistance.

AUGUST 25
MOST IMPORTANT PROBLEM

Interviewing Date: 7/22–25/83
Survey #218-G

*What do you think is the most important prob-
lem facing this country today?*

Unemployment 48%
Inflation; high cost of living 14
Fear of war 10
Economy (general) 7
International problems 6
Excessive government spending 5
Reagan budget cuts 5
Moral decline in society 4

Crime 2
All others 9
Don't know 3
                                    113%*

*Total adds to more than 100% due to multiple responses.

The following are the leading four problems named by key population groups:

By Sex
Male

Unemployment 45%
Inflation; high cost of living 13
Fear of war 9
Economy (general) 9

Female

Unemployment 50%
Inflation; high cost of living 16
Fear of war 11
Economy (general) 6

By Race
White

Unemployment 45%
Inflation; high cost of living 14
Fear of war 11
Economy (general) 8

Nonwhite

Unemployment 59%
Inflation; high cost of living 14
Fear of war 2
Economy (general) 6

By Education
College

Unemployment 41%
Inflation; high cost of living 13
Fear of war 13
Economy (general) 9

High School

Unemployment 51%
Inflation; high cost of living 15
Fear of war 10
Economy (general) 8

Grade School

Unemployment 54%
Inflation; high cost of living 15
Fear of war 2
Economy (general) 3

By Age
18–29 Years

Unemployment 48%
Inflation; high cost of living 13
Fear of war 15
Economy (general) 8

30–49 Years

Unemployment 46%
Inflation; high cost of living 15
Fear of war 9
Economy (general) 10

50 Years and Over

Unemployment 49%
Inflation; high cost of living 14
Fear of war 6
Economy (general) 4

By Politics
Republicans

Unemployment 42%
Inflation; high cost of living 13
Fear of war 9
Economy (general) 10

Democrats

Unemployment 55%
Inflation; high cost of living 16
Fear of war 8
Economy (general) 7

Independents

Unemployment 46%
Inflation; high cost of living 13
Fear of war 13
Economy (general) 6

Asked of those who named a problem: Which political party do you think can do a better job of handling the problem you have just mentioned—the Republican party or the Democratic party?

Republican 24%
Democratic 38
No difference 28
No opinion 10

Note: Although unemployment continues to be the dominant problem facing the nation in the eyes of most Americans, fear of war and other international problems are growing as the public's top concerns. In the latest Gallup survey, unemployment is cited by 48% as the most important problem facing the United States. This marks the first time since last August that fewer than 50% of the public have named joblessness as the top national concern. In surveys conducted in April of this year and October 1982, unemployment claimed the attention of 54% and 64%, respectively.

The possibility of war and other foreign policy issues, chiefly the nation's involvement in Central America, vie with the high cost of living as the second most prevalent problem. The 10% of the public currently citing the possibility of war, while still at a relatively low level, is up sharply since last October, when only 3% gave it top priority. In the April survey, 11% said the likelihood that the United States might find itself at war concerned them the most. The related issue of America's foreign policy is now the top national problem for 6% of survey respondents, up from 2% in April.

The high cost of living and the lingering effects of inflation are mentioned by 14% as the most important national concern. This, too, has receded slightly since earlier surveys. In both the April and October assessments, the high cost of living was named by 18% of survey participants.

Fear of war and other international problems have even greater significance for respondents who attended college, mentioned by 22%. By comparison, 15% of persons whose education ended at the high-school level, and 5% with less formal education than high school, cite international affairs, including war fears.

AUGUST 28
SATISFACTION INDEX

Interviewing Date: 8/5–8/83
Survey #220-G

In general, are you satisfied or dissatisfied with the way things are going in the United States at this time?

	Satisfied
National	35%
White	39
Black	13

National Trend

	National	White	Black
November 1982	24%	24%	12%
April 1982	25	28	5
December 1981	27	29	13
June 1981	33	35	15
January 1981	17	18	19
November 1979	19	18	19
February 1979	26	26	24

In general, are you satisfied or dissatisfied with the way things are going in your own personal life?

	Satisfied
National	77%
White	82
Black	50

National Trend

	National	White	Black
November 1982	75%	77%	56%
April 1982	76	80	49
December 1981	81	84	61

June 1981	81	84	59
January 1981	81	82	68
November 1979	79	83	50
February 1979	77	80	55

Note: The twentieth anniversary of the 1963 civil rights march on Washington finds an upbeat mood among white people in the nation but continuing pessimism among black Americans. The proportion of whites who express satisfaction with the way things are going in their own personal lives is now at 82%, compared to an already high 77% recorded in November. Among blacks, the current figure is 50% satisfied today, compared to 56% in the earlier survey.

Whites today also are considerably more satisfied with the way things are going in the nation than they were last fall, 39% compared to 24% in the earlier survey. Blacks, on the other hand, are as gloomy today as earlier, with 13% now saying they are satisfied with trends in the nation, compared to 12% in November.

Black teen-agers are considerably more optimistic about their own personal lives than are black adults, with 76% of black teens saying they are satisfied with the way things are going in their lives, not far below the figure of 84% recorded for white teen-agers in a recent Gallup Youth Survey. A wide gap in satisfaction levels, however, is found between white and black young people on satisfaction with trends in the nation, with twice the proportion of whites (43%) as blacks (20%) expressing satisfaction with the way things are going in the nation.

SEPTEMBER 1
PREJUDICE IN POLITICS

Interviewing Date: 4/29–5/2/83
Survey #213-G

Between now and the political conventions of 1984, there will be discussion about the qualifications of presidential candidates— their education, age, religion, race, and so on. If your party nominated a woman for president, would you vote for her if she were qualified for the job?

Would 80%
Would not 16
No opinion 4

By Sex
Male

Would 80%
Would not 16
No opinion 4

Female

Would 80%
Would not 16
No opinion 4

By Race
White

Would 80%
Would not 16
No opinion 4

Nonwhite

Would 80%
Would not 13
No opinion 7

By Education
College

Would 87%
Would not 10
No opinion 3

High School

Would 80%
Would not 17
No opinion 3

Grade School

Would 69%
Would not 22
No opinion 9

By Region

East

Would	85%
Would not	12
No opinion	3

Midwest

Would	80%
Would not	17
No opinion	3

South

Would	75%
Would not	18
No opinion	7

West

Would	82%
Would not	15
No opinion	3

By Age

18–29 Years

Would	89%
Would not	8
No opinion	3

30–49 Years

Would	83%
Would not	14
No opinion	3

50–64 Years

Would	72%
Would not	22
No opinion	6

65 Years and Over

Would	68%
Would not	25
No opinion	7

By Politics

Republicans

Would	74%
Would not	22
No opinion	4

Democrats

Would	79%
Would not	17
No opinion	4

Independents

Would	88%
Would not	9
No opinion	3

Interviewing Date: 3/11–14/83
Survey #211-G

If your party nominated a generally well-qualified man for president and he happened to be a black, would you vote for him?

Would	77%
Would not	16
No opinion	7

By Sex

Male

Would	77%
Would not	16
No opinion	7

Female

Would	78%
Would not	15
No opinion	7

By Race

White

Would	76%
Would not	18
No opinion	6

Nonwhite

Would	85%
Would not	4
No opinion	11

By Education
College

Would	85%
Would not	10
No opinion	5

High School

Would	78%
Would not	15
No opinion	7

Grade School

Would	59%
Would not	29
No opinion	12

By Region
East

Would	82%
Would not	12
No opinion	6

Midwest

Would	77%
Would not	19
No opinion	4

South

Would	68%
Would not	22
No opinion	10

West

Would	86%
Would not	6
No opinion	8

By Age
18–29 Years

Would	86%
Would not	10
No opinion	4

30–49 Years

Would	80%
Would not	15
No opinion	5

50–64 Years

Would	74%
Would not	15
No opinion	11

65 Years and Over

Would	64%
Would not	26
No opinion	10

By Politics
Republicans

Would	75%
Would not	19
No opinion	6

Democrats

Would	77%
Would not	16
No opinion	7

Independents

Would	80%
Would not	14
No opinion	6

Interviewing Date: 4/29–5/2/83
Survey #213-G

If your party nominated a generally well-qualified man for president and he happened to be a Catholic, would you vote for him?

Would 92%
Would not 5
No opinion 3

By Sex
Male
Would 92%
Would not 6
No opinion 2

Female
Would 92%
Would not 5
No opinion 3

By Race
White
Would 94%
Would not 4
No opinion 2

Nonwhite
Would 84%
Would not 8
No opinion 8

By Education
College
Would 96%
Would not 3
No opinion 1

High School
Would 93%
Would not 5
No opinion 2

Grade School
Would 81%
Would not 11
No opinion 8

By Region
East
Would 97%
Would not 2
No opinion 1

Midwest
Would 93%
Would not 5
No opinion 2

South
Would 85%
Would not 9
No opinion 6

West
Would 96%
Would not 3
No opinion 1

By Age
18–29 Years
Would 94%
Would not 4
No opinion 2

30–49 Years
Would 95%
Would not 3
No opinion 2

50–64 Years
Would 89%
Would not 9
No opinion 2

65 Years and Over
Would 88%
Would not 8
No opinion 4

By Politics

Republicans

Would	93%
Would not	4
No opinion	3

Democrats

Would	90%
Would not	7
No opinion	3

Independents

Would	96%
Would not	3
No opinion	1

If your party nominated a generally well-qualified man for president and he happened to be a Jew, would you vote for him?

Would	88%
Would not	7
No opinion	5

By Sex

Male

Would	87%
Would not	8
No opinion	5

Female

Would	88%
Would not	7
No opinion	5

By Race

White

Would	89%
Would not	7
No opinion	4

Nonwhite

Would	80%
Would not	12
No opinion	8

By Education

College

Would	95%
Would not	3
No opinion	2

High School

Would	89%
Would not	7
No opinion	4

Grade School

Would	71%
Would not	17
No opinion	12

By Region

East

Would	92%
Would not	4
No opinion	4

Midwest

Would	90%
Would not	7
No opinion	3

South

Would	80%
Would not	12
No opinion	8

West

Would	91%
Would not	6
No opinion	3

By Age

18–29 Years

Would	91%
Would not	6
No opinion	3

30–49 Years

Would 88%
Would not 6
No opinion 6

50–64 Years

Would 87%
Would not 8
No opinion 5

65 Years and Over

Would 82%
Would not 11
No opinion 7

By Politics
Republicans

Would 89%
Would not 6
No opinion 5

Democrats

Would 86%
Would not 9
No opinion 5

Independents

Would 93%
Would not 5
No opinion 2

If your party nominated a generally well-qualified man for president and he happened to be an atheist, would you vote for him?

Would 42%
Would not 51
No opinion 7

By Sex
Male

Would 48%
Would not 46
No opinion 6

Female

Would 37%
Would not 57
No opinion 6

By Race
White

Would 43%
Would not 51
No opinion 6

Nonwhite

Would 39%
Would not 54
No opinion 7

By Education
College

Would 54%
Would not 39
No opinion 7

High School

Would 43%
Would not 51
No opinion 6

Grade School

Would 16%
Would not 77
No opinion 7

By Region
East

Would 51%
Would not 41
No opinion 8

Midwest

Would 41%
Would not 53
No opinion 6

South

Would 31%
Would not 64
No opinion 5

West

Would 49%
Would not 46
No opinion 5

By Age
18–29 Years

Would 57%
Would not 36
No opinion 7

30–49 Years

Would 46%
Would not 48
No opinion 6

50–64 Years

Would 30%
Would not 63
No opinion 7

65 Years and Over

Would 23%
Would not 72
No opinion 5

By Politics
Republicans

Would 39%
Would not 55
No opinion 6

Democrats

Would 42%
Would not 53
No opinion 5

Independents

Would 47%
Would not 46
No opinion 7

By Religion
Protestants

Would 31%
Would not 64
No opinion 5

Catholics

Would 54%
Would not 38
No opinion 8

If your party nominated a generally well-qualified man for president and he happened to be a homosexual, would you vote for him?

Would 29%
Would not 64
No opinion 7

By Sex
Male

Would 27%
Would not 66
No opinion 7

Female

Would 31%
Would not 62
No opinion 7

By Race
White

Would 28%
Would not 66
No opinion 6

Nonwhite

Would 35%
Would not 53
No opinion 12

By Education
College

Would 42%
Would not 51
No opinion 7

High School

Would 27%
Would not 67
No opinion 6

Grade School

Would 12%
Would not 78
No opinion 10

By Region
East

Would 32%
Would not 62
No opinion 6

Midwest

Would 31%
Would not 63
No opinion 6

South

Would 22%
Would not 69
No opinion 9

West

Would 31%
Would not 61
No opinion 8

By Age
18–29 Years

Would 40%
Would not 53
No opinion 7

30–49 Years

Would 31%
Would not 62
No opinion 7

50–64 Years

Would 22%
Would not 71
No opinion 7

65 Years and Over

Would 13%
Would not 80
No opinion 7

By Politics
Republicans

Would 22%
Would not 73
No opinion 5

Democrats

Would 29%
Would not 62
No opinion 9

Independents

Would 35%
Would not 60
No opinion 5

By Religion
Protestants

Would 23%
Would not 70
No opinion 7

Catholics

Would	34%
Would not	60
No opinion	6

National Trend

Would vote for	1983	1978	1958
Woman	80%	76%	52%
Black	77	77	38
Catholic	92	91	68
Jew	88	82	62
Atheist	42	40	18
Homosexual	29	26	N.A.

Note: One of the more dramatic developments in the political scene over the past quarter century has been the growing willingness of the electorate to say they would vote for a Catholic, a Jew, a woman, or a black for president.

In 1958, 68% of the public said they would vote for a well-qualified man if he happened to be a Catholic; today the proportion is 92%.

In 1958, 62% indicated they would vote for a qualified Jewish presidential candidate; the current figure is 88%.

In 1958, 52% said they would have no trouble voting for a woman for president; in the latest survey, 80% express the same view.

In terms of their willingness to support a black man for president, the proportion vaulted from 38% in 1958 to 77% in 1978, a level maintained in the current survey.

While the barriers of race, religion, and sex have fallen dramatically during the last generation, the survey offers evidence that not all political discrimination has disappeared. Only 42% of respondents, for instance, say they would be willing to vote for an atheist for president, while even fewer (29%) would support a homosexual. Although it still lacks majority backing, the concept of an atheist for president has grown far more acceptable now than it was in 1958, when merely 18% of respondents indicated they would be willing to vote for an atheist.

The question of a homosexual for president was not asked in 1958; five years ago 26% said they would vote for a homosexual, statistically indistinguishable from the 29% who now express this opinion.

SEPTEMBER 4
PRESIDENTIAL TRIAL HEATS

Interviewing Date: 8/12–15/83
Survey #221-G

Asked of registered voters: Suppose the 1984 presidential election were being held today. If President Ronald Reagan were the Republican candidate and Walter Mondale were the Democratic candidate, which would you like to see win? [Those who named another candidate or who were undecided were asked: As of today, do you lean more to Reagan, the Republican, or to Mondale, the Democrat?]

Reagan	44%
Mondale	43
Other; undecided	13

National Trend for 1983

	Reagan	Mondale	Other; undecided
July 29–August 1	44%	42%	14%
May 13–16	42	47	11
February 25–28	41	47	12

Asked of registered voters: Suppose the 1984 presidential elections were being held today. If President Ronald Reagan were the Republican candidate and Senator John Glenn were the Democratic candidate, which would you like to see win? [Those who named another candidate or who were undecided were asked: As of today, do you lean more to Reagan, the Republican, or to Glenn, the Democrat?]

Reagan	40%
Glenn	46
Other; undecided	14

National Trend for 1983

	Reagan	Glenn	Other; undecided
July 29–August 1	41%	45%	14%
June 10–13	38	53	9
February 25–28.......	40	45	15

Asked of registered voters: If President Ronald Reagan were the Republican candidate running against Walter Mondale, the Democratic candidate, and John Anderson, an independent candidate, which would you like to see win? [Those who named another candidate or who were undecided were asked: As of today, do you lean more to Reagan, the Republican; to Mondale, the Democrat; or to Anderson, the independent?]

		Without Anderson
Reagan	41%	44%
Mondale	36	43
Anderson	11	–
Other; undecided	12	13

Asked of registered voters: If President Ronald Reagan were the Republican candidate running against Senator John Glenn, the Democratic candidate, and John Anderson, an independent candidate, which would you like to see win? [Those who named another candidate or who were undecided were asked: As of today, do you lean more to Reagan, the Republican; to Glenn, the Democrat; or to Anderson, the independent?]

		Without Anderson
Reagan	38%	40%
Glenn	40	46
Anderson	10	–
Other; undecided	12	14

Note: Former Vice-president Walter Mondale and President Ronald Reagan continue their neck-and-neck battle, with Mondale receiving 43% in the latest trial heat to 44% for the president. The previous survey showed Mondale with 42% and Reagan with 44%.

Senator John Glenn of Ohio has retained a slim lead over Reagan. Glenn receives the support of 46% of registered voters to 40% for the president. A survey conducted two weeks earlier showed similar results, with Glenn the choice of 45% and Reagan 41%.

The latest evidence indicates that a third-party candidacy by John Anderson would help Reagan in a contest against either Glenn or Mondale. When Anderson's name is included in the latest trial heats, the Glenn and Reagan race becomes virtually neck and neck, while Reagan pulls into a slight lead over Mondale.

Anderson, who expects to qualify for preelection federal financing of about $6 million, is now grappling with the practical and legal problems of registering his campaign as a third-party candidate on ballots in all fifty states. He has not yet announced whether he will run for the presidency next year.

SEPTEMBER 4
PRESIDENT REAGAN

Interviewing Date: 8/12–15/83
Survey #221-G

Do you approve or disapprove of the way Ronald Reagan is handling his job as president?

Approve 43%
Disapprove 45
No opinion 12

By Sex
Male

Approve 48%
Disapprove 41
No opinion 11

Female

Approve 38%
Disapprove 49
No opinion 13

By Race
White

Approve 49%
Disapprove 40
No opinion 11

Nonwhite

Approve 13%
Disapprove 69
No opinion 18

By Education
College

Approve 49%
Disapprove 43
No opinion 8

High School

Approve 42%
Disapprove 45
No opinion 13

Grade School

Approve 34%
Disapprove 50
No opinion 16

By Region
East

Approve 41%
Disapprove 47
No opinion 12

Midwest

Approve 43%
Disapprove 46
No opinion 11

South

Approve 42%
Disapprove 45
No opinion 13

West

Approve 48%
Disapprove 41
No opinion 11

By Age
18–29 Years

Approve 45%
Disapprove 42
No opinion 13

30–49 Years

Approve 41%
Disapprove 48
No opinion 11

50 Years and Over

Approve 44%
Disapprove 44
No opinion 12

By Income
$25,000 and Over

Approve 55%
Disapprove 37
No opinion 8

$15,000 and Over

Approve 51%
Disapprove 39
No opinion 10

Under $15,000

Approve 32%
Disapprove 53
No opinion 15

By Religion
Protestants

Approve 45%
Disapprove 43
No opinion 12

Catholics

Approve 46%
Disapprove 43
No opinion 11

By Occupation
Professional and Business

Approve 53%
Disapprove 39
No opinion 8

Clerical and Sales

Approve 38%
Disapprove 53
No opinion 9

Manual Workers

Approve 39%
Disapprove 48
No opinion 13

Nonlabor Force

Approve 40%
Disapprove 48
No opinion 12

Note: The stability over time in the standings of the candidates in trial heats is in part a reflection of stability in President Ronald Reagan's approval ratings.

The following is the 1983 trend for the past four months:

National Trend in 1983

	Approve	Dis- approve	No opinion
August 5–8	44%	46%	10%
July 29–August 1	44	42	14
July 22–25	42	47	11
June 24–27	47	44	9
June 10–13	43	45	12
May 20–23	46	43	11

May 13–16	43	45	12
April 29–May 2	43	46	11

SEPTEMBER 8
PRAYER IN PUBLIC SCHOOLS

INTERVIEWING DATE: 7/22–25/83
SURVEY #218-G

Have you heard or read about a proposed amendment to the U.S. Constitution that would allow voluntary prayer in public schools?

	Yes
National	82%

Asked of those who replied in the affirmative: Do you favor or oppose this proposed amendment? How strongly do you favor or oppose this proposed amendment—very strongly, fairly strongly, or not at all strongly?

Favor
  Very strongly 48%
  Fairly strongly 29
  Not at all strongly 4
Oppose
  Not at all strongly 2%
  Fairly strongly 5
  Very strongly 7
No opinion 5%

By Sex
Male

Favor 79%
Oppose 16
No opinion 5

Female

Favor 83%
Oppose 12
No opinion 5

By Race
White
Favor 79%
Oppose 15
No opinion 6

Nonwhite
Favor 91%
Oppose 7
No opinion 2

By Education
College
Favor 72%
Oppose 21
No opinion 7

High School
Favor 84%
Oppose 11
No opinion 5

Grade School
Favor 94%
Oppose 5
No opinion 1

By Region
East
Favor 81%
Oppose 16
No opinion 6

Midwest
Favor 85%
Oppose 10
No opinion 5

South
Favor 86%
Oppose 9
No opinion 5

West
Favor 67%
Oppose 25
No opinion 8

By Age
18–29 Years
Favor 77%
Oppose 18
No opinion 5

30–49 Years
Favor 79%
Oppose 15
No opinion 6

50 Years and Over
Favor 85%
Oppose 10
No opinion 5

By Politics
Republicans
Favor 85%
Oppose 10
No opinion 5

Democrats
Favor 81%
Oppose 14
No opinion 5

Independents
Favor 77%
Oppose 16
No opinion 7

By Religion
Protestants
Favor 84%
Oppose 11
No opinion 5

Baptists

Favor	91%
Oppose	6
No opinion	3

Methodists

Favor	82%
Oppose	11
No opinion	7

Catholics

Favor	84%
Oppose	10
No opinion	6

Which one of the following do you think is the most important in the religious and spiritual development of a child—the home, school, or the church?

Home	80%
School	2
Church	15
No opinion	3

Note: An overwhelming majority of Americans favors a constitutional amendment that would permit voluntary group prayer in public schools. The amendment would state: "Nothing in this Constitution shall be construed to prohibit individual or group prayer in public schools or other public institutions. No person shall be required by the United States or by any state to participate in prayer."

Among the eight in ten who have followed the pros and cons of the debate, 81% say they favor the proposed amendment, while 14% oppose it and 5% are undecided. Public support for such an amendment has remained firm over the fifteen months since President Ronald Reagan first proposed it. A May 1982 survey showed 78% of the aware group (also 82% in that survey) in favor of the Reagan proposal, with 16% opposed and 6% with no opinion.

Nearly half of the aware group (48%) say they strongly favor the proposed amendment, while 33% express mild support. On the disapproval side, 7% say they strongly oppose the amendment, while 7% express mild opposition. Although the public overwhelmingly favors permitting voluntary prayer in schools, the prevailing opinion among all groups and faiths is that the home is more important than either the church or school in the religious training of children.

SEPTEMBER 11
CONFIDENCE IN INSTITUTIONS

Interviewing Date: 8/5–8/83
Survey #220-G

I am going to read you a list of institutions in American society. Would you please tell me how much confidence you, yourself, have in each one—a great deal, quite a lot, some, or very little:

Church or organized religion?

	Great deal or quite a lot
National	62%

By Age

18–29 years	55%
30–49 years	61
50 years and over	69

National Trend

1981	64%
1979	65
1977	64
1975	68
1973	66

The military?

	Great deal or quite a lot
National	53%

By Age

18–29 years	49%
30–49 years	49
50 years and over	58

National Trend

1981	50%
1979	54
1977	57
1975	58
1973	66

Banks and banking?

	Great deal or quite a lot
National	51%

By Age

18–29 years	46%
30–49 years	44
50 years and over	59

National Trend

1981	46%
1979	60

U.S. Supreme Court?

	Great deal or quite a lot
National	42%

By Age

18–29 years	47%
30–49 years	42
50 years and over	38

National Trend

1981	46%
1979	45
1977	46
1975	49
1973	44

Public schools?

	Great deal or quite a lot
National	39%

By Age

18–29 years	34%
30–49 years	40
50 years and over	40

National Trend

1981	42%
1979	53
1977	54
1973	58

Newspapers?

	Great deal or quite a lot
National	38%

By Age

18–29 years	45%
30–49 years	34
50 years and over	36

National Trend

1981	35%
1979	51
1973	39

Congress?

	Great deal or quite a lot
National	28%

By Age

18–29 years	29%
30–49 years	25
50 years and over	30

National Trend

1981	29%
1979	34
1977	40
1975	40
1973	42

Big business?

	Great deal or quite a lot
National	28%

By Age

18–29 years	31%
30–49 years	24
50 years and over	29

National Trend

1981	20%
1979	32
1977	33
1975	34
1973	26

Organized labor?

	Great deal or quite a lot
National	26%

By Age

18–29 years	36%
30–49 years	22
50 years and over	22

National Trend

1981	28%
1979	36
1977	39
1975	38
1973	30

Television?

	Great deal or quite a lot
National	25%

By Age

18–29 years	23%
30–49 years	25
50 years and over	24

National Trend

1981	25%
1979	38
1973	37

Note: The public's confidence in the nation's most important institutions is no higher today than it was a decade ago in the days of Watergate. In the case of some of the institutions tested, confidence actually has fallen since 1973.

Institutions now accorded about the same degree of public confidence as ten years ago include: the church or organized religion, the U.S. Supreme Court, newspapers, big business, and organized labor. On the other hand, the public schools, Congress, and television now receive markedly lower confidence ratings than in the earlier survey.

Today, as in each of the previous surveys, the church or organized religion is the highest rated institution tested, with 62% of survey participants saying they have a great deal or quite a lot of confidence in it. In 1973, 66% expressed a similar amount of confidence in the church. Next is the military, with 53% saying they have a high degree of confidence, followed by banks and banking (51%).

In the tier below are the U.S. Supreme Court (42%), the public schools (39%), and newspapers (38%). Congress and big business each receives positive confidence ratings from 28% of the public. The last two institutions on this year's list are organized labor (26%) and television (25%); in the 1973 survey, organized labor was rated favorably by 30% of the public, and television by 37%.

The sharp decline in confidence in the public schools, from 58% in the 1973 survey to 39% at present, comes at a time of widespread public dissatisfaction with public education. This loss of confidence was recently reflected in the report of the bipartisan National Commission on Excellence in Education, which concluded: "The educational foundations of our society are presently being eroded by a rising tide of mediocrity that threatens our very future as a nation and as a people."

The current views of young adults (18 to 29 years old) offer little cause for optimism for the immediate future. The proportion of young people expressing a high degree of confidence is no higher than that of persons 30 and over in the case of five of the institutions tested, and in some cases is lower.

SEPTEMBER 15
DEMOCRATIC PRESIDENTIAL CANDIDATES

Interviewing Date: 8/19–22/83
Survey #222-G

Asked of Democrats and independents: Suppose the choice for president in the Democratic convention in 1984 narrows down to Walter Mondale and John Glenn. Which would you prefer to have the Democratic convention select?

Choice of Democrats

Mondale	49%
Glenn	30
Undecided	21

National Trend

	Mondale	Glenn	Undecided
June 1983	57%	31%	12%
February 1983	52	30	18
December 1982	59	28	13

Choice of Independents

Mondale	34%
Glenn	39
Undecided	27

National Trend

	Mondale	Glenn	Undecided
June 1983	38%	43%	19%
February 1983	42	35	23
December 1982	41	40	19

Asked of Democrats and independents: Suppose the choice for president in the Democratic convention in 1984 narrows down to Walter Mondale, John Glenn, and Jesse Jackson. Which would you prefer to have the Democratic convention select?

Choice of Democrats

		Without Jackson
Mondale	44%	49%
Glenn	30	30
Jackson	8	–
Undecided	18	21

Choice of Independents

		Without Jackson
Mondale	32%	34%
Glenn	35	39
Jackson	5	–
Undecided	28	27

Note: Former Vice-president Walter Mondale continues to lead Senator John Glenn for the 1984 Democratic presidential nomination, but the margin between the two men has narrowed since June. In the interim between the two surveys, many former Mondale supporters have moved into the ranks of the undecided.

In the latest survey, Mondale is the choice of 49% of Democrats to 30% for Glenn, with 21% undecided. In the June survey, Mondale was chosen by 57% of Democrats to 31% for Glenn and 12% undecided. While Mondale continues to lead Glenn among Democrats, the race is statistically a toss-up among voters who classify themselves as independents, a group representing nearly one-third of the electorate. In the current survey, Glenn wins 39% of the support of independents to 34% for Mondale. In June, Glenn was the choice of 43% to 38% for his rival.

If the 1984 choice for president in the Democratic convention narrows down to Mondale, Glenn, and the Reverend Jesse Jackson, who has given some indication that he may seek the nomination, the results show that Mondale's support among Democratic voters would be cut slightly, while Glenn would stay at his current level.

SEPTEMBER 18
VOUCHER SYSTEM IN EDUCATION*

Interviewing Date: 6/24–27/83
Survey #217-G

In some nations, the government allots a certain amount of money for each child for his education. The parents can then send the child to any public, parochial, or private school they choose. This is called the "voucher system." Would you like to see such an idea adopted in this country?

Favor 51%
Oppose 38
No opinion 11

By Sex
Male

Favor 50%
Oppose 41
No opinion 9

Female

Favor 51%
Oppose 35
No opinion 14

By Race
White

Favor 49%
Oppose 40
No opinion 11

Black

Favor 64%
Oppose 23
No opinion 13

*This study was sponsored by Phi Delta Kappa, the professional educational fraternity.

By Education
College

Favor 47%
Oppose 44
No opinion 9

High School

Favor 53%
Oppose 37
No opinion 10

Grade School

Favor 50%
Oppose 29
No opinion 21

By Region
East

Favor 55%
Oppose 35
No opinion 10

Midwest

Favor 52%
Oppose 40
No opinion 8

South

Favor 45%
Oppose 38
No opinion 17

West

Favor 50%
Oppose 40
No opinion 10

By Age
18–29 Years

Favor 60%
Oppose 29
No opinion 11

30–49 Years

Favor 52%
Oppose 40
No opinion 8

50 Years and Over

Favor 43%
Oppose 43
No opinion 14

By Politics
Republicans

Favor 48%
Oppose 41
No opinion 11

Democrats

Favor 52%
Oppose 38
No opinion 10

Independents

Favor 52%
Oppose 37
No opinion 11

By Religion
Protestants

Favor 46%
Oppose 42
No opinion 12

Catholics

Favor 63%
Oppose 29
No opinion 8

Public School Parents Only

Favor 48%
Oppose 41
No opinion 11

Nonpublic School Parents Only

Favor 64%
Oppose 30
No opinion 6

No Children in School

Favor 51%
Oppose 37
No opinion 12

National Trend

	Favor	Oppose	No opinion
1983	51%	38%	11%
1981	43	41	16
1971	38	44	18
1970	43	46	11

Note: As the new school year begins, a majority of Americans for the first time backs a voucher system for educating the nation's children. Under this system the government would provide a certain amount of money for the education of each child, regardless of whether the child attends a public, parochial, or other private secondary school.

In the latest survey, the voucher system is favored by a 51% majority of the adult public and opposed by 38%, with 11% undecided. As recently as two years ago, backers and opponents of the plan were about equal in number, with 43% in favor to 41% opposed. In surveys conducted in the early 1970s, opponents of the plan narrowly outnumbered proponents. The latest survey thus marks the first time majority support for the idea has emerged.

Not surprisingly, better than 2-to-1 support for the voucher system is found among parents of children attending parochial or independent, nonpublic schools. At the same time, a plurality of parents of children attending the public schools now favors it by a 48% to 41% margin.

Greater support for the voucher system is found among parents of children in parochial or private schools, blacks, Catholics, and young adults. Conversely, proportionately less support is expressed by parents of public-school children, whites, Protestants, and persons age 50 and older. In addition, roughly equivalent proportions of men and women favor the voucher system concept; Republicans, Democrats, and independents also back the plan by similar margins.

SEPTEMBER 22
POLITICAL AFFILIATION

Interviewing Date: July–August 1983
Various Surveys

*In politics, as of today, do you consider your-self a Republican, a Democrat, or an independent?**

Republican 25%
Democrat 45
Independent 30

By Sex
Male

Republican 26%
Democrat 42
Independent 32

Female

Republican 24%
Democrat 47
Independent 29

By Race
White

Republican 28%
Democrat 40
Independent 32

*Persons who say they belong to other parties or have no party allegiance (4% in the latest surveys) have been excluded.

Black

Republican 6%
Democrat 76
Independent 18

By Education
College

Republican 30%
Democrat 36
Independent 34

High School

Republican 24%
Democrat 46
Independent 30

Grade School

Republican 19%
Democrat 58
Independent 23

By Region
East

Republican 22%
Democrat 47
Independent 31

Midwest

Republican 27%
Democrat 40
Independent 33

South

Republican 21%
Democrat 51
Independent 28

West

Republican 32%
Democrat 39
Independent 29

By Age

18–29 Years

Republican 23%
Democrat 40
Independent 37

30–49 Years

Republican 23%
Democrat 44
Independent 33

50 Years and Over

Republican 28%
Democrat 49
Independent 23

By Income

$30,000 and Over

Republican 32%
Democrat 37
Independent 31

$20,000–$29,999

Republican 27%
Democrat 38
Independent 35

$10,000–$19,999

Republican 23%
Democrat 48
Independent 29

Under $10,000

Republican 19%
Democrat 55
Independent 26

By Religion

Protestants

Republican 29%
Democrat 44
Independent 27

Catholics

Republican 22%
Democrat 47
Independent 31

Jews

Republican 8%
Democrat 60
Independent 32

By Occupation

Professional and Business

Republican 31%
Democrat 35
Independent 34

Clerical and Sales

Republican 27%
Democrat 41
Independent 32

Blue Collar

Republican 20%
Democrat 48
Independent 32

Skilled Workers

Republican 22%
Democrat 43
Independent 35

Unskilled Workers

Republican 18%
Democrat 53
Independent 29

Farmers

Republican 33%
Democrat 37
Independent 30

By Location

Center Cities

Republican 18%
Democrat 54
Independent 28

Fringe of Cities

Republican 29%
Democrat 37
Independent 34

Other Locations

Republican 28%
Democrat 43
Independent 29

National Trend

	Republicans	Democrats	Independents
July–August 1983	25%	45%	30%
April–June 1983	23	46	31
January–March 1983 ..	24	46	30
1982	26	45	29
1981	28	42	30
1980	24	46	30
1979	22	45	33
1975	22	45	33
1972	38	43	29
1968	27	46	27
1964	25	53	22
1960	30	47	23
1954	34	46	20
1950	33	45	22
1946	40	39	21

Note: The downtrend in the proportion of Republicans in the electorate between 1981 and the second quarter of the current year has leveled out in the latest surveys. Still, only one adult in four (25%) currently claims allegiance to the GOP.

Republican affiliation reached a ten-year high point of 28% in 1981 in the aftermath of Ronald Reagan's landslide victory in November 1980. For the next eighteen months, Republican strength gradually ebbed to 23% in the second quarter of this year, undoubtedly affected by the recession.

With the economy starting to recover, there has been a modest upturn in the GOP's fortunes. In five Gallup surveys conducted during July and August with over 7,000 individuals, 25% classify themselves as Republicans, 45% as Democrats, and 30% as independents. The current findings, which show Democrats outnumbering Republicans by nearly a 2-to-1 margin, clearly point up the challenge facing Republican political candidates. To win, GOP candidates in the past have had not only to win a very high percentage of the votes of their own party members but also to win the support of a majority of independents and some Democratic votes as well.

The GOP is the minority party in every major demographic group but enjoys its greatest strength among whites, persons age 50 and older, the college educated, those from upper-income families, Protestants, persons living in households in which the chief wage earner is employed in business or the professions, farmers, westerners, and those living outside the core cities of the nation. Conversely, proportionately more Democrats are found among blacks, those age 50 and older, persons whose education ended at the grade-school level or earlier, those from lower-income families, Jews, unskilled workers, central city residents, and southerners.

It is interesting to note that President Reagan's gender gap—the propensity of far fewer women than men to approve of his policies and programs—is only moderately reflected in political allegiance. Although a slightly larger proportion of women than men claims affiliation with the Democratic party, approximately equal numbers of women and men say they are Republicans.

SEPTEMBER 25
RATING POLITICAL LEADERS

Interviewing Date: 8/12–15/83
Survey #221-G

You will note that the ten boxes on this scale go from the highest position of +5 for someone you have a very favorable opinion of all the way down to the lowest position of −5 for someone you have a very unfavorable opinion of. How far up or down the scale would you rate the following people:

Ronald Reagan?

Highly favorable ($+5$, $+4$)	.29%
Moderately favorable ($+3$, $+2$, $+1$)	.32
Moderately unfavorable (-1, -2, -3)	.16
Highly unfavorable (-4, -5)	.18
No opinion	. 5

By Sex
Male

Highly favorable	.31%
Moderately favorable	.33
Moderately unfavorable	.15
Highly unfavorable	.18
No opinion	. 3

Female

Highly favorable	.26%
Moderately favorable	.29
Moderately unfavorable	.18
Highly unfavorable	.20
No opinion	. 7

By Race
White

Highly favorable	.33%
Moderately favorable	.31
Moderately unfavorable	.16
Highly unfavorable	.17
No opinion	. 3

Nonwhite

Highly favorable	. 9%
Moderately favorable	.27
Moderately unfavorable	.22
Highly unfavorable	.29
No opinion	.13

By Education
College

Highly favorable	.30%
Moderately favorable	.31
Moderately unfavorable	.15
Highly unfavorable	.21
No opinion	. 3

High School

Highly favorable	.30%
Moderately favorable	.32
Moderately unfavorable	.15
Highly unfavorable	.19
No opinion	. 4

Grade School

Highly favorable	.21%
Moderately favorable	.31
Moderately unfavorable	.18
Highly unfavorable	.22
No opinion	. 8

By Region
East

Highly favorable	.28%
Moderately favorable	.30
Moderately unfavorable	.17
Highly unfavorable	.20
No opinion	. 5

Midwest

Highly favorable	.27%
Moderately favorable	.32
Moderately unfavorable	.19
Highly unfavorable	.20
No opinion	. 2

South

Highly favorable	.27%
Moderately favorable	.31
Moderately unfavorable	.16
Highly unfavorable	.17
No opinion	. 9

West

Highly favorable	34%
Moderately favorable	33
Moderately unfavorable	13
Highly unfavorable	19
No opinion	1

By Age
18–29 Years

Highly favorable	27%
Moderately favorable	36
Moderately unfavorable	15
Highly unfavorable	17
No opinion	5

30–49 Years

Highly favorable	26%
Moderately favorable	33
Moderately unfavorable	18
Highly unfavorable	18
No opinion	5

50 Years and Over

Highly favorable	33%
Moderately favorable	27
Moderately unfavorable	16
Highly unfavorable	20
No opinion	4

By Income
$25,000 and Over

Highly favorable	38%
Moderately favorable	30
Moderately unfavorable	14
Highly unfavorable	17
No opinion	1

$15,000 and Over

Highly favorable	34%
Moderately favorable	31
Moderately unfavorable	16
Highly unfavorable	16
No opinion	3

Under $15,000

Highly favorable	20%
Moderately favorable	31
Moderately unfavorable	18
Highly unfavorable	22
No opinion	9

By Politics
Republicans

Highly favorable	64%
Moderately favorable	25
Moderately unfavorable	3
Highly unfavorable	5
No opinion	3

Democrats

Highly favorable	12%
Moderately favorable	31
Moderately unfavorable	23
Highly unfavorable	30
No opinion	4

Independents

Highly favorable	25%
Moderately favorable	37
Moderately unfavorable	17
Highly unfavorable	16
No opinion	5

Walter Mondale?

Highly favorable ($+5$, $+4$)	25%
Moderately favorable ($+3$, $+2$, $+1$)	49
Moderately unfavorable (-1, -2, -3)	14
Highly unfavorable (-4, -5)	6
No opinion	6

By Sex
Male

Highly favorable	26%
Moderately favorable	48
Moderately unfavorable	16
Highly unfavorable	8
No opinion	2

Female

Highly favorable 25%
Moderately favorable 39
Moderately unfavorable 13
Highly unfavorable 5
No opinion 8

By Race

White

Highly favorable 24%
Moderately favorable 49
Moderately unfavorable 15
Highly unfavorable 7
No opinion 5

Nonwhite

Highly favorable 35%
Moderately favorable 40
Moderately unfavorable 7
Highly unfavorable 4
No opinion 14

By Education

College

Highly favorable 18%
Moderately favorable 51
Moderately unfavorable 20
Highly unfavorable 7
No opinion 4

High School

Highly favorable 26%
Moderately favorable 50
Moderately unfavorable 13
Highly unfavorable 6
No opinion 5

Grade School

Highly favorable 39%
Moderately favorable 36
Moderately unfavorable 9
Highly unfavorable 6
No opinion 10

By Region

East

Highly favorable 23%
Moderately favorable 57
Moderately unfavorable 10
Highly unfavorable 5
No opinion 5

Midwest

Highly favorable 25%
Moderately favorable 49
Moderately unfavorable 17
Highly unfavorable 6
No opinion 3

South

Highly favorable 31%
Moderately favorable 38
Moderately unfavorable 12
Highly unfavorable 7
No opinion 12

West

Highly favorable 21%
Moderately favorable 50
Moderately unfavorable 17
Highly unfavorable 7
No opinion 5

By Age

18–29 Years

Highly favorable 17%
Moderately favorable 60
Moderately unfavorable 14
Highly unfavorable 4
No opinion 5

30–49 Years

Highly favorable 25%
Moderately favorable 50
Moderately unfavorable 13
Highly unfavorable 6
No opinion 6

50 Years and Over

Highly favorable 31%
Moderately favorable 38
Moderately unfavorable 15
Highly unfavorable 9
No opinion 7

By Income

$25,000 and Over

Highly favorable 22%
Moderately favorable 52
Moderately unfavorable 19
Highly unfavorable 5
No opinion 2

$15,000 and Over

Highly favorable 22%
Moderately favorable 53
Moderately unfavorable 16
Highly unfavorable 7
No opinion 2

Under $15,000

Highly favorable 30%
Moderately favorable 43
Moderately unfavorable 10
Highly unfavorable 6
No opinion 11

By Politics

Republicans

Highly favorable 7%
Moderately favorable 50
Moderately unfavorable 24
Highly unfavorable 14
No opinion 5

Democrats

Highly favorable 42%
Moderately favorable 44
Moderately unfavorable 6
Highly unfavorable 3
No opinion 5

Independents

Highly favorable 17%
Moderately favorable 54
Moderately unfavorable 19
Highly unfavorable 5
No opinion 5

John Glenn?

Highly favorable ($+5$, $+4$) 24%
Moderately favorable ($+3$, $+2$, $+1$) 55
Moderately unfavorable (-1, -2, -3) ... 9
Highly unfavorable (-4, -5) 3
No opinion 9

By Sex

Male

Highly favorable 23%
Moderately favorable 56
Moderately unfavorable 10
Highly unfavorable 4
No opinion 7

Female

Highly favorable 25%
Moderately favorable 55
Moderately unfavorable 6
Highly unfavorable 2
No opinion 12

By Race

White

Highly favorable 24%
Moderately favorable 57
Moderately unfavorable 9
Highly unfavorable 3
No opinion 7

Nonwhite

Highly favorable 27%
Moderately favorable 47
Moderately unfavorable 5
Highly unfavorable 4
No opinion 18

By Education

College

Highly favorable 17%
Moderately favorable 65
Moderately unfavorable 9
Highly unfavorable 2
No opinion 7

High School

Highly favorable 27%
Moderately favorable 53
Moderately unfavorable 7
Highly unfavorable 3
No opinion 10

Grade School

Highly favorable 29%
Moderately favorable 44
Moderately unfavorable 8
Highly unfavorable 3
No opinion 16

By Region

East

Highly favorable 22%
Moderately favorable 58
Moderately unfavorable 8
Highly unfavorable 2
No opinion 10

Midwest

Highly favorable 26%
Moderately favorable 58
Moderately unfavorable 8
Highly unfavorable 2
No opinion 6

South

Highly favorable 26%
Moderately favorable 51
Moderately unfavorable 7
Highly unfavorable 4
No opinion 12

West

Highly favorable 20%
Moderately favorable 56
Moderately unfavorable 13
Highly unfavorable 2
No opinion 9

By Age

18–29 Years

Highly favorable 17%
Moderately favorable 62
Moderately unfavorable 9
Highly unfavorable 2
No opinion 10

30–49 Years

Highly favorable 24%
Moderately favorable 57
Moderately unfavorable 9
Highly unfavorable 2
No opinion 8

50 Years and Over

Highly favorable 29%
Moderately favorable 51
Moderately unfavorable 8
Highly unfavorable 4
No opinion 8

By Income

$25,000 and Over

Highly favorable 19%
Moderately favorable 66
Moderately unfavorable 8
Highly unfavorable 2
No opinion 5

$15,000 and Over

Highly favorable 23%
Moderately favorable 59
Moderately unfavorable 9
Highly unfavorable 3
No opinion 6

Under $15,000

Highly favorable	26%
Moderately favorable	51
Moderately unfavorable	7
Highly unfavorable	3
No opinion	13

By Politics
Republicans

Highly favorable	13%
Moderately favorable	61
Moderately unfavorable	15
Highly unfavorable	4
No opinion	7

Democrats

Highly favorable	35%
Moderately favorable	50
Moderately unfavorable	5
Highly unfavorable	3
No opinion	7

Independents

Highly favorable	20%
Moderately favorable	60
Moderately unfavorable	8
Highly unfavorable	3
No opinion	9

Here is a list of terms shown as pairs of opposites that have, been used to describe political candidates. Now, from each pair of opposites would you select the terms which best describe Ronald Reagan/Walter Mondale/John Glenn:

Bright, intelligent?

Reagan	53%
Mondale	56
Glenn	65

By Politics
Republicans

Reagan	74%
Mondale	50
Glenn	66

Democrats

Reagan	40%
Mondale	62
Glenn	64

Independents

Reagan	53%
Mondale	55
Glenn	70

Likeable?

Reagan	50%
Mondale	50
Glenn	63

By Politics
Republicans

Reagan	71%
Mondale	43
Glenn	67

Democrats

Reagan	36%
Mondale	57
Glenn	62

Independents

Reagan	52%
Mondale	50
Glenn	64

High moral principles?

Reagan	50%
Mondale	49
Glenn	58

By Politics

Republicans

Reagan 66%
Mondale 43
Glenn 61

Democrats

Reagan 40%
Mondale 55
Glenn 58

Independents

Reagan 51%
Mondale 46
Glenn 59

Colorful, interesting personality?

Reagan 50%
Mondale 33
Glenn 46

By Politics

Republicans

Reagan 71%
Mondale 27
Glenn 48

Democrats

Reagan 39%
Mondale 40
Glenn 46

Independents

Reagan 51%
Mondale 28
Glenn 46

Says what he believes?

Reagan 50%
Mondale 30
Glenn 39

By Politics

Republicans

Reagan 71%
Mondale 20
Glenn 40

Democrats

Reagan 37%
Mondale 40
Glenn 40

Independents

Reagan 52%
Mondale 25
Glenn 41

Decisive, sure of himself?

Reagan 48%
Mondale 41
Glenn 53

By Politics

Republicans

Reagan 69%
Mondale 33
Glenn 54

Democrats

Reagan 35%
Mondale 48
Glenn 52

Independents

Reagan 50%
Mondale 39
Glenn 55

Strong leadership qualities?

Reagan 47%
Mondale 36
Glenn 47

By Politics
Republicans

Reagan 70%
Mondale 23
Glenn 41

Democrats

Reagan 34%
Mondale 46
Glenn 49

Independents

Reagan 48%
Mondale 33
Glenn 51

Good judgment in crisis?

Reagan 44%
Mondale 40
Glenn 54

By Politics
Republicans

Reagan 64%
Mondale 32
Glenn 54

Democrats

Reagan 30%
Mondale 49
Glenn 55

Independents

Reagan 47%
Mondale 35
Glenn 55

Religious person?

Reagan 43%
Mondale 33
Glenn 33

By Politics
Republicans

Reagan 56%
Mondale 25
Glenn 30

Democrats

Reagan 37%
Mondale 39
Glenn 37

Independents

Reagan 40%
Mondale 32
Glenn 31

Well-defined program for progress?

Reagan 43%
Mondale 26
Glenn 27

By Politics
Republicans

Reagan 68%
Mondale 16
Glenn 22

Democrats

Reagan 29%
Mondale 36
Glenn 31

Independents

Reagan 41%
Mondale 20
Glenn 25

You know where he stands?

Reagan 41%
Mondale 35
Glenn 33

By Politics

Republicans

Reagan	63%
Mondale	27
Glenn	26

Democrats

Reagan	29%
Mondale	43
Glenn	37

Independents

Reagan	42%
Mondale	33
Glenn	34

Imaginative solutions to problems?

Reagan	37%
Mondale	31
Glenn	34

By Politics

Republicans

Reagan	55%
Mondale	24
Glenn	39

Democrats

Reagan	24%
Mondale	41
Glenn	42

Independents

Reagan	34%
Mondale	28
Glenn	43

Puts country's interests first?

Reagan	35%
Mondale	31
Glenn	46

By Politics

Republicans

Reagan	59%
Mondale	22
Glenn	27

Democrats

Reagan	24%
Mondale	39
Glenn	39

Independents

Reagan	36%
Mondale	28
Glenn	36

Exceptional ability?

Reagan	35%
Mondale	32
Glenn	41

By Politics

Republicans

Reagan	58%
Mondale	18
Glenn	42

Democrats

Reagan	22%
Mondale	43
Glenn	49

Independents

Reagan	34%
Mondale	28
Glenn	47

Takes moderate positions?

Reagan	34%
Mondale	45
Glenn	50

By Politics

Republicans

Reagan	50%
Mondale	38
Glenn	51

Democrats

Reagan	26%
Mondale	49
Glenn	50

Independents

Reagan	33%
Mondale	50
Glenn	52

You can believe in him?

Reagan	33%
Mondale	35
Glenn	47

By Politics

Republicans

Reagan	61%
Mondale	22
Glenn	44

Democrats

Reagan	18%
Mondale	47
Glenn	51

Independents

Reagan	33%
Mondale	31
Glenn	48

Sides with average citizen?

Reagan	23%
Mondale	38
Glenn	42

By Politics

Republicans

Reagan	42%
Mondale	28
Glenn	41

Democrats

Reagan	14%
Mondale	46
Glenn	44

Independents

Reagan	22%
Mondale	38
Glenn	41

Sympathetic to poor?

Reagan	21%
Mondale	44
Glenn	37

By Politics

Republicans

Reagan	39%
Mondale	39
Glenn	34

Democrats

Reagan	13%
Mondale	50
Glenn	42

Independents

Reagan	20%
Mondale	44
Glenn	34

Note: President Ronald Reagan and his leading Democratic rivals, Walter Mondale and John Glenn, generate only mild enthusiasm among the electorate at present, but a close look at the image each man projects to the public reveals some dramatic differences.

To measure enthusiasm for the candidates, a

10-point scale called the Stapel Scalometer is used. Reagan, Mondale, and Glenn are found to create about equal enthusiasm among the electorate, with 29% giving the president a highly favorable rating (the top two positions on the scale) to 25% for Mondale and 24% for Glenn. On the negative side, however, Reagan receives a highly unfavorable rating (the bottom two scale positions) of 18%, compared to only 6% for Mondale and 3% for Glenn.

In terms of positive personality traits, President Reagan outscores his rivals as a man who "says what he believes," "colorful, interesting personality," "you know where he stands" on issues, "religious person," and "well-defined program for progress." He fares less well than the two leading Democratic contenders as being "sympathetic to poor," "sides with average citizen," and "takes moderate positions."

Of the two Democrats, Glenn fares much better on many of the items but holds his widest leads over Mondale on "likeable," "colorful, interesting personality," "good judgment in crisis," and "puts country's interests first." Mondale beats Glenn on "sympathetic to poor" and closely matches Glenn on "imaginative solutions to problems," "you know where he stands," "well-defined program for progress," and "sides with average citizen."

SEPTEMBER 29
REAGANOMICS

Interviewing Date: 8/19–22/83
Survey #222-G

What effect do you think the Reagan administration's economic policies will have on your own and your family's financial situation? Do you feel your financial situation will be much better, somewhat better, somewhat worse, or much worse as a result of the Reagan economic policies?

Better 32%
Worse 44
Same (volunteered) 19
No opinion 5

By Sex
Male

Better 37%
Worse 39
Same (volunteered) 20
No opinion 4

Female

Better 27%
Worse 48
Same (volunteered) 19
No opinion 6

By Race
White

Better 35%
Worse 39
Same (volunteered) 21
No opinion 5

Nonwhite

Better 14%
Worse 65
Same (volunteered) 14
No opinion 7

By Education
College

Better 43%
Worse 34
Same (volunteered) 20
No opinion 3

High School

Better 30%
Worse 47
Same (volunteered) 19
No opinion 4

Grade School

Better 13%
Worse 51
Same (volunteered) 23
No opinion 13

By Region

East

Better	25%
Worse	50
Same (volunteered)	19
No opinion	6

Midwest

Better	36%
Worse	44
Same (volunteered)	16
No opinion	4

South

Better	36%
Worse	36
Same (volunteered)	21
No opinion	7

West

Better	29%
Worse	45
Same (volunteered)	24
No opinion	2

By Age

18–29 Years

Better	34%
Worse	49
Same (volunteered)	13
No opinion	4

30–49 Years

Better	37%
Worse	40
Same (volunteered)	19
No opinion	4

50 Years and Over

Better	25%
Worse	44
Same (volunteered)	24
No opinion	7

By Income

$25,000 and Over

Better	46%
Worse	32
Same (volunteered)	20
No opinion	2

$15,000 and Over

Better	40%
Worse	36
Same (volunteered)	21
No opinion	3

Under $15,000

Better	20%
Worse	54
Same (volunteered)	18
No opinion	8

By Politics

Republicans

Better	50%
Worse	24
Same (volunteered)	22
No opinion	4

Democrats

Better	21%
Worse	56
Same (volunteered)	17
No opinion	6

Independents

Better	35%
Worse	41
Same (volunteered)	20
No opinion	4

National Trend

	Better	Worse	Same	No opinion
August 1983	32%	44%	19%	5%
August 1982	23	56	15	6
August 1981	48	36	*	16

*Volunteered "same" response recorded with "no opinion."

How about the nation? What effect do you think the Reagan administration's economic policies will have on the nation's economic situation? Do you feel the nation's economic situation will be much better, somewhat better, somewhat worse, or much worse as a result of the Reagan economic policies?

Better 40%
Worse 43
Same (volunteered) 9
No opinion 8

By Sex
Male

Better 46%
Worse 40
Same (volunteered) 8
No opinion 6

Female

Better 35%
Worse 45
Same (volunteered) 10
No opinion 10

By Race
White

Better 44%
Worse 39
Same (volunteered) 9
No opinion 8

Nonwhite

Better 17%
Worse 64
Same (volunteered) 10
No opinion 9

By Education
College

Better 54%
Worse 35

Same (volunteered) 7
No opinion 4

High School

Better 38%
Worse 45
Same (volunteered) 9
No opinion 8

Grade School

Better 18%
Worse 49
Same (volunteered) 14
No opinion 19

By Region
East

Better 35%
Worse 47
Same (volunteered) 10
No opinion 8

Midwest

Better 43%
Worse 44
Same (volunteered) 5
No opinion 8

South

Better 44%
Worse 34
Same (volunteered) 13
No opinion 9

West

Better 38%
Worse 47
Same (volunteered) 8
No opinion 7

By Age

18–29 Years

Better 40%
Worse 47
Same (volunteered) 7
No opinion 6

30–49 Years

Better 45%
Worse 41
Same (volunteered) 9
No opinion 5

50 Years and Over

Better 37%
Worse 40
Same (volunteered) 11
No opinion 12

By Income

$25,000 and Over

Better 54%
Worse 37
Same (volunteered) 6
No opinion 3

$15,000 and Over

Better 50%
Worse 37
Same (volunteered) 8
No opinion 5

Under $15,000

Better 25%
Worse 53
Same (volunteered) 10
No opinion 12

By Politics

Republicans

Better 64%
Worse 20
Same (volunteered) 8
No opinion 8

Democrats

Better 27%
Worse 56
Same (volunteered) 10
No opinion 7

Independents

Better 42%
Worse 42
Same (volunteered) 9
No opinion 7

National Trend

	Better	Worse	Same	No opinion
August 1983	40%	43%	9%	8%
August 1982	32	54	7	7
August 1981	53	37	4	6

Note: Confidence that Reaganomics will improve one's own and the nation's financial situation has grown since the dark days of the recession in 1982, but it falls short of the optimism expressed when the economic program was launched in 1981. A total of 32% of the public currently says their own family financial situation will improve as a result of Reaganomics, while 44% say it will worsen. In August 1982, only 23% were optimistic, while 56% were pessimistic. Still earlier, in August 1981 shortly after the inception of the program, 48% were optimistic and 36% were pessimistic about the likelihood of its improving their financial situation.

In response to another question, 40% are currently bullish about the effect of Reaganomics on the nation's overall financial situation, while about the same proportion, 43%, are bearish. By contrast, 32% were optimistic in 1982, while 54% were pessimistic. In October 1981, when the first Gallup measurement on the subject was taken, optimists outnumbered pessimists 53% to 37%. Optimism in all major population groups dropped off sharply from the 1981 to 1982 period, and in the current survey it is still below the peak levels of 1981.

Consistently greater confidence in Reaganomics has been expressed by Republicans, men, whites, persons under age 50, and those with some college education. On the other hand, Democrats, women, blacks, persons age 50 and older, and those whose education ended at high-school level or earlier have been less optimistic about the effects of the administration's economic programs and policies.

OCTOBER 2
PRESIDENT REAGAN

Interviewing Date: 8/19–22/83
Survey #222-G

As I read off each of the following problems, would you tell me whether you approve or disapprove of the way President Ronald Reagan is handling that problem:

Economic conditions in this country?

Approve	37%
Disapprove	54
No opinion	9

By Sex
Male

Approve	44%
Disapprove	49
No opinion	7

Female

Approve	31%
Disapprove	58
No opinion	11

By Race
White

Approve	43%
Disapprove	49
No opinion	8

Nonwhite

Approve	8%
Disapprove	79
No opinion	13

By Education
College

Approve	55%
Disapprove	41
No opinion	4

High School

Approve	33%
Disapprove	59
No opinion	8

Grade School

Approve	15%
Disapprove	62
No opinion	23

By Region
East

Approve	31%
Disapprove	61
No opinion	8

Midwest

Approve	39%
Disapprove	54
No opinion	7

South

Approve	40%
Disapprove	47
No opinion	13

West

Approve	39%
Disapprove	53
No opinion	8

By Age

18–29 Years

Approve 38%
Disapprove 55
No opinion 7

30–49 Years

Approve 38%
Disapprove 56
No opinion 6

50 Years and Over

Approve 36%
Disapprove 50
No opinion 14

By Income

$25,000 and Over

Approve 53%
Disapprove 43
No opinion 4

$15,000 and Over

Approve 46%
Disapprove 47
No opinion 7

Under $15,000

Approve 24%
Disapprove 63
No opinion 13

By Politics

Republicans

Approve 65%
Disapprove 25
No opinion 10

Democrats

Approve 20%
Disapprove 70
No opinion 10

Independents

Approve 42%
Disapprove 53
No opinion 5

By Occupation

Professional and Business

Approve 51%
Disapprove 41
No opinion 8

Clerical and Sales

Approve 46%
Disapprove 46
No opinion 8

Manual Workers

Approve 33%
Disapprove 61
No opinion 6

Nonlabor Force

Approve 32%
Disapprove 55
No opinion 13

National Trend

	Approve	Dis-approve	No opinion
January 1983*	29%	64%	7%
April 1981**	60	29	11

*Low or near low point of trend to date
**High point of trend to date

Inflation?

Approve 41%
Disapprove 49
No opinion 10

By Sex

Male

Approve 48%
Disapprove 43
No opinion 9

Female

Approve 34%
Disapprove 55
No opinion 11

By Race
White

Approve 46%
Disapprove 45
No opinion 9

Nonwhite

Approve 12%
Disapprove 73
No opinion 15

By Education
College

Approve 59%
Disapprove 35
No opinion 6

High School

Approve 35%
Disapprove 56
No opinion 9

Grade School

Approve 23%
Disapprove 56
No opinion 21

By Region
East

Approve 36%
Disapprove 53
No opinion 11

Midwest

Approve 40%
Disapprove 54
No opinion 6

South

Approve 41%
Disapprove 45
No opinion 14

West

Approve 48%
Disapprove 43
No opinion 9

By Age
18–29 Years

Approve 42%
Disapprove 50
No opinion 8

30–49 Years

Approve 40%
Disapprove 52
No opinion 8

50 Years and Over

Approve 40%
Disapprove 47
No opinion 13

By Income
$25,000 and Over

Approve 58%
Disapprove 37
No opinion 5

$15,000 and Over

Approve 50%
Disapprove 43
No opinion 7

Under $15,000

Approve 27%
Disapprove 60
No opinion 13

By Politics

Republicans

Approve 61%
Disapprove 30
No opinion 9

Democrats

Approve 27%
Disapprove 63
No opinion 10

Independents

Approve 46%
Disapprove 47
No opinion 7

By Occupation

Professional and Business

Approve 56%
Disapprove 36
No opinion 8

Clerical and Sales

Approve 52%
Disapprove 38
No opinion 10

Manual Workers

Approve 34%
Disapprove 58
No opinion 8

Nonlabor Force

Approve 38%
Disapprove 48
No opinion 14

National Trend

	Approve	Dis- approve	No opinion
January 1983*	36%	56%	8%
April 1981**	58	28	14

*Low or near low point of trend to date
**High point of trend to date

Unemployment?

Approve 28%
Disapprove 62
No opinion 10

By Sex

Male

Approve 32%
Disapprove 59
No opinion 9

Female

Approve 24%
Disapprove 64
No opinion 12

By Race

White

Approve 31%
Disapprove 59
No opinion 10

Nonwhite

Approve 6%
Disapprove 80
No opinion 14

By Education

College

Approve 36%
Disapprove 56
No opinion 8

High School

Approve 26%
Disapprove 66
No opinion 8

Grade School

Approve 16%
Disapprove 59
No opinion 25

By Region

East

Approve 23%
Disapprove 67
No opinion 10

Midwest

Approve 26%
Disapprove 67
No opinion 7

South

Approve 30%
Disapprove 55
No opinion 15

West

Approve 33%
Disapprove 57
No opinion 10

By Age

18–29 Years

Approve 26%
Disapprove 68
No opinion 6

30–49 Years

Approve 29%
Disapprove 62
No opinion 9

50 Years and Over

Approve 28%
Disapprove 57
No opinion 15

By Income

$25,000 and Over

Approve 38%
Disapprove 56
No opinion 6

$15,000 and Over

Approve 34%
Disapprove 59
No opinion 7

Under $15,000

Approve 19%
Disapprove 66
No opinion 15

By Politics

Republicans

Approve 52%
Disapprove 38
No opinion 10

Democrats

Approve 13%
Disapprove 76
No opinion 11

Independents

Approve 29%
Disapprove 63
No opinion 8

By Occupation

Professional and Business

Approve 37%
Disapprove 55
No opinion 8

Clerical and Sales

Approve 39%
Disapprove 52
No opinion 9

Manual Workers

Approve 23%
Disapprove 69
No opinion 8

Nonlabor Force

Approve 23%
Disapprove 59
No opinion 18

National Trend

	Approve	Dis-approve	No opinion
January 1983	19%	73%	8%
March 1981	43	34	23

Note: Despite the brightening economic picture, President Ronald Reagan has a long way to go to regain majority approval for his handling of economic conditions in the nation. In the early "honeymoon" days of his presidency, approval outweighed disapproval by a wide 60% to 20% margin. In subsequent measurements approval declined steadily, to 29% in January of the current year. In the latest survey 37% approve, while 54% disapprove.

A similar pattern is found for the public's rating of Reagan's handling of inflation and unemployment. In an April 1981 survey of the president's handling of inflation, approval outweighed disapproval 2 to 1, or 58% to 28%. The approval rating then declined at a steady rate, reaching a low of 36% in January 1983. The president has succeeded in reversing this trend, but his gains on this issue are modest; in the latest survey, 41% approve and 49% disapprove.

Reagan has never scored well on the unemployment issue. In a March 1981 survey he won the approval of 43% of Americans on this issue, but approval then sank to 19% in January 1983. The president's rating has rebounded considerably since January, but the current approval figure (28%) remains unimpressive.

These three questions on Reagan's handling of the economy, inflation, and unemployment have been asked in twenty national Gallup surveys since March 1981.

OCTOBER 6
PARTY BETTER FOR PEACE AND PROSPERITY

Interviewing Date: 9/9–12/83
Survey #223-G

Which political party—the Republican party or the Democratic party—do you think will do a better job of keeping the country prosperous?

Republican 33%
Democratic 40
No difference (volunteered) 14
No opinion 13

By Sex
Male

Republican 38%
Democratic 38
No difference (volunteered) 15
No opinion 9

Female

Republican 29%
Democratic 42
No difference (volunteered) 13
No opinion 16

By Race
White

Republican 37%
Democratic 37
No difference (volunteered) 14
No opinion 12

Nonwhite

Republican 12%
Democratic 59
No difference (volunteered) 13
No opinion 16

By Education

College

Republican 48%
Democratic 29
No difference (volunteered) 14
No opinion 9

High School

Republican 27%
Democratic 46
No difference (volunteered) 15
No opinion 12

Grade School

Republican 21%
Democratic 42
No difference (volunteered) 11
No opinion 26

By Region

East

Republican 31%
Democratic 44
No difference (volunteered) 13
No opinion 12

Midwest

Republican 33%
Democratic 39
No difference (volunteered) 17
No opinion 11

South

Republican 32%
Democratic 41
No difference (volunteered) 11
No opinion 16

West

Republican 39%
Democratic 34
No difference (volunteered) 16
No opinion 11

By Age

18–29 Years

Republican 35%
Democratic 40
No difference (volunteered) 12
No opinion 13

30–49 Years

Republican 35%
Democratic 37
No difference (volunteered) 15
No opinion 13

50 Years and Over

Republican 31%
Democratic 43
No difference (volunteered) 14
No opinion 12

By Income

$25,000 and Over

Republican 48%
Democratic 29
No difference (volunteered) 14
No opinion 9

$15,000 and Over

Republican 42%
Democratic 34
No difference (volunteered) 14
No opinion 10

Under $15,000

Republican 22%
Democratic 49
No difference (volunteered) 13
No opinion 16

By Politics

Republicans

Republican 73%
Democratic 8
No difference (volunteered) 10
No opinion 9

Democrats

Republican 13%
Democratic 70
No difference (volunteered) 10
No opinion 7

Independents

Republican 33%
Democratic 25
No difference (volunteered) 22
No opinion 20

By Occupation

Professional and Business

Republican 50%
Democratic 29
No difference (volunteered) 10
No opinion 11

Clerical and Sales

Republican 31%
Democratic 45
No difference (volunteered) 15
No opinion 9

Manual Workers

Republican 25%
Democratic 43
No difference (volunteered) 15
No opinion 17

Nonlabor Force

Republican 33%
Democratic 40
No difference (volunteered) 11
No opinion 16

Labor Union Families Only

Republican 32%
Democratic 43
No difference (volunteered) 15
No opinion 10

Nonlabor Union Families Only

Republican 34%
Democratic 39
No difference (volunteered) 14
No opinion 13

National Trend

	Repub-lican	Demo-cratic	No opinion*
September 9–12, 1983	33%	40%	27%
October 1982	34	43	23
April 1981	41	28	31
September 1980	35	36	29
August 1976	23	47	30
September 1972	38	35	27
October 1968	34	37	29
October 1964	21	53	26
October 1960	31	46	23
October 1956	39	39	22
January 1952	31	35	34

*Includes "no difference"

Which political party do you think would be more likely to keep the United States out of World War III—the Republican party or the Democratic party?

Republican 26%
Democratic 39
No difference (volunteered) 21
No opinion 14

By Sex

Male

Republican 31%
Democratic 33
No difference (volunteered) 24
No opinion 12

Female

Republican 21%
Democratic 45
No difference (volunteered) 19
No opinion 15

By Race
White

Republican 28%
Democratic 37
No difference (volunteered) 22
No opinion 13

Nonwhite

Republican 12%
Democratic 53
No difference (volunteered) 17
No opinion 18

By Education
College

Republican 31%
Democratic 39
No difference (volunteered) 20
No opinion 10

High School

Republican 23%
Democratic 42
No difference (volunteered) 22
No opinion 13

Grade School

Republican 20%
Democratic 32
No difference (volunteered) 23
No opinion 25

By Region
East

Republican 21%
Democratic 44
No difference (volunteered) 22
No opinion 13

Midwest

Republican 29%
Democratic 35
No difference (volunteered) 25
No opinion 11

South

Republican 27%
Democratic 38
No difference (volunteered) 18
No opinion 17

West

Republican 26%
Democratic 40
No difference (volunteered) 22
No opinion 12

By Age
18–29 Years

Republican 25%
Democratic 48
No difference (volunteered) 15
No opinion 12

30–49 Years

Republican 24%
Democratic 39
No difference (volunteered) . . . . .23 .
No opinion 14

50 Years and Over

Republican 28%
Democratic 33
No difference (volunteered) 25
No opinion 14

By Income
$25,000 and Over

Republican 33%
Democratic 35
No difference (volunteered) 21
No opinion 11

$15,000 and Over

Republican 30%
Democratic 38
No difference (volunteered) 21
No opinion 11

Under $15,000

Republican 20%
Democratic 41
No difference (volunteered) 22
No opinion 17

By Politics

Republicans

Republican 65%
Democratic 10
No difference (volunteered) 16
No opinion 9

Democrats

Republican 8%
Democratic 67
No difference (volunteered) 17
No opinion 8

Independents

Republican 20%
Democratic 27
No difference (volunteered) 30
No opinion 23

National Trend

	Repub-lican	Demo-cratic	No opinion*
September 9–12, 1983	26%	39%	35%
October 1982	29	38	33
April 1981	29	34	37
September 1980	25	42	33
August 1976	29	32	39
September 1972	32	28	40
October 1968	37	24	39
October 1964	22	45	33
October 1960	40	25	35
October 1956	46	16	38
January 1952	36	15	49

*Includes "no difference"

Note: Despite the strengthening economy, the GOP has made little headway with voters on the politically potent issue of being able to bring prosperity to the United States. By a 40% to 33% margin, voters credit the Democrats as better able to keep the nation prosperous. These findings closely parallel those recorded in October 1982, when 43% of voters named the Democratic party and 34% cited the Republican party.

The Democrats also hold a wide lead on the peace issue, with 39% of voters currently crediting the Democratic party as more likely to keep the nation at peace and 26% naming the GOP. Again, the findings are similar to those recorded one year ago, when 38% saw the Democrats as better able to keep peace and 29% chose the Republicans.

The twin issues of peace and prosperity historically have been the key issues in national elections, with the party on top on both having a distinct advantage at election time. In the 1950s, 1960s, and most of the 1970s, the Democrats held wide leads on prosperity, while the GOP during this period tended to enjoy an advantage on peace. The high point for the GOP on the prosperity issue was recorded in April 1981, when 41% said the Republicans would do a better job of keeping the country prosperous and 28% named the Democrats. On the peace issue, the GOP reached its high-water mark in October 1956, during Dwight Eisenhower's presidency, when 46% said the Republicans and 16% named the Democrats as more likely to keep the nation out of another war.

OCTOBER 6
PRESIDENTIAL TRIAL HEATS

Interviewing Date: 9/16–19/83
Survey #224-G

Asked of registered voters: Suppose the 1984 presidential election were being held today. If President Ronald Reagan were the Republican candidate and Walter Mondale were the Democratic candidate, which would you like to see win? [Those who named another person or who were undecided were asked: As of today, do you lean more to Reagan, the Republican, or to Mondale, the Democrat?]

Reagan 48%
Mondale 44
Other; undecided 8

By Sex

Male

Reagan 52%
Mondale 43
Other; undecided 5

Female

Reagan 43%
Mondale 46
Other; undecided 11

By Race

White

Reagan 53%
Mondale 39
Other; undecided 8

Nonwhite

Reagan 9%
Mondale 80
Other; undecided 11

By Education

College

Reagan 56%
Mondale 38
Other; undecided 6

High School

Reagan 44%
Mondale 47
Other; undecided 9

Grade School

Reagan 36%
Mondale 57
Other; undecided 7

By Region

East

Reagan 49%
Mondale 40
Other; undecided 11

Midwest

Reagan 42%
Mondale 50
Other; undecided 8

South

Reagan 47%
Mondale 46
Other; undecided 7

West

Reagan 53%
Mondale 40
Other; undecided 7

By Age

18–29 Years

Reagan 49%
Mondale 46
Other; undecided 5

30–49 Years

Reagan 48%
Mondale 43
Other; undecided 9

50 Years and Over

Reagan 46%
Mondale 45
Other; undecided 9

By Income

$40,000 and Over

Reagan 60%
Mondale 34
Other; undecided 6

$30,000–$39,999

Reagan 61%
Mondale 32
Other; undecided 7

$20,000–$29,999

Reagan 53%
Mondale 42
Other; undecided 5

Under $20,000

Reagan 38%
Mondale 53
Other; undecided 9

By Politics
Republicans

Reagan 83%
Mondale 12
Other; undecided 5

Democrats

Reagan 18%
Mondale 74
Other; undecided 8

Independents

Reagan 53%
Mondale 35
Other; undecided 12

By Religion
Protestants

Reagan 50%
Mondale 43
Other; undecided 7

Catholics

Reagan 46%
Mondale 44
Other; undecided 10

National Trend

	Reagan	Mondale	Other; undecided
1983			
September 16–19 ...	47%	44%	9%
August 12–15	44	43	13
July 29–August 1 ...	44	42	14

June 10–13	41	50	9
April 29–May 2	43	49	8
February 25–28	41	47	12
1982			
December	40	52	8
April	46	46	8
1981			
October	54	37	9

Asked of registered voters: Suppose the 1984 presidential election were being held today. If President Ronald Reagan were the Republican candidate and Senator John Glenn were the Democratic candidate, which would you like to see win? [Those who named another person or who were undecided were asked: As of today, do you lean more to Reagan, the Republican, or to Glenn, the Democrat?]

Reagan 42%
Glenn 48
Other; undecided 10

By Sex
Male

Reagan 47%
Glenn 45
Other; undecided 8

Female

Reagan 35%
Glenn 52
Other; undecided 13

By Race
White

Reagan 46%
Glenn 44
Other; undecided 10

Nonwhite

Reagan 9%
Glenn 82
Other; undecided 9

By Education
College

Reagan 52%
Glenn 41
Other; undecided 7

High School

Reagan 34%
Glenn 55
Other; undecided 11

Grade School

Reagan 32%
Glenn 57
Other; undecided 11

By Region
East

Reagan 40%
Glenn 46
Other; undecided 14

Midwest

Reagan 38%
Glenn 55
Other; undecided 7

South

Reagan 43%
Glenn 45
Other; undecided 12

West

Reagan 46%
Glenn 47
Other; undecided 7

By Age
18–29 Years

Reagan 41%
Glenn 52
Other; undecided 7

30–49 Years

Reagan 42%
Glenn 47
Other; undecided 11

50 Years and Over

Reagan 41%
Glenn 48
Other; undecided 11

By Income
$40,000 and Over

Reagan 56%
Glenn 36
Other; undecided 8

$30,000–$39,999

Reagan 50%
Glenn 40
Other; undecided 10

$20,000–$29,999

Reagan 47%
Glenn 46
Other; undecided 7

Under $20,000

Reagan 33%
Glenn 57
Other; undecided 10

By Politics
Republicans

Reagan 78%
Glenn 17
Other; undecided 5

Democrats

Reagan 13%
Glenn 78
Other; undecided 9

Independents

Reagan 44%
Glenn 40
Other; undecided 16

By Religion
Protestants

Reagan 45%
Glenn 47
Other; undecided 8

Catholics

Reagan 39%
Glenn 48
Other; undecided 13

National Trend

	Reagan	Glenn	Other; undecided
1983			
September 16–19 ...	42%	48%	10%
August 12–15	40	46	14
July 29–August 1 ...	41	45	14
June 10–13	38	53	9
April 29–May 2	37	54	9
February 25–28	40	45	15
1982			
December	39	54	7

Asked of registered voters: Suppose the 1984 presidential election were being held today. If President Ronald Reagan were the Republican candidate and George McGovern were the Democratic candidate, which would you like to see win? [Those who named another person or who were undecided were asked: As of today, do you lean more to Reagan, the Republican, or to McGovern, the Democrat?]

Reagan 53%
McGovern 35
Other; undecided 12

By Sex
Male

Reagan 57%
McGovern 33
Other; undecided 10

Female

Reagan 49%
McGovern 38
Other; undecided 13

By Race
White

Reagan 59%
McGovern 30
Other; undecided 11

Nonwhite

Reagan 13%
McGovern 73
Other; undecided 14

By Education
College

Reagan 59%
McGovern 33
Other; undecided 8

High School

Reagan 51%
McGovern 36
Other; undecided 13

Grade School

Reagan 41%
McGovern 47
Other; undecided 12

By Region
East

Reagan 53%
McGovern 30
Other; undecided 17

Midwest

Reagan 47%
McGovern 41
Other; undecided 12

South

Reagan 57%
McGovern 34
Other; undecided 9

West

Reagan 55%
McGovern 38
Other; undecided 7

By Age
18–29 Years

Reagan 52%
McGovern 41
Other; undecided 7

30–49 Years

Reagan 52%
McGovern 38
Other; undecided 10

50 Years and Over

Reagan 54%
McGovern 31
Other; undecided 15

By Income
$40,000 and Over

Reagan 68%
McGovern 27
Other; undecided 7

$30,000–$39,999

Reagan 65%
McGovern 26
Other; undecided 9

$20,000–$29,999

Reagan 52%
McGovern 36
Other; undecided 12

Under $20,000

Reagan 46%
McGovern 42
Other; undecided 12

By Politics
Republicans

Reagan 86%
McGovern 9
Other; undecided 5

Democrats

Reagan 27%
McGovern 59
Other; undecided 14

Independents

Reagan 57%
McGovern 30
Other; undecided 13

By Religion
Protestants

Reagan 56%
McGovern 34
Other; undecided 10

Catholics

Reagan 52%
McGovern 34
Other; undecided 14

Note: Although Walter Mondale continues to be the top nomination choice of Democratic voters, he shows less strength against President Ronald Reagan in test races for 1984 than does his chief rival, John Glenn. In the latest Gallup test elections, Reagan receives the support of 48% of registered voters to 44% for Mondale. In the other contest, Reagan trails Glenn, 42% to 48%. These findings are similar to those obtained in earlier surveys.

Recently announced contender George McGovern, the defeated Democratic presidential candidate in 1972, loses to Reagan by a 35% to 53% margin in the first test of his vote-getting potential. McGovern makes a strong showing in the Midwest, losing to Reagan there by only 6 percentage points. His 9% share of Democrats' votes to be their 1984 standard-bearer places him third in the nomination race. Although he trails far behind leaders Mondale (37%) and Glenn (26%), McGovern now leads candidates Alan Cranston, Reubin Askew, Gary Hart, and Ernest Hollings.

OCTOBER 9
DEMOCRATIC PRESIDENTIAL CANDIDATES

Interviewing Date: 9/9–12/83
Survey #223-G

Asked of Democrats and independents: Which one of these persons [respondents were handed a card listing candidates] would you like to see nominated as the Democratic party's candidate for president in 1984?

Choice of Democrats

Walter Mondale	37%
John Glenn	26
George McGovern	9
Alan Cranston	5
Reubin Askew	3
Gary Hart	3
Ernest Hollings	1
None; don't know	16

National Trend

	July 1983	June 1983
Mondale	41%	41%
Glenn	25	24
McGovern	–	–
Cranston	7	8
Askew	2	3

Hart	4	3
Hollings	2	1
None; don't know	19	20

Choice of Independents

Glenn	28%
Mondale	27
McGovern	13
Cranston	5
Hart	4
Askew	2
Hollings	1
None; don't know	20

National Trend

	July 1983	June 1983
Glenn	31%	28%
Mondale	32	25
McGovern	–	–
Cranston	4	7
Hart	4	7
Askew	2	2
Hollings	2	2
None; don't know	25	29

Choice of Democrats with Jesse Jackson on List

Mondale	34%
Glenn	23
McGovern	8
Jackson	8
Cranston	5
Askew	3
Hart	3
Hollings	1
None; don't know	15

By Race
White

Mondale	35%
Glenn	26
McGovern	10
Jackson	2
Cranston	6
Askew	3

Hart 3
Hollings 1
None; don't know 14

Black

Mondale 28%
Glenn 11
McGovern 3
Jackson 34
Cranston 3
Askew 3
Hart .... *
Hollings .... *
None; don't know 18

*Less than 1%

Note: George McGovern's mid-September entry into the contest for the 1984 Democratic presidential nomination has had two immediate effects. First, it has catapulted the former South Dakota senator and 1972 Democratic presidential nominee into third place, with 9% of Democrats' votes, behind leading contenders Walter Mondale and John Glenn, but ahead of would-be nominees Alan Cranston, Reubin Askew, Gary Hart, and Ernest Hollings. Second, by drawing Democrats' votes away from the six original contenders, especially Mondale, McGovern's presence in the race has narrowed the once considerable gap between Mondale and Glenn.

In the latest Gallup survey, Mondale is the choice of 37% of Democrats for their party's nomination to 26% for Glenn, an 11-point lead for the former vice-president. In surveys conducted during June and July before the McGovern announcement, Mondale led Glenn by much larger 17- and 16-point margins, respectively. Although Mondale's lead over Glenn among Democrats has shrunk since McGovern's entry, the two leaders remain virtually deadlocked for the nomination among independents, who constitute almost one-third of the electorate and of whom many can vote in the Democratic primaries next year.

The latest survey also measured the possible impact of the Reverend Jesse Jackson, who has indicated he may enter the Democratic nomination contest. Among all Democrats in the survey, when Jackson's name is included he receives 8% of their nomination votes, placing him in a tie with McGovern. The Jackson vote is drawn about equally from backers of Mondale and Glenn; thus, while the presence of Jackson marginally decreases the overall vote for the leaders, it does not affect their relative standing.

In January 1972, candidate McGovern had the backing of only 3% of Democrats for their party's nomination. His support increased only a few percentage points over the next several weeks, but by April his standing had shot up to 17%. By May, he was even with his key rivals, winning 25% of the support of Democrats to 26% for George Wallace and 26% for Hubert Humphrey. By late June, as the Democratic convention neared, he moved ahead of his opponents, winning 30% of the vote to 27% for Humphrey and 25% for Wallace. In the 1972 presidential election, President Richard Nixon easily won his bid for a second term and defeated McGovern by a 62% to 38% margin.

OCTOBER 12
MONDALE-GLENN PATTERNS OF
SUPPORT TAKE SHAPE*

A reading of the Democratic candidate preference polls suggests that, as of now, Walter Mondale has the numbers but John Glenn has the intangibles. The contest for the top Democratic spot in 1984 seems to be a two-man race, according to surveys of the public and party pros. A September Gallup Poll of rank-and-file Democrats found 37% supported Walter Mondale, while 26% favored Glenn; George McGovern was a distant third at 9%. The sharp contrasts in how the two leading candidates are perceived and their support patterns may well dictate the eventual Democratic nominee.

The overriding difference between Glenn and Mondale is that the former vice-president is the

*This Gallup analysis was written by Andrew Kohut, president of the Gallup Organization Inc.

choice of traditional Democratic groups, while the Ohio senator is preferred by voters who are more on the periphery of the Democratic party. Mondale's core support is blue collar, black, urban, and lower income. On the other hand, Glenn's support tends to be greater among white, more affluent, and better educated Democrats. Almost all the polls show that Glenn has relatively greater strength among voters who consider themselves political independents. While Mondale is clearly the front-runner among Democrats, he and Glenn run about evenly among independents. One of the anomalies of Gallup's findings is that Glenn, who has relatively less strength among orthodox Democrats, also has less appeal to Democrats under 30 years old who are too young to remember his feats as an astronaut.

Mondale's current lead in the polls among rank-and-file Democrats may be a little more tenuous than is suggested by his overall margin. Glenn's level of support varies far less than Mondale's when Gallup tests the relative strength of the two front-runners against other well-known Democrats such as Jesse Jackson and Ted Kennedy. In particular, should Jackson enter the race, he could draw off a good deal of Mondale's black support in large primary states. For example, in July prior to McGovern's entry into the race, Mondale led Glenn 41% to 25%, but when a September Gallup Poll of Democrats retested with McGovern and Jackson in the race, Mondale's support dropped to 34%, while preference for Glenn was all but unchanged (23%).

The Ohio senator has a more sharply defined personal image than does the former vice-president. More people see him as likable, interesting, bright, principled, having good judgment and strong leadership qualities. Mondale is better regarded on policy rather than personal dimensions. In particular, Mondale, more than Glenn, is seen as sympathetic to the average citizen and the poor, qualities one would expect in a candidate whose core support is traditionally Democratic.

Mondale's traditional Democratic position and organizational strength brought him official labor union and women's groups' endorsements and also has made him the top choice of Democratic party

pros. Summer polls by ABC News of the Democratic National Committee found Mondale leading Glenn but with a large undecided vote. However, a September *Newsweek* poll of some 319 influential Democrats found 44% choosing Mondale, while 30% named Glenn as their top choice. This poll of influential Democrats, which included fifty-eight U.S. senators and representatives, twelve governors, and, in total, seventy Democratic National Committee members, showed that, while Mondale was seen as better organized and the sentimental favorite, Glenn was widely viewed as the candidate better able to defeat Ronald Reagan in 1984 by a majority of 51% to 34%.

This view is consistent with what the polls have shown over the past year: Glenn runs a considerably stronger race than Mondale in test elections against Reagan. The Ohio senator's greater appeal to independents accounts for this. It would seem that independents' support is an especially important asset in 1984 when members of both major parties can be expected to back their standard-bearers. Support for the president among Republicans probably will be in the high 80s and, judging from last year's congressional vote, traditional Democratic groups may well turn out heavily against the president.

In many respects, the polls suggest that the race for the Democratic nomination will pit Glenn's powerful personal image and his potential ability to attract a broader spectrum of voters against the loyalist appeal of Mondale. The earliest primaries may quickly indicate which of these factors holds the greatest sway.

OCTOBER 16
PRESIDENT REAGAN

Interviewing Date: 9/16–19/83
Survey #224-G

Do you approve or disapprove of the way Ronald Reagan is handling his job as president?

Approve 47%
Disapprove 43
No opinion 10

By Sex

Male

Approve 53%
Disapprove 40
No opinion 7

Female

Approve 42%
Disapprove 45
No opinion 13

By Race

White

Approve 53%
Disapprove 38
No opinion 9

Nonwhite

Approve 13%
Disapprove 71
No opinion 16

By Education

College

Approve 54%
Disapprove 42
No opinion 4

High School

Approve 44%
Disapprove 44
No opinion 12

Grade School

Approve 35%
Disapprove 48
No opinion 17

By Region

East

Approve 45%
Disapprove 44
No opinion 11

Midwest

Approve 48%
Disapprove 44
No opinion 8

South

Approve 49%
Disapprove 39
No opinion 12

West

Approve 46%
Disapprove 46
No opinion 8

By Age

18–24 Years

Approve 40%
Disapprove 49
No opinion 11

25–29 Years

Approve 49%
Disapprove 40
No opinion 11

30–49 Years

Approve 51%
Disapprove 42
No opinion 7

50–64 Years

Approve 48%
Disapprove 41
No opinion 11

65 Years and Over

Approve 43%
Disapprove 42
No opinion 15

By Income

$40,000 and Over

Approve	58%
Disapprove	35
No opinion	7

$30,000–$39,999

Approve	62%
Disapprove	36
No opinion	2

$20,000–$29,999

Approve	54%
Disapprove	37
No opinion	9

Under $20,000

Approve	57%
Disapprove	37
No opinion	6

By Politics

Republicans

Approve	81%
Disapprove	14
No opinion	5

Democrats

Approve	25%
Disapprove	66
No opinion	9

Independents

Approve	48%
Disapprove	39
No opinion	13

By Religion

Protestants

Approve	51%
Disapprove	40
No opinion	9

Catholics

Approve	44%
Disapprove	43
No opinion	13

By Occupation

Professional and Business

Approve	59%
Disapprove	34
No opinion	7

Clerical and Sales

Approve	45%
Disapprove	47
No opinion	8

Manual Workers

Approve	43%
Disapprove	48
No opinion	9

Nonlabor Force

Approve	37%
Disapprove	48
No opinion	15

By Community Size

One Million and Over

Approve	45%
Disapprove	45
No opinion	10

500,000–999,999

Approve	41%
Disapprove	51
No opinion	8

50,000–499,999

Approve	50%
Disapprove	39
No opinion	11

2,500–49,999

Approve 45%
Disapprove 45
No opinion 10

Under 2,500; Rural

Approve 51%
Disapprove 39
No opinion 10

Labor Union Families Only

Approve 40%
Disapprove 51
No opinion 9

Nonlabor Union Families Only

Approve 48%
Disapprove 41
No opinion 11

National Trend

	Approve	Dis-approve	No opinion
1983			
September 16–19	47%	43%	10%
September 9–12	47	42	11
August 19–22	43	46	11
August 12–15	43	45	12
August 5–8	44	46	10
July 29–August 1	44	42	14
July 22–25	42	47	11
June 24–27	47	44	9
June 10–13	43	45	12
May 20–23	46	43	11
May 13–16	43	45	12
April 29–May 2	43	46	11
April 15–18	41	49	10
March 11–14	41	49	10
February 25–28	40	50	10
January 28–31	35	56	9
January 21–24	37	53	10
January 14–17	37	54	9
1982			
December	41	50	9
November	43	47	10
October	42	48	10
September	42	48	10
August	41	49	10
July	42	46	12
June	45	45	10
May	45	44	11
April	43	47	10
March	46	45	9
February	47	43	10
January	49	40	11

Also asked of those who expressed an opinion of the way Reagan is handling his job as president: How strongly would you say you approve/disapprove—very strongly, or not so strongly?

Approve 47%
  Strongly 22
  Not so strongly 24
  No opinion 1
Disapprove 43
  Not so strongly 13
  Strongly 28
  No opinion 2
No opinion 10

By Sex
Male

Approve 53%
  Strongly 28
  Not so strongly 24
  No opinion 1
Disapprove 40
  Not so strongly 12
  Strongly 27
  No opinion 1
No opinion 7

Female

Approve 42%
  Strongly 16
  Not so strongly 24
  No opinion 2

Disapprove 45
    Not so strongly 15
    Strongly 29
    No opinion 1
No opinion 13

By Race
White

Approve 53%
    Strongly 24
    Not so strongly 27
    No opinion 2
Disapprove 38
    Not so strongly 12
    Strongly 25
    No opinion 1
No opinion 9

Black

Approve 12%
    Strongly 7
    Not so strongly 4
    No opinion 1
Disapprove 75
    Not so strongly 22
    Strongly 51
    No opinion 2
No opinion 13

Hispanics Only

Approve 41%
    Strongly 22
    Not so strongly 19
    No opinion .... –
Disapprove 39
    Not so strongly 10
    Strongly 27
    No opinion 2
No opinion 20

By Politics
Republicans

Approve 81%
    Strongly 51
    Not so strongly 28
    No opinion 2

Disapprove 14
    Not so strongly 4
    Strongly 9
    No opinion 1
No opinion 5

Democrats

Approve 25%
    Strongly 7
    Not so strongly 18
    No opinion .... –
Disapprove 66
    Not so strongly 18
    Strongly 46
    No opinion 2
No opinion 9

Independents

Approve 48%
    Strongly 18
    Not so strongly 29
    No opinion 1
Disapprove 39
    Not so strongly 15
    Strongly 23
    No opinion 1
No opinion 13

Note: President Ronald Reagan's job performance rating is now at its highest point in twenty-one months, with 47% of Americans saying they approve of his performance in office and 43% expressing disapproval. The last time the president's job rating was as high was in January 1982, when 49% approved and 40% disapproved.

Growing public optimism over the economy is clearly a major factor in the president's improved performance rating, with three persons in four in the current survey who express an opinion expecting the present economic recovery to last through the election year of 1984.

While public views on the economy are working in favor of Reagan today, the economic outlook of Americans was working against President Jimmy Carter at a comparable point in his presidency. In 1979 a late September-early October survey showed only 33% of Americans saying they approved of Carter's performance in office and 54% expressing disapproval. Continuing public concern over inflation and the energy crisis were key factors in disapproval of Carter's performance at that time.

Following the downing of the Korean jetliner by the Soviet Union on September 1, Reagan's approval rating increased 4 percentage points, a gain he has sustained in the latest survey. In a companion question, 52% of respondents express approval of Reagan's handling of the airliner incident, while 33% disapprove.

All persons in the current survey also were asked how strongly they approve or disapprove of Reagan's performance in office. The results show that one person in five nationally (22%) approves very strongly, while about three in ten (28%) disapprove very strongly. Men are twice as likely as women to say they approve very strongly—28% and 16% respectively, while fully one-half of blacks (51%) disapprove very strongly and only 7% approve very strongly.

Among Hispanics, 41% express approval of Reagan, not significantly different from the figure of 47% of the U.S. population as a whole, and 39% disapprove. Of all Hispanics, 22% approve very strongly, while 19% give mild approval to Reagan's performance. On the negative side, 10% of Hispanics express mild disapproval while 27% are in the strong disapproval category.

OCTOBER 20
SOVIET UNION/NATIONAL DEFENSE

Interviewing Date: 8/19–22; 9/16–19/83*
Survey #222-G; 224-G

Do you think President Ronald Reagan is being too tough in his dealings with the Soviet Union, not tough enough, or about right?

*The Korean jetliner was shot down by the Soviet Union on September 1.

	September 16–19	August 19–22
Too tough	5%	10%
Not tough enough	50	34
About right	38	41
No opinion	7	15

By Sex
Male

Too tough	5%	10%
Not tough enough	50	37
About right	40	43
No opinion	5	10

Female

Too tough	5%	11%
Not tough enough	50	31
About right	37	39
No opinion	8	19

By Race
White

Too tough	5%	9%
Not tough enough	50	34
About right	39	43
No opinion	6	14

Nonwhite

Too tough	4%	16%
Not tough enough	51	34
About right	30	32
No opinion	15	18

By Education
College

Too tough	10%	14%
Not tough enough	39	31
About right	49	46
No opinion	2	9

High School

Too tough	3%	9%
Not tough enough	56	37
About right	36	40
No opinion	5	14

Grade School

Too tough	3%	8%
Not tough enough	51	31
About right	33	33
No opinion	13	28

By Region

East

Too tough	4%	12%
Not tough enough	51	32
About right	39	41
No opinion	6	15

Midwest

Too tough	3%	9%
Not tough enough	52	34
About right	39	44
No opinion	6	13

South

Too tough	4%	8%
Not tough enough	50	37
About right	39	38
No opinion	7	17

West

Too tough	10%	15%
Not tough enough	47	34
About right	35	39
No opinion	8	12

By Age

18–24 Years

Too tough	8%	13%
Not tough enough	51	36
About right	33	36
No opinion	8	15

25–29 Years

Too tough	4%	17%
Not tough enough	48	26
About right	42	46
No opinion	6	11

30–49 Years

Too tough	5%	9%
Not tough enough	55	35
About right	34	43
No opinion	6	13

50–64 Years

Too tough	3%	8%
Not tough enough	49	36
About right	42	43
No opinion	6	13

65 Years and Over

Too tough	4%	9%
Not tough enough	43	34
About right	44	36
No opinion	9	21

By Politics

Republicans

Too tough	2%	4%
Not tough enough	48	36
About right	46	49
No opinion	4	11

Democrats

Too tough	6%	13%
Not tough enough	53	34
About right	34	36
No opinion	7	17

Independents

Too tough	6%	10%
Not tough enough	50	33
About right	37	44
No opinion	7	13

By Religion

Protestants

Too tough	3%	8%
Not tough enough	50	35
About right	41	42
No opinion	6	15

Catholics

Too tough	4%	10%
Not tough enough	53	34
About right	36	44
No opinion	7	12

By Occupation
Professional and Business

Too tough	6%	14%
Not tough enough	46	33
About right	44	45
No opinion	4	8

Clerical and Sales

Too tough	4%	5%
Not tough enough	51	29
About right	37	44
No opinion	8	22

Manual Workers

Too tough	5%	10%
Not tough enough	56	36
About right	33	41
No opinion	6	13

Nonlabor Force

Too tough	4%	11%
Not tough enough	43	35
About right	44	34
No opinion	9	20

By Community Size
One Million and Over

Too tough	6%	13%
Not tough enough	45	32
About right	39	39
No opinion	10	16

500,000–999,999

Too tough	6%	13%
Not tough enough	54	31
About right	31	38
No opinion	9	18

50,000–499,999

Too tough	5%	9%
Not tough enough	49	35
About right	40	43
No opinion	6	13

2,500–49,999

Too tough	3%	8%
Not tough enough	55	35
About right	38	47
No opinion	4	10

Under 2,500; Rural

Too tough	3%	8%
Not tough enough	53	37
About right	39	40
No opinion	5	15

Labor Union Families Only

Too tough	5%	9%
Not tough enough	52	35
About right	40	44
No opinion	3	12

Nonlabor Union Families Only

Too tough	5%	11%
Not tough enough	50	34
About right	38	40
No opinion	7	15

There is much discussion as to the amount of money the government in Washington should spend for national defense and military purposes. How do you feel about this: Do you think we are spending too much, about the right amount, or too little?

	September 16–19	August 19–22
Too much	37%	42%
About right	36	35
Too little	21	14
No opinion	6	9

By Sex

Male

Too much	34%	42%
About right	37	37
Too little	25	15
No opinion	4	6

Female

Too much	39%	41%
About right	35	34
Too little	18	13
No opinion	8	12

By Race

White

Too much	35%	40%
About right	38	37
Too little	22	15
No opinion	5	8

Nonwhite

Too much	49%	52%
About right	23	27
Too little	18	7
No opinion	10	14

By Education

College

Too much	46%	48%
About right	35	34
Too little	17	14
No opinion	2	4

High School

Too much	32%	40%
About right	39	36
Too little	24	15
No opinion	5	9

Grade School

Too much	35%	34%
About right	32	36
Too little	23	10
No opinion	10	20

By Region

East

Too much	40%	46%
About right	37	29
Too little	17	15
No opinion	6	10

Midwest

Too much	37%	44%
About right	39	36
Too little	20	12
No opinion	4	8

South

Too much	34%	31%
About right	33	38
Too little	26	19
No opinion	7	12

West

Too much	37%	47%
About right	35	39
Too little	22	9
No opinion	6	5

By Age

18–24 Years

Too much	42%	54%
About right	29	27
Too little	24	9
No opinion	5	10

25–29 Years

Too much	43%	54%
About right	33	36
Too little	16	7
No opinion	8	3

30–49 Years

Too much	35%	40%
About right	39	36
Too little	23	18
No opinion	3	6

50–64 Years

Too much	36%	34%
About right	38	44
Too little	21	15
No opinion	5	7

65 Years and Over

Too much	32%	35%
About right	38	32
Too little	19	14
No opinion	11	19

By Politics
Republicans

Too much	26%	30%
About right	47	44
Too little	22	19
No opinion	5	7

Democrats

Too much	42%	47%
About right	30	30
Too little	22	13
No opinion	6	10

Independents

Too much	39%	44%
About right	34	36
Too little	22	13
No opinion	5	7

By Religion
Protestants

Too much	34%	36%
About right	35	38
Too little	25	16
No opinion	6	10

Catholics

Too much	37%	44%
About right	43	38
Too little	15	10
No opinion	5	8

By Occupation
Professional and Business

Too much	39%	46%
About right	37	35
Too little	21	14
No opinion	3	5

Clerical and Sales

Too much	36%	38%
About right	36	41
Too little	23	11
No opinion	5	10

Manual Workers

Too much	35%	42%
About right	38	36
Too little	22	15
No opinion	5	7

Nonlabor Force

Too much	38%	37%
About right	32	33
Too little	22	15
No opinion	8	15

By Community Size
One Million and Over

Too much	41%	49%
About right	35	35
Too little	17	8
No opinion	7	8

500,000–999,999

Too much	36%	44%
About right	35	33
Too little	22	13
No opinion	7	10

50,000–499,999

Too much	39%	45%
About right	35	32
Too little	21	15
No opinion	5	8

2,500–49,999

Too much	35%	37%
About right	34	35
Too little	26	17
No opinion	5	11

Under 2,500; Rural

Too much	32%	33%
About right	38	40
Too little	24	17
No opinion	6	10

Labor Union Families Only

Too much	40%	47%
About right	35	36
Too little	22	12
No opinion	3	5

Nonlabor Union Families Only

Too much	36%	40%
About right	36	35
Too little	22	15
No opinion	6	10

Those Who Say Reagan Is Not Tough Enough in His Dealings With the Soviet Union*

Too much	34%
About right	35
Too little	28
No opinion	3

Those Who Say Reagan Is About Right in His Dealings With the Soviet Union*

Too much	34%
About right	45
Too little	16
No opinion	5

Those Who Say Reagan Is Too Tough in His Dealings With the Soviet Union*

Too much	77%
About right	8
Too little	12
No opinion	3

*Based on September 16–19 interviews

National Trend
(Defense Spending)

	Too much	About right	Too little	No opinion
Sept. 16–19, 1983	37%	36%	21%	6%
Aug. 19–22, 1983	42	35	14	9
Jan. 14–17, 1983	45	33	14	8
November 1982	41	31	16	12
March 1982	36	36	19	9
1981	15	22	51	12
1976	36	32	22	10
1973	46	30	13	11
1971	50	31	11	8
1969	52	31	8	9
1960	18	45	21	16

Note: In the aftermath of the Korean airliner incident, public support for defense spending cuts has fallen to its lowest level in more than a year. At the same time, Americans' perceptions that President Ronald Reagan is not being tough enough in his dealings with the Soviet Union have risen sharply.

In a Gallup survey conducted shortly before the Soviets shot down the unarmed Korean passenger airliner, 42% said they thought the United States was spending too much for defense and military purposes, while 35% said the amount was about right, 14% thought it was too little, and 9% had no opinion. After the airliner tragedy, those who said defense spending was too high dropped to 37%, while the belief that military spending is too little rose by 7 percentage points to 21%.

Before the shooting down of the airliner, 41%

said they thought Reagan's dealings with the Soviet Union were about right in severity, while 34% thought the president was not tough enough, 10% said he was too tough, and 15% did not express an opinion. After the international incident, there was a 16 percentage-point increase from 34% to 50% in those saying Reagan is not tough enough.

A surprising degree of unanimity among Americans of different political persuasions is found when the results of the surveys conducted before and after the incident are compared. As noted, the feeling that Reagan is not being tough enough with the Soviet Union increased by 16 points nationally. The event produced a 12-point increment in this sentiment among Republicans in the survey, and a comparable increase among Democrats (up 14 points) and independents (up 17).

OCTOBER 23
SOVIET UNION

Interviewing Date: 9/16–19/83*
Survey #224-G

You notice that the ten boxes on this card go from the highest position of +5 for a country you have a very favorable opinion of all the way down to the lowest position of −5 for a country you have a very unfavorable opinion of:

How far up the scale or how far down the scale would you rate the Soviet Union?

*The findings reported below are based on a rating device called the Stapel Scalometer. This scale not only determines whether an opinion is favorable or unfavorable, but it also registers the intensity with which that opinion is held. Values on the scale run from a high of +5 to a low of −5. The top five positions represent favorable opinions and the bottom five, unfavorable opinions.

Very favorable (+5, +4) 2%
Mildly favorable (+3, +2, +1) 7
Mildly unfavorable (−1, −2, −3) 22
Very unfavorable (−4, −5) 66
No opinion 3

By Sex
Male

Very favorable 2%
Mildly favorable 8
Mildly unfavorable 23
Very unfavorable 65
No opinion 2

Female

Very favorable 2%
Mildly favorable 6
Mildly unfavorable 22
Very unfavorable 67
No opinion 4

By Race
White

Very favorable 2%
Mildly favorable 6
Mildly unfavorable 22
Very unfavorable 67
No opinion 3

Nonwhite

Very favorable 2%
Mildly favorable 10
Mildly unfavorable 20
Very unfavorable 60
No opinion 8

By Education
College

Very favorable 3%
Mildly favorable 8
Mildly unfavorable 31
Very unfavorable 57
No opinion 1

High School

Very favorable 1%
Mildly favorable 6
Mildly unfavorable 21
Very unfavorable 70
No opinion 2

Grade School

Very favorable 2%
Mildly favorable 8
Mildly unfavorable 15
Very unfavorable 69
No opinion 6

By Region
East

Very favorable 2%
Mildly favorable 5
Mildly unfavorable 23
Very unfavorable 66
No opinion 4

Midwest

Very favorable 1%
Mildly favorable 6
Mildly unfavorable 18
Very unfavorable 72
No opinion 3

South

Very favorable 3%
Mildly favorable 6
Mildly unfavorable 19
Very unfavorable 69
No opinion 4

West

Very favorable 3%
Mildly favorable 11
Mildly unfavorable 18
Very unfavorable 56
No opinion 2

By Age
18–29 Years

Very favorable 2%
Mildly favorable 9
Mildly unfavorable 27
Very unfavorable 60
No opinion 3

30–49 Years

Very favorable 3%
Mildly favorable 7
Mildly unfavorable 21
Very unfavorable 67
No opinion 2

50 Years and Over

Very favorable 1%
Mildly favorable 6
Mildly unfavorable 19
Very unfavorable 70
No opinion 4

By Politics
Republicans

Very favorable 2%
Mildly favorable 3
Mildly unfavorable 23
Very unfavorable 70
No opinion 2

Democrats

Very favorable 2%
Mildly favorable 8
Mildly unfavorable 20
Very unfavorable 67
No opinion 4

Independents

Very favorable 2%
Mildly favorable 9
Mildly unfavorable 21
Very unfavorable 65
No opinion 3

National Trend

(Favorable Attitudes Toward the Soviet Union)

September 16–17, 1983*	9%
1982	21
1981	20
1980†	13
1979	34
1978	26
1976	21
June 1973‡	45
April 1973§	34
1967	19
1966	17
1956	5
1954	5
1953	1

*Downing of Korean airliner, September 1
†Afghanistan invasion, December 1979
‡Leonid Brezhnev's visit, June 1973
§SALT ratified, August 1972

Now, how would you rate the Soviet leaders?

Very favorable (+5, +4)	1%
Mildly favorable (+3, +2, +1)	6
Mildly unfavorable (−1, −2, −3)	21
Very unfavorable (−4, −5)	68
No opinion	4

By Sex

Male

Very favorable	2%
Mildly favorable	6
Mildly unfavorable	22
Very unfavorable	68
No opinion	2

Female

Very favorable	1%
Mildly favorable	5
Mildly unfavorable	21
Very unfavorable	68
No opinion	6

By Race

White

Very favorable	1%
Mildly favorable	5
Mildly unfavorable	22
Very unfavorable	69
No opinion	4

Nonwhite

Very favorable	*%
Mildly favorable	12
Mildly unfavorable	21
Very unfavorable	60
No opinion	7

By Education

College

Very favorable	2%
Mildly favorable	7
Mildly unfavorable	27
Very unfavorable	62
No opinion	2

High School

Very favorable	1%
Mildly favorable	3
Mildly unfavorable	23
Very unfavorable	71
No opinion	2

Grade School

Very favorable	1%
Mildly favorable	6
Mildly unfavorable	18
Very unfavorable	65
No opinion	10

By Region

East

Very favorable	2%
Mildly favorable	5
Mildly unfavorable	24
Very unfavorable	65
No opinion	4

Midwest

Very favorable 1%
Mildly favorable 6
Mildly unfavorable 19
Very unfavorable 70
No opinion 4

South

Very favorable 1%
Mildly favorable 6
Mildly unfavorable 17
Very unfavorable 72
No opinion 4

West

Very favorable 2%
Mildly favorable 5
Mildly unfavorable 27
Very unfavorable 63
No opinion 4

By Age

18–29 Years

Very favorable .... *%
Mildly favorable 6
Mildly unfavorable 29
Very unfavorable 62
No opinion 3

30–49 Years

Very favorable 2%
Mildly favorable 5
Mildly unfavorable 18
Very unfavorable 71
No opinion 4

50 Years and Over

Very favorable 1%
Mildly favorable 5
Mildly unfavorable 19
Very unfavorable 69
No opinion 6

By Politics

Republicans

Very favorable 1%
Mildly favorable 5
Mildly unfavorable 18
Very unfavorable 72
No opinion 4

Democrats

Very favorable 2%
Mildly favorable 4
Mildly unfavorable 22
Very unfavorable 69
No opinion 3

Independents

Very favorable 1%
Mildly favorable 6
Mildly unfavorable 24
Very unfavorable 64
No opinion 5

*Less than 1%

How would you rate the Soviet people?

Very favorable (+5, +4) 9%
Mildly favorable (+3, +2, +1) 40
Mildly unfavorable (−1, −2, −3) 30
Very unfavorable (−4, −5) 15
No opinion 6

By Sex

Male

Very favorable 12%
Mildly favorable 42
Mildly unfavorable 26
Very unfavorable 14
No opinion 6

Female

Very favorable 7%
Mildly favorable 37
Mildly unfavorable 33
Very unfavorable 16
No opinion 7

By Race

White

Very favorable 10%
Mildly favorable 42
Mildly unfavorable 31
Very unfavorable 12
No opinion 6

Nonwhite

Very favorable 9%
Mildly favorable 24
Mildly unfavorable 24
Very unfavorable 33
No opinion 10

By Education

College

Very favorable 12%
Mildly favorable 54
Mildly unfavorable 25
Very unfavorable 5
No opinion 4

High School

Very favorable 8%
Mildly favorable 37
Mildly unfavorable 32
Very unfavorable 19
No opinion 4

Grade School

Very favorable 8%
Mildly favorable 31
Mildly unfavorable 28
Very unfavorable 22
No opinion 12

By Region

East

Very favorable 9%
Mildly favorable 42
Mildly unfavorable 26
Very unfavorable 17
No opinion 7

Midwest

Very favorable 11%
Mildly favorable 38
Mildly unfavorable 32
Very unfavorable 14
No opinion 5

South

Very favorable 8%
Mildly favorable 33
Mildly unfavorable 35
Very unfavorable 17
No opinion 7

West

Very favorable 11%
Mildly favorable 47
Mildly unfavorable 25
Very unfavorable 11
No opinion 6

By Age

18–29 Years

Very favorable 10%
Mildly favorable 36
Mildly unfavorable 32
Very unfavorable 15
No opinion 7

30–49 Years

Very favorable 10%
Mildly favorable 42
Mildly unfavorable 29
Very unfavorable 14
No opinion 5

50 Years and Over

Very favorable 8%
Mildly favorable 40
Mildly unfavorable 29
Very unfavorable 16
No opinion 7

By Politics

Republicans

Very favorable	9%
Mildly favorable	46
Mildly unfavorable	36
Very unfavorable	14
No opinion	5

Democrats

Very favorable	8%
Mildly favorable	36
Mildly unfavorable	32
Very unfavorable	19
No opinion	5

Independents

Very favorable	11%
Mildly favorable	41
Mildly unfavorable	31
Very unfavorable	10
No opinion	7

Note: Reflecting national frustration and anger in the wake of the Korean airliner tragedy, favorable opinion of the Soviet Union is currently at its lowest point since 1956. In the latest survey, only 9% of U.S. adults hold a favorable opinion of the Soviet Union, while 88% express unfavorable views of that nation. One year ago, 21% held a favorable and 74% an unfavorable opinion of the Communist superpower.

Views about the Soviet leaders and people were assessed separately in the current survey, as well as views about the nation as a whole. The results show that much of the current animosity toward the Soviet Union is directed at the leaders rather than the people; only 7% hold a favorable opinion of the leaders and 89% an unfavorable opinion. In contrast, Americans lean to the positive side when asked to rate the Soviet people, with 49% holding favorable and 45% unfavorable views of Soviet citizens. Americans with a college background are even more positive, with 66% expressing favorable views toward the Soviet rank and file and 30% negative opinions. The views of the college educated about the Soviet leaders, however, closely match those of persons with less formal education.

As stated above, favorable attitudes toward the Soviet Union are lower today than at any other time since 1956, when only 5% held a favorable opinion. Still earlier, in August 1953, only 1% of Americans held a favorable opinion. By a ratio of 8 to 1, the public believed the Soviet Union was out to rule or dominate the world, a view that had persisted since the end of World War II.

Little change was recorded in the mid-1950s, but a decade later, in 1966, overall favorable ratings of the USSR had climbed to 17%. By that time, Americans had become far less antagonistic toward the Soviet Union, due in part to a shift in attitudes toward mainland China. The ideological split between the Soviet Union and the People's Republic had led many Americans to believe that Red China was a greater menace to world peace and that the Soviet Union would be on our side in the event of trouble between China and the United States.

At the time of Leonid Brezhnev's visit in 1973, positive ratings had climbed to 45%, the highest favorable vote recorded since the war; this reflected his agreement with President Richard Nixon to try to avert a military confrontation that might lead to nuclear conflict. In the ensuing years, however, this enthusiasm waned, and by 1976 only 21% held a favorable opinion of the Soviet Union. Positive feelings increased and in early 1979, 34% expressed favorable views. Then came the Afghanistan invasion in late 1979, draining much of the goodwill that had been building and causing favorable attitudes to plunge 21 percentage points.

OCTOBER 24
LEBANON SITUATION

Interviewing Date: 10/7–10/83
Survey #225-G

Do you think the United States made a mistake in sending the Marines to Lebanon, or not?

Yes, a mistake 51%
No 37
No opinion 12

By Sex

Male

Yes, a mistake 45%
No 45
No opinion 10

Female

Yes, a mistake 56%
No 29
No opinion 15

By Race

White

Yes, a mistake 49%
No 39
No opinion 12

Nonwhite

Yes, a mistake 61%
No 23
No opinion 16

By Education

College

Yes, a mistake 46%
No 45
No opinion 9

High School

Yes, a mistake 55%
No 34
No opinion 11

Grade School

Yes, a mistake 55%
No 26
No opinion 19

By Region

East

Yes, a mistake 58%
No 33
No opinion 9

Midwest

Yes, a mistake 46%
No 40
No opinion 14

South

Yes, a mistake 49%
No 36
No opinion 15

West

Yes, a mistake 51%
No 38
No opinion 11

By Age

18–29 Years

Yes, a mistake 56%
No 35
No opinion 9

30–49 Years

Yes, a mistake 51%
No 37
No opinion 12

50 Years and Over

Yes, a mistake 50%
No 37
No opinion 13

By Politics

Republicans

Yes, a mistake 36%
No 53
No opinion 11

Democrats

Yes, a mistake 61%
No 29
No opinion 10

Independents

Yes, a mistake 50%
No 36
No opinion 14

Those Who Approve of
President Reagan

Yes, a mistake 35%
No 54
No opinion 11

Those Who Disapprove of
President Reagan

Yes, a mistake 68%
No 23
No opinion 9

How likely do you think it is that the U.S. involvement in Lebanon could turn into a situation like Vietnam—that is, that the United States would become more and more deeply involved as time goes on? Would you say this is very likely, fairly likely, not very likely, or not at all likely?

Very likely 35%
Fairly likely 29
Not very likely 20
Not at all likely 8
No opinion 8

By Sex
Male

Very likely 31%
Fairly likely 26
Not very likely 25
Not at all likely 13
No opinion 5

Female

Very likely 39%
Fairly likely 32
Not very likely 15
Not at all likely 4
No opinion 10

By Race
White

Very likely 34%
Fairly likely 29
Not very likely 21
Not at all likely 9
No opinion 7

Nonwhite

Very likely 38%
Fairly likely 30
Not very likely 13
Not at all likely 7
No opinion 12

By Education
College

Very likely 23%
Fairly likely 31
Not very likely 29
Not at all likely 13
No opinion 4

High School

Very likely 42%
Fairly likely 27
Not very likely 17
Not at all likely 8
No opinion 6

Grade School

Very likely 38%
Fairly likely 23
Not very likely 16
Not at all likely 5
No opinion 18

By Region

East

Very likely	33%
Fairly likely	28
Not very likely	22
Not at all likely	11
No opinion	6

Midwest

Very likely	39%
Fairly likely	28
Not very likely	18
Not at all likely	8
No opinion	7

South

Very likely	34%
Fairly likely	28
Not very likely	19
Not at all likely	8
No opinion	11

West

Very likely	35%
Fairly likely	33
Not very likely	21
Not at all likely	6
No opinion	5

By Age

18–29 Years

Very likely	34%
Fairly likely	36
Not very likely	16
Not at all likely	10
No opinion	4

30–49 Years

Very likely	36%
Fairly likely	30
Not very likely	20
Not at all likely	7
No opinion	7

50 Years and Over

Very likely	34%
Fairly likely	23
Not very likely	23
Not at all likely	9
No opinion	11

By Politics

Republicans

Very likely	25%
Fairly likely	29
Not very likely	27
Not at all likely	12
No opinion	7

Democrats

Very likely	43%
Fairly likely	27
Not very likely	17
Not at all likely	6
No opinion	7

Independents

Very likely	34%
Fairly likely	32
Not very likely	20
Not at all likely	8
No opinion	6

Those Who Approve of President Reagan

Very likely	23%
Fairly likely	31
Not very likely	27
Not at all likely	12
No opinion	7

Those Who Disapprove of President Reagan

Very likely	47%
Fairly likely	27
Not very likely	15
Not at all likely	5
No opinion	6

Note: Even prior to the recent bomb blast in Beirut that killed more than 200 U.S. Marines (October 23), 51% of Americans had reached the conclusion that the United States made a mistake in sending Marines to Lebanon, with 64% saying it was either very or fairly likely that our involvement could turn into a situation like Vietnam.

OCTOBER 27
ECONOMIC RECOVERY

Interviewing Date: 9/16–19/83
Survey #224-G

> It is estimated that the federal government's budget deficit for fiscal 1984 will be as much as $200 billion—that is, it will spend more than it takes in—unless some steps are taken to reduce the size of this deficit. Do you approve or disapprove of raising income taxes as a way of reducing this deficit?

Approve 14%
Disapprove 79
No opinion 7

By Sex
Male

Approve 18%
Disapprove 78
No opinion 4

Female

Approve 12%
Disapprove 79
No opinion 9

By Education
College Graduates

Approve 23%
Disapprove 74
No opinion 3

College, Incomplete

Approve 15%
Disapprove 80
No opinion 5

High-School Graduates

Approve 11%
Disapprove 83
No opinion 6

Less Than High-School Graduates

Approve 9%
Disapprove 80
No opinion 11

By Income
$40,000 and Over

Approve 23%
Disapprove 74
No opinion 3

$30,000–$39,999

Approve 21%
Disapprove 74
No opinion 5

$20,000–$29,999

Approve 13%
Disapprove 82
No opinion 5

$10,000–$19,999

Approve 11%
Disapprove 81
No opinion 8

Under $10,000

Approve 11%
Disapprove 78
No opinion 11

By Politics
Republicans

Approve 15%
Disapprove 79
No opinion 6

Democrats

Approve 17%
Disapprove 77
No opinion 6

Independents

Approve 13%
Disapprove 82
No opinion 5

As you know, the economy has begun to recover from recession this year, with increased production, employment, and profits. Of course, no one knows for sure, but what is your best guess how long this recovery will last before the economy turns down again—will the recovery end this year, early next year, later next year, or later than that?

This year 6%
Early next year 11
Later next year 20
Later than that 38
Never (volunteered) 5
No opinion 20

By Politics
Republicans

This year 4%
Early next year 13
Later next year 20
Later than that 44
Never (volunteered) 5
No opinion 16

Democrats

This year 8%
Early next year 11
Later next year 19
Later than that 35
Never (volunteered) 5
No opinion 20

Independents

This year 6%
Early next year 12
Later next year 21
Later than that 38
Never (volunteered) 6
No opinion 18

For each item on this list, please tell me whether you think it will be a great threat, somewhat of a threat, or not much of a threat to continued recovery in the economy:

The federal government's budget deficit?

Great threat 42%
Somewhat 34
Not much 13
No opinion 11

By Politics
Republicans

Great threat 41%
Somewhat 38
Not much 15
No opinion 6

Democrats

Great threat 41%
Somewhat 32
Not much 13
No opinion 14

Independents

Great threat 45%
Somewhat 31
Not much 13
No opinion 11

High interest rates?

Great threat 61%
Somewhat 29
Not much 6
No opinion 4

By Politics

Republicans

Great threat 61%
Somewhat 31
Not much 6
No opinion 2

Democrats

Great threat 63%
Somewhat 26
Not much 5
No opinion 6

Independents

Great threat 60%
Somewhat 30
Not much 6
No opinion 4

The amount of taxes people pay?

Great threat 39%
Somewhat 35
Not much 20
No opinion 6

By Politics

Republicans

Great threat 34%
Somewhat 37
Not much 24
No opinion 5

Democrats

Great threat 43%
Somewhat 33
Not much 18
No opinion 6

Independents

Great threat 38%
Somewhat 34
Not much 22
No opinion 6

The rate of inflation?

Great threat 52%
Somewhat 32
Not much 10
No opinion 6

By Politics

Republicans

Great threat 51%
Somewhat 33
Not much 12
No opinion 4

Democrats

Great threat 53%
Somewhat 31
Not much 8
No opinion 8

Independents

Great threat 52%
Somewhat 32
Not much 11
No opinion 5

International trade problems such as the high value of the dollar, debts owed by countries like Brazil, Poland, etc.?

Great threat 43%
Somewhat 35
Not much 11
No opinion 11

By Politics

Republicans

Great threat 43%
Somewhat 37
Not much 13
No opinion 7

Democrats

Great threat 43%
Somewhat 34
Not much 10
No opinion 13

Independents

Great threat 46%
Somewhat 33
Not much 11
No opinion 10

Note: The American people are highly optimistic about the economic recovery, with six in ten predicting the economy will not begin to run out of steam until late next year, if then. In the latest survey, 20% say the economy might turn down late next year, while an additional 43% believe the recovery will last still longer.

On the less optimistic side, 6% predict an end to the recovery in the remaining months of 1983, while 11% think this may occur in early 1984. About one person in five, 20%, did not offer an opinion.

This bullish outlook for the recovery is only slightly stronger among Republicans, 69% of whom say an economic downturn may come late next year or beyond, than it is among Democrats (59%) and independents (65%).

In a companion question, high interest rates are considered a great threat to the recovery by 61% of respondents. Cited next often is the rate of inflation, with 52% saying it is a great threat. International trade problems, such as the high value of the dollar and the debts owed by developing nations, are rated a great threat by 43%, followed by the federal budget deficit according to 42% of the public. Finally, 39% say the amount of taxes people pay greatly threatens the recovery.

With comparatively few considering that personal income taxes might jeopardize the recovery and fewer still believing the upturn will be short-lived, it is not surprising that raising taxes to reduce the huge federal budget deficit is voted down by an overwhelming 5-to-1 margin. In all, 79% disapprove of tax hikes, while only 14% approve. Overwhelming majorities in all population groups, including Democrats, Republicans, and independents, reject higher taxes. Significantly larger proportions of college graduates (23%) and persons whose annual family income is $30,000 or more (22%) favor a tax increase; but even with these upscale groups, the weight of public sentiment is heavily against raising taxes.

OCTOBER 30
WOMAN FOR VICE-PRESIDENT

Interviewing Date: 10/7–10/83
Survey #225-G

Asked of registered voters: If a Democratic presidential nominee in 1984 selected a woman to be his vice-presidential running mate, would this make you more likely or less likely to vote for the Democratic ticket?

More likely 25%
Less likely 17
No difference (volunteered) 53
No opinion 5

By Sex
Male

More likely 20%
Less likely 17
No difference (volunteered) 56
No opinion 7

Male—Republicans

More likely 16%
Less likely 26
No difference (volunteered) 54
No opinion 4

Male—Democrats

More likely 24%
Less likely 12
No difference (volunteered) 56
No opinion 8

Male—Independents

More likely 21%
Less likely 17
No difference (volunteered) 57
No opinion 5

Female

More likely 29%
Less likely 17
No difference (volunteered) 50
No opinion 4

Female—Republicans

More likely	16%
Less likely	26
No difference (volunteered)	54
No opinion	4

Female—Democrats

More likely	40%
Less likely	12
No difference (volunteered)	44
No opinion	4

Female—Independents

More likely	25%
Less likely	15
No difference (volunteered)	56
No opinion	4

By Politics

Republicans

More likely	16%
Less likely	26
No difference (volunteered)	54
No opinion	4

Democrats

More likely	32%
Less likely	12
No difference (volunteered)	50
No opinion	6

Independents

More likely	23%
Less likely	16
No difference (volunteered)	56
No opinion	5

Note: If the 1984 Democratic presidential candidate were to select a woman as his running mate, his chances at the polls in November likely would be considerably enhanced. About one-half (53%) of all voters say that a woman as the vice-presidential candidate on the Democratic ticket would not affect their vote either way. But of those who think it would make a difference, a higher proportion (25%) say they would be more likely rather than less likely (17%) to vote for a Democratic ticket with a woman in the number two spot.

A Democratic ticket with a woman for vice-president would have particular appeal to women, who now account for 53% of the voting age population and in the last election voted at the same rate as men. By a 2-to-1 ratio, 29% to 17%, women say they would be more likely to vote for a ticket with a woman as vice-president. Another 50% of women say it would make no difference in their voting behavior. In the case of men, the addition of a woman to the Democratic ticket would make virtually no difference.

Since the question focused on the Democratic ticket, the views of Democratic voters are of prime importance. Among Democrats of both sexes, 32% say they would be more likely, 12% less likely to vote for a ticket with a woman. Among women Democrats, the comparable percentages are 40% to 12% and among men, 24% to 12%.

Many women think that the vice-presidency is the next logical step leading to the presidency. In the latest (May) Gallup survey on the subject, 80% say they would vote for a woman for president. The growth in the percentage of Americans who say they would be willing to vote for a woman for president is one of the most dramatic in polling annals. In a 1937 Gallup Poll, only 31% said they would vote for a woman for the highest office.

NOVEMBER 3
DEMOCRATIC PRESIDENTIAL CANDIDATES

Interviewing Date: 10/7–10/83
Survey #225-G

Asked of Democrats and independents: Which one of the persons on this card [card listed candidates] would you like to see nominated as the Democratic party's candidate for president in 1984?

Choice of Democrats

Walter Mondale	40%
John Glenn	21
Jesse Jackson	10

George McGovern 8
Alan Cranston 6
Gary Hart 3
Reubin Askew 1
Ernest Hollings 1
No opinion 10

White Democrats Only

Mondale 43%
Glenn 24
Jackson 3
McGovern 9
Cranston 6
Hart 4
Askew 1
Hollings 1
No opinion 9

Black Democrats Only

Mondale 30%
Glenn 10
Jackson 39
McGovern 5
Cranston 4
Hart .... *
Askew 1
Hollings 1
No opinion 10

Choice of Independents

Mondale 35%
Glenn 23
McGovern 9
Hart 5
Cranston 4
Jackson 3
Hollings 2
Askew .... *
No opinion 19

*Less than 1%

Note: Former Vice-president Walter Mondale has widened his lead over the field of Democratic presidential candidates and currently receives 40% of Democrats' nomination votes to 21% for Senator John Glenn. A September survey showed Mondale with 34% and Glenn with 23%.

In the current survey, completed just prior to the announcement of his candidacy, the Reverend Jesse Jackson is in third place, winning 10% of Democrats' votes nationwide. Jackson is the top choice of black Democrats with 39% of their support, but Mondale is a close second with 30% of the black vote. George McGovern receives 8% of the overall Democratic vote, followed by Alan Cranston with 6%, Gary Hart with 3%, Reubin Askew with 1%, and Ernest Hollings also with 1%.

In announcing that he will seek the 1984 Democratic presidential nomination, Jackson said he would try to choose a woman as his running mate. In view of this, it is interesting to note that 32% of Democrats in a recent Gallup survey said they would be more likely to vote for a Democratic ticket that included a woman, compared to 12% who would be less likely. The balance of 50% say it would make no difference either way. Among women Democrats, the ratio is even greater, with 40% saying they would be more likely, compared to 12% who would be less likely to vote for a Democratic ticket with a woman in the number two spot.

A black vice-presidential candidate on the Democratic ticket probably would neither hurt nor help. For every Democrat who would be more likely to vote for a Democratic ticket with a black as the vice-presidential candidate, an equal proportion (21%) would be less likely to do so. The remaining 57% either say it would make no difference or do not express an opinion.

The electorate is far more receptive to a black candidate for president today than in earlier decades, with the proportion saying they would be willing to vote for a black having grown from 38% in 1958 to 77% in a 1983 survey.

National Trend
(Vote for Black for President)*

	Would	Would not	No opinion
1983	77%	16%	7%
1978	77	18	5
1971	70	23	7
1969	67	23	10
1967	54	40	6

*From 1958 to 1978 the following question wording was used: *There's always much discussion about the qualifications of presidential candidates—their education, age, race, religion, and the like. If your party nominated a generally well-qualified man for president and he happened to be a Negro, would you vote for him?*

In 1983 the question was: *If your party nominated a generally well-qualified man for president and he happened to be black, would you vote for him?*

NOVEMBER 6
PRESIDENTIAL TRIAL HEATS

Interviewing Date: 10/7–10/83
Survey #225-G

> Asked of registered voters: Suppose the 1984 presidential election were being held today. If President Ronald Reagan were the Republican candidate and Walter Mondale were the Democratic candidate, which would you like to see win? [Those who named another person or who were undecided were asked: As of today, do you lean more to Reagan, the Republican, or to Mondale, the Democrat?]

Reagan 44%
Mondale 50
Other; undecided 6

By Politics
Republicans

Reagan 81%
Mondale 16
Other; undecided 3

Democrats

Reagan 17%
Mondale 78
Other; undecided 5

Independents

Reagan 48%
Mondale 44
Other; undecided 8

> Asked of registered voters: Suppose the 1984 presidential election were being held today. If President Ronald Reagan were the Republican candidate and Senator John Glenn were the Democratic candidate, which would you like to see win? [Those who named another person or who were undecided were asked: As of today, do you lean more to Reagan, the Republican, or to Glenn, the Democrat?]

Reagan 42%
Glenn 49
Other; undecided 9

By Politics
Republicans

Reagan 80%
Glenn 16
Other; undecided 4

Democrats

Reagan 18%
Glenn 73
Other; undecided 9

Independents

Reagan 44%
Glenn 46
Other; undecided 10

> Asked of registered voters: Suppose the 1984 presidential election were being held today. If President Ronald Reagan were the Republican candidate and George McGovern were the Democratic candidate, which would you like to see win? [Those who named another person or who were undecided were asked: As of today, do you lean more to Reagan, the Republican, or to McGovern, the Democrat?]

Reagan 50%
McGovern 41
Other; undecided 9

By Politics

Republicans

Reagan 84%
McGovern 13
Other; undecided 3

Democrats

Reagan 26%
McGovern 65
Other; undecided 9

Independents

Reagan 56%
McGovern 34
Other; undecided 10

Asked of registered voters: Suppose the 1984 presidential election were being held today. If President Ronald Reagan were the Republican candidate and the Reverend Jesse Jackson were the Democratic candidate, which would you like to see win? [Those who named another person or who were undecided were asked: As of today, do you lean more to Reagan, the Republican, or to Jackson, the Democrat?]

Reagan 64%
Jackson 24
Other; undecided 12

By Politics

Republicans

Reagan 89%
Jackson 8
Other; undecided 3

Democrats

Reagan 46%
Jackson 39
Other; undecided 15

Independents

Reagan 68%
Jackson 19
Other; undecided 13

Note: In the latest test election, Walter Mondale has regained the lead over President Ronald Reagan that he last held in June, while Senator John Glenn maintains the lead over the president which he has consistently held over a period of many months. In the latest survey, Mondale leads Reagan 50% to 44%, while Glenn's margin is 49% to 42%. Thus Glenn, who has trailed Mondale as the top choice of Democrats for the nomination, at least temporarily has lost the valuable campaign argument that he is the only Democrat who has greater vote-getting potential than President Reagan. The current survey was completed prior to the October 25th Grenada invasion, but a Gallup/*Newsweek* survey indicates that this event so far has had little impact on Reagan's popularity.

Senator George McGovern still trails the president by a fairly wide margin, 41% to 50%, but he has picked up support since mid-September when he lost by 35% to 53%.

The Reverend Jesse Jackson loses to Reagan, 24% to 64%, about the same as last summer when the figures were 22% to 61%. The impact of Jackson's announcement of his candidacy on his election standing will be measured in upcoming surveys. He hopes not only to win the support of a vast majority of blacks but also to build a coalition with Hispanic voters. Political observers point out that, if the nation's 6 million Hispanic citizens of voting age are added to 18 million blacks, there is a potential voting bloc that could easily swing an election. Jackson currently has the support of nine blacks in every ten but only three in ten Hispanics.

NOVEMBER 10
MONDALE/GLENN AND
PEACE/PROSPERITY ISSUES

Interviewing Date: 10/21–24/83
Survey #226-G

Asked of Democrats and independents: Which Democratic candidate, Walter Mondale or John Glenn, if elected president, do you think would be more likely to keep the United States out of World War III?

Views of Democrats

Mondale 41%
Glenn 25
No difference (volunteered) 19
No opinion 15

Views of Independents

Mondale 30%
Glenn 32
No difference (volunteered) 18
No opinion 20

Asked of Democrats and independents: Which Democratic candidate, Walter Mondale or John Glenn, if elected president, do you think would do a better job of keeping the country prosperous?

Views of Democrats

Mondale 43%
Glenn 27
No difference (volunteered) 14
No opinion 16

Views of Independents

Mondale 28%
Glenn 35
No difference (volunteered) 15
No opinion 22

Note: Walter Mondale holds a substantial advantage over his rival, John Glenn, as the candidate perceived by Democrats as better able to keep the nation prosperous and to keep the United States out of war. While Mondale currently leads Glenn on both issues among Democratic voters, he is tied with the Ohio senator among independents as the better candidate to keep the nation at peace. Glenn holds an edge over Mondale among independents as the candidate better able to keep the United States prosperous.

The twin issues of peace and prosperity have consistently been the key issues in every presidential contest. Gallup Poll history has shown that the presidential candidate with a lead on both issues almost invariably has won the election.

NOVEMBER 13
ILLEGAL ALIENS

Interviewing Date: 10/21–24/83
Survey #226-G

Do you think it should or should not be against the law to employ a person who has come into the United States without proper papers?

Should 79%
Should not 18
No opinion 3

By Sex
Male

Should 81%
Should not 17
No opinion 2

Female

Should 76%
Should not 20
No opinion 4

By Race
White

Should 79%
Should not 18
No opinion 3

Nonwhite

Should 73%
Should not 22
No opinion 5

Hispanics Only

Should 62%
Should not 29
No opinion 9

By Education
College

Should 80%
Should not 17
No opinion 3

High School

Should	78%
Should not	19
No opinion	3

Grade School

Should	69%
Should not	26
No opinion	5

By Region

East

Should	78%
Should not	19
No opinion	3

Midwest

Should	84%
Should not	14
No opinion	2

South

Should	80%
Should not	18
No opinion	2

West

Should	71%
Should not	24
No opinion	5

By Age

18–29 Years

Should	77%
Should not	20
No opinion	3

30–49 Years

Should	81%
Should not	16
No opinion	3

50 Years and Over

Should	77%
Should not	20
No opinion	3

By Politics

Republicans

Should	84%
Should not	15
No opinion	1

Democrats

Should	76%
Should not	20
No opinion	4

Independents

Should	77%
Should not	21
No opinion	2

By Occupation

Professional and Business

Should	78%
Should not	20
No opinion	2

Clerical and Sales

Should	64%
Should not	35
No opinion	1

Manual Workers

Should	81%
Should not	16
No opinion	3

Nonlabor Force

Should	81%
Should not	18
No opinion	1

National Trend

	Should	Should not	No opinion
October 1983	79%	18%	3%
1980	76	18	6
1977	72	23	5

Do you believe everyone in the United States should be required to carry an identification card such as a Social Security card, or not?

Should 66%
Should not 31
No opinion 3

By Sex
Male

Should 63%
Should not 34
No opinion 3

Female

Should 69%
Should not 28
No opinion 3

By Race
White

Should 66%
Should not 31
No opinion 3

Nonwhite

Should 68%
Should not 27
No opinion 5

Hispanics Only

Should 77%
Should not 23
No opinion .... −

By Education
College

Should 45%
Should not 49
No opinion 6

High School

Should 74%
Should not 23
No opinion 3

Grade School

Should 83%
Should not 15
No opinion 2

By Region
East

Should 62%
Should not 36
No opinion 2

Midwest

Should 70%
Should not 26
No opinion 4

South

Should 72%
Should not 25
No opinion 3

West

Should 57%
Should not 40
No opinion 3

By Age
18–29 Years

Should 68%
Should not 30
No opinion 2

30–49 Years

Should 60%
Should not 37
No opinion 3

50 Years and Over

Should 71%
Should not 25
No opinion 4

By Politics
Republicans

Should 64%
Should not 33
No opinion 3

Democrats

Should 69%
Should not 27
No opinion 4

Independents

Should 64%
Should not 34
No opinion 2

By Occupation
Professional and Business

Should 52%
Should not 44
No opinion 4

Clerical and Sales

Should 68%
Should not 30
No opinion 2

Manual Workers

Should 71%
Should not 26
No opinion 3

Nonlabor Force

Should 75%
Should not 22
No opinion 3

National Trend

	Should	Should not	No opinion
October 1983	66%	31%	3%
1980	62	33	5
1977	65	30	5

It has been proposed that illegal aliens who have been in the United States for seven years be allowed to remain in the United States. Do you favor or oppose this proposal?

Favor 42%
Oppose 51
No opinion 7

By Sex
Male

Favor 38%
Oppose 57
No opinion 5

Female

Favor 44%
Oppose 46
No opinion 10

By Race
White

Favor 41%
Oppose 52
No opinion 7

Nonwhite

Favor 46%
Oppose 45
No opinion 9

Hispanics Only

Favor 59%
Oppose 32
No opinion 9

By Education
College

Favor 47%
Oppose 47
No opinion 6

High School

Favor 37%
Oppose 56
No opinion 7

Grade School

Favor 43%
Oppose 43
No opinion 14

By Region
East

Favor 47%
Oppose 46
No opinion 7

Midwest

Favor 37%
Oppose 56
No opinion 7

South

Favor 42%
Oppose 50
No opinion 8

West

Favor 39%
Oppose 54
No opinion 7

By Age
18–29 Years

Favor 44%
Oppose 50
No opinion 6

30–49 Years

Favor 44%
Oppose 49
No opinion 7

50 Years and Over

Favor 38%
Oppose 54
No opinion 8

By Politics
Republicans

Favor 38%
Oppose 57
No opinion 5

Democrats

Favor 45%
Oppose 47
No opinion 8

Independents

Favor 39%
Oppose 53
No opinion 8

By Occupation
Professional and Business

Favor 41%
Oppose 51
No opinion 8

Clerical and Sales

Favor 55%
Oppose 39
No opinion 6

Manual Workers

Favor 41%
Oppose 55
No opinion 4

Nonlabor Force

Favor 35%
Oppose 54
No opinion 11

National Trend

	Favor	Oppose	No opinion
October 1983	41%	52%	7%
1980	37	52	11
1977	39	52	9

Note: The American public takes a hard line toward illegal aliens, with 79% in favor of a law which would make it illegal to employ a person who has entered the United States without proper papers. The latest results represent a slight but continuing increase in support of such a law, with 76% favoring such legislation in 1980 and 72% in a 1977 survey.

The public also strongly supports a proposal requiring all U.S. citizens and permanent resident aliens to carry an identification card. This would make it possible for prospective employers to distinguish illegal aliens from legal job-seekers. Two persons in three (66%) in the latest survey back such legislation, a slight increase since 1980 when the figure was 62%.

The public's views also were sought on a proposal to grant permanent resident status to all aliens who entered the United States illegally and have been in the country for seven years, a proposal first made by President Jimmy Carter. About one-half (51%) oppose this proposal, while 42% favor it, figures which closely parallel those recorded in surveys in 1980 and 1977.

Among Hispanics in the survey, support for a law against hiring illegal aliens outweighs opposition 62% to 29%, while 77% voice approval of requiring identification cards compared to 23% who disapprove, findings similar to those for the nation as a whole. On the other hand, opinion among Hispanics is 59% to 32% in favor of granting amnesty to aliens, whereas views are 5 to 4 in opposition among the nation as a whole. While the sample included only ninety-eight Hispanics and the percentages reported are subject to a 10 percentage-point deviation, the results reliably indicate the majority position taken by Hispanics on these issues.

The hard-line attitude of the public stems in considerable measure from concern over the state of the economy and fear that illegal aliens will take jobs from U.S. citizens. For example, persons engaged in manual work, particularly those in unskilled jobs, are more likely to favor an identification card than are persons in white-collar jobs.

The Simpson-Mazzoli bill, recently stalled in Congress, would set up a system of sanctions against employers who knowingly employ illegals and introduce a method intended to identify legal immigrants. It would also grant amnesty to immigrants who have lived in the United States for a certain period.

The problem of immigration and of illegal aliens, especially from Latin American countries, is likely to be of growing concern to the United States. A global survey conducted by Gallup International for the Charles F. Kettering Foundation found that one person in five in Latin America (South America, Central America, and the Caribbean) would like to emigrate to another country. The United States is their favorite choice as a future home. One-third of all Mexicans included in the survey said they would like to leave Mexico, and they too prefer the United States over other nations. Border officials estimate that between half a million and one million "illegals" cross from Mexico annually, driven by unemployment and population pressures at home.

NOVEMBER 17
ITEM VETO POWER

Interviewing Date: 10/21–24/83
Survey #226-G

> At the present time, when Congress passes a bill, the president cannot veto parts of that bill, but must accept it in full or veto it. Do

*you think this should be changed so that the
president can veto some items in a bill without vetoing the entire bill?*

Favor 67%
Oppose 25
No opinion 8

By Education
College Graduates

Favor 67%
Oppose 31
No opinion 2

College, Incomplete

Favor 66%
Oppose 27
No opinion 7

High-School Graduates

Favor 74%
Oppose 21
No opinion 5

Less Than High-School Graduates

Favor 60%
Oppose 24
No opinion 16

By Politics
Republicans

Favor 75%
Oppose 19
No opinion 6

Democrats

Favor 63%
Oppose 30
No opinion 7

Independents

Favor 66%
Oppose 26
No opinion 8

National Trend

	Favor	Oppose	No opinion
October 1983	67%	25%	8%
1978	70	19	11
1975	69	20	11
1945	57	14	29

Note: If the views of the American people were heeded, President Ronald Reagan would be permitted to veto specific items in bills passed by Congress instead of having to veto or approve an entire bill as at present. Two voters in three (67%) in the latest Gallup survey favor giving presidents item veto power, while 25% are opposed and 8% undecided. Solid support is found among all major population segments, including persons of all political stripes and those with different levels of educational attainment.

Large majorities in surveys spanning almost four decades have favored changing the present rule. When the issue was first presented to the public in 1945, 57% voted in favor of allowing chief executives to exercise item veto power.

Opponents of the present system say that giving presidents item veto power would stop "pork-barrel" legislation—the inclusion in the budget of items that primarily serve the narrow political interests of some members of Congress without regard to the wisdom of the measures on their own merits. Others contend that eliminating the expensive riders that are frequently tacked on to proposed bills would save millions of dollars. The main argument of those who favor the present system is that it gives the legislative branch more power by forcing a president to accept items, particularly in appropriations bills, which he might not otherwise accept.

The record $195 billion federal deficit for fiscal 1983, in the eyes of some political observers, lends new urgency to controlling government spending. President Reagan recently indicated he may seek line-item veto power in his budget proposal next year.

NOVEMBER 20
PRESIDENT REAGAN

Interviewing Date: 9/30–10/16; 10/26–27/;
10/28–11/13/83
Special Telephone Surveys*

Do you approve or disapprove of the way Ronald Reagan is handling his job as president?

	Oct. 28– Nov. 13	Oct. 26–27	Sept. 30– Oct. 16
Approve	53%	48%	46%
Disapprove	31	39	37
No opinion	16	13	17

	Percent Approving	
	Oct. 28– Nov. 13	Sept. 30– Oct. 16

By Sex

Male	58%	47%
Female	49	44

By Race

White	57%	49%
Nonwhite	33	26

By Education

College graduates	55%	54%
College, incomplete	55	53
High-school graduates	60	45
Less than high-school graduates	40	35

By Region

East	56%	45%
Midwest	53	43
South	53	47
West	51	45

*The October 26–27, 1983 telephone interviews were conducted by *Newsweek*.

By Age

18–29 years	54%	44%
30–49 years	56	47
50 years and over	51	45

By Politics

Republicans	84%	77%
Democrats	36	26
Independents	48	48

Note: President Ronald Reagan has registered a moderate gain in popularity in the aftermath of the momentous events in Beirut and Grenada. In a survey completed on November 13, 53% approved of Reagan's overall performance in office while 31% disapproved.

The president's upturn in popularity is found in most major population segments. Among Republicans, his approval score, at a high 77% prior to the foreign events, went still higher to 84% approval after those occurrences. Among Democrats, too, Reagan made a strong 10-point advance. Independents gave the president a 48% job approval rating both before and after the incidents.

As shown in the table, Reagan's popularity rose about equally among both whites and nonwhites. However, although his popularity increased with both sexes, the 5-point improvement among women failed to match an 11-point increase among men. Thus, on a relative basis, the Beirut and Grenada events served to widen rather than close the president's so-called gender gap.

In a similar survey conducted prior to the foreign incidents, Reagan received a 46% favorable job rating with 37% disapproving. The latest assessment, therefore, represents an improvement of 7 percentage points in the president's standing with the American people over a period of six weeks. His current rating is his highest in two years.

It is interesting to note that a survey conducted for *Newsweek* by the Gallup Organization on October 26–27—immediately after the Grenada invasion—showed virtually no change in Reagan's popularity. This suggests that the public's favorable response to his performance was a considered judgment that took some time to develop.

While Reagan's 7-point gain in popularity as a consequence of the Beirut and Grenada events can be characterized as moderate, the president has enjoyed a steady upward trend in popularity since early this year. His present 53% approval rating, in fact, represents the first time in almost two years that it has topped the 50% mark. In addition to the public goodwill that accrued to Reagan because of the foreign incidents, growing optimism about the economic recovery has contributed to a generally strong trend this year.

NOVEMBER 24
DEMOCRATIC PRESIDENTIAL CANDIDATES

Interviewing Date: 10/21–24/83
Survey #226-G

Asked of Democrats and independents: Will you please look over this list and tell me which of these persons you have heard of? Now, please tell me which of these persons you know enough about to have an opinion of?

Which one would you like to see nominated as the Democratic party's candidate for president in 1984? Now, for each of the persons on this list, please tell me whether that person would be acceptable or not acceptable to you as the Democratic presidential candidate in 1984?

Choice of Democrats

	Heard of	First choice
Walter Mondale	94%	34%
George McGovern	86	7
John Glenn	85	23
Jesse Jackson	81	8
Alan Cranston	52	3
Gary Hart	38	1
Reubin Askew	32	2
Ernest Hollings	30	1
No opinion	–	21

Choice of Independents

	Heard of	First choice
Mondale	92%	24%
McGovern	86	8
Glenn	82	25
Jackson	81	4
Cranston	51	2
Hart	38	1
Askew	35	2
Hollings	28	1
No opinion	–	33

Acceptability of Democratic Candidates
(Based on Democrats and Independents Familiar with Each Candidate)

	Acceptable	Not acceptable	No opinion
Glenn	83%	12%	5%
Mondale	77	15	8
Hart	63	23	14
Askew	59	31	10
McGovern	59	32	9
Cranston	58	29	13
Hollings	52	34	14
Jackson	38	55	7

Note: Democratic contender Walter Mondale's lead over Senator John Glenn has narrowed in the latest survey of the nomination choices of Democratic voters. Mondale currently leads Glenn 34% to 23%. In an early October survey Mondale was the choice of 40% of Democrats to 21% for his rival. In September the figures were 34% for Mondale and 23% for Glenn. As the trend reveals, there is considerable volatility in the choices of voters at this early stage in the race for the nomination.

The Reverend Jesse Jackson and 1972 presidential candidate George McGovern are in a statistical tie for third place, with Jackson having 8% of the vote and McGovern 7%. Next are Alan Cranston with 3%, Reubin Askew with 2%, and Gary Hart and Ernest Hollings each with 1%.

Every political hopeful faces three major hurdles in the race for the nomination: gaining name recognition, gaining general acceptability among voters, and winning the solid support of voters.

Mondale, Glenn, McGovern, and Jackson have high name recognition; upwards of eight in ten Democrats have heard of each. The name recognition scores of the other four candidates are far lower, with one-half or fewer of Democrats saying they have heard of Cranston, Hart, Askew, and Hollings.

All Democrats and independents in the survey who had heard of each candidate and had an opinion were then asked whether this person would be acceptable or unacceptable to them as the Democratic nominee for 1984. Three-fourths or more of the sample (which includes independents as well as Democrats to provide a larger sample base) say they would find Glenn and Mondale acceptable. In the next tier are Hart, Askew, McGovern, and Cranston, who are acceptable to approximately six in ten.

Acceptable to only about one-half, at least at present, are Hollings at 52% and Jackson at 38%. In the case of Jackson, it should be borne in mind that 16% of Democrats currently say they would not vote for a black for president, although the trend has been sharply downward over the last two decades.

Gallup Polls over the last four decades have shown that, at this point prior to a presidential election, the top choice of Democrats has not always gone on to win the nomination the following year. Here are the leading nomination choices of Democrats in surveys conducted approximately six months prior to the Democratic convention in each election since 1956:

Historical Patterns

October 1979

Edward Kennedy	39%
Jimmy Carter	32
Edmund "Jerry" Brown, Jr.	8
Henry Jackson	5
Other; no opinion	16

(1980 nominee: Carter)

October 1975

Hubert Humphrey	23%
George Wallace	19
Henry Jackson	11
George McGovern	9
Edmund Muskie	9
Sargent Shriver	8
Other; no opinion	21

(1976 nominee: Carter)

November 1971

Edward Kennedy	29%
Edmund Muskie	24
Hubert Humphrey	19
George McGovern	6
Other; no opinion	22

(1972 nominee: McGovern)

September 1967

Robert Kennedy	39%
Lyndon Johnson	37
Arthur Goldberg	8
Hubert Humphrey	6
Other; no opinion	10

(1968 nominee: Humphrey)

December 1963

Lyndon Johnson	68%
Robert Kennedy	16
Other; no opinion	16

(1964 nominee: Johnson)

December 1959

John Kennedy	27%
Adlai Stevenson	26
Lyndon Johnson	11
Estes Kefauver	10
Other; no opinion	25

(1960 nominee: Kennedy)

Adlai Stevenson 51%
Estes Kefauver 16
Averell Harriman 8
Other; no opinion 25

(1956 nominee: Stevenson)

NOVEMBER 27
CARDIO-PULMONARY
RESUSCITATION (C.P.R.)

Interviewing Date: 10/21–24/83
Survey #226-G

Have you heard or read about a lifesaving emergency first-aid technique for heart attack victims known as Cardio-Pulmonary Resuscitation, or C.P.R.?

Yes 87%
No 13

Asked of those who replied in the affirmative: Have you taken such a course on how to administer C.P.R.?

	1983 Have taken	1977 Have taken
National	21%	8%
By Sex		
Male	23%	10%
Female	19	6
By Education		
College	29%	16%
High school	15	6
Grade school	6	1
By Region		
East	16%	5%
Midwest	24	9
South	18	8
West	29	11
By Age		
18–29 years	29%	10%
30–49 years	23	10
50 years and over	12	5

By Community Size

One million and over	19%	6%
500,000–999,999	28	11
50,000–499,999	24	10
2,500–49,999	21	8
Under 2,500; rural	41	7

Asked of those who have heard or read about C.P.R. and who have not taken a course in C.P.R.: Would you be interested in taking a course on how to administer C.P.R., or not?

	Would be interested
National	64%

By Sex

Male	62%
Female	65

By Education

College	75%
High school	56
Grade school	31

By Region

East	67%
Midwest	67
South	55
West	68

By Age

18–29 years	78%
30–49 years	77
50 years and over	41

By Community Size

One million and over 62%
500,000–999,999 66
50,000–499,999 70
2,500–49,999 72
Under 2,500; rural 56

Also asked of those who have heard or read about C.P.R.: Do you think it would be a good idea or a poor idea to require all high-school students to take this course before they can graduate from high school?

Good idea 80%
Poor idea 17
No opinion 3

Note: The campaign to get Americans to take a course in C.P.R. has been extremely successful, with one adult in every five now saying that he or she has had such training, nearly triple the proportion recorded in a 1977 survey. In addition, the percentage of adults who have heard or read-about the emergency first-aid technique known as Cardio-Pulmonary Resuscitation has increased sharply since 1977 from two-thirds of the population (66%) to 87%, an extraordinarily high awareness figure. Furthermore, of the three-fourths of the adult population who have not taken such a course, almost two-thirds (64%) indicate an interest in doing so.

Used most often to revive heart attack victims, C.P.R. is also helpful in cases of electrocution, drowning, and other accidents where immediate restoration of breathing can make the difference between life and death. Because so many Americans die in accidents, some cities have undertaken C.P.R. programs to instruct citizens in the fundamentals of this technique—a combination of rhythmic external chest massage and mouth-to-mouth resuscitation.

DECEMBER 1
DEMOCRATIC PRESIDENTIAL CANDIDATES

Interviewing Date: 9/16–19; 10/7–10, 21–24/83
Survey #224-G; 225-G; 226-G

Asked of Democrats: Which one of the persons on this list would you like to see nominated as the Democratic party's candidate for president in 1984?

Walter Mondale 36%
John Glenn 22
Jesse Jackson 8
George McGovern 8
Alan Cranston 5
Gary Hart 3
Reubin Askew 2
Ernest Hollings 1
None; don't know .15

By Race—Democrats
White

Mondale 38%
Glenn 26
McGovern 9
Cranston 5
Hart 3
Askew 2
Jackson 2
Hollings 1
None; don't know .14

Black

Mondale 28%
Glenn 9
McGovern 4
Cranston 4
Hart . . . . *
Askew 1
Jackson 37
Hollings . . . . *
None; don't know .17

By Region—Democrats
East

Mondale 39%
Glenn 23

McGovern	8
Cranston	5
Jackson	5
Askew	2
Hart	2
Hollings	1
None; don't know	15

Midwest

Mondale	41%
Glenn	27
McGovern	8
Cranston	2
Jackson	9
Askew	1
Hart	3
Hollings	*
None; don't know	9

South

Mondale	35%
Glenn	21
McGovern	6
Cranston	1
Jackson	11
Askew	3
Hart	2
Hollings	1
None; don't know	20

West

Mondale	28%
Glenn	19
McGovern	10
Cranston	15
Jackson	8
Askew	2
Hart	4
Hollings	1
None; don't know	13

By Age—Democrats

18–24 Years

Mondale	35%
Glenn	18
Jackson	18
McGovern	8

Cranston	5
Askew	2
Hart	1
Hollings	*
None; don't know	13

25–29 Years

Mondale	34%
Glenn	19
Jackson	10
McGovern	12
Cranston	5
Askew	1
Hart	5
Hollings	*
None; don't know	14

30–49 Years

Mondale	29%
Glenn	26
Jackson	9
McGovern	10
Cranston	4
Askew	3
Hart	4
Hollings	1
None; don't know	14

50 Years and Over

Mondale	44%
Glenn	22
Jackson	4
McGovern	5
Cranston	4
Askew	2
Hart	1
Hollings	1
None; don't know	17

By Religion—Democrats

Protestants

Mondale	36%
Glenn	22
Jackson	11
McGovern	6
Cranston	4
Askew	2
Hart	2

Hollings 1
None; don't know 16

Catholics

Mondale 39%
Glenn 24
Jackson 3
McGovern 10
Cranston 4
Askew 2
Hart 3
Hollings 1
None; don't know 14

By Union Membership—Democrats

Members

Mondale 35%
Glenn 31
McGovern 10
Jackson 7
Cranston 4
Askew 2
Hart 2
Hollings .... *
None; don't know 9

Nonmembers

Mondale 37%
Glenn 20
McGovern 7
Jackson 9
Cranston 4
Askew 2
Hart 3
Hollings 1
None; don't know 17

*Less than 1%

Note: Although Walter Mondale with 36% of Democrats' votes and John Glenn with 22% lead the other six candidates for the Democratic presidential nomination by a wide margin, an analysis of the vote by groups reveals some surprising patterns. Mondale has the official backing of the AFL-CIO but manages no better than a statistical tie with Glenn among Democrats from labor union households. Ironically, Mondale holds a wide 37% to 20% lead over Glenn in nonunion households.

Jesse Jackson, tied with George McGovern for third place as the national choice of Democrats, runs neck and neck with Glenn for second place among the younger (18 to 24) Democratic voters. Jackson is the front-runner among black Democrats, but Mondale is not far behind. Blacks' choices for candidates other than Jackson, in fact, outweigh his own support. Among black Democrats, Glenn is a distinct also-ran at present.

Mondale and Glenn far outstrip their rivals in each of the four major regions of the nation, with the exception of the West, where Alan Cranston (with 15% of the vote compared to 5% nationally) vies for second place with Glenn and McGovern. The current choices of men and women are remarkably similar, with Mondale and Glenn topping both lists by almost identical margins.

DECEMBER 4
UNITED NATIONS

Interviewing Date: 10/7–10/83
Survey #225-G

In general, do you feel the United Nations is doing a good job or a poor job in trying to solve the problems it has had to face?

Good job 36%
Poor job 51
No opinion 13

By Education
College

Good job 34%
Poor job 60
No opinion 6

High School

Good job 36%
Poor job 49
No opinion 15

Grade School

Good job 35%
Poor job 41
No opinion 24

By Age

18–24 Years

Good job	41%
Poor job	45
No opinion	14

25–29 Years

Good job	38%
Poor job	51
No opinion	11

30–49 Years

Good job	39%
Poor job	50
No opinion	11

50–64 Years

Good job	29%
Poor job	57
No opinion	14

65 Years and Over

Good job	33%
Poor job	50
No opinion	17

By Politics

Republicans

Good job	36%
Poor job	52
No opinion	12

Democrats

Good job	38%
Poor job	49
No opinion	13

Independents

Good job	33%
Poor job	55
No opinion	12

National Trend

	Good job	Poor job	No opinion
October 7–10, 1983 ...	36%	51%	13%
1982	36	49	15
1980	31	53	16
1975	33	51	16
1971	35	43	22
1970	44	40	16
1967	49	35	16
1956	51	37	12

Do you think the United States should give up its membership in the United Nations, or not?

Should	12%
Should not	79
No opinion	9

By Education

College

Should	8%
Should not	89
No opinion	3

High School

Should	14%
Should not	78
No opinion	8

Grade School

Should	15%
Should not	65
No opinion	20

By Age

18–24 Years

Should	11%
Should not	80
No opinion	9

25–29 Years

Should	11%
Should not	80
No opinion	9

30–49 Years

Should 8%
Should not 85
No opinion 7

50–64 Years

Should 18%
Should not 75
No opinion 7

65 Years and Over

Should 16%
Should not 69
No opinion 15

By Politics
Republicans

Should 16%
Should not 80
No opinion 4

Democrats

Should 10%
Should not 81
No opinion 9

Independents

Should 12%
Should not 77
No opinion 11

Those Who Think the United Nations Is Doing a Good Job

Should 5%
Should not 92
No opinion 3

Those Who Think the United Nations Is Doing a Poor Job

Should 19%
Should not 75
No opinion 6

National Trend

	Should	Should not	No opinion
October 7–10, 1983 ...	12%	79%	9%
1982	12	79	9
1975	16	74	10
1967	10	85	5
1963	8	79	13
1962	9	86	5
1951	12	75	13

*Do you think the United Nations should move out of the United States, or not?**

Should 19%
Should not 67
No opinion 14

By Education
College

Should 20%
Should not 67
No opinion 13

High School

Should 19%
Should not 68
No opinion 13

Grade School

Should 18%
Should not 57
No opinion 25

By Age
18–24 Years

Should 14%
Should not 75
No opinion 11

*This question was asked for the first time.

25–29 Years

Should 12%
Should not 73
No opinion 15

30–49 Years

Should 17%
Should not 71
No opinion 12

50–64 Years

Should 26%
Should not 61
No opinion 13

65 Years and Over

Should 23%
Should not 58
No opinion 19

By Politics
Republicans

Should 24%
Should not 65
No opinion 11

Democrats

Should 16%
Should not 72
No opinion 12

Independents

Should 18%
Should not 65
No opinion 17

Note: Although most Americans currently hold negative opinions about the performance of the United Nations, relatively few would like to see the United States give up its membership in the world body. In addition, two of three persons interviewed in a recent Gallup survey reject the idea that the United Nations should move its headquarters out of the United States.

In the current survey, 36% think the United Nations is doing a good job in trying to solve the problems it has had to face, while 51% say it is doing a poor job. The latest findings are virtually unchanged from those recorded in a June 1982 survey. Americans have held more negative than positive views about the United Nations since 1970. In that year, a slim 44% to 40% plurality gave it a favorable performance rating.

Only one person in eight (12%) thinks the United States should withdraw from the world body, while eight in ten (79%) think we should not. This attitude has prevailed overwhelmingly in surveys conducted since 1951. The most widespread sentiment in favor of U.S. withdrawal was recorded in 1975, when 16% held this view. The low point of 8% was found in 1963.

Only one person in five (19%) in the current survey believes the United Nations should leave the United States, its headquarters since it was founded in 1946 following World War II. More than three times as many, 67%, disagree. Earlier this year a senior U.S. delegate voiced his frustration with the world forum by inviting the United Nations to leave. President Ronald Reagan suggested that it meet here for six months each year and in Moscow for the other six.

DECEMBER 8
PRESIDENTIAL POLITICS AND
THE HISPANIC VOTE

Six Separate Surveys Conducted during August, September, and October 1983*

> *Is your name now recorded in the registration book of the precinct or election district where you now live?*

*For results based on the subsample of Hispanics, one can say with 95% confidence that the deviation attributable to sampling and other random effects could be plus or minus 5 percentage points. The error for the entire sample could be 1 percentage point and for the subsample of blacks, 4 points in either direction.

National 72%
Hispanics 58
Blacks 69

In politics, as of today, do you consider your-self a Republican, a Democrat, or an independent?

Republican
National 27%
Hispanics 24
Blacks 6

Democrat
National 43%
Hispanics 51
Blacks 77

Independent
National 30%
Hispanics 25
Blacks 17

Do you approve or disapprove of the way Ronald Reagan is handling his job as president?

Approve
National 45%
Hispanics 40
Blacks 12

Disapprove
National 44%
Hispanics 42
Blacks 75

No opinion
National 11%
Hispanics 18
Blacks 13

Asked of Democrats: Which one of the per-sons on this list would you like to see nom-inated as the Democratic party's candidate for president in 1984?

	National	Hispanics	Blacks
Mondale	36%	35%	27%
Glenn	22	16	8
Jackson	9	7	36
McGovern	8	12	4
Cranston	4	7	4
Hart	2	1	*
Askew	2	1	1
Hollings	1	*	1
None; don't know ..	16	21	19

*Less than 1%

Asked of registered voters: Suppose the 1984 presidential election were being held today. If President Ronald Reagan were the Repub-lican candidate and Walter Mondale were the Democratic candidate, which would you like to see win? [Those who named another person or who were undecided were asked: As of today, do you lean more to Reagan, the Republican, or to Mondale, the Democrat?]

Reagan
National 45%
Hispanics 38
Blacks 8

Mondale
National 46%
Hispanics 46
Blacks 78

Other; undecided
National 9%
Hispanics 16
Blacks 14

Asked of registered voters: Suppose the 1984 presidential election were being held today. If President Ronald Reagan were the Repub-lican candidate and John Glenn were the Democratic candidate, which would you like to see win? [Those who named another per-son or who were undecided were asked: As of today, do you lean more to Reagan, the Republican, or to Glenn, the Democrat?]

Reagan

National 41%

Hispanics 40

Blacks 8

Glenn

National 48%

Hispanics 46

Blacks 75

Other; undecided

National 11%

Hispanics 14

Blacks 17

Note: President Ronald Reagan and the Republican party have relatively strong appeal to the nation's Hispanic voters despite the widespread assumption that Hispanics are solidly Democratic due to their generally low economic status. They are more oriented toward the Democratic party than is the overall adult population; however, a much smaller proportion of Hispanics (51%) than blacks (77%) identifies themselves as Democrats. Those who vote Democratic in the Hispanic population outnumber Republicans by a 2-to-1 ratio. In sharp contrast, black Democrats outweigh black Republicans in these surveys, 77% to 6%.

Both major parties are vying eagerly for the support of the 10 million Hispanics of voting age because of their potential impact in the key Sun Belt states. Those votes could well be decisive next year in California, Texas, and Florida—states with 97 electoral votes, more than one-third of the 270 needed to win the presidency.

In view of the importance of the Hispanic vote to both parties, the Gallup Poll recently measured the candidate choices and political leanings of this segment of the electorate. Here are the key findings, based on a combination of recent national surveys in order to have a sufficiently large number of Hispanics for analysis.

Hispanics are slightly less favorable than the general population in their appraisal of President Reagan's performance in office, with 40%

approving and 42% disapproving. The national findings show 45% approval and 44% disapproval. By way of comparison, only 12% of blacks in these surveys express approval, while 75% disapprove.

Hispanics who say they are Democrats most often choose Walter Mondale (35%) to be the 1984 Democratic presidential nominee, followed by John Glenn (16%); George McGovern (12%); and Alan Cranston and Jesse Jackson, each with 7%. Far fewer Hispanics than blacks (36%) favor Jackson for the nomination. In test elections for the presidency in 1984, Hispanics vote for Mondale over the president, 46% to 38%, and for Glenn over Reagan, 46% to 40%. The comparable figures for registered voters nationwide are Mondale 46%, Reagan 45%; and Glenn 48%, Reagan 41%.

Although the Hispanic vote could be decisive in the 1984 election, at least some of its potential impact could be diminished by the relatively low level of voter registration. A smaller proportion of Hispanics (58%) than either blacks (69%) or the total adult population (72%) is currently registered to vote. Evidence of their progress in political participation is seen in the fact that only 36% of Hispanics were registered to vote in the 1980 election.

DECEMBER 11
MOST IMPORTANT PROBLEM

Interviewing Date: 11/18–21/83
Survey #227-G

What do you think is the most important problem facing this country today?

	November 18–21, 1983	October 7–10, 1983*	October 2–5, 1982†
Fear of war; international problems ..	37%	23%	6%
Unemployment	32	42	62
Inflation; high cost of living	11	12	18
Moral decline in society	6	5	3
Excessive government spending	5	4	4

Reagan budget cuts	4	3	3
Economy (general) ...	3	4	11
All others	8	13	15
Don't know	3	4	2
	109%‡	110%‡	124%‡

*Survey #225-G
†Survey #183-G
‡Total adds to more than 100% due to multiple responses.

Note: International tensions and the threat of war are named by the American people, for the first time since the Vietnam War, as the top problems facing the United States today. A total of 37% names these and related problems compared to far fewer (23%) who did so in an early October survey, and merely 6% a year ago.

The two surveys bracketed the terrorist bombing of the Marine barracks in Beirut and the U.S. operation in Grenada. The later survey also may reflect the publicity surrounding the televised movie, "The Day After," viewed by roughly half of all adults.

With concern over war or the threat of war rising to the forefront, worries about the economy have subsided. A total of 32% today names unemployment as the top problem facing the nation compared to 42% in the October survey. Inflation and high living costs are cited by 11% in the current survey, statistically unchanged from the 12% recorded in October.

DECEMBER 15
PRESIDENT REAGAN

Interviewing Date: 11/18–21/83
Survey #227-G

Do you approve or disapprove of the way Ronald Reagan is handling his job as president?

Approve 53%
Disapprove 37
No opinion 10

By Politics
Republicans

Approve 91%
Disapprove 7
No opinion 2

Democrats

Approve 33%
Disapprove 57
No opinion 10

Independents

Approve 51%
Disapprove 36
No opinion 13

Now let me ask you about specific foreign and domestic problems. As I read off each problem, one at a time, would you tell me whether you approve or disapprove of the way President Reagan is handling that problem:

Economic conditions in this country?

Approve 48%
Disapprove 46
No opinion 6

By Politics
Republicans

Approve 81%
Disapprove 16
No opinion 3

Democrats

Approve 31%
Disapprove 65
No opinion 4

Independents

Approve 48%
Disapprove 45
No opinion 7

The situation in Grenada?

Approve 59%
Disapprove 32
No opinion 9

By Politics
Republicans

Approve 83%
Disapprove 12
No opinion 5

Democrats

Approve 45%
Disapprove 45
No opinion 10

Independents

Approve 62%
Disapprove 29
No opinion 9

Nuclear disarmament negotiations with the Soviet Union?

Approve 47%
Disapprove 37
No opinion 16

By Politics
Republicans

Approve 71%
Disapprove 17
No opinion 12

Democrats

Approve 36%
Disapprove 49
No opinion 15

Independents

Approve 46%
Disapprove 37
No opinion 17

Foreign policy?

Approve 46%
Disapprove 41
No opinion 13

By Politics
Republicans

Approve 75%
Disapprove 16
No opinion 9

Democrats

Approve 32%
Disapprove 58
No opinion 10

Independents

Approve 46%
Disapprove 39
No opinion 15

Relations with the Soviet Union?

Approve 46%
Disapprove 40
No opinion 14

By Politics
Republicans

Approve 70%
Disapprove 21
No opinion 9

Democrats

Approve 34%
Disapprove 52
No opinion 14

Independents

Approve 46%
Disapprove 40
No opinion 14

The situation in Central America?

Approve 36%
Disapprove 44
No opinion 20

By Politics

Republicans

Approve 59%
Disapprove 24
No opinion 17

Democrats

Approve 24%
Disapprove 58
No opinion 18

Independents

Approve 36%
Disapprove 42
No opinion 22

The situation in Lebanon?

Approve 34%
Disapprove 52
No opinion 14

By Politics

Republicans

Approve 54%
Disapprove 34
No opinion 12

Democrats

Approve 25%
Disapprove 63
No opinion 12

Independents

Approve 32%
Disapprove 53
No opinion 15

Note: Sustained by growing public optimism over the economy and favorable reaction to the operation in Grenada, President Ronald Reagan's job performance rating remains at its highest level in two years. In the latest survey, 53% express approval of Reagan's handling of the presidency, up a full 10 points from an August survey, while 37% disapprove. The last time the president's performance rating was significantly higher was in October 1981, when 56% approved and 35% disapproved.

The uptrend in the public's favorable response to the president's overall performance in office is paralleled by increases in approval of his handling of specific domestic and international problems. In fact, the current approval level for most of these problems represents the highest percentage recorded to date for Reagan.

Greatest support is found for his handling of the situation in Grenada, with 59% expressing approval and 32% disapproval. In the case of the other six problems studied, approval still falls below the 50% level.

Domestically, 48% now approve of Reagan's handling of economic conditions, up 11 points since August 1983 and the highest figure recorded since August 1981. On the international front, 46% approve of Reagan's overall handling of foreign policy, a jump of 15 points since August and the highest since December 1981. Approval is slightly up on Reagan's handling of the situations in Lebanon and Central America, but only a third express support for the president's efforts in each area.

Approval also has grown for the president's handling of relations with the Soviet Union, as well as the nuclear disarmament negotiations, but the trend has been fairly flat in both cases. While Reagan wins approval from nearly half of persons interviewed for his handling of nuclear disarmament, a parallel survey showed the public leaning heavily to the view that the president is not going far enough in trying to bring about an agreement with the Soviet Union on nuclear weapons. The figures were: not far enough, 48%; too far, 12%; about right, 28%; and no opinion, 12%.

DECEMBER 18
DEMOCRATIC PRESIDENTIAL
CANDIDATES

Interviewing Date: 11/18–21/83
Survey #227-G

Asked of Democrats and independents: Which one of the persons on this card would you like to see nominated as the Democratic party's candidate for president in 1984?

Choice of Democrats*

Walter Mondale	47%
John Glenn	19
Jesse Jackson	7
George McGovern	7
Alan Cranston	3
Reubin Askew	3
Gary Hart	2
Ernest Hollings	1
None; don't know	11

National Trend

	Oct. 21–24, 1983	Oct. 7–10, 1983	Sept. 1983
Mondale	34%	40%	34%
Glenn	23	21	23
Jackson	8	10	8
McGovern	7	8	8

*The variability observed in recent surveys in the nomination choices of Democrats is not attributable to sampling error. In the last two surveys, the percentage of Democrats choosing Mondale increased from 34% to 47%, a 13% difference. Any difference larger than 7%, given the sample sizes for Democrats in these surveys, is statistically significant.

In October, Mondale led Glenn by an 11% margin; his margin increased to 28% in November. In both surveys, the proportion of Democrats favoring Mondale over Glenn is statistically significant. In addition, the change in the spread between the two candidates is beyond the range of sampling error.

Cranston	3	6	5
Askew	2	1	3
Hart	1	3	3
Hollings	1	1	1
None; don't know	21	10	15

Choice of Independents

John Glenn	27%
Walter Mondale	27
George McGovern	9
Jesse Jackson	6
Gary Hart	3
Ernest Hollings	3
Reubin Askew	2
Alan Cranston	2
None; don't know	21

National Trend

	Oct. 21–24, 1983	Oct. 7–10, 1983	Sept. 1983
Glenn	25%	23%	26%
Mondale	24	35	26
McGovern	8	9	12
Jackson	4	3	6
Hart	1	5	3
Hollings	1	2	1
Askew	2	*	2
Cranston	2	4	4
None; don't know	33	19	20

*Less than 1%

Asked of Democrats: Suppose the choice for president in the Democratic convention in 1984 narrows down to Walter Mondale and John Glenn. Which one would you prefer to have the Democratic convention select?

Mondale	64%
Glenn	29
Undecided	7

National Trend

	Mondale	Glenn	Undecided
August 1983	49%	30%	21%
June 1983	57	31	12
February 1983	52	30	18
December 1982	59	28	13

Note: Former Vice-president Walter Mondale currently enjoys a commanding 47% to 19% lead over Senator John Glenn in an unusually volatile contest for the 1984 Democratic presidential nomination. Mondale's present 28 percentage-point advantage over Glenn is the largest recorded in six Gallup surveys this year. In a late October poll, Mondale led Glenn by an 11-point margin, 34% to 23%, while in early October, Mondale was the victor by 19 points, receiving 40% of Democrats' nomination votes to 21% for his closest rival, Glenn. Although Mondale has prevailed over Glenn in every 1983 nomination test, the widely fluctuating margins separating the two frontrunners are characteristic of contests in which voters are not strongly committed to their choice of candidates.

Consistent with earlier findings, none of the six other candidates as yet shows any sign of emerging from the pack to challenge leaders Mondale and Glenn. The Reverend Jesse Jackson and George McGovern each receives 7% of Democrats' nomination votes. Reubin Askew and Alan Cranston are the choice of 3% each; Gary Hart, 2%; and Ernest Hollings, 1%.

The results of nomination contests pitting just the two leaders against each other also offer valuable insights. In the current survey, Democrats choose Mondale over Glenn by a huge 35-point margin, 64% to 29%. In a similar showdown in August, Mondale beat Glenn by a narrower 49% to 30% edge. Virtually all of Mondale's 15-point increment between the two surveys came from a decrease in the proportion of Democrats who did not choose between the two men in the earlier survey. By contrast, Glenn suffered an insignificant 1% loss in the latest poll.

While Mondale has better than a 2-to-1 lead over Glenn as the nomination choice of Democrats, the race is dead even among voters who say they are independents, a group representing about one-third of the electorate. In the current survey, Mondale and Glenn each receives 27% of independents' votes, followed by McGovern with 9% and Jackson with 6%. Next are Hart and Hollings, each with 3%; and Askew and Cranston, each with 2%. With the exception of the early October survey in which Mondale held a 12-point lead over Glenn, independents have been closely divided between the two men.

DECEMBER 22
DEFENSE POLICIES

Interviewing Date: 11/18–21; 11/25–12/4/83*
Survey #227-G

Do you think the Reagan administration's defense policies have brought the United States closer to war or closer to peace?

Closer to war	47%
Closer to peace	28
No difference (volunteered)	15
Don't know	10

National Trend
August 1983

Closer to war	43%
Closer to peace	26
No difference (volunteered)	17
Don't know	14

Is President Reagan going too far or not far enough in trying to bring about an agreement with the Soviet Union on nuclear weapons?

Too far	12%
Not far enough	48
About right (volunteered)	28
No opinion	12

*The results reported are based on two surveys; the second, November 25–December 4, was a special telephone survey.

National Trend

August 1983

Too far	10%
Not far enough	34
About right (volunteered)	41
No opinion	15

Would you favor or oppose an agreement between the United States and the Soviet Union for an immediate, verifiable freeze on the testing, production, and deployment of nuclear weapons?

Favor	77%
Oppose	13
Don't know	10

National Trend

	May 1983	March 1983	November 1982
Favor	75%	70%	71%
Oppose	16	21	20
Don't know	9	9	9

Do you favor or oppose a freeze on the production of nuclear weapons whether or not the Soviet Union agrees to do the same?

Favor	23%
Oppose	68
Don't know	9

National Trend

May 1983

Favor	22%
Oppose	68
Don't know	10

How likely do you think we are to get into a nuclear war within the next ten years—very likely, fairly likely, fairly unlikely, or very unlikely?

Very likely	16%
Fairly likely	24
Fairly unlikely	28
Very unlikely	25
No opinion	7

National Trend

	October 1983	April 1982	June 1981
Very likely	18%	18%	19%
Fairly likely	26	29	28
Fairly unlikely	27	24	26
Very unlikely	24	21	23
No opinion	5	8	4

If we should happen to get into an all-out nuclear war, what do you think your own chances would be of living through it—very good, poor, or just 50-50?

Very good	3%
Poor	69
Just 50-50	25
Don't know	3

National Trend

	June 1981	Feb. 1963	Sept. 1961
Very good	5%	5%	9%
Poor	60	52	43
Just 50-50	32	37	40
Don't know	3	6	8

Russia is said to be spending many times more on civil defense to protect its people from nuclear attack than the United States is spending. Do you think we should do more than we are doing now, do less, or do you think our present efforts are about right?

Do more	42%
Do less	4
About right	44
No opinion	10

Note: By a 5-to-3 margin Americans today think the defense policies of the Reagan administration are bringing the United States closer to war than to peace. In the latest survey, 47% say closer to war, 28% closer to peace, 15% do not see a difference in either direction, and 10% are undecided.

The latest survey, conducted in the aftermath of a turbulent four months on the international scene, shows a substantial and growing number of Americans holding the view that President Ronald Reagan has not gone far enough in trying to bring about an agreement with the Soviet Union on nuclear weapons. A total of 48% holds this view, while 12% say he has gone too far, and 28% about right.

The latest survey also shows widespread public support (77%) for an immediate, verifiable bilateral freeze with the Soviet Union on the testing, production, and deployment of nuclear weapons. At the same time, the public continues to overwhelmingly reject a unilateral freeze, with only 23% saying they would favor a freeze on the production of nuclear weapons whether or not the Soviet Union agrees.

About one person in six (16%) believes that we are very likely to get into a nuclear war within the next ten years, while 24% think it is fairly likely, 28% fairly unlikely, and 25% very unlikely. While the current weight of opinion is clearly on the side that such a war is unlikely, as many as seven in ten think that if such a tragedy were to occur, their chances of living through it would be poor. The proportion saying "poor" has grown since June 1981, when the figure was 60%, and is considerably higher than the comparable percentage recorded in 1963 (52%) and in 1961 (43%).

About four in ten Americans today (42%) think the United States should spend more money on civil defense than we are now doing, while 4% think we should do less, and 44% believe our present efforts are sufficient.

DECEMBER 25
FEDERAL DEFICIT

Interviewing Date: 11/18–21/83
Survey #227-G

One proposal for reducing the deficit now being discussed in Congress calls for an even balance between reduced spending and increased taxes. Under this plan, there would be one dollar in increased taxes for every dollar in spending cuts. Does this sound like a good idea or a bad idea to you?*

Good idea 41%
Bad idea 41
No opinion 18

By Education
College Graduates

Good idea 45%
Bad idea 40
No opinion 15

College, Incomplete

Good idea 43%
Bad idea 44
No opinion 13

High-School Graduates

Good idea 35%
Bad idea 39
No opinion 26

Less Than High-School Graduates

Good idea 35%
Bad idea 39
No opinion 26

By Income
$20,000 and Over

Good idea 44%
Bad idea 41
No opinion 15

*None of the differences between those saying "good idea" and "bad idea" within each group is statistically significant.

Under $20,000

Good idea 39%
Bad idea 40
No opinion 21

By Politics
Republicans

Good idea 44%
Bad idea 42
No opinion 14

Democrats

Good idea 42%
Bad idea 39
No opinion 19

Independents

Good idea 40%
Bad idea 42
No opinion 18

Basically, there are two ways to reduce the federal budget deficit—by reducing government spending, including both defense and social spending, or by raising taxes. If you had to choose between them, which would you prefer: reducing government spending, or raising taxes?

Reducing spending 70%
Raising taxes 16
Some of each (volunteered) 9
No opinion 5

How important do you think it is to balance the federal budget: very important, fairly important, or not so important?

Very important 54%
Fairly important 32
Not so important 9
No opinion 5

By Education
College Graduates

Very important 41%
Fairly important 44
Not so important 14
No opinion 1

College, Incomplete

Very important 56%
Fairly important 33
Not so important 9
No opinion 2

High-School Graduates

Very important 57%
Fairly important 31
Not so important 8
No opinion 4

Less Than High-School Graduates

Very important 57%
Fairly important 23
Not so important 7
No opinion 13

By Income
$20,000 and Over

Very important 49%
Fairly important 39
Not so important 8
No opinion 4

Under $20,000

Very important 59%
Fairly important 25
Not so important 10
No opinion 6

Do you happen to know whether the federal government is or is not operating at a loss?

Yes, is 70%
No, is not 7
Don't know 23

Asked of those who were aware that the federal government is operating at a deficit: Just your best guess, what is the estimated size of the federal deficit for fiscal 1983?*

$200 billion or more (correct)	27%
$100–$199 billion	7
Less than $100 billion	17
Billions, millions, high, etc.	13
Don't know	36

Note: A proposal that would match cuts in government spending dollar for dollar with higher taxes in order to reduce the federal budget deficit receives a mixed reception from the public. The proposal, similar to some being discussed in Congress, is favored by 41% and opposed by the same proportion in the latest Gallup survey. At the same time, the public prefers further spending cuts over increased taxes—given the choice—by an overwhelming 70% to 16% margin.

The survey reveals growing public awareness that the federal government is running at a heavy loss: 70% now compared to 63% a year ago say the government is operating in the red. Furthermore, 27% of those aware of the deficit now cite $200 billion or more as the size of the deficit for fiscal 1983. Last November, the comparable figure was 16%.

All persons in the current survey were asked their opinion of the importance of balancing the federal budget. More than half, 54%, said this was "very important," while 32% said it was "fairly important." Only 9% rated a balanced budget "not so important," while 5% did not express an opinion. Similar surveys have shown the informed public to favor a constitutional amendment to balance the federal budget by 3-to-1 margins or better.

*The extent of the public's knowledge about the deficit does not materially affect its perceptions of the importance of a balanced budget. Roughly equivalent proportions of well- and poorly informed persons, for instance, think it is very important that the federal budget be balanced.

DECEMBER 29
LEBANON SITUATION

Interviewing Date: 11/28–21/83
Survey #227-G

Do you think the United States made a mistake in sending the Marines to Lebanon, or not?

Yes, a mistake	45%
No	45
No opinion	10

By Sex
Male

Yes, a mistake	42%
No	51
No opinion	7

Female

Yes, a mistake	48%
No	40
No opinion	12

By Race
White

Yes, a mistake	43%
No	48
No opinion	9

Nonwhite

Yes, a mistake	62%
No	23
No opinion	15

By Education
College

Yes, a mistake	43%
No	48
No opinion	9

High School

Yes, a mistake	44%
No	46
No opinion	10

Grade School

Yes, a mistake 48%
No 37
No opinion 15

By Region
East

Yes, a mistake 47%
No 45
No opinion 8

Midwest

Yes, a mistake 48%
No 42
No opinion 10

South

Yes, a mistake 42%
No 46
No opinion 12

West

Yes, a mistake 45%
No 46
No opinion 9

By Age
18–24 Years

Yes, a mistake 48%
No 43
No opinion 9

25–29 Years

Yes, a mistake 52%
No 39
No opinion 9

30–49 Years

Yes, a mistake 42%
No 50
No opinion 8

50–64 Years

Yes, a mistake 44%
No 45
No opinion 11

65 Years and Over

Yes, a mistake 48%
No 40
No opinion 12

By Income
$40,000 and Over

Yes, a mistake 40%
No 52
No opinion 8

$30,000–$39,999

Yes, a mistake 41%
No 50
No opinion 9

$20,000–$29,999

Yes, a mistake 47%
No 46
No opinion 7

$10,000–$19,999

Yes, a mistake 43%
No 47
No opinion 10

Under $10,000

Yes, a mistake 54%
No 32
No opinion 14

By Politics
Republicans

Yes, a mistake 29%
No 66
No opinion 5

Democrats

Yes, a mistake 56%
No 35
No opinion 9

Independents

Yes, a mistake 45%
No 44
No opinion 11

National Trend

	Yes	No	No opinion
November 18–21, 1983	45%	45%	10%
October 7–10, 1983 ...	51	37	12

Note: As President Ronald Reagan ponders his soon-to-be-announced decision on whether to seek reelection, he needs to be concerned about the political implications of any prolonged involvement in the Middle East, as well as the state of the economy. Americans have been involved in Lebanon for sixteen months since the Marines landed in Beirut in August 1982, with the limited purpose of escorting the Palestinian guerrilla chief, Yasir Arafat, and his men out of the area.

Although the percentage of Americans who say we made a mistake in sending the Marines to Lebanon has declined slightly over the last two months, nearly half (45%) presently hold this view. An earlier survey found 64% holding the belief that it is either very or fairly likely that our involvement in Lebanon could turn into a situation like Vietnam. The president's popularity at this point in time, however, continues at 53% approval, the highest level in two years, and is sustained in considerable measure by growing public optimism over the economy and favorable reaction to the operation in Grenada.

An examination of recent history shows that two of Reagan's predecessors—Harry Truman in 1952 and Lyndon Johnson in 1968—bowed out of the race for reelection largely because of mounting public opposition to U.S. involvement in the Korean and Vietnam wars. During Truman's presidency, shortly after we made a commitment to help South Korea, only 20% of Americans in August 1950 said our involvement was a mistake, and 43% approved of Truman's overall performance in office. By March 1951, after Communist China had invaded Korea, the percentage who said we had made a mistake shot up to 50%, while Truman's popularity rating declined to 28%. A similar pattern emerged during Johnson's presidency. In the first measurement in August 1965 of views on U.S. involvement in South Vietnam, only 20% said getting into that conflict was a mistake, and Johnson's job performance rating was 64%; by August 1968, those saying "a mistake" climbed to 53%, while Johnson's rating slipped to 35%.

Index

A

Abortion
legal under some circumstances or illegal, 140-42
national trend, 142
Supreme Court ruling on, 139-40
national trend, 140
Advertising practitioners
honesty rating, 144
AIDS (Acquired Immune Deficiency Syndrome)
cure will be found during next year or two, 125-26
likely to reach epidemic proportions, 124-25
Alcoholic beverages
how often you drink, 80
use of, 80
national trend, 80
see also Drinking age
Alcoholism
how serious a problem, 81
Anderson, John
as nominee for Republican presidential candidate, 30-31
choice without Reagan, 31
in trial heats vs. Reagan and Glenn, 170
in trial heats vs. Reagan and Mondale, 129-31, 170
Argentina
predictions for 1983 in, 1
Armstrong, William
as nominee for Republican presidential candidate, 31
choice without Reagan, 31
Askew, Reubin
as nominee for Democratic presidential candidate, 7-8, 67, 69, 93, 121-22, 147, 212-13, 239, 250, 253-55, 259, 264
choice with Jackson, 212-13
choice without Kennedy, 147
national trend, 212, 264
Assault
incidence of, 35-36
reported to police, 36

Atheists
vote for atheist for president, 166-67
national trend, 169
Australia
predictions for 1983 in, 1
Austria
predictions for 1983 in, 1
Authority
respect for, and 65-and-older group, 82
Average citizen
candidates side with, 192
fairly treated by Reagan administration, 59

B

Babbitt, Bruce
as nominee for Democratic presidential candidate, 7-8, 67, 69
Baker, Howard
as nominee for Republican presidential candidate, 30-31
choice without Reagan, 31
as Republican convention choice vs. Bush, 49
in trial heats vs. Glenn, 48-49
in trial heats vs. Mondale, 48
Bankers
honesty rating, 143
Banks and banking
confidence in, 175
national trend, 175
Begin, Menachem
as most admired man, 4
in 1981, 5
in 1980, 5
Belgium
how serious a problem is alcoholism in, 81
predictions for 1983 in, 1
Bentsen, Lloyd
as nominee for Democratic presidential candidate, 7-8, 67, 69, 93
Blacks
approval of Democratic nominees for presidential candidate, 259
approval of marriage between whites and, 96-98
national trend, 98
approval of Reagan in trial heats vs. Glenn, 259-60
approval of Reagan in trial heats vs. Mondale, 259
approval rating of Reagan, 83, 259
fairly treated by Reagan administration, 59
financially better off next year than now, 84
political party affiliation of, 84, 259
presidential performance ratings of Eisenhower through Reagan, 83
satisfaction with United States, 160
national trend, 160
satisfaction with your personal life, 160
national trend, 160-61

Blacks (*continued*)
  vote for black man for president, 70-72, 162-63
    national trend, 72, 169, 239
  your name recorded in precinct or election district, 258-59
Bradley, Bill
  as nominee for Democratic presidential candidate, 7-8, 67, 69, 93
Brazil
  debts owed by, as threat to continued U.S. recovery, 236-37
  predictions for 1983 in, 1
Brown, Edmund (Jerry), Jr.
  as nominee for Democratic presidential candidate, 7-8, 67, 69
Brown, John Y.
  as nominee for Democratic presidential candidate, 7-8, 67, 69, 93
Budget, federal
  important to balance, 268
  proposed amendment requiring government to balance, 126-27
    national trend, 127
  Reagan cuts in, as most important problem, 86, 158, 261
    national trend, 87
  see also Deficit, federal
Building contractors
  honesty rating, 144
Bumpers, Dale
  as nominee for Democratic presidential candidate, 67, 69
Burglary (home broken into)
  incidence of, 35-36
  reported to police, 36
Bush, George
  as nominee for Republican presidential candidate, 30-31
    choice without Reagan, 31
  as Republican convention choice vs. Baker, 49
  in trial heats vs. Glenn, 48
  in trial heats vs. Mondale, 47-48
Business
  big, confidence in, 176
    national trend, 176
  big, as threat to country, 127-29
    national trend, 129
Business executives
  fairly treated by Reagan administration, 60-61
  honesty rating, 144
Byrne, Jane
  as most admired woman, 5

C

Canada
  how serious a problem is alcoholism in, 81
  predictions for 1983 in, 1

Cardio-Pulmonary Resuscitation (C.P.R.)
  interested in taking a course on, 252-53
  require high-school students to take this course, 253
  taken a course on, 252
Car salesmen
  honesty rating, 144
Carter, Jimmy
  approval rating vs. Reagan, 11-12, 18, 83, 107, 146
    national trend, 18, 40
  as most admired man, 4
    in 1981, 5
    in 1980, 5
Carter, Rosalynn
  as most admired woman, 5
Catholics
  approval of marriage between Protestants and, 98-99
    national trend, 99
  vote for Catholic for president, 163-65
    national trend, 169
Central America
  should give military assistance to friendly governments in, 157-58
  situation in, handled by Reagan, 134-35, 263
  see also El Salvador
Chile
  predictions for 1983 in, 1
Cigarette smoking
  in past week, 137
    national trend, 137
Civil defense
  amount spent for, 266
Clergymen
  honesty rating, 143
Colombia
  predictions for 1983 in, 1
Congress
  approval of additional aid to El Salvador, 51-52
  approval rating, 108-09
    national trend, 109
  confidence in, 175
    national trend, 175
  and item veto by president, 247-48
    national trend, 248
  proposal to reduce deficit, 267-68
Congressmen
  honesty rating, 144
Connally, John
  as nominee for Republican presidential candidate, 30-31
    choice without Reagan, 31
Constitutional amendments, proposed
  allowing voluntary prayer in public schools, 172-74
  requiring government to balance federal budget, 126-27
    national trend, 127
Consumer opinion
  at odds with protectionism (analysis by A. Kohut), 138-39

Cost of living
    amount needed each week by your family, 50
    amount needed each week for family of four, 49
        national trend, 50
    amount spent on food each week, 44
        national trend, 44
    as most important problem, 86, 158-60, 260
        national trend, 87
Crane, Philip
    as nominee for Republican presidential candidate, 31
        choice without Reagan, 31
Cranston, Alan
    as nominee for Democratic presidential candidate, 7-8,
        67, 69, 93-94, 121-22, 147, 212-13, 239, 250,
        253-55, 259, 264
    choice with Jackson, 212-13
    choice without Kennedy, 147
    national trend, 94, 212, 264
Crime
    afraid to walk alone at night, 32-33
        national trend, 33
    afraid to walk alone during daytime, 33-34
    feel safe at home at night, 32
        national trend, 32
    happened to you in last twelve months, 34-36
    more crimes in this area than a year ago, 34
        national trend, 34
    as most important problem, 87, 159
        national trend, 87

D

Danforth, John
    as nominee for Republican presidential candidate, 31
        choice without Reagan, 31
Defense
    national, handled by Reagan, 20, 89
        national trend, 20
Defense policies
    brought United States closer to war or peace, 265
        national trend, 265
Defense spending
    amount spent for national defense, 37-38, 221-24
        national trend, 38, 224
    cuts in, to reduce federal deficit, 28-29
Deficit, federal
    cuts in defense spending to reduce, 28-29
    cuts in "entitlement" programs to reduce, 29-30
    cuts in social programs to reduce, 26-27
    estimated size of, for fiscal 1983, 25, 269
    even balance between reduced spending and increased
        taxes to reduce, 267-68
    government operating at a loss, 24-25, 268
    raise income taxes to reduce, 25-26, 234-35
    reduce government spending or raise taxes to reduce,
        268
    as threat to continued recovery, 235

Deformed infants
    parents asked doctors not to keep baby alive, 102-03
Democratic party
    affiliation of blacks with, 84, 259
    affiliation of Hispanics with, 259
    affiliation with, 42-43, 180-82, 259
        national trend, 43, 182
    better for handling most important problem, 87-88, 160
        national trend, 88
    better for keeping country prosperous, 202-04
        national trend, 204
    more likely to keep United States out of war, 204-06
        national trend, 206
    nominees for presidential candidate, 7-8, 66-67, 69,
        93-94, 121-22, 147, 177, 212-13, 238-39, 250,
        253-55, 259, 264-65*
    historical patterns (1955-80), 251-52
        national trend, 94, 212, 264-65
    presidential front-runners compared to eventual nomi-
        nees (1952-76), 6
    woman as vice-presidential running mate, 237-38
Denmark
    how serious a problem is alcoholism in, 81
    predictions for 1983 in, 1
Dentists
    honesty rating, 143
Diana, Princess of Wales
    as most admired woman, 5
Doctors
    honesty rating, 143
Dole, Robert
    as nominee for Republican presidential candidate, 30-
        31
    choice without Reagan, 31
Dollar
    high value of, as threat to continued recovery, 236-37
Drinking age
    raised in all states to 21, 15
Druggists
    honesty rating, 143
Durenberger, David
    as nominee for Republican presidential candidate, 31
        choice without Reagan, 31

E

Economic conditions
    handled by Reagan, 19, 90, 197-98, 261
        national trend, 19, 198
    see also Reaganomics; Recession
Economy
    as most important problem, 86, 158-60, 261
        national trend, 87
Education
    like to see "voucher system" in, 178-79
        national trend, 179

Education reforms
  developing best educational system in world, 86
  elementary-school children work too hard, 85
  extending school day by one hour, 86
  extending school year by 30 days, 86
  high-school students required to pass standard examination to get diploma, 85
  students in high schools work too hard, 85
  subjects required for high-school students, 85
  wide variety or more basic courses in high schools, 85
Eisenhower, Dwight
  approval rating vs. Reagan, 11-12, 18, 83, 107, 146
    national trend, 18, 40
Elderly people
  fairly treated by Reagan administration, 60
  review of 65-and-older group, 81-83
Elizabeth II, Queen
  as most admired woman, 5
El Salvador
  additional military aid for, 51-52
  increase number of U.S. advisers in, 52-54, 152-53
  permit U.S. advisers to enter combat areas, 153-55
  same thing will happen in other Latin American countries, 56-58, 92
  U.S. involvement could turn into a Vietnam, 54-56, 92, 132-34, 135, 155-56
    national trend, 157
Energy situation
  handled by Reagan, 90
Engineers
  honesty rating, 143
Environment
  handled by Reagan, 90-91
Exercise
  do anything regularly, 17
  happen to jog, 16
  how far do you usually jog, 16

F

Family size
  ideal number of children, 38-39
    national trend, 39
Family ties
  emphasis on, and 65-and-older group, 82
Farmers
  treated fairly by Reagan administration, 61
Finances see Personal finances
Finland
  predictions for 1983 in, 1
Fonda, Jane
  as most admired woman, 5
Ford, Betty
  as most admired woman, 5
Ford, Gerald
  approval rating vs. Reagan, 146

national trend, 40
  as most admired man, 4
    in 1981, 5
    in 1980, 5
Foreign policy
  handled by Reagan, 20, 91, 262
    national trend, 20
France
  how serious a problem is alcoholism in, 81
  predictions for 1983 in, 1
Front-runners
  early, as losers (analysis by A. Kohut), 6-7
Funeral directors
  honesty rating, 143
Future see Predictions for 1983

G

Gallup analyses
  education reforms, 84-86
  President Reagan's gender gap, 145-46
  review of the 65-and-older group, 81-83
  see also Kohut, Andrew, analysis by
Gandhi, Indira
  as most admired woman, 5
Glenn, John
  approval rating by degree, 186-88
  better than Mondale for keeping country prosperous, 242
  better than Mondale for keeping United States out of war, 241-42
  as Democratic convention choice vs. Mondale, 8, 67-68, 122, 177
    national trend, 177
  as Democratic convention choice vs. Mondale and Jackson, 177
  as nominee for Democratic presidential candidate, 7-8, 66-67, 69, 93-94, 121-22, 147, 212-13, 238-39, 250, 253-55, 259, 264
    choice with Jackson, 212-13
    choice without Kennedy, 147
    national trend, 94, 212, 264-65
  and patterns of support (analysis by A. Kohut), 213-14
  perceived personality traits of, 188-92
  in trial heats vs. Baker, 48-49
  in trial heats vs. Bush, 48
  in trial heats vs. Mondale, 264
    national trend, 265
  in trial heats vs. Reagan, 2-3, 46, 47, 92, 123, 149-50, 169, 208-10, 240, 259-60
    by Hispanics and blacks, 259-60
    national trend, 93, 123, 150, 170, 210
  in trial heats vs. Reagan and Anderson, 170
Government
  big, as threat to country, 127-29
    national trend, 129

Italy
how serious a problem is alcoholism in, 81
predictions for 1983 in, 1

J

Jackson, Jesse
as Democratic convention choice vs. Mondale and Glenn,
177
as most admired man, 4
in 1981, 5
as nominee for Democratic presidential candidate, 122,
212-13, 238-39, 250, 253-55, 259, 264
national trend, 264
in trial heats vs. Reagan, 150-52, 241
in trial heats vs. Reagan and Mondale, 104-06
Japan
how serious a problem is alcoholism in, 81
predictions for 1983 in, 1
United States losing lead to, in science and technology,
86
Jews
approval of marriage between non-Jews and, 99-101
national trend, 101
vote for Jew for president, 165-66
national trend, 169
John Paul II, Pope
as most admired man, 4
in 1981, 5
in 1980, 5
Johnson, Lyndon
approval rating vs. Reagan, 146
national trend, 40

K

Kemp, Jack
as nominee for Republican presidential candidate, 31
choice without Reagan, 31
Kennedy, Edward
as most admired man, 4
in 1981, 5
in 1980, 5
as nominee for Democratic presidential candidate, 147
Kennedy, John
approval rating vs. Reagan, 11-12, 18, 83, 107, 146
national trend, 18, 40
King, Coretta
as most admired woman, 5
Kissinger, Henry
as most admired man, 4
in 1981, 5
in 1980, 5
Kohut, Andrew, analysis by
Early Front-runners Are Generally Losers, 6-7
Mondale-Glenn Patterns of Support Take Shape, 213-
14

Protectionism and Consumer Opinion at Odds, 138-39
*Significant Parallels in Public Response to Reagan and
Thatcher*, 111-12
Social Security—A Credible Crisis, 41-42

L

Labor
big, as threat to country, 127-29
national trend, 129
organized, confidence in, 176
national trend, 176
Labor union leaders
honesty rating, 144
Labor unions
endorsement of presidential candidate, 109-11
Lawyers
honesty rating, 144
Laxalt, Paul
as nominee for Republican presidential candidate, 31
choice without Reagan, 31
Lebanon
situation in, handled by Reagan, 263
United States made mistake in sending Marines to, 230-
32, 269-71
national trend, 271
U.S. involvement could turn into a Vietnam, 232-34
Lugar, Richard
as nominee for Republican presidential candidate, 31
choice without Reagan, 31
Luxembourg
predictions for 1983 in, 1

M

McGovern, George
as nominee for Democratic presidential candidate, 7-8,
66-67, 69, 212-13, 239, 250, 253-55, 259, 264
choice with Jackson, 212-13
national trend, 264
in trial heats vs. Reagan, 210-11, 240-41
Man, most admired
choice for, 4
in 1981, 5
in 1980, 5
Marijuana use
acceptance of, and 65-and-older group, 82
Marriage
between blacks and whites, 96-98
national trend, 98
between Catholics and Protestants, 98-99
national trend, 99
between Jews and non-Jews, 99-101
national trend, 101
Medicaid
cuts in, to reduce federal deficit, 29-30

Middle East situation
  handled by Reagan, 21, 91
  see also Lebanon
Middle-income people
  fairly treated by Reagan administration, 60
Military
  amount spent for national defense and, 221-24
    national trend, 224
  confidence in, 174
    national trend, 175
Military force
  building strongest in world, 86
Mondale, Walter
  approval rating by degree, 184-86
  better than Glenn for keeping country prosperous, 242
  better than Glenn for keeping United States out of war, 241-42
  as Democratic convention choice vs. Glenn, 8, 67-68, 122, 177
    national trend, 177
  as Democratic convention choice vs. Glenn and Jackson, 177
  as nominee for Democratic presidential candidate, 7-8, 66-67, 69, 93-94, 121-22, 147, 212-13, 238-39, 250, 253-55, 259, 264
    choice with Jackson, 212-13
    choice without Kennedy, 147
    national trend, 94, 212, 264-65
  and patterns of support (analysis by A. Kohut), 213-14
  perceived personality traits of, 188-92
  in trial heats vs. Baker, 48
  in trial heats vs. Bush, 47-48
  in trial heats vs. Glenn, 264
    national trend, 265
  in trial heats vs. Reagan, 3-4, 46-47, 93, 103-04, 122, 148-49, 169, 206-08, 240
    by Hispanics and blacks, 259
    national trend, 93, 123, 149, 169, 208
  in trial heats vs. Reagan and Anderson, 129-31, 170
  in trial heats vs. Reagan and Jackson, 104-06
Money
  emphasis on, and 65-and-older group, 82
Moral decline in society
  as most important problem, 86, 158, 260
    national trend, 87
Moynihan, Daniel (Pat)
  as nominee for Democratic presidential candidate, 7-8, 67, 69, 93
    national trend, 94

N

Netherlands (Holland)
  how serious a problem is alcoholism in, 81
  predictions for 1983 in, 1
Newspaper reporters
  honesty rating, 143

Newspapers
  confidence in, 175
    national trend, 175
Nixon, Richard
  approval rating vs. Reagan, 11-12, 18, 83, 107, 146
    national trend, 18, 40
  as most admired man, 5
Norway
  predictions for 1983 in, 1
Nuclear arms freeze
  agreement between United States and Soviet Union for immediate freeze, 72-74, 266
    national trend, 74, 266
  continuation of arms buildup or United States falling behind Soviet Union, 74-76
    national trend, 76
  United States or Soviet Union stronger in nuclear weapons, 74
    national trend, 74
  whether or not Soviet Union agrees to do the same, 266
    national trend, 266
Nuclear disarmament
  negotiations with Soviet Union, 262
Nuclear war
  likely to get into, 266
    national trend, 266
  your chances of living through, 266
    national trend, 266
Nuclear weapons
  agreement with Soviet Union on, 265
    national trend, 266

O

O'Connor, Sandra Day
  as most admired woman, 5

P

Packwood, Robert
  as nominee for Republican presidential candidate, 31
  choice without Reagan, 31
Peace
  Reagan's defense policies have brought United States closer to, 265
    national trend, 265
  United States doing all it can to keep, 76-78
    national trend, 78
  USSR doing all it can to keep, 78-79
    national trend, 79
Peace (keeping out of war) *see* Democratic party; Glenn, John; Mondale, Walter; Republican party
People like yourself
  fairly treated by Reagan administration, 60
Percy, Charles
  as nominee for Republican presidential candidate, 30-31
  choice without Reagan, 31

Personal finances
    effect of Reaganomics on, 22-23, 62-64, 193-94
        national trend, 23, 194
    see also Blacks
Peru
    predictions for 1983 in, 1
Pharmacists
    honesty rating, 143
Philippines
    predictions for 1983 in, 1
Poland
    debts owed by, as threat to continued U.S. recovery,
        236-37
Policemen
    honesty rating, 143
Political affiliation
    of blacks, 84, 259
    of Hispanics, 259
    by party, 42-43, 180-82
        national trend, 43, 182
    of 65-and-older group, 82
Political officeholders, local
    honesty rating, 144
Political officeholders, state
    honesty rating, 144
Political philosophy
    of 65-and-older group, 82
Poor people
    candidates sympathetic to, 192
    fairly treated by Reagan administration, 58-59
Prayer in public schools
    home, school or church in religious development of
        child, 174
    proposed amendment to allow voluntary, 172-74
Predictions for 1983
    in developing nations, 1
    in industrial nations, 1
        national trend in United States, 1
Presidential candidates
    endorsement of, by labor unions, 109-11
    prejudice in voting for, 161–69
        national trend, 169
    see also Blacks; Democratic party; Front-runners; His-
        panics; Republican party; Women
Presidential trial heats
    Baker vs. Glenn, 48-49
    Baker vs. Mondale, 48
    Bush vs. Glenn, 48
    Bush vs. Mondale, 47-48
    Mondale vs. Glenn, 264
        national trend, 265
    Reagan vs. Glenn, 2-3, 46, 47, 92, 123, 169, 208-10,
        240, 259-60
        by Hispanics and blacks, 259-60
        national trend, 93, 123, 170, 210
    Reagan vs. Glenn and Anderson, 170
    Reagan vs. Jackson, 150-52, 241
    Reagan vs. McGovern, 210-11, 240-41

Reagan vs. Mondale, 3-4, 46-47, 93, 103-04, 122, 148-
    49, 169, 206-08, 240, 259
    by Hispanics and blacks, 259
    national trend, 93, 123, 149, 169, 208
Reagan vs. Mondale and Anderson, 129-31, 170
Reagan vs. Mondale and Jackson, 104-06
Problems
    most important, 86-89, 158-60, 260-61
    national trend, 87, 88
Prosperity
    Mondale or Glenn better at keeping country prosperous,
        242
    party better at keeping country prosperous, 202-04
        national trend, 204
Protectionism
    at odds with consumer opinion (analysis by A. Kohut),
        138-39
Protestants
    approval of marriage between Catholics and, 98-99
        national trend, 99
Public schools
    confidence in, 175
        national trend, 175
    see also Education reforms; Prayer in public schools

R

Reagan, Nancy
    as most admired woman, 5
Reagan, Ronald
    approval rating, 8-10, 17, 39-40, 44-45, 61, 106-08,
        120, 123, 135, 146, 170-72, 214-17, 249, 259,
        261
        national trend, 10, 40, 41, 123, 172, 217
    approval rating by black Americans, 83, 259
    approval rating by degree, 135-36, 183-84, 217-18
    approval rating by Hispanics, 259
    approval rating in terms of gender gap, 145, 146
    approval rating vs. predecessors, 11-12, 18, 83, 107,
        146
        national trend, 18, 40
    choices for presidential candidate without, 31, 49
    compared to Margaret Thatcher (analysis by A. Kohut),
        111-12
    and economic conditions, 19, 90, 197-98, 261
        national trend, 19, 198
    and energy situation, 90
    and environment, 90-91
    and foreign policy, 20, 91, 262
        national trend, 20
    and gender gap (Gallup analysis), 145-46
    his defense policies have brought United States closer
        to war or peace, 265
        national trend, 265
    and inflation, 19, 89-90, 198-200
        national trend, 19, 200
    like to see him run for president in 1984, 12-13, 120
        national trend, 13, 120

and Middle East situation, 21, 91
as most admired man, 4
  in 1981, 5
  in 1980, 5
and national defense, 20, 89
  national trend, 20
and nuclear disarmament negotiations with Soviet Union,
    262
perceived personality traits of, 188-92
and relations/dealings with Soviet Union, 20-21, 90,
    219-21, 262
  national trend, 21
says recession is ending, 45
and situation in Central America, 134-35, 263
and situation in Grenada, 262
and situation in Lebanon, 263
treats fairly the average citizen, 59
treats fairly blacks, 59
treats fairly business executives, 60-61
treats fairly elderly people, 60
treats fairly farmers, 61
treats fairly middle-income people, 60
treats fairly people like yourself, 60
treats fairly poor people, 58-59
treats fairly small-business people, 61
treats fairly wealthy people, 59-60
treats fairly women, 59
in trial heats vs. Glenn, 2-3, 46, 47, 92, 123, 149-50,
    169, 208-10, 240, 259-60
  by Hispanics and blacks, 259-60
  national trend, 93, 123, 150, 170, 210
in trial heats vs. Glenn and Anderson, 170
in trial heats vs. Jackson, 150-52, 241
in trial heats vs. McGovern, 210-11, 240-41
in trial heats vs. Mondale, 3-4, 46-47, 93, 103-04, 122,
    148-49, 169, 206-08, 240, 259
  by Hispanics and blacks, 259
  national trend, 93, 123, 149, 169, 208
in trial heats vs. Mondale and Anderson, 129-31, 170
in trial heats vs. Mondale and Jackson, 104-06
trying to bring about agreement with Soviet Union on
    nuclear weapons, 265
  national trend, 266
and unemployment, 19, 91, 200-02
  national trend, 20, 202
will run for president in 1984, 13, 120
  national trend, 13, 120
Reaganomics
  effect on nation's economic situation, 23-24, 64-65,
    195-96
    national trend, 24, 65, 196
  effect on nation's economic situation a year from now,
    65
  effect on nation's economic situation over the long run,
    65-66
  effect on your financial situation, 22-23, 62-64, 193-
    94
    national trend, 23, 64, 194

Realtors
  honesty rating, 144
Recession
  ending, according to Reagan, 45
  how long will recovery last, 235
  as most important problem, 86
    national trend, 87
  threats to continued recovery, 235-37
Religion
  church or synagogue attendance, 14
    national trend, 14
    national trend, of Protestants and Catholics, 14
  church or synagogue membership, 13-14
    national trend, 14
  confidence in church or organized, 174
    national trend, 174
  see also Prayer in public schools
Religious beliefs
  and 65-and-older group, 82
Republican party
  affiliation of blacks with, 84, 259
  affiliation of Hispanics with, 259
  affiliation with, 42-43, 180-82, 259
    national trend, 43, 182
  better for handling most important problem, 87-88, 160
    national trend, 88
  better for keeping country prosperous, 202-04
    national trend, 204
  more likely to keep United States out of war, 204-06
    national trend, 206
  nominees for presidential candidate, 30-31
  presidential front-runners compared to eventual nomi-
    nees (1952-80), 6
Robbery (money or property taken by force)
  incidence of, 35-36
  reported to police, 36
Rockefeller, Jay
  as nominee for Democratic presidential candidate, 7-8,
    67, 69, 93
    national trend, 94

S

Sadat, Anwar
  as most admired man, 5
Satisfaction
  with United States, 160
    of 65-and-older group, 83
    national trend, 160
  with your personal life, 160
    of 65-and-older group, 82
    national trend, 160-61
  see also Blacks
Science and technology
  United States losing lead in, to Japan and Germany, 86
Senators
  honesty rating, 144

Sexual freedom
acceptance of, and 65-and-older group, 82
Small-business people
treated fairly by Reagan administration, 61
Social programs
cuts in, to reduce federal deficit, 26-27
Social Security
credible crisis (analysis by A. Kohut), 41-42
cuts in, to reduce federal deficit, 29-30
Soviet Union (USSR, Russia)
agreement on nuclear weapons, 265
national trend, 266
agreement with United States for immediate nuclear
weapons freeze, 72-74, 266
national trend, 74, 266
agrees or not on freeze on nuclear weapons, 266
national trend, 266
approval rating, 225-26
national trend, 227
approval rating of Soviet leaders, 227-28
approval rating of Soviet people, 228-30
continuation of arms buildup or United States falling
behind, 74-76
national trend, 76
doing all it can to keep peace, 78-79
national trend, 79
nuclear disarmament negotiations with, 262
relations/dealings with, handled by Reagan, 20-21, 90,
219-21, 262
national trend, 21
stronger than United States in nuclear weapons, 74
national trend, 74
Spain
how serious a problem is alcoholism in, 81
predictions for 1983 in, 1
Stockbrokers
honesty rating, 144
Strauss, Robert
as nominee for Democratic presidential candidate, 7-8,
67, 69
Supreme Court
confidence in, 175
national trend, 175
ruling on abortion, 139-40
national trend, 140
Sweden
predictions for 1983 in, 1
Switzerland
predictions for 1983 in, 1

T

Taxes
amount people pay, as threat to continued recovery,
236
see also Deficit, federal

Teachers
honesty rating, 143
Television
confidence in, 176
national trend, 176
Television reporters and commentators
honesty rating, 143
Teresa of Calcutta, Mother
as most admired woman, 5
Thatcher, Margaret
compared to Ronald Reagan (analysis by A. Kohut),
111-12
as most admired woman, 5
Theft of car
incidence of, 35-36
reported to police, 36
Theft of money or property
incidence of, 34-36
reported to police, 36
Trade problems
international, as threat to continued recovery, 236-37
Trucks, tandem rigs
law prohibiting, on major interstate highways, 94-95
law prohibiting such vehicles on other roads, 95

U

Udall, Morris
as nominee for Democratic presidential candidate, 7-8
Unemployment
handled by Reagan, 19, 91, 200-02
national trend, 20, 202
as most important problem, 86, 89, 158-60, 260
national trend, 87
United Nations
approval rating, 255-56
national trend, 256
should move out of United States, 257-58
United States should give up membership in, 256-67
national trend, 257
United States
doing all it can to keep peace, 76-78
national trend, 78
how serious a problem is alcoholism in, 81
importance of developing best educational system, most
efficient industrial production system, or strongest
military force, 86
losing lead in science and technology to Japan and Germany, 86
party better for keeping country prosperous, 202-04
national trend, 204
party more likely to keep out of war, 204-06
national trend, 206
predictions for 1983 in, 1
national trend, 1
Reagan's defense policies have brought closer to war
or peace, 265

national trend, 265
satisfaction with way things are going in, 160
of 65-and-older group, 83
national trend, 160
should give military assistance to friendly governments
in Central America, 157-58
and Soviet Union *see* Soviet Union (USSR, Russia)
Uruguay
predictions for 1983 in, 1

V

Vandalism of property
incidence of, 34-36
reported to police, 36

W

Walesa, Lech
as most admired man, 4
Walters, Barbara
as most admired woman, 5
War
fear of, as most important problem, 86, 158-60, 260
national trend, 87

party more likely to keep United States out of, 204-06
national trend, 206
Reagan's defense policies have brought United States
closer to, 265
national trend, 265
see also Nuclear war
Wealthy people
fairly treated by Reagan administration, 59-60
Weicker, Lowell
as nominee for Republican presidential candidate, 31
choice without Reagan, 31
West Germany
how serious a problem is alcoholism in, 81
predictions for 1983 in, 1
United States losing lead to, in science and technology,
86
Woman, most admired
choice for, 5
Women
fairly treated by Reagan administration, 59
vote for Democratic ticket with woman as vice-
president, 237-38
vote for woman for president, 112-14, 161-62
national trend, 114, 169
Working hard
emphasis on, and 65-and-older group, 82